34324

D0687375

GODDESSES AND THE DIVINE FEMININE

Rosemary Radford Ruether

· GODDESSES AND
THE DIVINE FEMININE

A Western Religious History

University of California Press

Berkeley Los Angeles London

University of California Press
Berkeley and Los Angeles, California

University of California Press, Ltd.
London, England

© 2005 by The Regents of the University of California

The author and publisher have made considerable effort
to contact copyright holders and to secure permission
prior to publication. Any copyright holder who remains
unacknowledged may contact the publisher, who will
correct the oversight at the earliest opportunity.

Library of Congress Cataloging-in-Publication Data

Ruether, Rosemary Radford.
    Goddesses and the divine feminine : a Western
religious history / Rosemary Radford Ruether.
        p. cm.
    Includes bibliographical references and index.
    ISBN 0-520-23146-5 (alk. paper)
    1. Goddesses.   2. Women and religion.
3. Goddess religion. I. Title.
BL325.F4R84 2005
202'.114—dc22   2004029226

Manufactured in the United States of America

14   13   12   11   10   09   08   07   06   05
10 9 8 7 6 5 4 3 2 1

The paper used in this publication meets the minimum
requirements of ANSI/ NISO Z39.48–1992 (R 1997)
(Permanence of Paper).

CONTENTS

ILLUSTRATIONS

ACKNOWLEDGMENTS

I wish to thank many people who have given me critical feedback on this work. This list includes Gale Yee of the Episcopal Divinity School in Cambridge, Massachusetts, and Cheryl Anderson of Garrett-Evangelical in Evanston, Illinois, for reading the chapter on Hebrew scripture; Luise Schottroff of the Pacific School of Religion in Berkeley for reading the section on the New Testament; Margaret Conkey and Carolyn Merchant of the University of California at Berkeley for reading the material on anthropology; David Lawrence of the Swedenborgian Institute at the Pacific School of Religion for reading the section on Swedenborg; Moses Penumaka, doctoral student at the Graduate Theological Union, for his extensive work in scanning and preparing the pictures for the book; and the students in the Spring 2003 course "Goddesses and the Spiritual Feminine," for their reflections on what the material in this book means to them.

INTRODUCTION

My interest in goddesses of the ancient Near East and Greece goes back to 1954, when I began studying the religious worldviews of these societies.[1] In a course on Greek tragedy with Robert Palmer (translator of Walter Otto's work on Dionysus), I read writers such as Jane Harrison and was introduced to the theory that a matriarchal society had preceded the rise of patriarchy in ancient Greek and Mediterranean societies.[2] As I continued to pursue these interests at Scripps College and the Claremont Graduate School, I focused on the classics and early Christianity. In particular, I studied the Greek and Near Eastern background of Hebrew and early Christian thought, Platonism and Neoplatonism,[3] and various religious movements, such as the mystery religions of the Hellenistic and Greco-Roman worlds, in which Cybele, Isis, and other goddesses were central. It became evident to me that the Hebrew religion and Christianity, far from simply repressing and leaving behind these "pagan" religious worldviews, had appropriated and reinterpreted them. The Christianity that emerged in the first to fourth century was, in many ways, a reinterpreted synthesis of the religious worldviews of the ancient Mediterranean world.

In studying the Hebrew Bible and early Christianity side by side with ancient paganism, I found myself attracted to the prophetic traditions that sided with the poor and oppressed and denounced the rich and powerful. As I became involved in the civil rights and antiwar movements of the 1960s, this spiritual lineage undergirded my commitment to justice. Although the ancient pagan religions that I had been studying seemed to lack this prophetic social justice tradition, I nevertheless continued to regard them as offering valid spiritual worldviews, as did my mentors, such as Robert Palmer, who frankly preferred ancient paganism to Christianity.

I began to think in terms of complementary spiritualities—pagan, prophetic, and contemplative.[4] Pagan spirituality, typical of most indigenous religions, focuses on the renewal of the earth and human life within the changing seasons. Prophetic spirituality focuses on the struggle to restore just and harmonious relations among humans and with the earth in a covenantal relation with a creating and redeeming God, over against a world dominated by great systems of oppression and injustice. Contemplative spirituality withdraws from the "illusions" of transitory existence and seeks to unite the soul with the permanent source of reality.

I saw ancient Judaism building on pagan spirituality and reinterpreting it in the light of a historical and prophetic viewpoint. In the Hellenistic era, Jewish thinkers such as Philo appropriated Neoplatonic thought and used it to develop a mystical hermeneutics and a contemplative practice of Judaism. Christianity also built on and reinterpreted these many layers of spirituality. In its focus on ascetic, monastic life, it emphasized the contemplative path for more than a millennium, but it never lost the seasonal spirituality on which the church year was based. Periodically, prophetic spirituality was recovered in order to struggle against systems of injustice, including those within the church itself. Today, modern ecological movements have rediscovered the spirituality of earth renewal, marrying it to prophetic critique. Thus, each of these spiritualities not only has a distinct validity but also continually interacts with the others in new and creative ways.

In 1968, a feminist critique of male-dominated societies started to emerge in the civil rights movement. In the early sixties, I had already questioned the way Catholicism treated women's sexuality and reproductive role.[5] Now I began to reflect on how women had been marginalized throughout the whole of religious history, asking what had been the causes of this long history of domination and what might be sources for the affirmation of women as full and equal persons. My first essay on this subject, written originally in the late sixties, had the provocative title "Male Chauvinist Theology and the Anger of Women."[6]

In 1972, I was invited to teach for a year at Harvard Divinity School "under" the Chauncey Stillman Chair of Roman Catholic Studies.[7] There, I developed a course that attempted to sort out this religious history from the perspective of women, going from the prehistoric period to the era of the Hellenistic mystery religions and the emergence of early Christianity. Drawing on E. O. James's 1959 book *The Cult of the Mother Goddess*, I started by talking about the thesis that a Mother Goddess had been universally worshipped in the prehistoric Near East.[8] I showed pictures of the Paleolithic and Neolithic female figures that were said to represent this Mother Goddess.

I was surprised and intrigued when my students, almost all feminist women, were repelled by these images. The large breasts, bellies, and buttocks of these figures, with truncated hands and feet and a head that lacked facial features, struck them as exploitative images of the female. To their minds, the societies that made these images valued women's bodies as a source of sex and nurture but did not value women's person or agency. The students argued that these prehistoric images depicted a woman as all buttocks, breasts, and belly, not as a person with facial features who saw, thought, or spoke, not as a person who moved around on her own two feet and took charge of things with her hands.

Until then, I had assumed that the existence of these ancient female figurines was "proof" that women had been respected and had wielded power in these ancient matriarchal, or at least prepatriarchal, societies. Later in the 1970s, a new movement of "Goddess" religion would emerge that would again interpret these ancient figurines as testimony of a positive view of women. For example, Anne Barstow, in her article "The Prehistoric Goddess," talks of being thrilled by these images and feeling that, for the first time, her female body had been affirmed.[9] Other books on prehistoric goddesses similarly celebrated these fat, faceless, handless, feetless images with large breasts, buttocks, and bellies—such as the Venus of Willendorf (c. 25,000 BCE) (fig. 1)—as evidence of a time when women held leading positions in society and were revered and worshipped as primary exemplars of the divine. But my students' negative reaction to these same images made me aware that both of these responses are projections from our modern context and that neither view may have much to do with what the creators of these images actually had in mind.

Also in the 1970s, I began to read in the emerging field of feminist anthropology, which questioned the entire theory of "matriarchal origins" and explored the more complex ways in which gender and male-female relations developed in various societies.[10] I also became aware of how much the concept of an original matriarchal society, superseded by patriarchy, was itself a product of nineteenth-century European societies marked by their own acute conflicts between "masculine" and "feminine" constructions of gender—conflicts that reflected the beginning of the feminist movement and the efforts to marginalize and repress it. In the 1950s and early 1960s, I had encountered this theory of matriarchal origins in the works of classical archaeologists and historians, and I now began to reread these accounts more as products of their own European context and less as reliable accounts of prehistoric antiquity.

FIGURE I

Venus of Willendorf, c. 25,000 BCE. Limestone statuette with traces of red coloring, height 4⅜ in., from Willendorf, Wachau, Lower Austria. The ample volume of the sacred female celebrates her capacity for nurture. (Naturhistorisches Museum, Vienna; photo: Erich Lessing / Art Resource, NY)

The emerging movement of Goddess spirituality took hold of these nineteenth-century writings, however, interpreting them uncritically as proof of an ancient matriarchal society overthrown by patriarchy. Several women students in theological schools, seeking more positive sources for a feminist theology, gravitated to these Goddess movements and attempted to discredit any effort to draw on Jewish and Christian sources. Some of these Goddess "thealogians," such as Carol Christ, criticized persons like myself and Elizabeth Fiorenza for not being "radical" enough, for remaining mere "reformers" because we failed to embrace the Goddess and continued to mine Jewish and Christian sources of tradition.[11]

I wrote responses to these views, and for a few years a heated interchange took place between myself and the emerging Goddess feminists.[12] I felt the need both to explicate the reasons for my perspective and to warn against a simplistic appropriation of a thesis of matriarchal origins. I also questioned the "essentialist" view of the female as embodiment of nurturing, life-affirming virtues, vis-à-vis the male as paradigm of aggressive militarism, that often lurked behind these modern Goddess spiritualities. Goddess feminists, however, misread these warnings as a rejection of their own option for a new path of spiritual development. Some assumed that I was motivated by the belief that the Jewish and Christian traditions were the only valid religions and that no one should leave them for some alternative path.

This was not at all my view at that time, nor has it been my view in the years that followed. I have taken for granted since the 1950s that Christianity is one religion among others and that all religions have their negative sides, including marginalizing women to one degree or another. Feminists have no perfect option from some past tradition. This means that we can choose from various options such as Judaism, Christianity, or Buddhism, or we can pursue new options by seeking to recover other ancient traditions. But as we go deeper into these traditions, we find the need to be "reformers" and reinterpreters of those traditions. A fully pro-woman feminist theology and spirituality did not exist in the past in any clearly recoverable sense, although all these traditions contain many hints of alternative perspectives.

Only in the second half of the twentieth century and into the twenty-first have women been in a position to seek a more adequate alternative religion that will fully affirm us as women. I object to any Christian exclusivism and also to any simplistic reversal of Christian exclusivism that sets a prehistoric goddess religion as the true source of feminist faith, defining Christianity and Judaism as totally worthless. Feminists need to recognize that in whatever tradition we choose to stand, we are reinterpreting from our own context.

Another point of contention, recently revived, charges Christian feminists with arguing that Goddess feminists "have no ethics."[13] Goddess feminists such as Starhawk, a person who demonstrates the deep prophetic ethics being developed by a major leader of the Goddess tradition, are cited as evidence to the contrary. But this conflict misinterprets what I have said. In my own experience, as I have explained, the ancient pagan traditions lacked the prophetic spirituality that I discovered in the Hebrew tradition. But this does not mean that ancient paganisms had no other valuable spiritualities. It also does not suggest that modern feminist pagans lack a prophetic social justice ethic. For me, feminism itself is a prophetic social justice ethic. Modern feminist pagans are developing their thought not simply from the effort to recover ancient paganisms but also from the background of Western religious traditions from which they come. A feminist pagan such as Starhawk, coming from the Jewish tradition, synthesizes both prophetic and earth-renewal spiritualities from roots in her own Jewish history as well as from the pagan traditions she has adopted.

The twenty-five years since these debates began have seen some shifting and realignment of the cultural terrain in western Europe and North America. On the one hand, Goddess and neopagan movements have become increasingly "normalized," finding their place in academe and in gatherings of world religions, such as the Parliament of the World's Religions. (Adherents of these movements have even become chaplains in the U.S. Army.) Their spokespersons have nuanced their articulation of their own assumptions, recognizing the degree to which their views are a new interpretation of spirituality and not simply a literal recovery of something prehistoric. Either-or dichotomies between good paganism and bad Christianity, or vice versa, have given way to the beginning of ecumenism, in which all movements that seek a feminist earth-renewal spirituality in various traditions can see one another as partners.

On the other hand, new conflicts between various feminist perspectives have also arisen. In the 1980s, Goddess feminists appropriated the work of archaeologist Marija Gimbutas as proof of prehistoric matriarchal or matricentric societies overthrown by invading patriarchalists, a viewpoint popularly disseminated by writers such as Charlene Spretnak and Riane Eisler.[14] The emerging community of feminist paleo-archaeologists, alarmed by what they saw as bad archaeology, responded with a critique of Gimbutas's work. They sought to define a feminist archaeological standpoint that was neither an argument for recovery of original matriarchy nor a defense of universal patriarchy. This academic critique, popularized by writers such as Cynthia Eller, led to renewed charges of "betrayal" from Goddess feminists.[15]

At the same time, a surge of extremely aggressive patriarchal fundamentalism has appeared in all the dominant world religions—Christianity, Judaism, Islam, and even in Asian religions—that seeks to beat women back into "their place," by force, if necessary, as well as by various methods of blame and shame. Feminists and feminism have become targets worldwide. In the administration of U.S. President George W. Bush, evangelical Christian fundamentalism merged with American militarism and an aspiration for world domination, spurring efforts to dismantle women's reproductive rights, environmental protections, and international cooperation among nations.

Yet, the unmasking of this unilateral U.S. aggression has itself sparked a worldwide peace movement in opposition to the American attack on Iraq, a movement that has also attempted to link together all the various protest movements against military and economic domination and to envision a global alternative. It seems to me that the moment has come for various feminist movements not only to ally with one another but also to align themselves with this global movement to build an alternative way of being together on this one planet.

Goddess and Christian feminists need to see that they share many of the same values and even a similar theo/alogy, which views divinity not as a male transcendent Other of dominating power, but rather as the energy of sustaining and renewing life. This emergent common theo/alogy is also shared with other religious movements and activists, such as those engaged in ecological rethinking of the various world religions, liberation theologians who are incorporating ecological and feminist challenges into their thought, and indigenous peoples whose theologies seek to resurrect their ancient traditions and to confront the threat of neoliberalism to their traditional ways of life.[16]

These many religious movements themselves need to ally with women's, labor, peasant, antiwar, and environmental movements in a global front of resistance and alternative development of society. In the slogan that emerged from the World Social Forum in Porto Alegre, Brazil, we all need to join hands in a common declaration that "a different world is possible."[17]

I hope that this book can be a small contribution to shaping one piece of this global alliance. It seeks to sort out that piece of history that connects ancient Near Eastern societies, as they rose from their Neolithic roots, with the contemporary Western feminist efforts to reevaluate how they are linked to those roots today. This book restates my own ongoing reflection on this history over a fifty-year period. It expresses a critique of theories of ancient matriarchy, while at the same time affirming the movements that seek to reinterpret those roots today for a feminist-ecological spirituality. My hope is to further an alliance among the many forms of religious feminism, while recognizing that we are all reinterpreting ancient traditions and imagery that are ambivalent and whose ancient meaning is partly lost to us. I believe that we share mostly common values, and I also believe that we are all being beaten with the same stick by fundamentalists, for whom "lesbian feminist witch" is the common label for us all.[18]

Chapter 1 attempts to sort out this question of gender and prehistory, particularly in the conflict between those who endorse the perspective of Marija Gimbutas and the feminist archaeologists who have critiqued it. In this chapter and in the first part of chapter 2, I suggest a mediating way of viewing this development from prehistoric to early patriarchal societies, which sees the earlier societies as more egalitarian but probably not female-dominated.

The second part of chapter 2 focuses on four major goddesses of the ancient Mediterranean world: Inanna/Ishtar, Anat, Isis, and Demeter. In my view, it is not evident that these goddesses ever existed in order to express a matricentric society. In the form in which their stories have come down to us, the first three goddesses express a construction of female divinity that sacralizes not only male but also royal or class-dominated societies. The figure of the Goddess Demeter seems to me more ambivalent, both assuming patriarchal rule and protesting against its abuse of women, while sustaining earth renewal and hope for life after death.

Chapter 3 looks at the gradually diminishing presence of the female consort of El/Yahweh in Hebrew thought, as well as the re-creation, after the exile, of a new Hebrew Goddess in the figure of Wisdom. But this Hebrew Goddess is hardly a feminist. She is juxtaposed to a hostile view of the "bad foreign woman" and functions primarily to link males to males, a male divine father to human sons, and human fathers, as parents and teachers, to human sons. This raises the question, which I take up in the conclusion of this work, of why men need the Goddess. Instead of the expected story line in which patriarchal religion suppresses all female imagery of the divine, what we see in some lines of Jewish and Christian history is a periodic reinvention of goddesses by men to serve male interests.

For me, this is a major part of the difficulty in any effort by women, either historically or today, to lay hold of these goddesses for feminist purposes. In order to have them become resources for feminism, we need to come to terms with the way these goddesses and female divine symbols reflect male constructions of the female, at least in the form they have come down to us. This is why I titled this book *Goddesses and the Divine Feminine*. I believe that the term "feminine" (as distinct from "feminist") signals an androcentric shaping of the female image.

The fourth chapter looks at how goddesses and female symbols of the divine functioned in two major movements that sought religious salvation in the context of Greco-Roman society, the mystery religions and gnosticism. Although both have been passed down to us shaped by a male point of view, both included women as priestesses, religious leaders, and adherents. Unfortunately, we have no texts by women in which we can glimpse how women saw their relation to the goddesses of the mystery religions. Gnosticism is even more complex: despite its androcentric view of divinity, it had powerful female deities and suggested a kind of subversion of the whole dominant patriarchal society and cosmos. Perhaps we glimpse here a proto-feminist movement in the context of an international, colonized society of antiquity.

Chapter 5 traces female symbols in early Christianity from the first to the fourth century. Here, we see a further masculinization of female symbols, such as Wisdom, that Christianity appropriated from its Jewish roots. At the same time, however, a powerful new set of female symbols of the divine and the redeemed human, as female Holy Spirit, Mother Church, bridal soul, and finally as Mary, Mother of God, began to be elaborated.

The sixth chapter continues the account of this development of Mariology through the medieval world. The chapter then turns to five medieval women mystics who laid hold of these female symbols—Wisdom, Mother Church, and bridal soul—to affirm their own spiritual journeys as women empowered to speak, write, teach, and guide other women.

Chapter 7 detours from western European religious history to see how female images of the divine played out in the violent encounter of the Aztec world with its Spanish conquerors in Mexico in the sixteenth century. In Aztec society, we find an aggressive, militarist patriarchy, whose religious worldview culminated in a continual round of human sacrifice to sustain a fragile sun and cosmos. Somewhat more egalitarian societies with some female leadership may have existed before the Aztecs, but this knowledge is hard to recover, given our sources, which mostly come from the Franciscan friars who sought to convert the indigenous peoples to Christianity. Yet Aztec and pre-Aztec Mesoamerican worldviews were rooted in a vision of the dialectical interconnection of male and female divinity in the ultimate source of life, played out on every level of cosmic and human reality.

The Spanish sought to repress all these gods and goddesses in favor of a devotion to the Christian God the Father and his crucified son. Yet the very shock of this meeting and the mixture of the two peoples produced many apparitions of the central female symbol of Spanish Christianity, Mary, most notably in the apparition of Mary as Virgin of Guadalupe. Guadalupe, as the "Goddess of the Americas," has been and continues to be today a multivalent symbol that can both validate reactionary trends of the patriarchal Mexican church and society and nonetheless be endlessly reappropriated and interpreted from revolutionary, liberative, and feminist perspectives. Again, we are faced with the complex story of how men create goddesses for their own purposes and how, nonetheless, some women claim these goddesses for themselves in creative ways.

The eighth chapter returns to the world of sixteenth-century Europe, in the German context of the Reformation. Here, we see the most extensive effort of patriarchal Christianity to repress all female symbols of the divine. Wisdom, Mother Church, and bridal soul, as well as Mary and female saints, are swept away by church Reformers in favor of an exclusive focus on God the Father and his crucified son. It is this Protestant history that stands behind the assumption of modern Western feminists that patriarchal religion normally seeks to purge all female symbols of the divine. This assumption has obscured the way in which patriarchal religions have continually created new (androcentric) goddesses.

But this view of a patriarchal Protestantism with exclusively male symbols is itself too simple. Protestants have failed to recognize, and to appropriate as part of their tradition, continual waves of mystical and millennialist Protestantism from the seventeenth to the nineteenth centuries, which redeveloped the Wisdom symbol and re-created a vision of God and the human being as androgynous. This Protestant Goddess, Wisdom, was elaborated mainly by men, who sought to affirm their own "feminine side" and to devote themselves to a deity that included the female. Consequently, this renewed Wisdom theology is hardly feminist. Most of this theology of divine and human androgyny either marginalized women entirely or firmly put them in their place as auxiliary to male spiritual development. Yet here, too, women found ways to appropriate this Goddess and reaffirm her from their own perspective.

Chapter 9 takes us to nineteenth-century western Europe and America, where contested gender identities take a more strident form with the emergence of feminism. In response, patriarchal cultures made rigorous efforts to reassert either women's natural inferiority or their idealized complementarity to male roles as rulers of public society. It is in this context that waves of male historians and archaeologists who studied the ancient Mediterranean world sought to reread the roots of European society as a story of the rise of patriarchy from an earlier matriarchy.

This theme was taken up by socialism and early feminism and reinterpreted to affirm liberative hopes for an emerging socialist and/or feminist society. Thus, the Victorian theory of original matriarchy was shaped by two quite different story lines. One line of thought tells it as a story of ascent from an inferior female-dominated society to a superior male-dominated one. Another tells it as a fall-redemption story of an originally harmonious and good world, distorted by a "fall" into evil patriarchy, to be overcome by the emergence of a higher socialist and/or feminist society today.

Chapter 10 recounts how the renewed feminist movement, from the 1970s to today, reappropriated these nineteenth-century theories of matriarchal fall and redemption, seeking a pro-woman spirituality. It traces the emergence of this movement as it developed complex ritual practices for individuals and groups and as theoreticians arose to elaborate its theological and ethical vision for a comprehensive social transformation. Although still seeing this movement as countercultural, leaders of Goddess spirituality have sought to normalize themselves both in the academy and within the spectrum of religious diversity in American society. I believe that Christian feminists should heartily support both of these developments, recognizing our largely common values as well as our common enemies in fundamentalist patriarchal religions.

The book's conclusion recapitulates the argument of the book and also advocates new alliances among ecofeminist perspectives in various religious contexts. Such mutual support is possible without embracing theories about gender in human social evolution that are not historically tenable. One can affirm the validity of alternative Goddess spiritualities in the contemporary context without insisting that everyone accept the thesis of a literal "feminist Eden" in prehistoric human existence.

We need to acknowledge the validity of the many paths from which feminists mine their traditions—whether those traditions are Jewish, Christian, Buddhist, Hindu, Chinese, Korean, or Celtic. All are historically problematic, and yet all have some potential. Finally, I believe that our hope rests in a new way of imagining and enacting our relation to one another and the earth, a way that never fully existed in any of our ancient worlds but that is vitally necessary today to save our planet from destruction.

ONE · Gender and the
Problem of Prehistory

IMAGINING PREHISTORY

To examine the contested issue of gender in ancient Near Eastern prehistory, I begin with a definition of the period. Prehistory is the time before the invention of writing (which took place around 3500 BCE in the ancient Near East). This period is divided into several major eras of human development in eastern Europe and the ancient Near East: late Paleolithic (c. 30,000–9000 BCE), proto-Neolithic and Neolithic (c. 9000–5600 BCE), and Calcolithic (5600–3500 BCE). In the European late Paleolithic, we begin to have some evidence of human creative consciousness in the form of cave paintings, figurines, and tools decorated with designs or with figures of animals or humans. The Neolithic is divided from the Paleolithic by the movement from food gathering (hunting and collecting fruits, nuts, and plants) to food growing and domestication of animals. The Calcolithic describes a time of more developed agriculture (including the use of the plow and irrigation) as well as trade and early urbanization.

The Neolithic revolution took place gradually in the ancient Near East between 9000 and 7000 BCE. At first, herds of wild animals or areas of wild grains were cordoned off and controlled by more settled human groups; later, with full domestication, animals were bred for food, milk, or skins, and seeds were conserved for planting grains. These innovations developed along parallel lines in several places in the ancient Near East and spread to other nearby areas. There was not a uniform, straightforward pattern of development. Agriculture might have been started in one area and then abandoned when water supplies gave out; the group that had begun to grow food might then have migrated and become pastoral. Earlier Paleolithic patterns of hunting and gathering continued in societies near those that had moved on to agriculture and stock breeding. Many Neolithic societies mixed stock breeding and agriculture with hunting wild animals and gathering wild plants.[1]

A variety of female figurines with markedly large breasts, buttocks, and bellies are found in Neolithic sites. These figurines are often seen as reflecting a view that links the female body with fecundity, likely an inheritance from the Paleolithic period.[2] The development of pottery around 7000 BCE offers new artifacts with geometric designs, often molded in human and animal shapes. But without writing, it is very difficult to determine the actual thoughts or intentions of those who created these images. Even early writings, such as texts from third-millennium Sumerian cities, are not easy to interpret, a topic explored in the following chapter. With no writing, and with only those artifacts that happen to be made of materials capable of longer survival (stone, metal, baked clay, bone), determining what a group of people *meant* by particular images is guesswork, an area into which trained archaeologists venture with great caution.

Yet humans, including trained archaeologists, are driven to know what such things meant and thus what they might mean for us today. This is why such quests for evidence of the lives of earlier peoples are undertaken. How does knowing the paths trod by humans in the past inform us about what we are, about our potential as humans? Prehistory—precisely because one can say so little about it or about the inner life of its people with certainty—easily becomes a tabula rasa on which to project our own theories about what humans necessarily are or should be and hence must have once been. Questions of gender roles, in particular, have reflected the social assumptions of the archaeologists.

Archaeological studies of prehistory reflect sharply contrasting lines of interpretation of gender roles. The dominant line in archaeology, which continues today, simply assumes that, however much human society might change in terms of technology and movement from hunting and gathering to agriculture and stock breeding to industrialism, gender roles are fixed by biology. This interpretation holds that the male is the dominant food provider, that from the dawn of human development he was the one who left the home base to secure food, primarily by hunting animals. The focus of many paleoanthropologists, then, has been on "man the hunter." This view assumes that the primary diet of early humans was meat and that the role of hunter was filled exclusively by males. Males are also seen as the primary innovators of social and technological advances: hunting generated both social cooperation among men and the impetus to create implements such as spears, axes, and knives.[3]

This view casts women as passive recipients of the food brought back to the home base by the males. Women's primary work was maternal, producing and raising babies. They also did secondary food processing, grinding and cooking grains or meat. This image of Paleolithic humans has had an overwhelming impact on anthropological museums throughout the world as well as pictorial representations in introductory anthropology books.[4] Representations of "early man" picture males as mobile, working in groups, hunting, fishing, and shaping tools for the hunt; women are isolated, sedentary, caring for children, cooking food.

Archaeologists have typically assumed that males created and used most of the surviving stone or bone tools from Paleolithic peoples. Thus, a rounded implement is likely to be interpreted as a mace used by males to kill animals, rather than as a pounding tool used by women to process grain or nuts.[5] Such depictions of Paleolithic "man" reproduce the presumed sexual division of labor within the Western industrial middle class, with its split between "home" and "work," with men as providers and women confined to domestic work and child raising.

In the mid-nineteenth century, a different picture of prehistoric humans, as originally matriarchal and only later developing patriarchal societies, was advanced by a few Western thinkers, based more on traditions of classical literature than on field studies. The pioneering exposition of this thesis of original matriarchy was the three-volume work *Myth, Religion, and Mother Right*, published by German classicist J. J. Bachofen in 1861. This work had a major impact on nineteenth-century thought. It shaped the way classicists such as Jane Harrison and archaeologists such as Sir Arthur Evans, who explored the ruins of the palace of Knossus in Crete, looked at the evidence of pre-Hellenic societies.[6]

Lewis Morgan, in his study *Ancient Society* (1877), on American Indians, also read his evidence through the lens of the idea that human society passed through an original matriarchal stage. From Morgan's work, the idea entered Marxist discourse and became a permanent part of Marxist theory as it described stages of social development. Frederick Engels, in his treatise *The Origin of the Family, Private Property, and the State* (1884), drew from Morgan the concept of an original stage of "mother right" that had been superseded by patriarchal property holding and lines of descent.[7]

Bachofen did not see original matriarchy as a time of high civilization. Rather, he considered the end of matriarchy and the development of patriarchy as the triumph of the "masculine" qualities of rationality over the inferior "feminine" qualities of instinct. Engels, however, drawing on patterns of Western thought that posited an original "Eden" followed by a "fall," described original matriarchy as a time of "primitive communism," contrasting it to the ascendance of patriarchy that followed, with its unjust domination of the male over the female. As Engels put it, "the overthrow of mother right was the world historic defeat of the female sex."[8] This, for Engels, was the cellular model of all subsequent oppressive class relations between owner and worker. He argued that civilization had been built on a series of unjust systems of exploitation, but that this history would culminate in a final transformation, in which women would be emancipated and communism would reappear as a higher and final stage. Late Victorian feminist theorists, such as Matilda Joslyn Gage, in her 1893 treatise *Woman, Church, and State*,[9] also imagined the time of original matriarchy as one of high civilization, followed by a fall into violence and oppression under patriarchal rule.

But these nineteenth-century theories of a fixed sequence of social stages, in which original "promiscuity" was followed by matriarchy and then by patriarchy, were discredited in the new anthropology pioneered by Franz Boas in the 1920s.[10] Boas considered such theories of universal social evolution to be unscientific and argued that they should be entirely abandoned in favor of painstaking research on particular local societies. Each society, he believed, was sui generis and needed to be studied for its own distinct configurations rather than being fit into a universal theory of stages of development. Boas's methods have helped to provide a foundation for modern scientific anthropology and archaeology.

The link between nineteenth-century concepts of early matriarchy and both feminism and Marxism perhaps made this theory particularly objectionable to American male anthropologists of the twentieth century. Robert Lowie, author of *Primitive Society* (1920), sought to demolish this hypothesis as it had been advanced in Morgan's study of indigenous American societies. In this work, Lowie asserts that there has never been an instance of actual matriarchy—that is, rule by women that parallels patriarchy. He goes on to claim that matrilineal descent has had no universal priority in human history. In his view, it occurs only rarely and only as an anomaly when normative paternal rule is temporarily interrupted. But it is inherently unstable and soon disappears.[11] For Lowie, paternal descent and male dominance are the natural and universal human patterns.

The primacy of patriliny became a widely shared consensus in American anthropology into the 1960s, as theories of the evolution of society and the search for the origins of certain developments assumed to be normative in human society came back into favor.[12] Elman Service's *Primitive Social Organization: An Evolutionary Perspective* (1962) reflects this consensus. Service traces the organization of human society back to the earliest emergence of hominids from prehuman primates. Although the mother-child dyad may be the core of the human family, he assumes that prolonged human infantile dependency and the change from seasonal to continual sexuality in females created the necessity of protecting women from sexually aggressive males and the need for males to provide for women and children. The conjugal male-female bond developed to satisfy these needs, he argues.[13]

Service concedes that females gathered plant foods, but he seems to regard this as a very inadequate food supply compared to the animal protein derived from hunting by males. He also sees females as incapable of forming organizations among themselves and describes them as gathering plants alone with dependent children. Males, in contrast, developed hunting as the main human food supply early in human history, an activity that inherently created cooperation among groups of men. The need to defend one's own group against other males, presumed to be always aggressive, made war necessary. Thus, men bonded through hunting and war.[14] This theory of male bonding in the context of hunting and war as uniquely masculine activities was popularized in the era of the Vietnam war, reflecting the first wave of antifeminist backlash in books such as Lionel Tiger's *Men in Groups* (1969).[15]

Described as physically weaker by nature, unable to travel far or run swiftly because of continual pregnancy and child care, the female necessarily submitted to the male to receive food for herself and her offspring and protection from the sexual aggression of other males. The male, superior in strength and mobility, decreed virilocal residence as the normal family pattern: the female was transferred from her natal family to that of her husband, while the sisters of her husband were similarly transferred to the households of other males. Service argues that this exchange, or "reciprocal giving," of women was the first expression of "human" sharing, and itself reflected the emergence of a truly human capacity to organize and plan for the future, as distinct from prehuman primates.[16] Through such reasoning, Service construes something very much like the monogamous, male-dominant family, with male provider-protector and dependent female, as the original and universal human family.

This view was challenged by a growing number of women anthropologists in the 1960s and 1970s. Studies of existing foraging and gardening societies conducted by male anthropologists were shown to be skewed by the men's inability to actually observe and speak with the women in such settings. Female anthropologists who could locate themselves in the women's community saw a very different picture. Their studies of foraging societies showed that female gathering of plants, nuts, and berries not only was an equal source of food for many communities but for some supplied the predominant food source.[17] In addition, related females and their children generally gathered as a group, not in isolation.

Females also bonded with one another. Particularly in matrilocal societies (in which a male joins his spouse in the location of her mother's family), they worked together in procuring and processing food. Women, too, were toolmakers. They fashioned digging tools, invented weaving and basket making, and created slings to carry children, freeing their hands to gather food. Women invented tools for chopping and grinding gathered foods and containers for cooking and storage. Women in their work as gatherers and food processors were the primary creators of the technology that turned the raw into the cooked, plant and animal matter into clothes and containers. In their role as plant gatherers, they were probably the first to learn to scatter seeds to grow new plants.[18]

Some women paleoanthropologists also challenged the dogma of a primordial division of labor between male hunters and female gatherers dating to early hominid or even prehuman primates. They suggested that a long period of scavenging young, weak, or dead animals preceded organized hunting, with both males and females participating equally in such scavenging.[19]

In their landmark book *The Female of the Species*, M. Kay Martin and Barbara Voorhies describe matrilineal and matrilocal social organization as enduring and stable rather than rare and aberrant. Starting from the premise that the mother-child dyad is the core human group, they regard matrilineal and matrilocal societies as originally much more widespread in early foraging societies than they are now, although not universal. In these societies, the grandmother was the central ancestress, with her children and grandchildren clustered around her in an extended family. Men, rather than women, moved between matricentric extended households. The male gained access to a wife through serving her and her family, although he retained his relationship to his own mother's household and lineage. Male leadership was provided by brothers of the matrilineal group.[20]

Matrilineal societies flourished particularly in situations of relative abundance, where there was not severe competition for resources. Such situations were common for early human foragers, who gathered food in regions that later became sites for the development of agriculture. In a 1965 symposium on "man the hunter," the mostly male contributors disputed the assumption that foraging societies were driven by scarcity and were always on the brink of starvation. On the contrary, they described this way of life as "the most successful and persistent adaptation man has ever achieved"—much more successful than the way of life initiated by the agricultural revolution and industrialization, which the writers saw as bringing humans to the brink of annihilation in the second half of the twentieth century. This early abundance and the ease of the foraging lifestyle that sustained humanity for 99.9 percent of its history have been obscured as patriarchal agricultural and industrial societies have taken over these regions, pushing foragers into marginal areas of the world.[21]

Martin and Voorhies point out that matriliny and patriliny are not fixed alternatives. Humans throughout history have created a complex variety of kinship patterns that include both paternal and maternal kin. Bilineal descent is common in many societies. For example, in the Tiwi culture in Australia, men trace their ancestors patrilineally for the purpose of allotting territory, whereas marriage is organized matrilineally through a common grandmother.[22] Women's status varies greatly in patrilineal societies, depending on the extent to which women retain control of the fruits of their own labor, which they allocate to the family or market, and on whether they inherit and control land or other means of wealth from their own families. Simply proving that women have a large work role in a society says nothing about women's status unless one can also show that they control the means of production and the fruits of their work.

Although men tend to be the hunters of large game and women the gatherers of plant food in surviving foraging societies, this division of labor is by no means fixed. When animals are hunted by driving them into a trap, men and women both participate. Women often hunt and catch smaller animals. In the Tiwi culture, women both gather plant food and hunt smaller land animals, while the men primarily focus on fishing and catching birds.[23] The work assigned to women varies greatly in different societies. In some fishing cultures, women are the primary fishers or the gatherers of shellfish.[24] The basic rule of foraging societies is that no one, except the very young, is a passive, dependent nonproducer. The work involved in procuring and processing food demands the skills of both male and female, beginning at an early age. The model of family based on a male provider and a female dependent is a product of projecting the ideology of the industrial middle-class household of modern society back onto Paleolithic times.

Martin and Voorhies see patrilineal and patrilocal societies developing in foraging and early gardening societies in two contexts: in regions of scarcity and harsh competition for resources; and in situations of abundance, when early agriculture and trade create the possibility of surplus wealth.[25] With the development of gardening, very likely initiated by female food gatherers, people begin to claim particular plots of land for ongoing use, and this land is marked off as controlled by specific cultivators. Domestication of plants allows the accumulation and storage of food. Trade develops, as people exchange food, artisan work such as pottery, and especially useful materials, such as obsidian or special kinds of stone or wood, between different regions.[26] Work to accumulate wealth replaces a less hurried way of life in which food was simply gathered for each day. The accumulation and storage of wealth creates divisions between wealthier and poorer members of the society, in contrast to the community of foragers, in which food was not accumulated and all shared on a relatively equal level.

In this new situation of the quest for surplus wealth, the female role as worker, not the female as helpless dependent, is the root of her subjugation in developing patrilineal and patrilocal societies. Men accumulate wealth by accumulating a female workforce. Women are married out of their natal households and located in the household of their husbands, where they lose the support system of their own parents, sisters, and brothers. Polygyny is the way in which males accumulate wealth, by acquiring many female workers. Yet not all polygyny is experienced as oppressive by women. In some cases, especially when the wives are related, they bond, work as a team, and effectively control their common husband.[27]

Anthropologists such as Martin and Voorhies generally describe foraging societies as egalitarian, but this primarily means that there is no class hierarchy, although some individuals may be given higher status. Men and women play complementary roles in hunting and food gathering, but these roles can be organized in various ways that may or may not concede decision-making roles to women. Some hunting-gathering or hunting-gardening societies in which women have a large work role and provide the majority of the food can nevertheless feature male violence against women.[28] Thus, work role complementarity in foraging and gardening societies cannot necessarily be idealized as a blissful time of equality between men and women.

REDISCOVERING "ORIGINAL MATRIARCHY"

As women anthropologists struggled to map the complexity of male-female roles and actual power relations in preindustrial societies, a renewed feminist movement was raising questions about the origins of patriarchy. In this context of the 1970s, the nineteenth-century theory of original matriarchy as a time of female power, harmony, and justice resurfaced. The writings of nineteenth-century matriarchalists such as Bachofen, Gage, and Harrison were rediscovered and heralded as a revelation of the true history of gender relations, long concealed by triumphant patriarchy.

This literature, however, had been totally discredited among professional anthropologists and archaeologists. Women archaeologists became increasingly concerned with the way in which archaeology was being cited as proof of this story of original matriarchy. They wanted to clearly distinguish their own carefully scientific studies, which vindicated larger roles for women in early human societies, from such revived matriarchal theory.[29] But their critique was not widely known outside professional circles. It did not deter the popularity of the theory among a new wave of cultural feminists, often linked with a reclaimed Goddess worship, seen as the original religion of humanity.

A major authority for the new matriarchalism and Goddess quest of the 1980s and 1990s has been Marija Gimbutas, archaeologist and cultural historian of Neolithic "Old Europe" and author of such treatises as *Goddesses and Gods of Old Europe* (1982) (originally *Gods and Goddesses of Old Europe*, 1974), *The Language of the Goddess* (1989), and *The Civilization of the Goddess* (1991). Gimbutas's credentials as an archaeologist gave scientific credibility to the new matriarchalism for popularizers such as Riane Eisler (*The Chalice and the Blade*, 1987) and Charlene Spretnak (*The Politics of Women's Spirituality*, 1982.)[30]

In her successive books, which are copiously illustrated, Gimbutas not only describes the extraordinary pottery and figurines of Neolithic cultures in the Balkans from 7000 to 3000 BCE but also embeds these images and artifacts in a story of great mythic power. It is this narrative that has caught the imagination of those women and men who are engaged in a search for a more life-sustaining deity and spirituality in the midst of modern dehumanization and threatened ecocide. This narrative is so symbolically compelling that it has become a kind of dogma for many people involved in this Goddess quest. Disputing its details is treated as a treasonous heresy directed against feminist hopes, perpetrated by heartless academics. The emotionality of this debate indicates the high stakes it involves.[31]

What are the stakes involved in this debate? The Gimbutas narrative tells of a time before patriarchy, war, and violence when humans lived together peacefully and were in harmony with nature, a time when both men and women revered the female as the immanent power of renewal in nature that carried life through creation, growth, decline, death, and renewal of life. Gimbutas suggests that this egalitarian, peaceful time reigned from human beginnings well into the Neolithic agricultural revolution, not only in a restricted region of the Balkans and the northeastern Mediterranean but worldwide, and was also the original culture of all the great civilizations of Asia.[32]

In her view, this happy time was destroyed by a small group of militaristic, patriarchal nomads who originated in the Russian steppes and swept down on horseback into southern Europe in successive waves (4400–4300 BCE, 3500 BCE, and 3000 BCE), conquering the unprotected, peaceful peoples of these regions and imposing their patriarchal culture and way of life on them. The matricentric, goddess-worshipping folk of Old Europe and the eastern Mediterranean eventually amalgamated with their conquerors, although they kept remnants of their own cultures, which are preserved in the surviving goddess figures from the historic cultures of the Near East, Greece, and Rome. This goddess-centered subculture also survives in European folklore down to our own time.

This narrative is a powerful identity myth for some European and American women and men. It allows them to imagine a peaceful, matricentric, and ecologically sustainable culture as their own "original culture" and to disown the patterns of patriarchy, violence, and domination that have characterized Western culture from its alleged roots in the ancient Near East and Greece. By imagining a time—indeed, the primeval time—before this culture of violence and domination, one can also imagine a time after it, a day when Euro-Americans can reclaim their original and more authentic mothering, peaceful, ecologically sustainable cultural selves. The culture of patriarchal domination of women and nature thus loses its claim to primacy and "naturalness" and becomes a "bad interlude" that can be overcome.

This narrative provides a basis for a modern countercultural identity that is very empowering for those who seek such an alternative to the looming disasters of modern industrialism and militarism. Two questions need to be asked, however. First, is this narrative historically true? Asking this question is not simply academic quibbling. It goes to the heart of how we tell the story of our past in order to mediate our future. If we tell the story of our past in a way that significantly distorts the knowable evidence, we may not understand how we got to be the way we are and, more important, what we really need to do to change. Second, as a myth, does this narrative mediate real liberating transformation for women and men? We must consider the possibility that it contains the very assumptions that have caused our problems and hence may tie us to and reproduce these same problems rather than helping us overcome them.

These two questions are asked and answered in the negative in Cynthia Eller's book *The Myth of Matriarchal Prehistory: Why an Invented Past Won't Give Women a Future*.[33] I am in basic agreement with this book; yet the critique needs further discussion. We should give Gimbutas's work its due, while also recognizing its faults. To this end, I recount Gimbutas's argument in further detail.

Before she embarked on her major publications, Marija Gimbutas was an established archaeologist who had participated in major excavations in regions such as Yugoslavia, Macedonia, and the Balkans[34] and who had amassed a huge inventory of Neolithic artifacts, pottery, and figurines from the entire area of southern Europe and the eastern Mediterranean. Her first major interpretive work was published in 1974 under the title *Gods and Goddesses of Old Europe*. Its republication in 1982, with a new title that reversed the relation of gods to goddesses, framed the images she described more explicitly in the context of a story of an original peaceful "paradise" and the "fall" into violent patriarchy. In the ten years between the first and second editions of this book, Gimbutas had apparently become convinced that the existing artifacts must be understood by placing them into this narrative frame.[35]

But this interpretive frame does not deeply penetrate the main text itself. We read of Neolithic village cultures located in regions of Greece and the Balkans into the mid-Danube that had successfully domesticated a range of plants and animals, produced sophisticated pottery and figurines, and established trade and commerce. Gimbutas's main contribution is that she validated this region as an area of autonomous cultural achievements, not simply as an outpost of the developments in the Near East and Greece.

In this second edition, we hear about a predominance of female figures, with a focus on fat buttocks, breasts, and bellies as well as elaborate costumes, hair arrangements, masked faces. There are miniature models of houses in which bulls' horns and female figures are featured together with domestic implements, ovens, grindstones, and chimneys. These Gimbutas interprets as representations of "shrines." A large number of animals are part of the imagery: snakes, fish, birds, bears, bees, butterflies, pigs. Almost all the images are seen as expressions of a unitary Goddess who governs birth, death, and regeneration. The identification of these images as expressions of the Goddess is carried primarily by Gimbutas's assertions; there often seems to be little reason to see fish, bears, or birds as female rather than as male, or as not gendered at all.

Gimbutas concedes that a few images, such as those of phalluses and figures with prominently erect penises, are indeed male, but she describes male representations as marginal to the overwhelming predominance of images associated with the Goddess. She also concedes that snakes represent the male penis. We are told dogmatically that this was a female-dominated culture, but the author cites little to prove this assertion, other than the assumption that the existence of many female images means a female-dominated culture. But we know all too well from other cultures, such as contemporary India or even the Christian Middle Ages, that the existence of many female religious images does not equal female domination.

Gimbutas's next major publication, *The Language of the Goddess* (1989), attempts to gather the symbols found on these figurines and pottery into a comprehensive system in order to interpret their meaning. Gimbutas sees the various decorative patterns—Vs, Ms, zigzags, and the like—as a proto-writing for a form of pre–Indo-European language that is as yet indecipherable. Much of this attempt to identify symbols with definite meanings seems overly assertive. Are zigzags always rain? Are Vs always pubic triangles? It challenges credulity when Gimbutas confidently identifies megalithic stone altars in temples in Malta that have a slightly tapering lower end as "pubic triangles."[36] Reviewers have questioned Gimbutas's penchant for finding definite female gender symbols in every cross, double or triple line, or circle.[37]

In *The Language of the Goddess*, Gimbutas develops what she sees as the underlying religion of the Goddess. She claims that these ancient peoples did not worship a variety of images of life in localized expressions. Instead, she argues, they had one unified understanding of the Goddess as the power of creation and re-creation underlying all life and renewal of life throughout the whole region (the whole world?). All these many images of females in various forms, of diverse animals, and of natural phenomena such as rain were understood as expressions of a unitary female deity. Symbolic colors such as black and white had a meaning opposite from the one they acquired later in patriarchal cultures; black, for instance, symbolized the fertile earth, while white was the expression of death. Stiff, white female figurines represented the Goddess in her death aspect.

Gimbutas thus defines belief in a monotheistic Goddess, the unitary power of life and renewal of life underlying the process from gestation and birth to death and rebirth, as a shared religion of all these peoples. The earth as the place of burial was identified with the mother's womb. In descending into the earth for burial in womb-shaped underground temples, one was at the same time affirming a faith in the rebirth of nature from death. These ancient people thus had no fear of death, understanding it as an integral part of the life process. This is an attractive worldview for contemporary ecofeminist spirituality, but can we know that this is what ancient people understood as their own worldview? Much of Gimbutas's reconstruction of the Goddess religion seems eisegesis—that is, it involves reading into ancient artifacts a predetermined worldview in which she already has come to believe.

In her culminating tome, *The Civilization of the Goddess* (1991), Gimbutas offers more definite data to support her view of an original matricentric society overrun by patriarchal militarists. For nonarchaeologists who have not seen this data firsthand, this book seems to be her most convincing work. But the fact that other archaeologists who have studied this same data, including women with a feminist perspective, strongly dispute her interpretations should give one pause.[38] In this work, Gimbutas insists that she is not talking about a primitive *matriarchy*. In other words, women did not hold dominating power over men in a way that paralleled male power over women in patriarchy. Rather, she claims that Neolithic European archaeological evidence discloses societies that were matricentric and matrilineal. The female descent group stayed together, and men married into the female-headed clan. This, Gimbutas says, can be deduced from evidence from graves in which the females are related to each other but the males are strangers.[39] She does not ask where these women's brothers are. They would have been related to the females, and matrilineal societies usually give leadership to brothers/uncles. She simply assumes that the males in the graves were all from other groups.

In her reconstruction of the social structure of these societies, Gimbutas seems reluctant to assign the males any leadership roles at all, hardly a pattern that has been observed in actual matrilineal peoples, including the famous matrilineal Iroquois, whose council of mothers stood behind and monitored the council of Iroquois chiefs.[40] According to Gimbutas, the societies of Old Europe were run exclusively by a council of women from the leading clans, headed by a priestess-queen. Men performed skilled roles as artisans and engaged in trade and commerce, but women governed the society as a whole, centered in its religious rites.

Despite the use of terms such as "queen," Gimbutas insists that she is talking about totally egalitarian societies in which men and women were fully equal. Men apparently were satisfied to ply their trades while ceding religious and political rule to women. It is hard to imagine males who have control of the sources of wealth in their hands yielding religious and political power exclusively to women for thousands of years. Archaeologists counsel caution in assuming that existing gatherer and horticultural peoples who have survived into modern times exhaust the possibilities of what might have existed in prehistory.[41] Yet it is significant that feminist anthropologists such as those cited earlier have found no societies with exclusively female leadership, as Gimbutas describes, among the varied options.

In existing matrilineal societies, major spheres of power are given to males, even if their leadership roles are derived from their mothers. No society gives women all the public power roles in government and religion. Moreover, relative egalitarianism does not in itself prove that a society is matrilineal and matrilocal. Foraging societies are egalitarian in the sense of lacking class hierarchy, but they are not necessarily matrilineal and matrilocal. Although matriliny may have once been more common than it is now, recall that Martin and Voorhies see patrilineal and patrilocal societies developing even in foraging societies in the context of food scarcity and a struggle for resources. (Perhaps such a situation explains the origins of Gimbutas's patriarchal, militarist horsemen from the Russian steppes.)

But the societies Gimbutas describes are not made up of foragers but of agriculturalists, with domesticated animals and plants, a developed material culture, and trade. Such a society allows accumulation of surplus wealth, a situation in which one would expect some class hierarchy to develop. Patrilineal and patrilocal patterns generally predominate in these societies. Gimbutas's efforts to explain away the existence of larger and smaller houses—and even palaces, in the case of Minoan society—by arguing that they are not evidence of class hierarchy seems highly strained. Indeed, her predilection for the term "queen" to refer to the presumed female clan head of these societies hardly squares with a lack of class hierarchy.

Gimbutas insists that all the artifacts she has uncovered point to overwhelming female predominance. Males are hardly represented at all, never as fathers, and not in any way that suggests dominance. But she strengthens this impression by assigning virtually all the symbolism to women, unless a particular symbol is clearly and obviously phallic—snakes, phalluses, and male figurines with erect penises, for example. The minimizing of male presence in the symbolic system rests on several other questionable assumptions. One is that the people of these societies failed to recognize any relation between the male sexual act and female gestation. Fatherhood was unknown, Gimbutas repeatedly asserts. Yet she explains the prominence of phallic symbols as representing the male "stimulating" principle—that is, the stimulation of the Goddess's fertility. It is hard to know what this means if it does not connect male insemination with female fertility.

Gimbutas also contradicts herself on the question of recognized paternity. In the conclusion of *Goddesses and Gods of Old Europe*, she states that "phallicism certainly had no obscene allusion; in the context of religious ritual it was a form of catharsis, not of symbolic procreation. There is no evidence that in Neolithic times mankind understood biological conception." Yet in the introduction to *The Language of the Goddess*, she dates the lack of knowledge of paternity back to Paleolithic times, asserting that Neolithic people were very keen observers of nature and certainly understood "the paternal role in the process of reproduction."[42]

One very prominent set of symbols in many of the Neolithic cultures Gimbutas examines involves the heads and horns of bulls. Sculptured bulls' heads (bucrania) and bulls' horns are found in many of the shrines she describes throughout the region, from the Balkans to the eastern Mediterranean. They are, for example, central to the shrines of the seventh-millennium Anatolian town of Çatal Hüyük. The bull cult also played a major role in Minoan culture, and memories of the Mediterranean bull cult survive in the Spanish tradition of bull fights. In cattle-raising societies, bulls are generally located in the male sphere of power, and bull symbolism is associated with male virility, power, and wealth.

Gimbutas, however, removes this entire set of symbols from the male to the female sphere. She does this by arguing that these horned heads actually represent the female womb and fallopian tubes. She shows a representation of these female reproductive organs from a modern medical book, in which they appear, with some imagination, somewhat like a bull's head and horns.[43] But the likelihood of Neolithic people observing these organs at all, much less perceiving a resemblance to a bull's head and horns, is far-fetched indeed. By transferring bucrania from the male to the female sphere, Gimbutas conveniently redefines what was probably the most central symbol of male virility in her cultural artifacts.

Perhaps the most dramatic part of *Civilization of the Goddess* is the concluding chapter, "The End of Old Europe: The Intrusion of Steppe Pastoralists from South Russia and the Transformation of Europe."[44] In this chapter, Gimbutas describes the successive invasions of the people she calls "Kurgans" (from the name of their barrow-type funeral mounds). Unlike the inhabitants of Old Europe, the Kurgans had domesticated the horse and used horses for military forays against neighboring peoples. The Kurgans lacked the sophisticated agriculture, the artisan work, and the trade of the peoples of Old Europe, but they had a developed arsenal of weapons.

Drawing evidence from excavations of graves and villages, Gimbutas details what she describes as the decisive shift that overtook the peoples of Old Europe with the successive incursions of these invaders from the north. The graves of earlier times, she writes, showed little difference between men and women in the goods buried with the deceased, and the villages lacked hill forts. But with the arrival of the Kurgans, new patterns developed: rich grave goods of gold and weapons in the barrows of leading males, hilltop forts, and evidence of violent death and human sacrifice. Gimbutas sees these incursions as the sole impetus for the transformation of the cultures in southern Europe and the Mediterranean from peaceful, matricentric cultures to patriarchal, militaristic ones. Some island areas, such as Crete, were not affected as early and thus retained their matricentric, egalitarian societies into the second millennium, but they too eventually succumbed to the new patriarchal ways. Other peoples, such as the Etruscans, who preceded the Romans in central Italy, also preserved the old matricentric culture.[45]

Several archaeologists who have worked in some of the same areas as Gimbutas question her interpretation, however. Ruth Tringham, for example, believes that Gimbutas has ignored evidence of fortification, inequality, and human sacrifice in earlier sites in order to fit her thesis.[46] One need not dispute the possibility that invasions of nomadic peoples, covetous of the wealth of agricultural settlements, had some effect in spurring the development of military defense in settlements in southern Europe and the Mediterranean. But these settlements did not experience one commanding series of invasions from a single place, the Russian steppes. Rather, there were continual invasions of surrounding peoples from many directions, who entered more settled areas and amalgamated culturally with the existing societies. Gimbutas's thesis that peaceful, goddess-worshipping, matriarchal societies experienced waves of invasions from one area by patriarchal militarists with a completely different culture is not history.

Gimbutas compares the Kurgans' invasion of undefended, peaceful southern Europe to the horse-riding Spaniards who swept through Central and South America, quickly overcoming a people who lacked war horses.[47] But the comparison begs the question. The indigenous peoples of Mexico and Peru, who lacked both horses and wheeled vehicles, had already developed, over more than a thousand years, a patriarchal, militarist, highly stratified class society that practiced human sacrifice. Clearly, the presence or absence of horses is not the sole determinant for the development of such societies.

The major archaeological site often used as "proof" of a peaceful, matricentric, goddess-worshipping culture in the Neolithic era of Old Europe has been the town of Çatal Hüyük, which flourished in the central plain of Anatolia between 6500 and 5600 BCE. The discovery and excavation of Çatal Hüyük by British archaeologist James Mellaart pushed back the history of urban development in the ancient Near East several millennia and showed that well-developed centers of trade existed in Anatolia long before the urban centers of the Sumerians in the Tigris and Euphrates delta.[48] The people of Çatal Hüyük domesticated more than a dozen types of plants. They also domesticated sheep and goats, which were probably used primarily for wool and milk, and had begun to domesticate cattle. Large game hunting played a key role in the cultural life of the people of Çatal Hüyük, who hunted aurochs (a species of cattle), wild pigs, deer, and leopards. Leopards were especially valued for their skins, which were used in ritual hunting dances. The domesticated dog played a role in hunting.

The site of Çatal Hüyük is distinguished by its elaborate wall paintings and plastered reliefs in what Mellaart describes as domestic shrines scattered within the houses. Many of these wall paintings seem to portray woven wall hangings, indicating the extensive development of textiles. Some of the designs are still seen in woven rugs in the area today.[49] Mellaart speculates that the limited area of the town excavated during the period from 1961 to 1963 had probably been the "priestly quarter," because it contained a larger number of these domestic shrines than other areas did.

The architecture of Çatal Hüyük consisted of one-story houses linked together to form a continuous outer wall. Inhabitants entered the main rooms through a hole in the roof, from which a ladder descended. Small passageways connected the main rooms with adjoining storage rooms and courtyards used to dispose of trash and human waste. The interior of the main rooms contained sleeping and work platforms as well as a hearth and an oven positioned so that the smoke could ascend through the opening in the roof. Twelve successive building levels were constructed, one over the other, during the settlement's eight-hundred-year history, until the site was abandoned for unknown reasons. There is no evidence that the town was ever conquered by outsiders.

Mellaart's feminist interpreters have exaggerated his descriptions considerably, claiming to see in the unbroken longevity of Çatal Hüyük evidence of a time before war and violence in human relations. They describe the town as unwalled and lacking any evidence of weapons.[50] But this contradicts Mellaart's interpretation. He views the continuous wall formed by the linked houses and the rooftop openings as a very effective defense system, which prevented neighboring peoples who might have coveted the settlement's wealth from conquering it. "Even if an enemy succeeded in breaching the wall he found himself in a closed room from which the ladder has no doubt been removed with the defenders waiting for him on the roof. To take the settlement would involve close fighting from house to house in a maze of dwellings which would be enough to discourage the attacker. . . . It is also clear that the people of this city were sufficiently well equipped with slingshot, bow and arrow, lance and spear to keep any attacker well away from the foot of the wall."[51] Likewise, Mellaart does not consider relations among Çatal Hüyük's residents to have been particularly peaceful. He notes a number of head wounds on the skeletons and suggests that there had been much quarreling and fighting among the inhabitants, reflecting the "rabbit-warren" nature of the closely packed quarters.[52]

Mellaart believes that the people of Çatal Hüyük disposed of their dead by exposing them on platforms well away from the site. When vultures and insects had stripped the bodies of their flesh, the bones were collected and buried under the platforms in the houses. Women and children were buried under the larger platforms, while only adult males were buried under the smaller platforms. Grave goods provide evidence of female and male cultural differentiation: females are typically buried with cosmetics, mirrors, and jewelry; males are buried with weapons and belt fasteners.[53]

Feminist interpreters of Mellaart, such as Anne Barstow, note that the female platforms were larger than those of the males, citing this as evidence that women enjoyed a higher status than men.[54] But this is not Mellaart's assumption. Rather, he

FIGURE 2

Bull, bucrania, and bulls' horns, seventh millennium BCE. Drawing from bas-relief, Çatal Hüyük. Life-size silhouettes of the bull, lively and naturalistic, were cut into the plaster wall and painted bright red. Bucrania (stylized bulls' heads) and horns set on pillars served as altars and ritual benches. (From James Mellaart, *Çatal Hüyük: A Neolithic Town in Anatolia* [London: Thames and Hudson, 1967])

sees the female platforms as larger because women not only slept there but also did indoor work with their children. Males worked outdoors and used their platforms for sleep. More recent excavations on the site by Ian Hodder have further eroded the impression that larger platforms identified with women meant that the women had higher status than the men.[55]

Gimbutas, Eisler, and others describe Çatal Hüyük as centered on the worship of a Mother Goddess, writing that the shrines were dominated by images of a goddess giving birth. They also argue that the importance of this Mother Goddess was evidenced by the many small figurines of females with large breasts and buttocks found in niches of the houses and grain bins. However, a study of Mellaart's reconstruction of the sculptured and painted decorations of the domestic shrine rooms presents a much more complicated picture. Some paintings focus on hunting scenes, with representations of bulls, bears, or stags surrounded by excited figures, some waving weapons, others dressed in leopard skins. Some seem to be dancing, while others

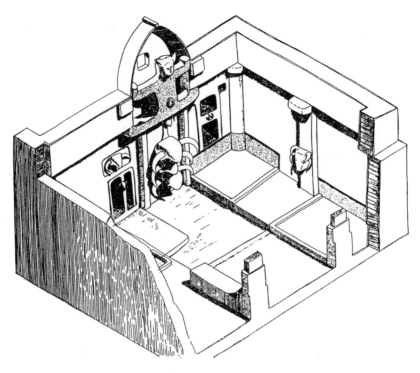

FIGURE 3

Leaping figure with catlike ears, above bulls' heads, seventh millennium BCE. Drawing from bas-relief, Çatal Hüyük. Three life-size plaster heads are superimposed in the wall below; actual skull plates with attached horns of the animals are embedded in the plaster. (From James Mellaart, *Çatal Hüyük: A Neolithic Town in Anatolia* [London: Thames and Hudson, 1967])

are tumbling over the backs of the animals. These human figures in hunting scenes portray what was perhaps a ritualized form of the hunt, in anticipation of actual hunts. Mellaart sees the human figures as entirely male, led by male priests clad in leopard skins.[56]

The majority of the shrine rooms are dominated by the image of the bull. Large painted figures of bulls, bulls' heads, multiple bulls' horns are strikingly evident (fig. 2). In some of the shrines, an anthropomorphic figure with arms raised and legs spread apart horizontally from the body with feet straight up was placed in plaster relief above the bulls' heads (fig. 3). This figure Mellaart interprets as a "goddess giving birth." His interpretation of this figure was decisive for his own view that a "cult of fertility" played a central role in Çatal Hüyük, though others have

FIGURE 4

Leaping figure, seventh millennium BCE. Drawing from bas-relief, Çatal Hüyük.
The youthful figure has her arms and legs stretched wide, her hair floating behind her.
(From James Mellaart, *Çatal Hüyük: A Neolithic Town in Anatolia* [London: Thames
and Hudson, 1967])

disputed this labeling.[57] The spread-legged figure with raised arms typically does
not have breasts, usually has a flat belly with what appears to be an umbilical "but-
ton," has no pubic triangle or vulva, but often does have what look like cat's ears.[58]
The body position of this figure is hardly that normally assumed by women giving
birth. The raised arms might suggest an "orante," or praying figure. But the ears,
the horizontal legs, and the upturned feet suggest a partly feline figure that appears
to be leaping.

A similar plaster figure, with legs extended horizontally on both sides, head turned,
and hair streaming backward, is clearly leaping or flying through the air (fig. 4).
Sometimes two such anthropomorphic figures of the same size appear together.
These Mellaart interprets as a paired goddess, the Great Mother and Daughter.[59] In
several cases, however, one figure has breasts and the other does not, prompting one
to at least ask whether they might be male and female. Nevertheless, one cannot escape noticing that the shrines are overwhelmingly dominated by bulls—large paintings of bulls and bulls' heads and horns—suggesting that these are highly important symbols for the culture. Mellaart unhesitatingly views these as expressions of
male virility. However one interprets the plaster figures above the bulls' heads,
whether birthing or leaping, it would appear that the people of Çatal Hüyük were
particularly preoccupied with bulls, probably linked specifically with male hunting
and hunting rites, if not virility.

A third type of symbolism in the shrines seems to focus on the rites of the dead.

FIGURE 5
Vultures with wingspans of five feet swoop down on headless human corpses, seventh
millennium BCE. Drawing from bas-relief, Çatal Hüyük. Three vultures fly toward
the right, four toward the left in a continuous mural that wraps around the walls of
the shrine. (From James Mellaart, *Çatal Hüyük: A Neolithic Town in Anatolia* [London:
Thames and Hudson, 1967])

Giant vultures are pictured surrounding and pecking at headless stick figures (fig.
5). Sometimes other human figures are portrayed trying to fight off the vultures, a
representation that is puzzling, given Mellaart's assumption that the community willingly exposed its dead to excarnation by these vultures.[60] Several shrines also contain rows of rounded reliefs molded over jaws of carrion birds in such a way that
the beaks stick out in the middle. Mellaart interprets these as women's breasts,[61] suggesting that the mother's breast was identified both with nurturing the young after
birth and with stripping away flesh after death. The female breast is thus connected
with the cycle of birth and death; the lactating breast is also the breast of death. If
this is true, what does this mean about the view of women as "mothers" held by
these people (or by Mellaart)? But since breasts usually come in pairs, not rows, one
has to wonder about this interpretation.[62]

In addition to the bulls' heads, plaster reliefs, and wall paintings, a number of small
sculptures in the round have been found in Çatal Hüyük, many of them not in the
shrines but in niches in the walls of the houses. The most striking is that of a female
with large buttocks and breasts seated on a chair with arms resting on two leopards
(fig. 6). Mellaart describes this as "the goddess giving birth."[63] But this description
again seems questionable. A side view of the piece shows the female figure at ease,

FIGURE 6
Seated female figure between two leopards, seventh millennium
BCE. Çatal Hüyük. (Ankara Museum of Anatolian Civiliza-
tions; photo from James Mellaart, *Çatal Hüyük: A Neolithic
Town in Anatolia* [London: Thames and Hudson, 1967])

resting back on her buttocks in a way that is not an obvious pose for giving birth.
Her knees are almost together, and the round object between her feet does not appear to be an infant.

Several of the other figurines also depict females with large breasts and buttocks,
although not with the distended bellies that might suggest advanced pregnancy. One
rests her hands on her knees, another holds her breasts, while yet another holds animal cubs. One sculpture features four figures, two of which appear to be a male and
a female in sexual union and the other two a mother and a child.[64] This sculpture
seems to show an explicit connection between male-female sexual union and the
mother-child relationship. The people of Çatal Hüyük were doubtless interested in
sexual union and childbirth, but was it as dominating an idea as Mellaart and others
assume?

When one studies the many "fat" female figurines collected by Gimbutas and others from the European Paleolithic and Neolithic eras, it is remarkable how seldom these figures are either clearly pregnant, giving birth (that is, a child emerging from a female figure who is in a squatting, pushing position), or holding a child. Peter Ucko has studied hundreds of Neolithic figures from these regions and finds only six showing a female with child.[65] This relative absence of reference between these fat female figures and birth or children raises the question of whether archaeologists' interpretation of these rotund figures has not focused on the Mother Goddess— the deified female as birth giver—to the exclusion of other possible references.

The location of such figures in grain bins or in proximity to hearths and ovens might suggest a focus on food rather than birth. Perhaps their fatness celebrates the hope for abundant food rather than reproductive success as the major concern of the makers of these statues. Because the ability of humans to accumulate and retain body fat was a key way to survive periods of famine, fatness might have been prized.[66] The figures might have also referred to human fecundity, of course, although not necessarily as the only or main reference. Since women were connected with grain in all its phases, from planting, harvesting, and storage to grinding grain and baking bread, one might well imagine females as the creators of the small female figurines at Çatal Hüyük, in the context of promoting abundance of staple grains. My point in this suggestion is not to claim to know what those who made these objects had in mind, but simply to open the imagination to other options rather than prematurely closing it by declaring all such female figures to be "fertility goddesses," pregnant and giving birth.

The concept of the Goddess as a monotheistic focus of religion, or even the idea of gods and goddesses as the references for figurines, itself needs to be questioned. How do we know that these people separated the natural forces in and around them from some "higher" or divine world of entities that they then thought of as "gods" or "goddesses"? Was there a "religion" separate from daily life? Feminist archaeologists, as noted earlier, have been highly critical of Gimbutas's reconstruction of an idyllic, matricentric world in Europe and the Mediterranean area during Paleolithic and Neolithic times, overthrown by Kurgan invaders from the Russian steppes. They have also questioned Mellaart's too ready interpretation of certain figures as representing a cult of the Mother Goddess in Çatal Hüyük, although he has not been the focus of a sustained critique.[67]

Feminist archaeology, emerging in the mid-1980s, has been slower to develop than feminist anthropology, reflecting the greater difficulty women have had establishing themselves in the archaeological field. Feminist archaeologists such as Rita Wright, Margaret Conkey, Ruth Tringham, and Joan Gero have sought to establish careful methodologies for both fieldwork and interpretation that counter the established dogmas of "man the hunter" propounded by structural-functionalism and sociobiology. Their aim has been to uncover a world of ancient humans that probably had a multiplicity of local economies, a world in which women were not simply helpless dependents but active participants in producing food; making and using tools; making pottery, baskets, and clothing; and creating symbolic representations.[68]

This effort to establish credible feminist approaches to archaeology has been threatened by Gimbutas's work, with her claims to archaeological credentials. The enormous enthusiasm for the work of Gimbutas and her followers in the popular culture and the disdain in which it is nonetheless held by most professional archaeologists put feminist archaeologists between a rock and a hard place. They needed to make clear their own critique of such work as professional archaeologists, while at the same time defending the appropriateness of raising feminist questions in archaeology, albeit in a way that would not be confused with Gimbutas's approach.

This double critique is represented in a number of articles written by feminist archaeologists, featuring both discussion of methodological questions and their interpretations of particular excavations. These articles include several book reviews as well as more extended critiques such as Lynn Meskell's "Goddesses, Gimbutas, and New Age Archaeology" and Margaret Conkey and Ruth Tringham's "Archaeology and the Goddess: Exploring the Contours of Feminist Archaeology." These reviews and articles severely question Gimbutas's work, both for reading into her data an a priori worldview that cannot be proven by the archaeological findings and for ignoring or distorting data to bolster her conclusions.

As Tringham puts it in her review of *The Civilization of the Goddess*, "In page after page [Gimbutas] attempts to convince us of her interpretation of figures as representations of particular manifestations of the Goddess (p. 242), or buildings as shrines (p. 326), and of carvings as snakes and vulvas (p. 304), as well as that traditional archaeologists are mistaken or narrow-minded (p. 338) and that the evidence exists unequivocally to support *her* interpretation. Alternative interpretations are denied any validity or are often not considered at all." The heart of Tringham's critique is represented by the following statement: "Feminist archaeological research is based on a celebration of the ambiguity of the archaeological record and the plurality of its interpretation, and the subjectivity of the prehistories that are constructed as a part of its discourse. Gimbutas, however, has mystified the process of interpretation and has presented her own conclusions as objective fact."[69]

Meskell's overview of Gimbutas's work offers similar criticism. Far from undoing sexist interpretations of prehistory, Meskell argues, Gimbutas and other followers of gynecentric theories have simply created a reversed sexist myth, which they have imposed on the data. "Thus they do not promote credibility; rather they damage and delimit the possible attributes of gender-based research, due to their poor scholarship, ahistorical interpretations, fictional elements and reverse sexism." For Meskell, Gimbutas's work is not only problematic in itself; in addition, its lack of credibility threatens the efforts of feminist archaeologists who want "the question of gender studies to be taken seriously in archaeological circles."[70]

Feminist archaeologists are fighting to defend the standing of their own work in a male-dominated field in which feminist questions are likely to be dismissed in advance. To have their efforts confused with the untenable ideologies and poor critical methods of Gimbutas would be a professional kiss of death. That they are not "neutral" critics of Gimbutas (and, indeed, their own methodology precludes such simplistic notions of "objectivity") does not, in my opinion, negate the validity of their criticism, although it has perhaps prevented them from giving attention to those parts of Gimbutas's work that might still have validity.

I believe that Gimbutas has given us an enormous number of intriguing images of ancient cultural artifacts that leave no doubt about the creativity of peoples in the Neolithic Balkans, regions that were previously not recognized as areas of autonomous culture. But I see the overall interpretative framework as lacking credibility. This failing threatens the validity of her interpretation at many points in her account and leads one to question whether evaluation of evidence may have been biased to build up the credibility of the overall story. Archaeologists who employ both a feminist perspective and careful methods of sifting data may be able to give us better-grounded accounts of the possible economies of early peoples in particular sites. But these archaeologists are hesitant to generalize from one site to another. They see any determination of the social organization of a community to be tentative, and reconstruction of a people's inner worldview even more so. Thus, feminist archaeologists usually do not try to define the "big picture" that many long for in order to understand "how we got the way we are." This leaves a large void, which myth-makers such as Gimbutas step in to fill.

I certainly cannot claim to provide the "big picture" of the social organization and inner life of early peoples and the transformation into the patriarchal, hierarchical patterns we find in early historical societies, such as that of the Sumerians in the third millennium BCE. Yet I can at least suggest some of the ways this development is likely to have happened. This tentative sketch is shaped by two questions. First, are we stuck with only two choices: a view based on "man the hunter," with patriarchy as biologically determined and unchanging; or a view based on the existence of an early matriarchy that was later overthrown by violent patriarchalists? Second, is the story of "original matriarchy violently overthrown" the myth that we need today to overcome the deleterious effects of male domination and violence on subjugated peoples and on the earth? My answer to both questions is no.

Although a detailed and comprehensive answer to the first question may never be attainable, it is possible, thanks to feminist work in anthropology and archaeology, to state the outlines of a more likely story. Human prehistory from hominids through the Paleolithic and Neolithic worlds did not consist of men providers and protectors sheltering and feeding dependent women whose main job was cooking and caring for children. Such a model of the human family is an ideology born of the nineteenth-century, postindustrial British and American middle class. Most human families, even in modern times, have depended on the productive work of both adult women and adult men, as well as that of their children. Only in a small sector of the middle class in the nineteenth and twentieth centuries did the male "head of family" have such a large income that he could afford to dispense with the productive work of women and children. The "man the hunter" view of prehistory misreads not only prehistory but most of recent human history as well.[71]

Towns in the Neolithic Near East, such as Çatal Hüyük, also depended on the work of both males and females. Women very likely predominated in certain areas of endeavor, such as spinning and weaving. This would suggest that the stunning textiles found represented on the walls of the town were their creations. Food processing was undoubtedly in their hands. Probably they helped sow and harvest the grains and other plant food. The storage of grain was very likely also their sphere. Fat female figurines perhaps reflect the connection of the female and the hope of abundant bread. Males probably predominated in hunting, but women are likely to have milked the goats and made dairy products.

The so-called shrines do not represent one gender at the expense of the other, but a complex world of life and death—excited hunters dancing around powerful animals, bulls' heads, and flying cat-eared human figures that are not clearly gendered. Men and women alike knew that their bodies would finally be stripped in death and their bones interred under the areas where they slept and worked. There is no reason to assume that the spectacle of great vultures tearing human flesh did not hold an element of terror for them. But the idea that they identified the female breast with these scavenging beaks of birds of death seems more a modern projection than a certain interpretation of the data.

There were probably no priestess-queens ruling the society and dominating the religious sphere exclusively, if indeed the religious sphere was so clearly differentiated from daily life. If a priestly class existed, males and females likely each had their roles in it. Both men and women contributed to the products of daily survival; both sexes shaped the culture. But perhaps all was not well between them. They may have looked at each other with some suspicion, as one sex claimed power in hunting weapons and the energy of great bulls, and the other monopolized the storage bin and provision of grains. Conflict and tension between men and women are not precluded by collaboration for survival.

But the route that led from such early Neolithic towns—still based partly on hunting, but with agriculture, domesticated animals, textiles, and trade—to the hierarchical, slave-owning cities of the Sumerian world, with their royal and priestly classes, great temples, palaces, and organized war three millennia later, is doubtless a complex one, not a straight evolutionary line. The major stimulus for this development came less from outside nomadic invaders and their horses and more from internal developments triggered by the accumulation of wealth. As wealth began to be monopolized in the hands of the few, the majority, males and females, became subjugated as exploited labor for this leisured, ruling class who came to control most of the land.

One key shift from the early gardening and hunting societies of the Neolithic era took place with the development of plow agriculture and irrigation, probably during the fourth millennium BCE in some areas of the Near East. When hunting begins to disappear as a male occupation, men turn to larger-scale agriculture, using as a labor force the cattle they have come to control. Ethnographic studies show that plow agriculture generally displaces women from their earlier role in hand-hoed gardening. Men then control both sources of food supply, grains and animals. Women still have major work roles, particularly in expanded textile production and food processing. But male plow agriculture reshapes land ownership in a way that decisively moves societies in the direction of both class hierarchy and male domination over women.[72]

That story is elaborated further in the next chapter. The second question, whether we need a myth of prehistoric matriarchy today, is answered more fully through the arguments of successive chapters. I have reservations about the usefulness of this myth for two reasons. First, it is not history and so cannot really help us understand how we got the way we are and how to change. Second, and even more important, it duplicates what I suspect is one of the key roots of the need of males to dominate females—namely, it identifies women predominantly as the representatives of the "natural."

If women, and women alone, personify the forces of nature in the cycles of birth and death, either they need to be dominated by men in order to control these forces of nature, or they are the primary gender that will somehow "save" us from the destructive effects of millennia of male domination of nature. I suggest instead that the only way we can, as human beings, integrate ourselves into a life-sustaining relationship with nature, is for both males and females to see ourselves as equally rooted in the cycles of life and death and equally responsible for creating a sustainable way of living together.

TWO · Goddesses and World Renewal
in the Ancient Mediterranean

This chapter focuses on particular patterns of mythic thought in the ancient cultures of the Near East, Egypt, and Greece in which goddesses play a central role in world renewal. It looks specifically at the figure of Innana/Ishtar of the Sumero-Akkadian traditions of the third and second millennia BCE and makes some comparisons with three other goddesses: Anat in Canaanite Ugaritic myth, Isis in Egypt, and Demeter in Greece. All of these goddesses are closely related to a beloved—a male lover or husband in the first three cases, a daughter in the fourth—who is connected with food production or rain in the face of threatened drought and whose resurrection, through the intervention of the goddess, restores life to the earth. These myths are not only about nature renewal, however. The first three have been reinterpreted in their historic forms in relationship to state formation and kingship. Thus, I also attempt to examine the difficult question of the relationship of these powerful and enduring female divine figures to the status of women in the societies that fostered their myths and cults.

INNANA/ISHTAR AND OTHER GODDESSES
IN SUMERO-AKKADIAN SOCIETY

Mesopotamia, the land between the Tigris and Euphrates Rivers, has been called the "cradle of civilization." It was here that a group of early cities emerged, bureaucracies and social hierarchies were elaborated, and religious institutions were reshaped to express the ideologies of ruling elites of temple and palace. Here writing was developed, originally as an extension of earlier forms of storage accounts for goods such as grain and oil. Between the end of the fourth millennium BCE and the middle of the third millennium, cuneiform (wedge-shaped symbols of a pictorial nature) was translated into the representation of syllables of speech and was used to record literary compositions such as hymns and myths.[1]

This system of writing, developed first for the Sumerian language and then used for the Semitic Akkadian language, gives us our first glimpse into the thought of an ancient people. (The earlier Sumerian culture was eventually absorbed into Akkadian society, becoming the Sumero-Akkadian culture.) Writing became highly specialized, the province of a schooled elite. Women were not admitted to these schools, even though, it is interesting to note, the Sumerian divine patron of the scribal art was the Goddess Nisaba, herself connected with grain storage.[2] This link between writing and storage takes us back to the early origins of writing, in storage accounts, and perhaps to a time when women, associated with grain storage in Neolithic times, had a hand in shaping these methods of record keeping. Outside the scribal elite, most Sumerians were illiterate, yet some females did attain literacy. There was the occasional priestess writer, such as Enheduanna, appointed by her father, Sargon, as high priestess of the moon God at Ur and the author of many hymns. Some *naditu* (cloistered priestesses) also seem to have been trained as scribes.[3]

Archaeologists have pushed the history of the region back to the fifth millennium BCE, when villages began to develop, practicing a mixture of farming and animal husbandry along with hunting and plant gathering. Small temples were found in these villages, and there is evidence of some differences of wealth. The fourth millennium saw a movement toward urbanization. Larger temples became the focus of urban centers, where more specialized workers gathered. A stratified society began to take shape, with larger landowner and temple ruling elites, administrators, and accountants. Military actions brought in prisoners of war as a slave workforce. Lacking much stone or wood, early Mesopotamian society made creative use of its local resources, such as reeds and clay. Extensive agriculture was made possible by channeling the rivers into a network of irrigation ditches.[4]

Temple leaders used slave and corvée labor to dig and maintain these vital irrigation canals. The city elites accumulated wealth primarily through exacting tribute. A portion of agricultural produce and artisan goods, such as grain and textiles, was extracted from households, where most of the labor was done. The system of corvée labor required each household to provide a certain number of days of labor to serve the central institutions. The elites justified these exactions primarily by claiming to represent the gods, the ruling forces of the cosmos, and hence the foundations of society's collective maintenance.[5] Thus, they presented the requirement of service to the gods as the destiny and common lot of all humans.

This view is reflected in the Sumerian myth of the creation of humans. According to this myth, originally the gods themselves had to do their own work, laboring to grow and harvest their food and dig the irrigation canals. The gods began to complain about this labor to Enki, the God of the sweet waters and of technological knowledge. Enki was sleeping, but he was awakened by Nammu, the primal mother who gave birth to all the gods. Enki directed the primal mother and her daughter deities to shape clay forms and turn them into living humans. These humans were charged with performing corvée service to the gods as their destined purpose for existence, and the gods were thereby freed from labor.[6]

This myth reflects the basic Sumerian view of the relation of humans to gods as one of servant to master. Rulers also portrayed themselves as servants of the gods. The myth reflects but also masks the emerging relationship of subjugated workers to a leisured aristocracy. The elites were freed for rule, and for military and cultural activities, by the labor of others, who contributed a portion of their products and labor to these elites.

The third millennium saw greatly expanded urbanization, with much of the population gathered in urban centers. Corvée labor was used to build monumental temples raised on high platforms and large city walls that served for defense and for displaying the power of the rulers. Competition between city-states brought chronic warfare. Military leaders, once appointed for temporary leadership in time of war, become hereditary kings with standing armies. The concentration of population in cities created a crisis in the older system of tribute that exacted a portion of the products and labor of households in the countryside. Large estates belonging to the kings, members of the royal family, high officials, and temple priests and priestesses came to control large amounts of labor and to draw on resident workforces of men and women to do the agricultural and artisan labor. These workers were paid in regular rations, in the form of allotments of grain, oil, and wool.[7]

Some of the workers were slaves, procured from among prisoners of war. Slave status became defined as hereditary, making their descendants permanent property of masters. Other workers owed temporary service as a result of debt: women and children could be handed over to other households to pay debts incurred by the head of a family. Most of the agricultural labor was performed not by large slave crews but by dependents who had been given allotments of land to work with their own family members, paying a portion of the produce to the estate owners.[8] In contrast to the earlier tribute system, the large estates came to own the land and leased it to workers in return for produce or payment in silver.

The records of these large estates of the third millennium give us a glimpse of the class and gender hierarchy of Sumerian society. Class stratification divided the elite class of temple, royal, and wealthy estate owners from a descending hierarchy of smaller landowners, semi-free dependent labor, and slaves. Women were defined as secondary within each class, but the lives of elite women were very different from those of the poorest slave women. Sumerian society saw women as able workers and administrators. Female members of the aristocracy—wives, sisters, and daughters of kings and high officials—were appointed to administer large estates belonging to the extended family.[9]

Other female family members were sometimes appointed priestesses of temples, where they not only officiated in the cult but also administered the large estates of the temple. Although evidence indicates that at least two independent queens ruled in Sumerian history, women were generally excluded from the highest royal power, which was entrusted with military defense, and thus were positioned primarily to represent the extended family as priestesses in its temple holdings. Some daughters of the elite became *naditu,* cloistered priestesses who did not marry and lived together in households in a walled compound. This institution seems to have developed partly as a way of keeping land that had been given to daughters within the family, by endowing temple lands that then remained under family control. A *naditu* could not marry or bear children but could adopt a son, who then belonged to her paternal line. She also engaged in business activities.[10]

One has less of a glimpse of middle-level women in Sumerian society, but records of property transactions show that they had legal rights and could sell and buy land. The poorest women, female slaves, are documented primarily through estate accounts that record their labor in large workshops that produced textiles. These women did not have independent households and were not given allotments of land. Their small children worked with them, though males were excluded when they reached adolescence. Ration records indicate that these women were the lowest paid, being given thirty to forty liters of barley monthly, with ten to twenty liters per child according to age, while male slaves received sixty or more liters and were often allowed time and land to produce their own goods for market.[11] Women slaves also performed other tasks on estates, such as milling grain, but the primary female sphere of labor involved textiles, in all stages of production. Spinning and weaving became closely associated with the definition of womanhood.

Thorkild Jacobsen, leading interpreter of Sumero-Akkadian religion, observes that the concept of the gods evolved through several stages that reflected changes in society.[12] In the fourth millennium, the gods were seen primarily as the vital power in natural phenomena—sky and earth, the power of the spring rains, the fertilizing power of the rivers, the sap that rises in growing plants, the shaping of the embryo in the womb, the sexual attraction that generates life. Each local village and region had its own array of deities that embodied the natural powers around them. The centralizing of villages into cities, and city-states into coalitions and empires, eventually connected these many deities into a more schematic pantheon. The gods of each city, including that city's patron deity, were believed to gather in a ruling assembly, where cosmic decisions were made. The shaping of these theories of the gods as a cosmic system and polity was likely the work of the temple scribal intelligentsia. But the names for the gods remained myriad, and the relations of the gods shifted as new cities rose to power and claimed supremacy for their patron god or goddess.

The concepts of the relations among the gods were shaped through several key social metaphors. One of these was the extended family. The pantheon of the gods resembled a family with an originating pair of parents, father and mother, who brought forth daughters and sons who, in turn, married and generated children and grandchildren. The original pair was represented by Sky (An) and Earth (Ki). Nammu, the Goddess of the watery deep, can also be portrayed as the original mother of the gods, from whom all the other gods were born. Ninhursag, representing the power of the ground and of wildlife in the hills and seen as the birthing Goddess, was also among the primal circle of deities. The offspring of the primal pair were Enhil, associated with the power of the wind and representative of his father, An, in lordship over the world system; and his younger brother, Enki, associated with the power of sweet waters and technological cunning.[13]

Enhil and his wife, Ninlil, associated with air and wind and patrons of the city of Nippur, were the parents of the moon God and Goddess, Nanna and Ningal. From the moon was born the sun God, Utu, as well as his sister Inanna, associated with love and the evening and morning stars. The counterpart to these deities of sky, air, water, and earth was the underworld, the realm of the dead, originally seen as ruled by the powerful Goddess Ereshkigal. Like many royal families, the family of the gods was quarrelsome, with younger members vying to equal and replace the power of their elders.

Another social metaphor for the relationships among the gods was based on the administrative staff of great temple estates. The patron god or goddess was viewed as the owner of the estate, served by a large bureaucracy of deities that mirrored the human bureaucracy. Certain gods fulfilled the roles of high constable, steward, chamberlain, and military protector. Lesser deities prepared the god's bath, bed, and meals; sang and played music; brought petitions; and carried the god on journeys. Others supervised the plowing and harvesting of fields and the care of fisheries, flocks, and wildlife. The entire cosmos, then, could be seen as the extended estates of a divine royal family, with various deities appointed to specific offices. This metaphor signaled a change in the relation of the gods to natural phenomena. Earlier, people had conceived of gods and goddesses as immanent within natural phenomena; now these phenomena came to be seen as spheres of administration, to which the gods were appointed by a divine lord and his representative.[14]

This concept is reflected in the myth of Enki, known as the organizer of the cosmic system on behalf of his father, An. First, Enki organizes the various lands and peoples and decrees their respective fates. He then turns to the various spheres of human needs. After filling the Tigris and Euphrates with fertilizing waters ejaculated from his penis, Enki puts the rivers under the God Enbilulu, inspector of canals. Enki appoints a fish deity to control the marshes, a sea goddess to control the sea, and a rain god to control the waters of the heavens. The fields and plowing, the tools of house construction, the wildlife of the steppes, the sheepfolds, and the textile industry are likewise put under the control of their respective deities. After organizing the administrative system of the cosmos, Enki is then challenged by Enhil's ambitious granddaughter Inanna, who complains that he has given her no sphere of administration. Enki replies that he has already given her a vast sphere that encompasses the power of kings in both love and war.[15]

Inanna's ambition for an enlarged sphere of rule is also portrayed in a second myth, which involves Enki, patron of the city of Eridu. In this story, Inanna sets out to visit Enki in Eridu. He welcomes her, and the two settle down to a prolonged drinking bout. In his drunken state, Enki proceeds to promise Inanna a series of *me*, cosmic spheres of power such as rulership, religious office, descent and ascent from the underworld, sexual arts, powerful speech, musical arts, military power, crafts, and others. Inanna gathers in each group of *me*, amassing a total of fourteen groups. She then takes them all and departs in her boat to return to her city of Erech. Enki, recovering from his drunken state, realizes what he has done and tries to prevent Inanna from reaching her city by sending a series of monstrous beings to stop her. But Inanna defeats each attack and arrives home triumphantly, thus justifying the restoration of her city to its supremacy in the Sumerian coalition. Enki ends by conceding the regained supremacy of Erech.[16]

Another key metaphor for relations among the gods was the political assembly in which leaders of each city in the Sumerian coalition met, gathering in the holy city of Nippur to appoint a king during military crises. The gods thus came to be seen as a political and juridical assembly that appointed or dismissed kings and decreed the fates of cities in war. The gods themselves were imagined as kings, warriors, and judges. They rode out in battle and judged appeals that were brought to them, ruling on cases involving other gods as well as humans. The wild and arbitrary powers of storm and flood in nature were fused with the devastating violence of war, both represented by gods. Before these arbitrary powers, humans could only weep and lament, hoping to avert divine wrath, but ultimately were forced to bow to the fate that the gods decreed.[17]

The development of these metaphors, from natural powers to extended family, estate management, and political assembly—themselves reflections of the increasingly hierarchical centralization of society—seems to have had various effects on the status of female deities in the divine pantheon. The earliest metaphors of immanent natural powers suggested parallel gods and goddesses, with the gender of deities associated with sky, earth, plants, animals, and waters often fluid, as nature itself demands a fluid interchange of male and female powers. The family metaphor also required equal numbers of female and male members: father and mother, sister and brother, daughters and sons. But the later myths had a tendency to marginalize the goddesses as wives. They became shadowy auxiliaries to dominant gods rather than distinct personalities in their own right. The metaphor of the political assembly marginalized goddesses even more. Upper-class women may have administered estates, but they were not members of the military and political assemblies.[18]

Three sets of myths express the marginalization of specific goddesses in the pantheon. One involves the rivalry of Enki and Ninhursag, Goddess of wildlife and birth. In the original pantheon, Ninhursag is third in ruling status, next to the father, An, and his son Enhil (Ki and Nammu, the primal mothers, already have become shadowy in this scheme). Enki wishes to displace Ninhursag and take her place as the third in rank. He challenges her to various contests. In one story, he impregnates her and then seduces and impregnates her daughter and granddaughter. He tries to repeat this with her great-granddaughter, but Ninhursag blocks this until he brings gifts. She then punishes Enki by implanting in him a series of herbs that cause him to fall gravely ill. She finally relents and brings forth from him eight healing deities. In another contest, Enki claims that for each human that Ninmah (Ninhursag) creates with various handicaps, such as blindness and deafness, he will find a job in society. But then Ninmah is unable to find a job for a particularly deformed creature created by Enki.[19] The upshot of these tales of rivalry between Enki and Ninhursag is that she is displaced and he becomes third in the pantheon. This downsizing of Ninhursag perhaps itself reflected a privatizing of the female powers of birth and household management vis-à-vis the public power of male administration and rule.

A second Goddess who became marginalized in Sumero-Akkadian tradition was Ereshkigal, ruler of the underworld. In early myths, she rules this realm alone; but in a later story, she is forced to accept a husband, Nergal, formerly a celestial God. In this story, Ereshkigal is invited to partake in a feast held by the gods in the heavenly world. She sends a representative to bring her some delicacies, but one God, Nergal, refuses to offer her deputy his respects. Ereshkigal demands that Nergal be sent to the underworld so that she can kill him. But when Nergal arrives, he grabs her by the hair, pulls her from her throne, and throws her on the ground to kill her. She pleads for her life, offering him marriage and rule over the underworld. Ereshkigal then becomes a dependent wife under the control of her husband.[20]

The most significant myth of male divine power displacing the female occurs in the Babylonian creation story, the Enuma Elish. This story in its extant form was probably shaped in the Old Babylonian period, in the early second millennium BCE, to herald the ascendancy of the God Marduk, patron of Babylonia, over the more ancient deities. The story begins with the emergence of creation from the primordial mother, Mummu-Tiamat, and her consort Apsu, representing the commingled waters from which all life emerged. From this pair, successive generations of gods and goddesses come forth. Then a conflict arises between the primordial mother, Tiamat, and the younger gods. Tiamat seeks to avenge the death of Apsu. She rallies the ancient gods, portrayed as monstrous powers of chaos that threaten the new order of the younger gods.

The divine assembly meets and appoints Marduk as its champion. Marduk then goes out and defeats Tiamat in single combat. He splits her body in half, using one half to shape the sky and the other half the earth below. After shaping the cosmos out of the dead body of Tiamat, Marduk then sacrifices her second consort, Kingu, and from his blood mixed with clay creates humans to serve the gods, relieving the gods of the need to labor.[21] This creation myth, designed to justify the ascendancy of Marduk over the other gods, pictures the ancient world of the divine as originating in and led by a powerful primordial goddess who is overthrown and dismembered, her body becoming the matter shaped by the male warrior god into the present cosmic order.

Despite these stories that marginalized goddesses (and perhaps reflected the

FIGURE 7
The Goddess Inanna, with signs of her ruling power, her foot on the back of a lion, 2334–2154 BCE. Cylinder seal, Mesopotamia. (Courtesy of the Oriental Institute of the University of Chicago)

increasingly subordinate position of women vis-à-vis the males of their families in second-millennium Babylonian law and society),[22] goddesses did not disappear from the imagination of divine power. Indeed, one, the Goddess Inanna, seemed to rise and take on expanded power—witness the tales of her complaints to Enki over his failure to give her a large enough sphere of power in the cosmos and her daring appropriation of the *me*, which she carried back to her city of Erech. In Sumero-Akkadian myth, Inanna (her Akkadian name is Ishtar) was typically pictured as impetuous, imperious, ambitious, ready to fight for her own prerogatives, and generally succeeding in her exploits (fig. 7). Her ascendancy owed something to Sargon, ruler of Akkad, who sought to create a united empire of Sumer and Akkad under his hegemony shortly after 2350 BCE.

Sargon shaped an Inanna/Ishtar royal myth to validate his own rise to power. According to one legend, Sargon was the son of a priestess and an unknown father. In a story that was perhaps later adapted to Moses in Hebrew scripture, his mother put the baby in a basket of rushes and set it adrift on a river. The baby was picked up and raised by Akki, a drawer of water, who made the boy his gardener. In that capacity, Sargon became the lover of Ishtar,[23] a story that reflects the myth of the sacred marriage, in which Inanna mates with a gardener. (This was a kingly title, for the king was seen as a shepherd and also as a gardener or farmer, key economic roles. In the temple, the king or priest poured the Waters of Life on the Tree of Life.) Sargon thus positioned himself as one put on the throne through union with Ishtar.

Sargon consolidated his power over Sumer by naming his brilliant daughter, Enheduanna, as high priestess of Ur. From this princess-priestess, we have a cycle of hymns to Inanna that express the royal ideology of the new dynasty. In her long poem on Inanna's exaltation, Enheduanna praises the Goddess as the "lady of all the *me*" (governing powers) and an equal to An, the sky father. Her image is all powerful, uniting the uncontrollable forces of storms and war: "In the van of battle, everything is struck down by you . . . in the guise of a charging storm, you charge, with a roaring storm you roar." All the other gods flutter away like bats before Inanna's powerful advent.[24]

Enheduanna then laments her own displacement from her position as priestess of Ur during an uprising against her father's rule. But the hymn ends with the confident hope that her position will be restored, even as Inanna's power will be exalted throughout the earth: "That you are lofty as Heaven, be known! That you are broad as earth, be known! That you devastate the rebellious land, be known! . . . that you attain victory, be known! [That,] Oh my lady, has made you great, you alone are exalted."[25]

Inanna owed her continued importance not only to her exaltation as patron of the Sumero-Akkadian dynasty of Sargon. That exaltation itself was rooted in her identification with two key mythic cycles central to kingship ideology: namely, the sacred marriage, and the descent and ascent from the underworld. Inanna incarnates heated female sexuality. She is the female side of courtship and sexual union, but never the dutiful wife or mother. She does not patronize motherhood, child care, or weaving. She establishes kings on their thrones, but she does so as a nubile bride who never becomes a submissive wife. In the poems of the courtship of Inanna and Dumuzi, we see Inanna in her relationship to the courting bridegroom.

Inanna's brother, the sun God Utu, initiates the courtship by telling her that he will bring her the bridal bedsheet of woven flax. He then introduces Dumuzi the shepherd as the prospective bridegroom, but Inanna dismisses the thought of marriage to a shepherd (seen by Sumerian society as a semi-nomadic, uncivilized bumpkin). She demands a farmer as her husband, someone who can fill her storehouses with heaped-up grain. Utu argues that the produce of the shepherd is equally valuable. Dumuzi then speaks, comparing his produce with that of the farmer. If the farmer brings black flour, Dumuzi will bring black wool. If the farmer brings white

FIGURE 8
The courtship of Inanna and Dumuzi,
Old Babylonian period, c. 2000–1600
BCE. Clay plaque, Mesopotamia. (Photo:
Erlenmeyer Collection, Basel)

flour, he will bring white wool. If the farmer brings beer, he will bring sweet milk.
If the farmer brings bread, he will bring honey cheese.[26]

Dumuzi then arrives at Inanna's door with his gifts, and Ningal, Inanna's mother,
persuades her to accept him. Inanna then prepares herself for the marriage bed with
scented oils, white robe, and precious jewelry. Inanna cries out in delight in her expectation of sexual pleasure, using the metaphors of a plowman plowing a field ripe
for planting: "Who will plow my vulva? Who will plow my high field? Who will
plow my wet ground? . . . Who will station the ox there?" Dumuzi declares that he
indeed will plow her vulva, to which Inanna replies: "Then plow my vulva, man of
my heart, plow my vulva" (fig. 8).[27]

In the scene of sexual union that follows, we see the fusion of agricultural luxu-
riance with the establishment of a king on his throne through his union with Inanna.
"Plants grew high by their side. Grains grew high by their side. Gardens flourished
luxuriantly." Dumuzi is the fertilizing power that makes the plants burgeon, while

FIGURE 9
Inanna, riding ahead of a war chariot, Akkad period. Cylinder seal,
Mesopotamia. (Collection of Pierpont Morgan Library, New York)

Inanna is the field that pours out grain. Dumuzi hymns, "O Lady, your breast is your
field. Inanna, your breast is your field. Your broad field pours out plants. Your broad
field pours out grain." Agricultural wealth, not a human child, is the anticipated outcome of this sexual union. This outpouring of food culminates in Inanna's enthronement of Dumuzi as king: "The Queen of Heaven, the heroic woman, greater than
her mother, who was presented with the *me* by Enki, Inanna, the first daughter of
the Moon, decreed the fate of Dumuzi." Inanna gives Dumuzi both military victory and kingly power (figs. 9 and 10):

> In battle I am your leader . . . on the campaign I am your inspiration . . . you
> the king, the faithful provider of Uruk . . . in all ways fit: to hold your head
> high on the lofty dais, to sit on the lapis lazuli throne, to cover your head with
> the holy crown, to wear long clothes on your body, to bind yourself with the
> garments of kingship, to carry the mace and the sword . . . you the sprinter,
> the chosen shepherd, in all ways are you fit. May your heart enjoy long days.

Assured of this outcome, Dumuzi proceeds to the sacred union with Inanna: "The
king went with lifted head to the holy loins. He went with lifted head to the loins of
Inanna. He went to the queen with lifted head. He opened wide his arms to the holy
priestess of heaven."[28]

FIGURE 10

Inanna/Ishtar, as Goddess of war, bringing captives to the king, 2300 BCE. Drawing from a clay tablet. (From Andrew Harvey and Anne Baring, *The Divine Feminine* [York Beach, Maine: Conari Press, 1996])

Though established on the throne by Inanna and assured of an outpouring of agricultural prosperity, Dumuzi find that his days are numbered. As the vitality of natural life, he dies with the searing heat of summer that kills the foliage and brings a long drought, during which the populace waits anxiously for the new rains that will allow new growth. The relation of Dumuzi to the dying and rising vegetation is reflected in the greatest of the Inanna myths, her descent to the underworld. In the Sumerian and Akkadian versions of this myth, it is Inanna who initiates the descent and thereby threatens the life of nature, while Dumuzi functions only as her forced surrogate.

Inanna undertakes this descent as an expression of her ambition, her desire to add the realm of the underworld, ruled by her sister Ereshkigal, to her own realms of power in heaven and earth. "From the great above the goddess opened her ear to the great below. . . . My Lady abandoned heaven and earth to descend to the underworld."[29] But lest she be defeated in her goal and be unable to return, Inanna alerts her servant Ninshubur to intervene for her with the elder gods Enhil, Nanna, and Enki. Inanna then proceeds through the seven gates of the underworld. At each gate, she knocks and demands to enter but is allowed to pass through only by being stripped, piece by piece, of the royal regalia that signifies her powers: her crown, her jewelry, her breastplate, her gold ring, her measuring rod and line, and finally her royal robe.

Naked and bowed low, Inanna enters the throne room of her sister Ereshkigal. There, she is judged by the Annuna, the judges of the underworld. Ereshkigal fixes her with the "eye of death" and turns her into a corpse, which she hangs from a hook on the wall like a piece of rotting meat. When Inanna fails to return, her faithful servant Ninshubur begins a lament for her and makes the rounds of the gods to intervene on her behalf. Enhil and Nanna ignore Ninshubur's pleas, but crafty Enki is willing to help. He fashions two sexually neutral creatures from the dirt of his fingernails and sends them to the underworld to aid Ereshkigal, who is moaning like a woman in labor. The two creatures offer to relieve her pains and in return demand the corpse of Inanna. In gratitude for their help, Ereshkigal releases the corpse of Inanna; but Inanna, now revived, cannot ascend back to the world above without providing a surrogate.

As Inanna emerges, she looks for a suitable substitute. She rejects the idea of using her faithful servant Ninshubur, who has saved her. She also refuses to send her two children, Shara and Lulal, who have mourned her absence. But then her eye fixes on her husband, Dumuzi, who has not mourned her but instead is enjoying the powers of kingship, "dressed in his shining *me*-garments. He sat on his magnificent throne." Falling into a rage at his uncaring behavior, "Inanna fastened on Dumuzi the eye of death. She spoke against him the word of wrath. She uttered against him the cry of guilt: Take him! Take Dumuzi away."[30] The story continues with the intervention of Dumuzi's loving sister Geshtianna, who seeks to save him. Through her efforts, Dumuzi's fate is modified. He will remain in the underworld only part of the year (the drought season) and during the rest of the year may ascend again. When he ascends, new life will be restored to the earth.

The figure of Inanna is fascinating to contemporary feminists seeking ancient goddess role models because of her autonomy, sexual enjoyment, and power. Some have asked whether she represents some prepatriarchal time when women enjoyed such power and vitality. But I believe that this is the wrong question. The image of Inanna in this ancient culture was not shaped as a "role model for women," much less as a remembrance of powers once available to women. Rather than beginning with modern gender ideology, one must reckon with her first by understanding the Sumero-Akkadian view of deity. Inanna's power and autonomy stem from her identity as a god, not as a human woman. For the Sumerians, a vast gulf separated humans and gods. Gods were immortal, and humans mortal. In the words of the Gilgamesh epic, "Only the gods live forever under the sun. As for mankind, numbered are their days."[31]

Humans were created to serve the gods with their labor. Their proper relation to the gods was praise and lament. Through praise, they hoped to win the favor of the gods; through lament, to turn away their wrath. But the gods were by nature imperious and capricious. Even kings were finally servants of the gods, knowing that, at any moment, the gods could fasten on them "the eye of death" and send them weeping into the underworld of death and decay. Prayers of praise and lament addressed to deities, whether god or goddess, thus had a similar formula.

One prayer of lament to Ishtar, probably originating in the middle of the second millennium, first addresses her by praising her greatness, particularly her power in war: "I pray to you, O Lady of Ladies, goddess of goddesses, O Ishtar, queen of all peoples, who guides mankind aright. . . . O most mighty princess, exalted is thy name. Thou indeed are the light of heaven and earth, O valiant daughter of Suen [the moon] , who determines battle."[32]

Having thus exalted Ishtar as the greatest of the gods, the lamenter then pours out his troubles to her in a fashion familiar to us from the Hebrew psalms, which were modeled on these Babylonian hymns. (I use the term "his" for the lamenter because the economic and political nature of his misfortunes reflects primarily the reality of powerful males, not that of women or poorer men.) The lamenter describes his sickness, his misfortunes, the conspiracy of his foes against him. He then pleads that any mistakes he has committed be revealed to him and asks to be forgiven: "Forgive my sin, my iniquity, my shameful deeds and my offense. Overlook my shameful deeds, accept my prayer, loosen my fetters, secure my deliverance." He begs that her wrath be averted: "How long, O my Lady, will thou be angered so that thy face is turned away?" The prayer ends with hopes that the Goddess will turn back to him and restore his fortunes so that he can once again prosper and triumph over his enemies: "My foes like the ground let me trample." The hymn ends with final words of praise: "The lady indeed is exalted, the Lady indeed is Queen, Irnini, the valorous daughter of Suen, has no rival."[33]

As an immortal, no god or goddess can be literally a "role model" for humans, yet these deities were also shaped as immortal "projections," to use a modern term, of the power and behavior of kings (and occasionally queens). Royal power was dimly reflected in the all-dominating power of gods, but always as temporary and always through acknowledgment of the rulers' dependency on and servitude to their patron deity. Any human woman who might have attempted to emulate Inanna would have been a powerful queen or a royal priestess, not an ordinary woman, just as the relation of rulers to ruled was modeled after the relation of gods to humans. Inanna was the Goddess of kings and queens, of powerful men and exceptional royal women, not a Goddess from which ordinary women could expect much succor in their daily lives as they struggled with childbirth, healing, or the toil of spinning and weaving. Here, a Goddess such as Ninhursag would be more the helper.

The figure of Inanna does have an aspect of carnival, of times of celebration in which the normal hierarchies of class and gender were dismantled and the limits and order of society breached. At such times, all women and men in society could join in celebration of Inanna. The wearing of transgendered clothes by her devotees reflects this time of upset of normal boundaries. But this aspect of Inanna's cult functioned as a temporary relief of class and gender separations, not a real change in these divisions.[34]

The combination of Inanna's divine power and sexual femaleness is linked to kingship ideology. Here, I believe the liminality of Inanna is important. As sexually aggressive, as the "hot" courtesan who attracts the male lover (but would be dangerous and inappropriate as a wife), Inanna also mediates between the divine and the human worlds. One probably should not interpret this as an indication that "sacred prostitution" was practiced in Sumero-Akkadian temples. How sacred marriage itself was enacted ritually also needs more study. Since the high priestess was herself often a mother, daughter, or sister of a king, it is not certain that such a marriage was always performed in a literally sexual way.[35]

Rather, we should see Inanna's sexuality as expressing the power through which the divine as female touched the highest ranks of the male human world, the realm of kings. Through marriage to her, kings were exalted, put on the lapis lazuli throne, and vested with the powers of rule. Kings could never become immortal, although some might have briefly pretended to be. They were, finally, humans and shared the common fate of humans, death. But through marriage to Inanna, kings could temporarily imagine themselves to be like gods, sharing in their power and glory. It is this boundary role of Inanna that helps to explain not only her contradictions but also her centrality for Sumerian royal mythology.

ANAT IN UGARITIC MYTH

The figure of Anat in Ugaritic myth both resembles and differs from that of Innana/ Ishtar in Sumero-Akkadian myth. Anat too is a war Goddess, with an aggressive, impetuous personality, and is linked to kingship ideology. Ugaritic myths were uncovered between 1929 and 1932 in the excavations of ancient Ugarit, a city on the

Syrian coast that flourished between 1500 and 1200 BCE. The many tablets found in these excavations are in seven languages—Akkadian, Cypro-Minoan, Egyptian, Hittite, Hurrian, Sumerian, and Ugaritic—testifying to the city's role as a center of international trade.[36]

The Ugaritic language was quickly deciphered because of its affinities to early Hebrew. The tablets include trade and tax lists, diplomatic letters, and lists of sacrifices to be performed to different deities at different times of the month.[37] Most important for our purposes is a series of mythological texts. Anat plays a key role in those texts in relation to the fortunes of Baal, the storm God, and in the story of the birth and death of the hero Aqhat. This discussion analyzes her nature and role by focusing on these two groups of texts.

The stories of the fortunes of Baal were edited by the scribe Ilimilku, apparently as part of the efforts to establish the claims of King Niqmad II to the throne.[38] The composition brings together groups of material copied from earlier tablets. The fragmentary nature of many of the surviving tablets makes it difficult to interpret some of the story. Overall, the Baal texts fall into three main sections. The first recounts the struggle between Baal and Yam, the God of the sea, in which Baal emerges victorious. The second involves the struggle to establish Baal's "house," or temple, and his sovereignty among the gods. In the third sequence, Baal is defeated by Mot, the God of death and the underworld. Anat searches for his body, recovers it, and performs the funerary rites. Baal is then restored to life and power.

The major deities in these stories are El, the father God, and Athirat-of-the-sea (Asherah), his wife and progenitress of the gods, and their three major offspring, Yam, Mot, and Anat. Baal is described as the "son of Dagan," a Hurrian God, although sometimes he is also called the son of El. His struggle for sovereignty perhaps reflects the effort to integrate the God of the Hurrian people into the Ugaritic pantheon.[39] In the first sequence, on the struggle of Baal and Yam, El initially favors Yam and declares his enthronement as king. Baal is enraged, attacks and kills Yam, and establishes his own rule. Anat appears at the beginning of these texts, when her father, El, summons her as the war Goddess to "grasp your spear and your mace, let your feet hasten to me, . . . bury war in the earth, set strife in the dust, . . . pour a libation into the midst of the earth."[40] These activities set the stage for Yam's intended coronation.

In the second sequence, on the establishment of Baal's house, Anat plays a central role as Baal's advocate. There is a feast for Baal in his palace. Anat is then described in terms of her activities as a war Goddess. She embodies the frenzy of battle that rages between two towns. Decapitated heads pile up beneath her, and she decks herself with severed hands and heads. She wades in the gore of warriors to her knees. This scene of warfare is then repeated in her temple. Here, she ritually sets up chairs and tables as representatives of armies and again steeps herself in the frenzy of war: "Her liver shook with laughter, her heart was filled with joy, the liver of Anat with triumph."[41] Her palace is then purified of the blood of soldiers, including her act of washing her hands in the blood of warriors. This second ritual war in her palace perhaps has to do with the cultic establishment of her victory and the conditions of peace (fig. 11).[42]

Baal meanwhile is strumming his lyre amid his wives. He sends a commission to Anat, asking her to establish conditions of victorious peace. Again, as in the summoning of Anat by El, Anat is called to come with these words: "Bury war in the earth; set strife in the dust, pour a libation into the midst of the earth . . . grasp your spear and your mace, let your feet hasten toward me." Anat is at first fearful that Baal has suffered some setback in his struggle for sovereignty. She cries out, "What manner of enemy has arisen against Baal, what foe against the Charioteer of the clouds?" She asks if she has not already defeated Yam and other foes of Baal: "Surely I smote the Beloved of El, Yam? Surely I exterminated Nahar, the mighty god? Surely I lifted up the dragon, I overpowered him?"[43]

Baal's messengers assure her that no new foes have arisen against Baal and that he summons her to establish conditions of victorious peace. Anat agrees to come, again claiming that she will "bury war in the earth." At the arrival of "his sister," "his father's daughter," Baal dismisses his harem. He sets a feast before her, while she purifies herself: "He set an ox before her, a fat ram in front of her. She drew water and washed herself with the dew of heaven . . . she made herself beautiful."[44]

A missing section may have contained a scene of sexual copulation between the two. Other text fragments describe Baal as he sees Anat approaching and then as he bows before her. There follows a vision of cows mating and giving birth. Baal exclaims, "Like our progenitor I shall mount you." "Baal advanced, his penis tumescent," while "moist was the nethermouth [vagina] of Anat." In another fragment, the sexual congress of the two is described in this way: "Baal was aroused and grasped her by the belly [vagina]; Anat was aroused and grasped him by the penis" . . . "Embrace, conceive and give birth."[45] Clearly, part of the relation of Baal and Anat is one of sexual delight, bringing fertile birth.[46] This relation is described in cattle imagery: Baal as a bull, the birthing ones as cows, the offspring a young male heifer. These images express the hopes for the power and wealth of kings.

Baal then complains to Anat that, unlike the other gods, he has no house. Anat vows to intervene with her father, El, threatening to thrash him if he does not accede

FIGURE 11

The Goddess Anat on a war chariot,
second millennium BCE. Stone stele.
(Private collection, Cairo)

to her demands: "I will make his gray hair run with blood, the gray hair of his beard
with gore, if he does not give a house to Baal like the gods." Anat then "stamped
her feet and the earth shook; she set her face toward El."[47] Arriving at El's sanctuary, she repeats her threats. El mollifies her, declaring that he knows her to be im-
placable. Baal and Anat then appeal to Athirat, asking her to intervene with El to
build a house for Baal. Athirat journeys to El's tent and makes this appeal: "Your
word, El, is wise, you are everlastingly wise, a life of good fortune is your word."
Athirat then calls for Baal's sovereignty: "Our king is Valiant, Baal is our Lord and
there is none above him." Once in power, Baal will ensure abundant rain: "And now
the season of his rains may Baal appoint, the season of his storm-chariot."[48]

El accepts this appeal, and Anat goes to tell Baal. "Virgin Anat rejoiced: she
stamped her feet and the earth shook. Then she set her face toward Baal. . . . Virgin
Anat laughed: she lifted up her voice and cried, Rejoice, Baal, good news I bring."
A vast palace of silver and gold is then erected for Baal, and sacrifices and feats are
performed to dedicate it. Baal tours his kingdom and throws down a challenge to
his remaining enemy, Mot, the God of death, declaring that "I alone, it is who will
rule over the gods."[49]

The third section of the Baal texts portrays this struggle between Mot and Baal,
in which Anat plays a key role. Mot declares that because he did not receive an invitation to Baal's feast, he will devour Baal and bring him down into the nether-

world of death. Baal trembles with fear and declares himself Mot's servant. Baal descends to earth and seeks to ensure his progeny by lying with a heifer, who bears him a young male. He then descends into the underworld. A cry is set up: "Dead was Valiant Baal, perished was the Prince, the Lord of the earth." El descends from his throne and sits on the ground, pouring ashes on his head and gashing himself in rites of mourning.[50]

Now it is Anat's turn to seek out Baal. She searches to the ends of the earth, going down into the underworld beyond the shores of death. There, Baal is found. She too performs rites of mourning, weeping and gashing herself. With the help of an assistant, Anat lifts Baal onto her shoulders and takes him to "the uttermost parts of Saphon," the holy mountain of the gods, where she performs the funerary rites, slaughtering groups of seventy bulls, oxen, sheep, stags, goats, and antelope.[51]

Anat's feelings of compassion for Baal are described as maternal: "Like the heart of a cow for her calf, . . . so the heart of Anat went out to Baal." She seizes and destroys Mot, her actions described in language reminiscent of a harvesting rite: "With a knife she split him, with a fan she winnowed him, with fire she burned him, with millstones she ground him, with a sieve she sifted him, in the field she sowed him, in the sea she sowed him."[52]

This ritual destruction of Mot is followed by El's vision of Baal's resurrection and the restoration of fertilizing rains to the earth: "Let the skies rain oil, let the *wadis* run with honey. And then I shall know that Valiant Baal is alive, that the Prince, Lord of the earth, exists."[53] Baal arises, is enthroned, and claims domination: "And Baal went up to the throne of his kingship." But Mot, not quite defeated, reemerges and complains of his treatment by Anat. After a struggle with Baal, Mot finally accepts Baal's dominion: "Let Baal be installed on the throne of his kingship."[54]

The story of the hero Aqhat, recounted in the second group of texts, reveals a different side of Anat's personality. The good king Daniel had prayed to the gods for a son and received a heroic boy, who is given a special bow and a set of arrows by the gods. Anat covets this bow and demands that Aqhat give it to her, promising him gold and silver and then immortal life. But Aqhat scorns her, declaring that he knows mortality is his lot as a human and that bows are for males, not females. As a huntress Goddess, Anat is affronted, and she arranges to kill Aqhat, an action that she then regrets. Aqhat's death brings a period of infertility to the land. His sister sets out to avenge him by killing the vulture that killed her brother.[55] It is possible that the hero is then resurrected and restored to his father, but that ending is missing from our tablets.[56]

With these two sets of stories, what can we say of Anat's role and personality?

Anat is violent and war-loving, yet she also establishes conditions of peace in the land. She is imperious yet fiercely loyal to her beloved Baal. She is sexual and brings forth offspring without ever ceasing to be a maiden. She is not Baal's wife, but his companion, what Latin Americans call a *compañera*,[57] although in the story of Aqhat she acts independently and against Baal's interests and is put in a questionable position as a result. In the Baal poems, she is his advocate, establishing his sovereignty and restoring him to life by rescuing his body, performing the funerary rites, and defeating his enemies. Like Inanna/Ishtar, she is the power behind the throne, both the throne of Baal and that of the king as representative of Baal. Through her, the kings of Ugarit are assured of their dominion, of the fertilizing rains on which agricultural plenty is based.

ISIS OF EGYPT

The figure of the Egyptian Goddess Isis developed over three thousand years, from before the first dynastic period (3000 BCE). In the Ptolemaic period (the reign of the Greek kings of Egypt, who ruled from 323 to 30 BCE), the cult of Isis and Osiris was reshaped as a mystery religion, similar to the Eleusinian mysteries, and became a religion of personal salvation disseminated throughout the Greco-Roman world.[58] Chapter 4 takes up this later phase of the story of Isis. Here, I attempt to sketch something of the figure of Isis before her Hellenistic transformation. This task is difficult because we have no complete Egyptian text of the story of Osiris's death and his restoration by Isis. This tale is found only in a heavily hellenized version by Plutarch, written in the early second century CE.[59]

In the cosmology shaped at the religious center of Heliopolis in the early dynastic period, Isis and Osiris belonged to the fourth generation of the gods. Creation was envisioned as emerging from the primal waters in the form of a hillock, much as the fertile hillocks of mud, on which Egypt's agricultural life depends, emerge from the annual inundation by the Nile. This original hillock was Atum, the creator. From him was brought forth the male God Shu (air, light) and the female Tefnut (moisture); they in turn brought forth the God Geb (earth) and the Goddess Nut (sky), who were separated from each other by Shu. From Geb and Nut came two pairs of gods and goddesses, Osiris and Isis, Seth and Nephthys. These nine made up the great gods, or the Ennead (to which was sometimes added an elder Horus).[60]

Isis and Osiris were said to have loved each other from their mother's womb, while Seth was depicted as the adversarial brother who seeks to kill Osiris and claim the sovereignty of Egypt. Nephthys, although said to be Seth's wife, acted as a helper

FIGURE 12
The Goddess Isis in her aspect as a
mother, suckling an infant pharaoh,
Ptolemaic period. Small statue.
(Museo Gregoriano Egizio, Vatican
Museums, Vatican State; photo:
Scala /Art Resource, NY)

and was the twin sister of Isis. The two were paired at the head and foot of the bier
of the dead Osiris, at the head and foot of the sarcophagi of pharaohs, and on the
doors leading to tombs, as two goddesses who assured the dead pharaoh, identified
with Osiris, of life after death.[61] Isis carried on her head the symbol of the royal
throne, while Nephthys bore the symbol of the palace.[62] Thus, together, they represented the basis for kingly power, the house in which the pharaoh was enshrined,
the seat upon which he was enthroned.

Isis, as the wife of the dead king resurrected into immortal life, was the mother
of the living king, Horus, whom she generated from the dead body of her husband-
brother, Osiris. The throne from which the pharaoh reigned was the lap of Isis, upon
which he was seated as a baby, nourished by her milk. In contrast to Inanna and Anat,
wifely and maternal devotion were central to the nature of Isis. A favorite image of
Isis and Horus shows the young king seated on her lap as she suckles him from her
breast (fig. 12),[63] an image that would be taken over into Christianity as the image
of Mary suckling the baby Jesus on her lap.

FIGURE 13
Isis and Nephthys stand behind Osiris, who sits on the throne, c. 1310 BCE.
Painting, Book of the Dead of Hunefer. (From Andrew Harvey and Anne
Baring, *The Divine Feminine* [York Beach, Maine: Conari Press, 1996])

Osiris, as king of the dead, presided over the hall of judgment into which each
dead person was led. Each individual's heart was weighed to see whether he or she
was worthy of being reborn to immortal life. Isis and Nephthys typically stood behind the enthroned Osiris, supporting him (fig. 13).[64] In the early dynastic period,
Osiris also became identified with the new grain that rises from the earth, fructified
by the Nile's waters. He is pictured lying as a mummy beneath the grain, which
sprouts from his body, while a priest pours water on him (fig. 14). Mats of earth with
sprouting grain were placed in the tombs of the dead, thus making the connection
between the grain that rises yearly from the earth and immortal life that rises in the
resurrected Osiris.[65] A similar identification of the seed that "dies" in the earth only
to rise as the new grain and the body resurrected to immortal life is used by Paul in
the New Testament (1 Cor. 15:37–38).

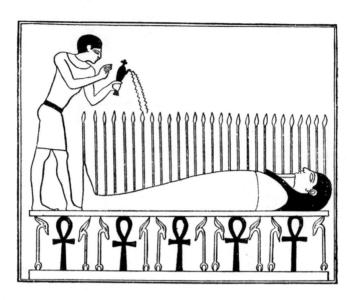

FIGURE 14
Osiris with wheat growing from his body, watered by a priest, with
the *ankh* life-sign and the *was*-scepter of divine prosperity beneath
him, Ptolemaic period. Bas-relief, Ptolemaic Temple of Isis at Philae.
(From Ernest Alfred Thompson Budge, *Osiris: The Egyptian Religion
of Resurrection* [New Hyde Park, NY: University Books, 1961])

There are several versions of the death of Osiris. In a story found in the theology of Memphis, Osiris falls into the risen Nile and drowns. The young Horus entreats
the Goddesses Isis and Nephthys to rescue Osiris. They draw him from the waters
and install him in the Great Seat, the temple of Ptah at Memphis, called the "mistress of all life, the Granary of the God through which the sustenance of the Two
Lands is prepared." Here, Osiris is explicitly identified with the grain "drowned"
in the waters of the Nile and then risen to new life. His son Horus is installed as
king of the Two Lands, the northern and southern kingdoms of Egypt, "in the embrace of his father Osiris" through taking his seat in this center of control over the
grain supply.[66]

Other versions of Osiris's death connect it to rivalry with Seth. Two successive
stages of this murder are found in Plutarch's treatise on Isis and Osiris. Plutarch's
account is a syncretistic conflation of Osiris with Dionysus and Isis with Demeter,
read through the lens of Neoplatonic philosophy, but the core stories go back to

earlier Egyptian tradition. In the first stage of the story, Tryphon (Seth) created a chest made to fit Osiris's body. He brought it into a banqueting hall and promised to give it to the person who fit inside. When Osiris lay in the chest, Seth slammed the lid and secured it with bolts and molten lead. Thrown into the Nile, it floated out to the sea, eventually washing ashore in the land of Byblos. There, a heath tree grew up around it until the chest was enclosed in its trunk. The tree was cut down and used as a pillar to support the roof of the palace owned by the king of Byblos.

Isis is depicted as wandering throughout the earth seeking the body of Osiris. She eventually reaches Byblos, where she becomes a nurse to the child of the king and queen. She then obtains the pillar and cuts out the chest containing the body of Osiris. Carrying it off with her, she opens the chest and lies on the body of Osiris, embracing him. Plutarch's account adds elements taken from the story of Demeter's quest for her daughter, Persephone. It is likely that the identification of Byblos as the place where Osiris's coffin ended up was part of a later cult of Osiris in that land.[67]

Earlier Egyptian rites seem to have enacted a play about the death of Osiris in which he was carried in a coffin. He is also identified with a pillar that is erected with the help of Isis and the pharaoh. Isis in the form of a bird is pictured as hovering over the mummified body of Osiris, whose rising life is depicted through his erect phallus (fig. 15). Isis takes his seed into her and conceives the child Horus.[68] Plutarch's source for the story of her embrace of the dead body of Osiris likely included this idea of Isis conceiving Horus through copulation with the erect phallus of the dead Osiris (Plutarch may have excluded this detail because he deemed it lacked dignity).

The story of the conception of Horus is found in several Egyptian texts. In one hymn to Osiris, we read:

Thy sister Isis acted as protectress of thee. She drove away thine enemies, she averted seasons [of calamity], she recited formulae with the magic power of her mouth. . . . She went about seeking him untiringly. She flew round and round over the earth uttering wailing cries of grief and she did not alight on the ground until she had found him. She made light appear from her feathers; she made air to come into being by her two wings, and she cried out the death cries for her brother. She made to rise the helpless members of him whose heart was at rest, she drew from him his essence and she made therefrom an heir. She suckled the child in solitariness, and none knew where his place was, and he grew in strength and his arm increased in strength in the House of Keb [Geb, earth].[69]

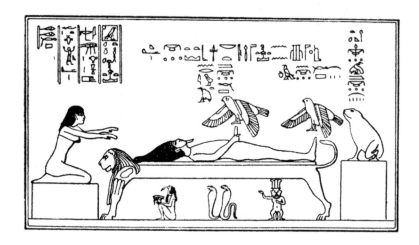

FIGURE 15
Osiris begetting Horus by Isis, who, in the form of a hawk, hovers over Osiris's
raised penis. The second hawk is Nephthys. At the head of the bier sits Hathor,
and at the foot sits the frog-Goddess Heqet. Drawing from sarcophagus art. (From
Ernest Alfred Thompson Wallis Budge, *Osiris: The Egyptian Religion of Resurrection*
[New Hyde Park, NY: University Books, 1961])

Another text tells the story of Horus's birth in the papyrus swamp of the delta
near the city of Buto. Here, the pregnant Isis flees from where Seth has imprisoned
her, giving birth and hiding the child in the papyrus swamp (fig. 16). One day, while
obtaining food, she returns to find the child dead of a scorpion sting. Isis utters loud
lamentations, and her sister Nephthys comes to her aid, appealing to the God Thoth,
who gives Isis magic incantations to draw out the poison and revive the child.[70]

In Plutarch's story, Isis hides the chest with the body of Osiris in the swamp, where
it was found by Typhon (Seth). He cuts the body into fourteen parts and scatters
them. Isis then embarks on a second search, now for the scattered parts of Osiris's
body. Sailing through the marshes in a papyrus boat, she finds all the parts of the
body except the phallus, which has been swallowed by a fish. Isis fashions a likeness
of the phallus and "consecrates" it, "in honor of which the Egyptians even today
hold festival." No Egyptian text has this idea that the phallus of Osiris was lost and
a likeness fashioned by Isis. Plutarch does not say that Isis impregnated herself with
Osiris's phallus in order to conceive the child Horus. Rather, he details how the many
shrines to Osiris throughout Egypt are depicted as places where Isis buried different parts of his body.[71]

FIGURE 16

The birth of Horus in the papyrus swamps. (From Ernest Alfred
Thompson Wallis Budge, *Osiris: The Egyptian Religion of Resurrection*
[New Hyde Park, NY: University Books, 1961])

The young Horus is nurtured by Isis and then trained by his father, Osiris, from
the land of the dead to become a powerful warrior. Horus avenges Osiris by doing
battle with their enemy Seth in order to vindicate his right to inherit the throne of
the Two Lands of Egypt.[72] References to the conflict of Seth and Horus are found
in various texts. One rather bawdy version from the twentieth dynasty (twelfth century BCE) has the two adversaries contending over a prolonged period. Isis continually intervenes on her son's behalf, until Seth refuses to take part in the contest while
Isis is present. Seth and Horus withdraw to an island. Seth charges the ferryman not
to transport any woman resembling Isis. But Isis bribes the ferryman and makes her
way there, tricking Seth into validating the claims of Horus.

The gods award the office to Horus, but Seth challenges him to an ordeal in which
both become hippopotamuses, with the award going to the one who stays under water
the longest. Isis harpoons Seth, but she withdraws the harpoon when Seth appeals
to her as his sister. Horus is enraged at Isis and cuts off her head (which is restored

by giving her a cow's head). Seth takes out Horus's eyes and buries them in the earth, but his sight is restored by Hathor (the cow Goddess with whom Isis has been identified). Seth and Horus then engage in a contest with rival ships, trying to sink each other's vessel.

Finally, the gods appeal to the judgment of Osiris, who emphatically demands that Horus be given the throne, as the son of the one who gave grain to the gods. Eventually, Seth concedes to Horus the right to rule as the son of Isis and Osiris. Seth is also granted his own sphere of rule in the heavens, as the thunder God.

> Then Horus, the son of Isis, was brought, and the white crown set upon his head. And he was put in the place of his father Osiris. And it was said of him: You are the good king of Egypt; you are the good Lord—life, prosperity, health—of every land up to eternity and forever. Then Isis gave a great cry to her son Horus, saying, "You are the good king! My heart rejoices that you light up the earth with your color."[73]

The central role of Isis in promoting Horus as king and heir of Osiris is supplemented by another story of her guile on behalf of her son. Two texts from the nineteenth dynasty (1350–1200 BCE) tell how Isis was able to obtain the secret name of the supreme God Re. In this text, Isis is described as "a clever woman. Her heart was craftier than a million men; she was choicer than a million gods; she was more discerning than a million of the noble dead. There is nothing which she did not know in heaven and earth, like Re, who made the content of the earth." To complete her knowledge, "the goddess purposed in heart to learn the name of the august god."[74]

Isis gathers spittle dropped from the God's mouth and kneads it with earth, fashioning a poisonous snake that bites the God on his daily stroll. When the God's suffering grows unbearable, Isis offers to heal him but only if he tells her his secret name. Finally, Re agrees to impart this name to her but only if she then shares this knowledge with Horus, vowing him to secrecy. Re tells her to incline her ears and draw the name from his body into her body. Isis revives Re, while drawing from him his highest power, with which she endows her son, Horus. The text ends with the jubilant cry, "The poison is dead, through the speech of Isis, the Great, the Mistress of the gods, who knows Re by his [own] name."[75]

Isis, like Inanna and Anat, is a "kingmaker" who sets the royal heir on the throne. She does so as lover and faithful wife of the dead king and as devoted mother of the new king, her son. Her instruments of power are not military vigor, but magic powers guilefully employed. Using these, she resurrects Osiris, heals Horus and Re, and learns the deepest secrets of the universe, which she passes on to her child, conceived through her power to revive the phallus of the dead Osiris. Horus, suckled at her breast, is enthroned on her lap, the seat of power. These evocative symbols make dramatically clear the ancient Near Eastern supposition that while men rule as kings and lords, it is the power of goddesses that puts them on their thrones.

DEMETER AND PERSEPHONE OF GREECE

The Demeter-Persephone myth and cult in Greece are unique because they privilege the mother-daughter bond rather than the relation of young goddess and king, as in the Inanna and Anat stories, or the royal family triad of husband, wife, and male child, as in the Egyptian story. (None of these stories feature a Mother Goddess and son-lover.)[76] The story of Demeter and Persephone is dramatically told in a late seventh-century BCE text that probably reflects the official story of the Eleusinian mysteries.[77]

The story opens with the rape of Persephone. A beautiful young girl, she is playing and gathering flowers with the daughters of Oceanus. She reaches for the narcissus flower, and the earth opens. Pluto in his horse-drawn chariot rises from below, seizes her, and carries her off to his underground realm. Persephone continually cries out, but her laments at first are heard only by Hecate and Helios, the sun God. Eventually, however, her mother, Demeter, also hears them. Demeter speeds across the earth with flaming torches, seeking her daughter. On the tenth day, she is met by Hecate, who tells her that she too heard the cries. They go to Helios, who reveals that Persephone has been taken to be the bride of Pluto, a union sanctioned by Zeus himself, father of Persephone. Helios advises Demeter to accept this as a fait accompli.

Demeter refuses to do so and becomes more savagely angry. She will not attend the assemblies of the gods in Olympus and instead disguises herself as an old woman. Wandering through towns and fields, she eventually comes to Eleusis, where she sits down at the maidens' well. There, she is met by the four daughters of Celeus, lord of Eleusis. She offers herself for hire as a housekeeper and is taken into this household to nurse the late-born son of the king. Demeter, who has been fasting, refuses wine offered by the matron of the house, Metaneira, but breaks her fast with a barley drink. A woman servant, Iambe, cheers her up with ribald jests.

The disguised Demeter not only nurses the child but also seeks to give him immortality by dipping him in fire by night. Metaneira spies on her one night and screams when she sees Demeter putting her child in the fire. Demeter is enraged,

FIGURE 17

Demeter and Kore (Persephone), early fifth century BCE.
Marble bas-relief. (Louvre, Paris; photo: Erich Lessing /
Art Resource, NY)

throws the child on the ground, and castigates the mother for her stupidity. She then
reveals her divine nature and demands that a temple be built. King Celeus calls the
people together, and they build the temple. Demeter withdraws into it and calls down
a blight on the land, causing no seeds to grow. In this way, she seeks to punish the
Olympian gods for their connivance in the rape of her daughter, by denying them
the sacrifices that would be brought to them by humans (and thereby destroying human life as well).

Zeus seeks to mollify Demeter by sending Iris to summon her to Olympus. When
the summons is refused, he sends one god after another, but their entreaties are rejected. Demeter declares that no seed will spring from the ground until her daughter is restored to her. Finally, Zeus agrees to release Persephone and sends Hermes
to fetch her. But Pluto secretly inserts pomegranate seeds in her mouth as she is de-
parting, forcing her to taste them. In a touching scene, Demeter and Persephone are
reunited, rushing into each other's arms (fig. 17). But Demeter immediately senses
that something is wrong and asks her daughter if she has tasted food in the underworld. Persephone confesses that Pluto forced her to do so.

Zeus sends their mother, Rhea, to Demeter to propose a compromise. Persephone
will spend a third of the year in the underworld as Pluto's wife, but for the other eight

months she will live with her mother and the Olympian gods. Demeter accepts this proposal and lifts the blight on the earth, restoring its fertility. She then goes to the leaders of the Eleusinians, among them Triptolemus and Eumolpus, and teaches them how to conduct her rites. Those who are initiated into them are assured of a happy life in the hereafter: "Happy is one among humans on earth who have seen these mysteries; but the one who is uninitiate and who has no part in them, never has a lot of like good things once he is dead, down in the darkness and gloom."[78]

This text is foundational for the Eleusinian mysteries, which were probably celebrated as local rites as far back as the Bronze Age (c. 1500 BCE). They became an all-Greek festival in the sixth century BCE and were gradually opened to the larger Greco-Roman world. The precinct where they were celebrated was continually enlarged into the second century CE, and the rites persisted there into the fifth century, when they were closed down by barbarian raids and Christian hostility.[79]

The story reflects key aspects of the rites. Triptolemus, referred to in the story, was said to have been given the knowledge of grain cultivation by Demeter, which he then carried throughout the world. The Eumolpids were a priestly family of Eleusis who held the leading offices of Hierophant (chief priest) and two assistant priestesses from the time the mysteries were founded into the last days of these rites in the late Roman period.[80] The rites were celebrated in late September and early October over a nine-day period. They were open to all Greek-speakers, men and women, even slaves, if they were innocent of shedding blood.

The rites began in Athens, with the fasting initiates purifying themselves in the sea, followed by a sacrifice of suckling pigs. Then there was a procession to Eleusis, followed by a torchlight enactment of the sorrowful search of Demeter for her daughter and their joyful reunion. The fast of the initiates was broken by drinking the barley drink. A dramatic exposure of holy objects followed; initiates were sworn to strict secrecy about these parts of the ritual. The initiates then departed for their homes, assured that their experiences would fortify them for a better life in the world to come.[81]

Lesser rites honoring Demeter were also conducted in different Greek cities. One, which took place over three days, was the Thesmophoria, a festival open only to women. On the first day, pigs were sacrificed in an underground chamber, and the decayed remains of the previous year's sacrifice were brought up and made available to farmers to fertilize their fields. On the second day, the women sat on the ground imitating the deep mourning of Demeter for her daughter. On the third day, this mourning was transformed into celebration with a banquet.[82] This rite seems linked primarily with agricultural fertility, but perhaps also with hopes for "good birth" for the women involved in the ritual.[83] The exclusion of men marked it as a rite for women to bond with one another in their shared experiences of loss and hope.

In the strictly gender-segregated society of classical Greece, the Demeter-Persephone story must have held deep meaning for women, especially the matrons who led the Thesmophoria rites. The special bond of mother and daughter in the women's part of the segregated household must have often been rudely broken by a powerful father who snatched away a beloved daughter into a marriage with one of his older male companions, with little consultation with the mother or daughter. Mothers and daughters must have experienced this as rape, when daughters, usually in their early teens, were carried off wailing into an unknown life. The return of such a daughter to visit her mother must also have reenacted something of the joy found in the Demeter story.

Demeter in some ways is Greek woman writ large. As corn Goddess, she gives the gift of grain and the land's fertility. Her gift of weaving provides the cloth that clothes society. But she is also subject to rape, to arbitrary male violence. Demeter herself was said to have been raped by Zeus and also by Poseidon.[84] She responds to the rape of her daughter by withholding the gift of fertility. Before this power, even the Olympian gods stand helpless. So, too, were women in Greek society deeply vulnerable to male power, but they had as their weapon of last resort the withholding of their sexuality and fertility. Tradition credits women with stopping the fratricidal Peloponnesian Wars by withholding sex from men.[85]

The ancient Greek world did not see the tale of Demeter as only a woman's story. It was a drama assumed to appeal to all, one that allowed men and women to experience sorrow, loss, and joyful reunion of mother and child. It also carried with it two profound reassurances, symbolically linked: the return of springtime fertility after a season of earth's barrenness; and the hope that, in the terrifying journey from this life to the next, one would find kindly gods in the world below. Thus, we find in both the Isis and the Demeter myths and cults keynotes that would become increasingly central to ancient religion. Agricultural plenty and political stability were important but insufficient. Immortal life had been deemed unavailable to mortals in Babylonian and Canaanite cultures, but this hope for immortality became central in Greco-Roman piety. Hope for life after death increasingly supplanted the hopes for renewal of agricultural life central to earlier Mediterranean religion.

THREE · The Hebrew God and Gender

The traditional understanding of deity in Hebrew scripture has assumed that Yahwism was always monotheistic, that the Hebrews had a unique religious perspective totally different from and opposed to that of their ancient Near Eastern neighbors. This view holds that they worshipped one god, male and transcendent, and rejected the validity of all other gods. The disappearance of goddesses, then, is seen as a result of the male monotheism of Hebrew religion. New interpretations of Hebrew scripture, however, informed through recent archaeological finds from both Hebrew society and the religions of the ancient Near East, have drawn a much more complex picture of the development of the Hebrew understanding of deity.

The picture of Hebrew religion as originating among desert nomads who fled slavery in Egypt and adopted a covenant binding themselves to an exclusive relationship with a national god at Sinai, entering Palestine as foreign invaders, has been thrown into question. Norman Gottwald, particularly, has pioneered a view of Israel that describes its origin in a confederation of tribes in the Canaanite highlands who were opposed to oppression by the tributary system of the coastal cities. This group of tribes adopted a distinct national identity, represented by a national god, but they did not differ in material culture from their Canaanite neighbors. The story of the exodus from Egypt may represent the experience of a small group of former Egyptian slaves who joined this confederation. The story may have been appropriated by Israel's first king, Saul, as a national charter myth to dramatize resistance to Canaanite tributary oppression, characterizing it as a revolt against the great empire of the era, Egypt. But the exodus, in this view, was not actually a shared historical experience of most of the tribes that became Israel.[1]

YAHWEH AND THE GODS AND GODDESSES OF CANAAN

Studies of early Israel have suggested that the Hebrews in the period of the judges and early monarchy were not monotheists in the fashion that developed later. These early people did not believe that Yahweh was the only god and that all other gods were simply nonexistent, nor did worship of Yahweh as the primary national god exclude other gods from the cult of Yahwism itself. The later war against the worship of Baal or Asherah does not reflect an Israelite fall into apostasy, with the people defecting to other religious cults foreign to Yahwism, as the biblical reformers interpret it, but an effort by later reformers to purge plural elements from an earlier Yahwism.[2] These earlier Canaanite elements included the identification of Yahweh as El, enthroned over an assembly or council of gods. Thus, Psalm 82 opens with these words: "God has taken his place in the divine council; in the midst of the gods he holds judgment." This divine council of gods was later interpreted as angels, or the "heavenly host" (1 Kings 22:19, Isa. 6:1–8, Jer. 23:18, Ps. 89:5–8).

Early Yahwism also identified Yahweh, like Baal, as a God of storm and fructifying rain and possibly identified Asherah, the consort of El, as the consort of Yahweh-El.[3] Symbolism from the Canaanite background of the tribes of Yahweh was part of the early cult of Yahweh, including "high places" (hilltop cult sites) and trees or wooden poles symbolic of trees (*asherah*, meaning the cult object, as distinct from Asherah, the name of the Goddess). By the time of the early monarchy, these *asherah* were probably seen as representing an aspect of Yahweh rather than a separate deity. But they continued to appear in official as well as popular Yahwism to the time of the exile in Babylonia. An inscription on a pillar in a burial cave at Khirbet el-Qom, near Hebron, dated from the eighth century BCE, speaks of Yahweh and "his Asherah" blessing someone called Uryahu and protecting him from his enemies. Two eighth-century BCE inscriptions on jars found at Kuntillet Ajrud, in the Sinai between Gaza and Aqabah, read, "I bless you by the Yahweh of Samaria and by his Asherah," and "I bless you by the Yahweh of Teman and by his Asherah."[4]

These inscriptions have excited fierce debate among scholars about whether they testify to the worship of Asherah as a Goddess consort of Yahweh or whether the term "his *asherah*" reflects the symbolic tree pole as a cult object associated with Yahweh but no longer viewed as a separate deity.[5] Evidence of popular veneration of a female figure has also been found in two sites, one near Jerusalem and another in

FIGURE 18
Asherah figurine from the period of the Hebrew monarchy.
Height 7⅞ in. Tell Duweir, Palestine. (The Metropolitan
Museum of Art, Gift of Harris D. Colt and H. Dunscombe
Colt, 1934 [34.126.53])

Samaria, both from the eighth century BCE. These areas have yielded female figurines with molded heads and breasts, sometimes with arms holding the breasts, on
pillar bases that flare at the bottom. Additionally, these pillar figurines have often
been found in domestic settings from the eleventh century BCE (fig. 18).[6] Thus, some
association of a female figure or her cult representation was common in Yahwism
down to the sixth century BCE.

The reform movements of the ninth and eighth centuries BCE, associated with
the prophets Elijah, Elisha, and Hosea, insisted on a strict monolatry, the worship
of Yahweh alone. These movements did not take the form of an attack on the *asherah*

or other cult symbols that had been part of earlier Yahwism; instead, they attacked the worship of Baals from surrounding peoples with whom Israel's kings were allying. The reformers believed that these alliances with powers outside Israel would subjugate the people to those who would milk the Israelite peasantry for tribute and who would also bring in their cults and set them up side by side with that of Yahweh.[7] The prophets denounced this Baal worship as apostasy and a rejection of Israel's national god, but their denunciations did not involve expelling the *asherah*, associated with an indigenous Yahwism.[8]

In the seventh-century Deuteronomic reform movements, these symbols of *asherah* and altars in high places fell under suspicion as being contrary to the strict worship of Yahweh. They were then purged from Israelite worship by reformers who sought to centralize the cult of Yahweh in Jerusalem and abolish other sites of worship in the "high places."[9] This stricter reform movement, however, did not necessarily deny that other gods existed for other nations; it asserted only that Israel should worship Yahweh alone. A more complete movement from monolatry to monotheism did not take place until the exile in the sixth century BCE. When Hebrews found themselves in exile in Babylonia, they felt the need to insist on God's exclusive role over all nations, even those who did not "know" Yahweh.[10] Thus, Second Isaiah declares, "I am the Lord and there is no other; besides me there is no god" (Isa. 45:5).

The shaping of the characteristics of the Hebrew God from the time of the judges and early monarchy to the exile shows a process of convergence in which roles played by Canaanite gods such as El, Baal, and Asherah, and perhaps Anat, were attributed to Yahweh. This was followed by a process of separation in which the cult of Yahweh was strictly distinguished from worship of the Baals associated with other peoples. This distinction did not, however, prevent Yahweh from continuing to be depicted in the role of a storm and rain God, drawn from the influence of Baalism in indigenous Yahwism. As Tikva Frymer-Kensky has shown, a picture emerged of Yahweh as an omnicompetent deity who brought together in "himself" most of the roles associated formerly with a pantheon of male and female deities.[11]

But convergence of divine roles in the person of Yahweh had its limits. Yahweh was male and could take over roles associated with female deities, especially sexuality and reproduction, only in limited ways. Although male, Yahweh is never depicted as having a penis or as actively sexual, unlike other male gods such as Enki or Baal.[12] Yahweh is also separate from the realm of death. He is a warrior who kills but is not vulnerable to death. Unlike Baal, he does not die or descend into the underworld. Thus, sex and death become realms of the unholy, from which God is separated, and from which those who worship him must separate themselves in order to come into the presence of the holy.[13]

Early on, Yahweh is identified with El, the high God of Canaanite religion. The Hebrew Bible contains no polemic associated with El, perhaps because no separate cult was associated with El at the time. El was the original God of the peoples who became Israel. The name Isra-el was itself an El name, not a Yahwist name.[14] Yahweh is even seen as one of the sons of El, who has been given Israel as his particular people among the nations (Deut. 32:8–9). El comes to be a generic word for God. It is assumed in the priestly tradition (Gen. 4:26, 15:2) that El was the name under which Yahweh was known in the time of the Patriarchs, with the name Yahweh being revealed only to Moses during the exodus: "And God said to Moses, 'I am Yahweh. I appeared to Abraham, to Isaac and to Jacob as El Shadday, but by my name of Yahweh I did not make myself known to them" (Exod. 6:2–3).

Yahweh takes over all the functions associated with El as high God, an elderly, fatherly figure enthroned amid a divine council. Like El, Yahweh is seen as compassionate and merciful. The El cult center at Shechem was taken over by Yahwists. Like El (and Baal), Yahweh is sometimes represented as a bull—for example, at the Yahwist shrines at Dan and Bethel, sponsored by the king Jeroboam.[15] But these representations were attacked as idolatrous by the Deuteronomist reformer who recorded the story (1 Kings 12:28–31).

Yahweh also takes over the characteristics of Baal as a storm God who brings fructifying rain. Indigenous Baal figures were often tolerated within Israel's national religion by being identified with Yahweh.[16] But Baal cults of other peoples were seen as primary rivals of Yahweh precisely because they claimed to bring the same gifts as Yahweh to humanity: rain and the harvests of grain, oil and wine, wool and flax. In Hosea, Israel's apostasy is described as looking to foreign Baal cults to give "her" these gifts, which are Yahweh's province:

> For she said, "I will go after my lovers, they bring me my bread and my water,
> my wool and my flax, my oil and my drink." . . . she did not know that it was
> I who gave her the grain, the wine and the oil. . . . therefore I will take back my
> grain in its season, and my wine in its season and I will take away my wool and
> my flax. (Hosea 2:5b, 8a, 9a)

Like Baal, Yahweh is a storm God whose voice is thunder and whose glory is shown in flashes of lightning: "The voice of the Lord is over the waters, the God of glory thunders, the Lord over mighty waters, . . . the voice of the Lord flashes forth flames of fire" (Ps. 29:3, 7). He rides the sky chariot of the dark rain clouds: "He rode on a cherub and flew, he came swiftly on the wings of the wind, he made darkness his covering around him, his canopy thick clouds dark with water" (Ps. 18:10–11). Rain becomes preeminently the province of Yahweh.

As Yahweh's global reach increases, it is even said that other nations are foolish to think that they can receive rain apart from him. In Jeremiah's words, "Can any idol of the nations bring rain? Or can the heavens give showers?" (Jer. 14:22). For Zechariah, all nations will eventually be defeated and come up to Jerusalem to worship Yahweh and keep the festival of booths. Those who do not will receive no rain (Zech. 14:16–17). The withholding of rain is the central way that God punishes Israel's apostasy and the evils of other nations. Thus, Amos sees God as punishing Israel and seeking to recall her from her apostasy by sending no rain or sending it only erratically (Amos 4:7–8).

Another area in which Yahweh appropriates the roles of Baal is the subduing of Yam, or the sea. Yahweh's work in laying the foundations of the cosmos is often referred to as his conquest of the sea and the monsters of the deep, Rahab and Leviathan. In the Baal texts, it is Baal who defeats Yam, although Anat is said to have defeated Yam as well. This is also reminiscent of Marduk's defeat of Tiamat, the dragon of chaos.[17] Job asserts that "by his power he stilled the Sea; by his understanding he struck down Rahab" (Job 26:12). Psalm 74 declares, "You divided the sea by your might; you broke the heads of the dragons in the waters, you crushed the heads of Leviathan" (13–14; also Ps. 89:9–10).

God's future deliverance of Israel from oppression is summoned by recalling God's primordial work in subduing Rahab. Thus, Isaiah cries out, "Awake, awake, put on strength, O arm of the Lord! Awake, as in days of old, the generations of long ago! Was it not you who cut Rahab in pieces, who pierced the dragon?" (Isa. 51:9). Isaiah also declares, "On that day the Lord with his hard and great and strong sword will punish Leviathan, the fleeing serpent, Leviathan the twisting serpent, and he will kill the dragon that is in the sea" (27:1).

Yahweh is preeminently a war god, a role often linked with the destructive aspects of storm gods and goddesses. The language for Yahweh's violence in war is reminiscent of that of Anat, who wades in blood up to her hips, who is drunk with war lust, who heaps up corpses and laughs in derision at her enemies.[18] In Hebrew scripture, too, the slaughter of enemies is compared to a harvest. In Deuteronomy 32:42, Yahweh promises, "I will make my arrows drunk with the blood, and my sword shall devour flesh, with the blood of the slain and the captives." God laughs at the nations that conspire against him: "He who sits in the heavens laughs, the Lord has them in derision. Then he will speak to them in his wrath and terrify them in his fury" (Ps. 2:4–5).

The corpses are heaped up, stink, and rot: "The Lord is enraged against the nations and furious against their hoards; he has doomed them, has given them over for slaughter. Their slain will be cast out, and the stench of their corpses shall rise; the mountains shall flow with their blood. All the host of heaven shall rot away. . . . " (Isa. 34:2–4). The blood bath is compared to treading the wine harvest; God's robes are red like those who trample the grapes: "I have trodden the wine press alone, and from the peoples no one was with me; I trod them in my anger and trampled them in my wrath; their juice spattered on my garments and stained all my robes" (Isa. 63:3). The time for divine vengeance is compared to harvest time: "Put in the sickle for the harvest is ripe. Go in, tread, for the wine press is full. The vats overflow, for their wickedness is great" (Joel 3:13).

This martial imagery was probably not derived directly from the tales of Anat's military prowess. Anat is never mentioned in Hebrew scripture and apparently was not an indigenous deity for Yahwist Canaanites. These descriptions seem to have become a part of monarchical traditions and were shared by the Hebrew monarchy, which assigned them to Yahweh.[19] War in the ancient Near Eastern cultures was generally the sphere of males and particularly of kings, although victory was attributed to war goddesses such as Inanna/Ishtar and Anat. In Israel, the male god controls this sphere on behalf of his elect, Israel.

Yahweh takes over not only spheres of gods and goddesses that had come to be seen as socially male but also the sphere that was primarily regarded as the realm of women and the work of mother goddesses: conception, the shaping of the child in the womb, birth, and child care. The original shaping of humanity from the clay of the earth—the role of the Mother Goddess Ninhursag in Sumerian myth—is transferred to Yahweh in Genesis. It is "the Lord God [who] formed man from the dust of the ground and breathed into his nostrils the breath of life, and man became a living being" (Gen. 2:7). In Genesis 1:27, God creates both male and female together "in the image of God" and blesses them, commanding them to be "fruitful and multiply and fill the earth and subdue it."

In Genesis 2, God creates only the male from the dust of the earth and creates the animals as his partners. But when these prove inadequate companions, God then creates the woman out of the man's own flesh in order to give him a partner that is "bone of my bones and flesh of my flesh" (Gen. 2:21–23). Thus, Genesis seems to imagine a time, somewhat like that in the Gilgamesh epic, in which the male was wild and animals were his companions, followed by a time when his life was humanized through relationship with a female.[20]

God not only creates the first humans; he is also responsible for successful human conception. It is he who "opens or shuts the womb," either allowing male insemination to cause pregnancy or preventing it from doing so. This, as Howard Eilberg-Schwartz points out, curtails the sexual potency of the Hebrew male. It is God, not the male, who determines whether sexual insemination causes the woman to become pregnant.[21] God is seen as shaping the child in the womb, bringing it to birth, and keeping it safe throughout its development.

These roles are also attributed to God in relation to Israel as a whole. Here, too, God is the power of conception and successful birth; God is the compassionate mother who guides Israel's footsteps.[22] Thus, in Deuteronomy 32:18, Israel is rebuked for its unfaithfulness to God, by comparing it to those forgetful of their mothers: "You were unmindful of the Rock that bore you; you forgot the God who gave you birth." In Numbers 11:12, Moses complains that the burden of being responsible for Israel's well-being is too heavy for him, declaring that it is God, not he, who is Israel's mother: "Did I conceive this people? Did I give birth to them, that you should say to me, 'Carry them in your bosom, as a nurse carries a suckling child'?"

God's labor on behalf of Israel can be compared to a mighty warrior and to a woman in labor: "Now I will cry out like a woman in labor; I will gasp and pant" (Isa. 42:14). In Psalm 22:9–10, a cry for God's help takes the form of reminding God of this role: "Yet it is you who took me from the womb; you kept me safe on my mother's breast." In Isaiah 42:3, it is God who reminds Israel that it "has been borne by me from your birth, carried from the womb."

God's motherly care extends throughout Israel's life. It is both creational and salvific: "Even to your old age I am he, even when you turn gray I will carry you. I have made and I will bear. I will carry and will save." God's loving care for Israel exceeds even that expected of mothers: "Can a woman forget her nursing child or show no compassion for the child of her womb? Even if these may forget yet I will not forget you" (Isa. 49:15). These descriptions do not make God female, but they do make him the mothering father who supersedes actual fathers and mothers as the reliable parent.[23]

ISRAEL, GOD'S WIFE: THE REVERSAL OF SACRED MARRIAGE

As we saw in chapter 2, ancient Near Eastern societies developed a powerful metaphor for the special relationship of kings and deities—namely, the sacred marriage, in which a goddess espouses a king and establishes him on his throne. Inanna/Ishtar and Anat, who are the divine side of the sacred marriage, are not visualized as docile wives but as impetuous, sexually aggressive, independent queens who bestow their favors where they will. Inanna/Ishtar is the patron of prostitutes as well as the divine consort of kings. The lusty behavior of these goddesses links them to storms and war.

The portraits of these goddesses defy later Western stereotypes of acceptable female behavior—behavior that could also be seen as questionable by the ancient patriarchal societies of the Near East. Such judgments seemed to happen in those moments when the culture shifted from seeing these goddesses as deities, whose arbitrariness must be accepted by dependent humans, to seeing them as females in relation to dominant males. In this optic, the goddesses could be derided as misbehaving women. In the Gilgamesh epic, for example, Gilgamesh responds contemptuously to Inanna's offer of marriage, condemning her as sexually promiscuous: "Which of your lovers have you loved forever? Which of your little shepherds have continued to please you? Come, let me name your lovers for you."[24] As chapter 2 recounts, the hero Aqhat in the Ugaritic myths derides Anat for demanding his bow, claiming that such a weapon is inappropriate for a female.

In Israel, female deity is eliminated, with motherly qualities taken over by a divine father. As Eilberg-Schwartz points out, this creates a dilemma for the appropriation of sacred marriage symbolism, since the marital relation of a male god and a male king would be homosexual. The only way to assimilate this language heterosexually is to feminize Israel as a bride or wife of God.[25] But when the prophets described Israel as God's bride, they were addressing the male elites, including kings and the leadership class of officials and priests. Thus, these male elites had to imagine themselves collectively as female in relation to God. Hebrew females were then even more severely distanced from the places of power and communication with God, lest they imagine that they, and not the male leadership class, were the primary object of this spousal relationship of God and Israel.

The prophets who developed this language casting Israel as God's bride primarily used it to condemn and polemicize against the male elites for their alliances with the foreign powers around them—Egypt, Assyria, and smaller powers such as Tyre—which jeopardized the independence of Israel. These alliances typically brought foreign cults into the capital cities of Israel and Judah, Samaria and Jerusalem. Ahab, for instance, ruler of the northern kingdom, created an alliance with the king of Tyre, marrying his daughter Jezebel, who was then allowed to bring her Phoenician Baal cult, seen as idolatrous by the prophets, to Samaria.[26] But the primary reference of the prophetic polemic was political. It was not simply the danger of foreign cults but the political alliances themselves that were threatening. Alliances with larger foreign powers meant accepting them as overlords and paying tribute to them, further impoverishing the Israelite peasantry, already bowed under taxes to the Israelite elites themselves.[27]

The prophets, then, used the metaphor of Israel as an unfaithful wife to God in order to denounce the elites for entering into these alliances. This metaphor was shaped to imagine Israel as wife turned harlot, engaging in promiscuous sexuality, prostituting herself to foreign powers. Israel is not just occasionally unfaithful. She is depicted as willful, impetuous, and voraciously sexual, a language reminiscent of Inanna/Ishtar and Anat, but used here to condemn the kings of Israel for their political relationships. The image of the harlot-bride goddess, revered as the patron of human kings in the ancient Near Eastern sacred marriage, is reversed to depict a patriarchal God punishing a human harlot-wife, symbol of an unfaithful nation and its kings.

The vividness of this sexual metaphor of harlotry, of imagining unfaithfulness to Yahweh as "whoring" after other nations, has misled modern interpreters into assuming that the primary sin being denounced was sexual. Drawing on Herodotus's questionable description of prostitution in the Babylonian temple, interpreters have also assumed that temple prostitution was characteristic of ancient Baal worship,[28] and thus that idolatrous worship of these gods entailed engaging in ritual prostitution. Exactly who was prostituting themselves is not clear: Israelite men going to Canaanite temple prostitutes, or Israelite women becoming temple prostitutes?

This framework of sacred prostitution as the context for the interpretation of Israel as the "whoring wife" is increasingly being discarded by a better understanding, both of ancient Near Eastern religion and of Israel's political and economic situation vis-à-vis foreign powers. Studies of the extensive personnel records of ancient temples show no evidence of any such practice of sacred prostitution. Although ordinary prostitutes were common enough in all these societies, including Israel, there is no evidence that sexual orgies were a part of official temple worship or that a class of priestesses performed as sacred prostitutes.[29]

Once this misleading hypothesis is cleared away, it becomes possible to explore the metaphor of Israel as a sexually promiscuous wife as a vivid way of denouncing the unfaithfulness of the male elites for their political alliances with foreign powers. Yet the vividness of this metaphor, as it is elaborated by the prophets Hosea, Jeremiah, and Ezekiel, is startlingly graphic in its description of the wife's voracious promiscuity and God's sexually punishing wrath. This graphic detail makes it hard to remember that the primary activity being denounced as "whoring" is not female sexual promiscuity but male elite political alliances.

This metaphor is first developed in the eighth century BCE by the prophet Hosea, who described himself as marrying "a wife of whoredom" and having "children of whoredom," whom he names Jezreel, Lo-Ruhamah (unpitied), and Lo-Ammi (not my people), in order to symbolize the unfaithfulness of Israel to God and God's threatened punishment. These children are told to plead with their mother (Israel) that "she is not [God's] wife and [God is] not her husband, that she put away whoring from her face and her adultery from between her breasts" (Hosea 1:2). God threatens not only to abandon Israel for her misdeeds but also to punish her. God will withdraw his rain and make her (the land) a wilderness and a parched land, withdrawing the harvest with which God has previously fed and clothed her (wine, grain and oil, flax and wool). This withdrawal of rain and the subsequent drought and impoverishment are imaged as sexual punishment: "I will strip her naked and expose her as in the day she was born" (2:3); "I will uncover her shame in the sight of her lovers and no one will rescue her out of my hand" (2:10).

Hosea's predictions of disaster would be fulfilled by the Assyrian conquest of the northern kingdom in 721 BCE. By the time of the prophets Jeremiah and Ezekiel—on the eve of the Babylonian conquest in 587 BCE and the two decades that followed—the focus had shifted to Judah and the city of Jerusalem.[30] God's unfaithful wife is embodied in Jerusalem, the capital city, the center of the political intrigues with foreign powers that risk bringing on the threatened disasters. Jeremiah excoriates the unfaithfulness of the people of the city as worse than that of any married woman, for most women would not forget their bridal gifts or their wedding day: "Can a girl forget her ornaments or a bride her attire? Yet my people have forgotten me, days without number" (Jer. 2:32). Her forgetfulness will be punished, and she will be led away as a captive to a conquering power, just as the northern kingdom was subjugated by Assyria: "How lightly you gad about, changing your ways! You shall be put to shame by Egypt, as you were put to shame by Assyria. From there also you will come away, with your hands on your head" (2:36).

Jeremiah throws in the question of whether God will ever restore Jerusalem to independence, asking whether a man can take back a divorced wife: "If a man divorces his wife and she goes from him and becomes another man's wife, will he return to her?" He suggests that the land itself would be polluted by such a restoration, just as the sexual act is polluted if a man takes back a woman who has been with another man: "Would not such a land be greatly polluted? You have played the whore with many lovers; and would you return to me? says the Lord" (Jer. 3:1). Jerusalem is seen as having prostituted herself in every place: "Where have you not been lain with? By the wayside you have sat, waiting for lovers." This promiscuity has "polluted the land with your whoring and wickedness" (3:2).

But the city's punishment is at hand. It is already desolate, even as it futilely negotiates to fend off disaster, like a prostitute who vainly decks herself with finery as her lovers are about to kill her: "And you, O desolate one, what do you mean that you dress in crimson, that you deck yourself with ornaments of gold, that you enlarge your eyes with paint? In vain you beautify yourself. Your lovers despise you. They seek your life" (Jer. 4:30). Jerusalem will be violated like a woman who is gang-raped: "It is for the greatness of your iniquity that your skirts are lifted up and you are violated" (13:22). God himself will hand her over to public rape: "I myself will lift up your skirts over your face and your shame will be seen" (13:26).

Ezekiel, writing shortly after Jerusalem's destruction, develops in still more vivid detail the metaphor of the unfaithful wife, whom God himself punishes by handing her over to be raped by her former lovers.[31] In chapter 16, Ezekiel recalls the mixed Canaanite heritage of Jerusalem before it became a Yahwist capital, by comparing it to a bastard infant girl born of mixed parentage who was exposed to die, put out naked in the blood of her birth: "Thus says the Lord God to Jerusalem: your origin and your birth were in the land of the Canaanites, your father was an Amorite and your mother a Hittite. As for your birth, on the day you were born, your navel was not cut, nor were you washed with water to cleanse you, nor rubbed with salt, nor wrapped with cloths . . . but you were thrown out in the open field" (Ezek. 16:1–5).

God passes by this exposed infant girl and decrees that she should not die. When she grows into nubile girlhood, he adopts her as his wife. He washes her and adorns her with all the ornaments of a beloved bride of a rich husband. But Jerusalem vainly trusts in her beauty, not realizing that it depends totally on God, and she turns to other relationships: "You . . . played the whore because of your fame, and lavished your whoring on any passerby." She uses God's gifts to enter into relations with many peoples, Egyptians, Philistines, Assyrians, Chaldeans. Unlike typical prostitutes, who take money for their favors, Jerusalem paid for her relations to these "lovers." The tribute that Jerusalem had to pay to these other nations is compared to a whore who pays lovers to come to her (Ezek. 16:31–34).

Because of all these abominations, God will hand Jerusalem over to these same lovers to punish her: "Therefore O whore, hear the word of the Lord, . . . I will gather your lovers with whom you took pleasure, all those you loved and all those you hated: I will gather them against you from all around and will uncover your nakedness to them" (Ezek. 16:35–37). These "lovers" will strip Jerusalem bare, destroy her monuments, and loot her wealth. This looting by foreign conquerors is compared to an adulterous woman exposed in the public square, with a mob invited to stone her to death: "They shall bring up a mob against you and they shall stone you and cut you to pieces with their swords" (16:40).

In chapter 23, Ezekiel develops an extended metaphor that compares the two kingdoms and their capitals, Samaria and Jerusalem, to two sisters of one mother, both of whom are married to God.[32] But both prove to be voracious whores. Even when Samaria is punished by God for her promiscuity by being carried into captivity by Assyria, her sister does not learn from this but becomes an even worse whore. She had played the whore in Egypt in the days of her youth, and as she turns to new paramours, she fondly remembers the outsized penises of her former lovers, "whose members were like those of donkeys, and whose emissions were like that of stallions" (Ezek. 23:20). But God will bring up all these lovers (nations with whom Jerusalem has entered into alliances) to assault her: "They will cut your nose and your ears [as one taken into slavery] and your survivors will fall by the sword" (23:25). This terrible suffering is only what Jerusalem deserves: "Your lewdness and your whoring have brought this upon you, because you have played the whore with the nations and polluted yourself with their idols" (23:29–30).[33]

Although these punishments sound terminal, the prophets assume that they are temporary, a deserved punishment, but one to be followed by reconciliation with God and restoration to the land, once Israel has repented. Unlike an ordinary patriarchal husband who turns over an adulterous wife for stoning, God takes back the rejected wife in some future time of reconciliation. Hosea speaks of this future reconciliation most endearingly. Yahweh not only will take back his unfaithful wife but also will restore their original love relationship, as it existed when she was young and pure in the desert era, before the entrance into the land: "Therefore I will now allure her and bring her into the wilderness, and speak tenderly to her" (Hosea 2:14).

This reconciliation will also restore all the gifts of prosperity that God has taken from her in his wrath. She will again have lush vineyards. She, in turn, will pledge her undying loyalty to her true husband, and they will never again be parted. Peace and justice will then flow in the land: "I will abolish the bow and the sword and war from the land and make you lie down in safety. And I will take you for my wife forever. I will take you for my wife in righteousness and in justice, in steadfast love and in mercy. I will take you for my wife in faithfulness and you shall know the Lord" (Hosea 2:18–20).

This extended metaphor for the relation of Israel and God seems to demand an extraordinary double consciousness on the part of Israel's male elites. On the one hand, they must see their own political wheeling and dealing in the optic of an unfaithful wife who has prostituted herself to numerous paramours. They must identify the terrible violence that has been afflicted on them by conquering foreign powers—burning their cities, raping their wives, killing their children, leading them into slavery—as deserved punishment for their sins. At the same time, they must take the side of God even in his grim rage, which punishes an adulterous wife by handing her over to gang rape, mutilation, and dismemberment, knowing that they and their families are actually the ones being described. Their hope lies in some indefinite future, when they have given up such alliances and God will again love them and restore them to well-being. As males, they must then imagine themselves wooed and caressed by this same God who has battered them.[34]

SEXUAL LOVE REDEEMED: THE SONG OF SONGS

From this punitive, patriarchal use of the marriage metaphor for God and Israel, one turns with relief and surprise to the Song of Songs (also known as the Song of Solomon). This collection of love poems was probably assembled sometime between the fifth and third centuries BCE. It began to be accepted as sacred literature sometime in the first century BCE, interpreted as an allegory of the love relation between God and Israel.[35] By the second century CE, this interpretation had become official, and Rabbi Akiva (50–135 CE) forbade singing it in secular banquet halls (an indication that it was still being used as popular literature).[36]

But the world of sexual love portrayed in the Song of Songs is radically different from the world portrayed by Hosea, Jeremiah, and Ezekiel. One might suggest that they represent divine-human marital love gone awry. By contrast, the Song of Songs pictures such love as it should be, that original idyllic bliss in which God first espoused Israel in the desert and the future restoration of that blissful love.[37] But what the Song of Songs depicts is not wedded bliss but premarital young love. Here, romantic sexual delight is a paradise in and for itself; it is not tied to marriage, reproduction, family, or national interests.

The relationship of the loving couple is egalitarian and mutual, not hierarchical. The social world is woman-centered. The young woman operates out of her "mother's house"; no father or paternal authority is present. Her quest for her male lover takes place in a realm of bonding among female peers. She appeals to her women friends to help her. The male lover operates on the margins, in the outside world of nature, coming in and out of the picture. The young woman is the dynamic center and speaks the majority of the lines. She moves out of and back into her matricentric world, her "mother's house," seeking the young man in the city, hesitating to let him in when he comes to her window, drawing him into her garden.

The egalitarian and female-centered characteristics of these poems have suggested to some a female authorship.[38] In the context of ancient Israel or other ancient Near Eastern societies, this is not a far-fetched idea. Women are known to have been professionals in music and poetry for celebrations and laments, functioning in the secular sphere of culture rather than the official world of male-dominated cult and text.[39] The viewpoint of the poems is secular, ahistorical, nonnational, personal; perhaps this was the sphere of female rather than male culture at the time.

The language abounds with innocent sensual delight that knows no guilt. Our senses are intoxicated with perfumes, the scents of flowers, the voice of the turtle dove, the soft fur of fawns, the tastes of sweet wine and delicious fruits. The season is springtime, when nature awakes, when trees and plants bud, the time of singing and flowers, when the earth recalls paradise. Above all, we are intoxicated by the promise of sexual love yet unspoiled, its seeking and finding, its kisses and caresses, sweet-smelling bodies lying in night-long embrace in soft bowers and gardens of delight, asking only that their happiness not be interrupted prematurely: "Do not bestir or awaken love before its time" (Song of Sol. 2:76).

The first poem opens with the maiden's appeal for the lover's kisses: "Let him kiss me with the kisses of his mouth. For your love is better than wine, your anointing oils are fragrant, your name is perfume poured out" (Song of Sol. 1:1–3). The maiden is suntanned from working in the vineyards, consigned to this task as a little sister by her "mother's sons." But she appeals to her lover not to disregard her, because she is "dark but beautiful."[40] The two lovers lie entwined, her body exuding the fragrance of nard, his body, lying "between my breasts," compared to sweet-smelling spices and blossoms, myrrh and henna flowers (1:12–14).

The young woman compares herself to a "rose of Sharon, a lily of the valley, a lily among brambles," small flowers that grow wild, while the young man is "an apple tree among the trees of the wood" (2:1–3). She longs for his sweet taste and embrace: "Sustain me with raisins, refresh me with apples, for I am faint with love. O that his left hand were under my head and that his right hand embraced me" (2:5–6). The young man is like a gazelle or a young stag who bounds over the mountains, who comes up to her window and whispers to her to "arise, my love, my fair one, and come away, for now the winter is past, the rain is over and gone" (2:8–11).

The young man appears and disappears. The young woman calls to him from her bed, but he gives no answer. She rushes out of her house, seeking him in the city streets. She appeals to the sentinels who keep the night watch to help her find him. She finds him and brings him home, to her mother's house. Again he appears at her window, puts his hand through the lattice, and calls for her to open it. But she hesitates; and when she rises, he is gone. Again she rushes into the streets to find him. This time, the sentinels beat her for being out at the wrong time of night and snatch off her light mantle. She appeals to her female friends, the daughters of Jerusalem, to help her find him. In response to their joking question, "What is your beloved more than another beloved?" (5:9), she sings the praises of his radiant beauty. Already, she is directing her steps to where he has gone: "Down to his garden, to the beds of spices, to pasture his flock in the garden and to gather lilies" (6:2). In anticipation of this love nest, she can declare their union: "I am my beloved's and my beloved is mine" (6:3).

As she praises his beauty, so he praises hers: "How graceful are your feet in your sandals, O queenly maiden! Your rounded thighs are like jewels, the work of a master hand. Your navel is a rounded bowl that never lacks mixed wine. Your belly is a heap of wheat encircled with lilies. Your breasts are like two fawns, twins of a gazelle." The lover compares her to a stately palm, her breasts like its date clusters. He vows to "climb the palm tree and lay hold its branches" (7:7–8). Or her breasts are like grape clusters, her kisses like wine (7:8–9). The maiden responds: "I am my beloved's and his desire is for me" (7:10). She calls him to "go forth into the fields" with her, to go to the vineyards to see whether the vines have budded, the grape blossoms have opened, the pomegranates are in bloom: "There I will give you my love" (7:10–12).

The last poem appeals to the hope for permanence in their love: "Set me as a seal upon your heart, as a seal upon your arm" (8:6). Her brothers still think of her as a girl: "We have a little sister and she has no breasts" (8:8), but she is already mature: "My breasts are like towers" (8:10).[41] The song ends with a final promise that her vineyard is for him, her prince, and an appeal for her loved one to come quickly: "Make haste, my beloved, and be like a gazelle or a young stag upon a mountain of spices" (8:14).

How did such love poetry, which never mentions God and ignores the rules of patriarchal marriage, become the "holy of holies" of Hebrew scripture?[42] Most scholars today insist on the complete secularity of the poetry, believing that it lacks any allegorical reference to the union of God and Israel. Michael Fox sees a close parallel to Egyptian love poetry of the twelfth and eleventh centuries BCE.[43] Like the Song of Songs, this Egyptian poetry is secular and personal, celebrating non-marital love play between a young man and a young woman. Both praise each other's beauty and moan about their love sickness. In one such poem, the beloved is described by the boy as "lovely of eyes," "sweet her lips," "long of neck, white of breast, her hair like true lapis lazuli, her arms surpass gold, her fingers like lotuses." The girl longs to see and kiss him: "My heart leaps up to go forth to make me gaze on my brother tonight. How lovely it is to pass by."[44] Although a thousand years older than the Hebrew poem, this Egyptian poetry was widely known in ancient culture and could have inspired a similar poetry in Israel.

Samuel Noah Kramer, pioneer scholar of Sumerian texts and culture, supports a different approach. He believes that the background of the Song of Songs is the ancient Near Eastern sacred marriage ritual. He suggests that this ritual was adopted under the monarchy and that Solomon, mentioned as author and archetypal king in the Song, engaged in an adaptation of the sacred marriage with a priestess representing the Goddess Astarte.[45] Kramer points to elements that are all reminiscent of the sacred marriage of Inanna and Dumuzi: the similarity of the language that describes the lover as king and shepherd, both titles of Dumuzi; the lush imagery of agricultural abundance, with flocks, grains, fruits, wine, perfumes, and flowers; and the description of the couple drawing into the garden to make love.

But the Song of Songs lacks the key purposes of the sacred marriage: the renewal of nature through the couple's lovemaking and the installation of the king on his throne through the love of the goddess. Nature is indeed lush in the Song, but it is the natural reality of springtime. It is not made fertile through the lovers' embraces. There is no evidence that sacred marriage rites were actually carried out in Israel, and it is unlikely that the Song is derived from the text of such a rite. Yet the lush language of love in vineyards and gardens of agricultural abundance, found in the poetry of the goddess and the king from Babylonia and Urgarit, may well have provided conventions for the celebration of young love, tropes which then passed into secular poetry. This seems to me a more likely explanation for the similarity of language in the Sumero-Akkadian and Hebrew poetry.

But why did the rabbis appropriate these poems and make them sacred writ? Taken on the literal level, the description of nonmarital sexual pleasure was offensive to their moral outlook, and thus they tried to guard against a literal reading. It is not enough to say that the rabbis needed to appropriate the poems because they were popular in the Hebrew secular culture; in fact, much that was popular was judged as immoral and repudiated. One can only assume that the rabbis themselves loved the poems; they appealed to a deep longing in them for innocent and blissful love. They were able to rationalize the appropriation of the poems by claiming that they represented the love between God and Israel—the true love between God and his people as it originally was, as it should be, as it will be in redemptive times.

The allegorizing of the Song of Songs as the love between God and Israel fundamentally masks its meaning. Its sensuality becomes spiritualized as a love of the mind, not the body. Indeed, its Christian monastic interpreters insist that it can be safely read only by those who have transcended and purged themselves of the temptations of physical erotic desires.[46] Its egalitarian mutuality between girl and boy is transformed into a hierarchical relation between an all-powerful male God and a feminized, dependent Israel. Nonmarital sexual pleasure is construed as spiritual marriage. Female initiative is transformed into feminine passivity, awaiting the coming of the dominant male. A woman's optic is transformed into that of patriarchal males who interpret themselves collectively as the "brides" of a male God in a way that hides a homoerotic spirituality beneath symbolic heterosexuality.[47]

WISDOM, GOD'S FEMALE "SIDE"?

The Wisdom literature—Proverbs, Job, Ecclesiasticus (also known as the Wisdom of Jesus ben Sirach), and the Wisdom of Solomon—contains a personified female figure, Wisdom, that seems at times to be a secondary manifestation, or hypostasis, of God. Scholars of this literature have debated whether Wisdom is simply a literary device, a metaphor for God's wisdom, or a being that has ontological status "alongside" Yahweh.[48] The background or origin of this figure is also the subject of inconclusive controversy. Some argue that Wisdom was drawn from the Egyptian Goddess Ma'at, who represented the wisdom of the gods, or from the Goddess Isis.[49] Others have seen reflections of Canaanite or Mesopotamian goddesses such as Astarte or Inanna.[50] John Day has pointed to Western Semitic literature, such as the Wisdom of Ahiqar, where wisdom is personified in language similar to that found in Proverbs.[51]

Other scholars have seen in Wisdom a reappearance of the Hebrew Goddess Asherah, whose tree pole long existed within Yahwist worship. Her fertile "tree of life" was appropriated into Yahweh's identity, even as her residual symbol, the tree pole, was purged from Yahwist cult sites by the time of the exile. Judith Hadley suggests that Wisdom is not so much a survival of Asherah as a compensation for her loss. With her functions absorbed into Yahweh, she is reconceived as a female expression of God, mediating between God and "man" (Hebrew male religious leaders).[52]

My view is that many of these ideas about the background of Wisdom are plausible. But they are neither mutually exclusive nor exhaustive; rather, they are elements in a broad array of possible cultural influences. The Wisdom figure of Hebrew literature is an original creation that transformed these influences into a new configuration, which has no exact precedent in these past expressions. But who were the creators, and what was the social context of this new configuration?

Leo Perdue fixes the sociohistorical context for the first development of the Wisdom figure in the book of Proverbs as the early periods of exile (late sixth and fifth centuries BCE) in the colony of Yehud (Judea), under Persian rule. The Zadokite priests of the restored temple in Jerusalem were the local leaders of the colony recognized by the Persian administration. A class of sages formed the scholarly supporters of this priestly leadership. These leaders, recently returned from exile through Persian patronage, sought to establish their legitimacy as the continuation of the Hebrew monarchy, which had reached its height under Solomon. They also were anxious to reclaim land that had passed into the hands of foreigners and those of mixed parentage during the exile.[53]

Perdue views the figure of Wisdom as a creation of this scholarly class and a representative of their interests. She epitomizes their claims that their teachings represent both historical continuity with Solomon and the ongoing expression of God's wisdom. By rooting Wisdom in God's creation of the world "in the beginning," their teachings become permanent and unchangeable, representing the foundations of the cosmos itself. Only through schooling oneself in these teachings does one have life. This way of life is also the way to wealth and worldly success. Those who accept it adhere to the established world order, identified as rooted in God's cosmic order, with its promise of patronage through the local leadership class and its imperial sponsors. Those who defy or reject it are on the path of disaster, and ultimately of death.

The call issued by Wisdom to come and learn from these sages and thereby become one of them is addressed to young men of families affluent enough to spare their sons from gainful labor for a time. These young men stand at the crossroads between various "calls" and temptations—some are tempted to dally among the pleasures of the city and neglect the hard work of intellectual discipline, for example, while others might be tempted to leave the strict endogamy of the renewed Jewish community for marriage into families of mixed parentage and culture. Still others could be tempted to follow dissident apocalyptic visionaries who would resist

Persian rule, hoping for divine intervention to overthrow it and restore an idealized, independent Davidic monarchy—revolutionary schemes that could bring on the punishing wrath of Persia, as would happen later in Roman times.

The counterpart to Lady Wisdom in the book of Proverbs is Dame Folly, who sums up all the temptations that lure young men to such disasters.[54] Ultimately, the crossroads at which these young, unschooled men stand lead in opposite directions, between life and death. To choose the way of Wisdom is to choose life; to follow Dame Folly is to sink down into Sheol, the dark underworld of the dead.

The stark contrast between these two female mediators, one who leads to life and the other to death, is established in the first chapter of Proverbs. The sage addresses the potential student as father to son. His teachings are the continuation of the wisdom learned in the family from his parents: "Hear my child, your father's instruction and do not reject your mother's teachings" (Prov. 1:8). Here, father and mother stand as a unified voice for the young man, urging him to move toward success and avoid the path of death. The "sinners" who tempt the young man in the wrong direction are presented not simply as idlers but as a gang of robbers and murderers. They say, "Come with us, let us lie in wait for blood; let us wantonly ambush the innocent. . . . We shall find all kinds of costly things, we shall fill our house with booty. Throw in your lot with us; we shall all have a common purse" (1:11, 13–14).

Having warned the young man against this rival gang, Wisdom speaks in the first person, crying out in the streets, the city squares, the busy corners, and at the entrance to the city gates. Her voice is one of stern rebuke, warning of impending calamity for those who fail to heed her call. In language reminiscent of war and storm goddesses such as Inanna/Ishtar, this calamity is imagined as a "panic" that "strikes you like a storm," a "whirlwind," bringing "distress and anguish." When this just retribution befalls those who reject Wisdom's call, it will be too late to call for her help. Anat's bloodthirsty laughter echoes in Wisdom's threat: "I also will laugh at your calamity, I will mock when panic strikes you" (1:26–27).

But all is not yet lost. There is still time to repent. If those who stray turn and accept Wisdom's call, the good life awaits: "Those who listen to me will be secure and will live at ease, without dread of disaster" (1:33). The wisdom promised here involves not only the inward cultivation of the soul but also concrete material benefits: to be "healthy, wealthy, and wise," protected from ill fortune; to be assured of "length of days and years of life," "abundant welfare," "favor and good repute in the sight of God and of the people," "healing of your flesh and a refreshment for your body," "your barns . . . filled with plenty," "your vats . . . bursting with wine" (3:2, 4, 8, 10). In Wisdom's right hand is "long life"; in her left hand, "riches and honor" (3:16). In an ancient metaphor reminiscent of the tree goddess of plenty, Wisdom is "the tree of life to those who lay hold of her; those who hold her fast are called happy" (3:18).

Lady Wisdom, with all the promises of the "good life" in her hands, is again and again contrasted with the "other woman," a seductress with "smooth words" who appears to promise happiness but whose ways lead to death (2:16–19). Her lips "drip honey and her speech is smoother than oil, but in the end she is bitter as wormwood, sharp as a two-edged sword. Her feet go down to death, her steps follow the path to Sheol" (5:3–5). In chapter 5, this woman represents the temptation to marry into "alien" families of non-Jews, or those of mixed parentage. The young man is warned that such intermarriage enriches others instead of building up his own group: "You will give your honor to others, . . . strangers will take their fill of your wealth and your labors will go to the house of an alien" (5:9–10).

The solution is strict endogamy, embracing a wife from one's own group and clinging to her all life long: "Drink water from your own cistern. . . . Let them be for yourself alone and not for sharing with strangers." The faithful wife from one's own group is hymned in the love language of the Song of Songs: "Rejoice in the wife of your youth, a lovely deer, a graceful doe. May her breasts satisfy you at all times; may you be intoxicated always by her love" (Prov. 5:18b-19).[55]

The "other woman" from outside one's group is defined as an adulteress, one who is already married but who seeks to seduce the young man whose feet are straying into other pastures. The threat here is not sex with prostitutes, but marriage with a woman of another group. The "smooth tongue of the adulteress," with her beauty and seductive ways, is distinguished from the prostitute: a prostitute can be bought for the price of "a loaf of bread," but this "wife of another . . . stalks a man's very life" (6:24–26).

In chapter 7, we are treated to a steamy scene of this "other woman," who lies in wait for the young man in the streets, "decked out like a prostitute," "loud and wayward." As he wanders by, she seizes and kisses him, enticing him into her house with the promise of a night of lovemaking while her husband is away. In the language of love poetry, she says: "I have decked my couch with coverings, . . . I have perfumed my bed with myrrh, . . . come let us take our fill of love until morning, let us delight ourselves with love, for my husband is not at home" (7:10–19). This scene gains vividness because it has been glimpsed through a lattice window (by whom?

Wisdom as the teacher who stays inside the home?): "For at the window of my house I looked out through my lattice and I saw . . . I observed"(7:6, 7).[56]

The culminating picture of these two rival women, Wisdom and Folly, is found in chapter 9 of Proverbs. Here, Wisdom is the hostess who invites the untutored to her banquet. In a language reminiscent of a Near Eastern goddess who builds a "house" (temple) as the seat of her presence and lays out a feast, Wisdom has "built her house, hewn her seven pillars. She has slaughtered her animals, she has mixed her wine, she has also set her table" (9:1–2). She sends out her servant girls (teachers as representatives of Wisdom?), who call the prospective students from "the highest places in the town." Her invitation to "eat of my bread and drink of my wine" is the call to spiritual growth: "Lay aside simpleness and live, walk in the way of insight" (9:5–6).[57]

Wisdom's rival, Folly, is described as a deceptive "look-alike." She too takes her seat "at the high places of the town, calling to those who pass by . . . you who are simple turn in here" (9:14, 16). But her drink and bread are stolen pleasures, tasted in secret; her guests are already on their way down to Sheol (9:17–18).[58] If the call of Wisdom and that of Folly look and sound so much alike, how can the "simple" tell them apart? The surest way is to stay close to home and not to stray into the houses of "aliens."

Despite the superficial similarity of Wisdom and Folly, they are polar opposites. Wisdom not only brings life; she is the life principle of the cosmos itself. Folly belongs to the realm that God does not enter, a realm that is outside creation itself—Sheol, the underworld of the dead. This identification of Wisdom with the foundation of God's creation is revealed several times in Proverbs. "The Lord by wisdom founded the earth, by understanding he established the heavens" (3:19–20). The description of her cosmological role in chapter 8 asserts that Wisdom was created by God "at the beginnings of his work, the first of his acts of long ago." Before anything else was created, "depths, . . . springs abounding in water, . . . mountains, . . . earth and fields or the world's first bits of soil, . . . I was there" (Prov. 8:22, 24, 25, 26, 27).

Wisdom is described as God's first creation. She is his child and his assistant, who was "beside him" as he "marked out the foundations of the earth" (8:22–30).[59] Wisdom's role in creation is not just as a "helper," however. She is the place where God's joy and satisfaction in his creation, and especially in the creation of humans, overflow: "I was daily his delight, rejoicing with him always, and delighting in the human race" (8:30b–31).[60] Wherever God rejoices in his creation, she is there.

This cosmological role of Wisdom is repeated with variations in Ecclesiasticus and Job. Ecclesiasticus (the Wisdom of Jesus ben Sirach) declares that "all wisdom is from the Lord and with him it remains forever" (Ecclus. 1:1). Thus, Wisdom is not a separate divine hypostasis, but simply God's wisdom. Yet she is also God's creation: "She was created before all other things . . . it is he who created her, he saw her and took her measure." This created wisdom was poured out "upon all God's works." She is also the special gift of those who love God, "created with the faithful in the womb, an eternal foundation among humans and among their descendants she will abide faithfully" (1:4, 9, 14–15). Although Wisdom permeates all creation and is given to all who seek the Lord, her definitive "incarnation" is the Torah.[61] It is in the commandments of Moses that she was given her "resting place," taking "root in an honored people, in the portion of the Lord, his heritage." All those who obey these commandments "will not sin" (24:11, 22).

Job has a more skeptical take on the capacity of humans to know Wisdom and obey her commands. Only God knows the way to wisdom; it is hidden from all human eyes. It dwells with God in the secret places of the cosmos, far beyond human experience. Humans have technical skills, but God's wisdom is mysterious, like God's ways themselves, far transcending human capacity to know and understand (Job 28).[62]

In the Wisdom of Solomon, a work of the Hellenistic Jewish community of Egypt from the early first century BCE, Wisdom's cosmological role expands.[63] She is the inner spiritual life of the soul, which is, at the same time, the immanence of God's divine spirit that permeates the cosmos: "She pervades and permeates all things, for she is the breath of the power of God and a pure emanation of the glory of the almighty." In language that would later be echoed in the Christian doctrine of the cosmological Logos, "she is the reflection of eternal light, a spotless mirror of the working of God and the image of his goodness" (Wisd. of Sol. 7:24–25, 26).

Wisdom is the divine presence that accompanies God's people, Israel, throughout their journey, protecting them from idolaters. To love her, to commune with her, is to connect God's eternal spirit with the human soul and thereby ensure immortal life.[64] Here, Wisdom takes on a distinctly Hellenistic soteriological role, the assurance of eternal life (perhaps to rival the Isis mystery religion, discussed in chapter 4). She answers questions about the soul's capacity to survive death and to ascend to live forever with God and even suggests that it is better to die unmarried and without children. This assertion seems to valorize the sort of ascetic life found in the Egyptian Jewish sect of the Therapeutae (examined in chapter 4).

We have left the earlier Hebraic world, where life was bounded by human finitude, and a grim Sheol after death, and which saw children as the chief means to

FIGURE 19
Shekinah holds the baby Moses, third century CE. Wall mural, Dura synagogue.

affirm ongoing life. The soul now has a heavenly future, and Wisdom is its means and guide to heaven. This concept of Wisdom would be continued and transformed in Christianity. Rabbinic Jewish thought would replace it with the feminine figure of Shekinah, the immanent presence of God in the Jewish community (fig. 19).

Where are women in the vision of Wisdom? At first glance, Wisdom seems to give women an exalted identity as quasi-divine mediators between God and "men." But a more careful examination reveals the androcentrism of this vision. Although the picture of Wisdom may contain whispers of real women as counseling wives and mothers, women as seekers of knowledge and teachers of wisdom are absent or invisible.[65] The world of wisdom is defined by relations between men, between human men and a male God, played out in relations between fathers and sons, male teachers and students.[66] Femaleness appears as two contrary liminal symbols on the borders of this male world, between human males and God, and between human males and death, the polar opposite of God. Women as agents, as seekers of wisdom in their own right, cannot insert themselves into this world of male-male relations without fundamentally reconstructing its gender symbolism.

FOUR · Savior Goddesses
in the Mystery Religions
and Gnosticism

THE MYSTERY RELIGIONS IN THE HELLENISTIC WORLD

In 333 BCE, Alexander the Great conquered Persia, the great rival of the Greeks, and two years later extended his power to Egypt. At his death, the ancient kingdoms of the Near East and Egypt were integrated into Hellenistic empires. Greek became the lingua franca of the educated elite. The religions of the ancient Near East were hellenized, and symbols of those religions were assimilated into the Greek deities. Two and a half centuries later, the Romans would sweep across the area, conquering Egypt and the Near East and appropriating this hellenized culture as they brought the region under their own imperial sway.

This loss of political independence and their subordination to the Greek and then the Roman empires changed the relation of the religious leadership classes to their earlier traditions. Their religions no longer functioned to shore up the well-being of independent kings, city-states, and kingdoms. Now they prayed for the well-being of Greek and Roman overlords. Their languages and cultures were overlaid by those of the imperial colonizers. At the same time, imperial unification of the Mediterranean allowed a new internationalism. Educated elites and merchants moved readily across the leading cities of the Near East, Greece, and Italy. Cities became multicultural and multiethnic.

This mixing of many peoples brought a mingling of their diverse religious cults. The Eleusinian mysteries remained tied to their historical location, but people flocked from across the empire to participate in these rites. The Dionysian rites, never tied to one place, were celebrated throughout the hellenized world. The rites of Cybele, the Magna Mater (Great Mother) of Phrygia, as well as the rites of the hellenized cult of Isis and Serapis of Egypt and the cult of Mithra from Persia, among others, spread across the Greco-Roman world and even into the far-flung reaches of Roman conquest in Gaul and England. These cults were hellenized, and elements from one were often assimilated into another. They became focused on individual personal salvation. Ordinary people (usually those of some means) could become initiates of the rites of the Great Mother, of Isis, or of Mithra.

In the late nineteenth and early twentieth centuries, studies of the mystery rites by the History of Religions School saw in them evidence of a general turn to eschatology in late Greco-Roman society, or what Gilbert Murray called a "failure of nerve."[1] Some scholars argued that the rites were influenced by the "irrationality" of "oriental" culture that flowed into the Western world, corrupting its self-confidence. They described earlier Greek societies such as classical Athens and early imperial Rome as "rational" and "this-worldly," worshipping deities that sacralized abundant earthly life. Late antique society, however, under "oriental" influence, lost this healthy optimism and focused increasingly on the hope for life after death.

This view of a turn to pessimism and eschatology is summed up in Gilbert Murray's *Four Stages of Greek Religion:*

Anyone who turns from the great writers of classical Athens, say Sophocles or Aristotle, to those of the Christian era, must be conscious of a great difference of tone. There is a change in the whole relation of the writer to the world around him. The new quality is not specifically Christian; it is just as marked in the Gnostics or Mithra-worshippers as in the Gospels and the Apocalypse, in Julian and Plotinus as in Gregory or Jerome. It is hard to describe. It is a rise of asceticism, of mysticism, in a sense, of pessimism; a loss of self-confidence, of hope in this life and of faith in normal human effort; a despair of patient inquiry, a cry for infallible revelation; an indifference to the welfare of the state; a conversion of the soul to God. It is an atmosphere in which the aim of the good man is not so much to live justly, to help the society to which he belongs and enjoy the esteem of his fellow creatures, but rather, by means of a burning faith, by contempt for the world and its standards, by ecstasy, suffering and martyrdom, to be granted pardon for his unspeakable unworthiness, his immeasurable sins. There is an intensifying of certain emotions; an increase of sensitiveness, a failure of nerve.[2]

The early twentieth-century scholars of the mystery religions saw them as examples of how earlier this-worldly cults of seasonal renewal had been converted to a pessimism that turned to eschatological hope. Through sharing in the death of Osiris or Attis and experiencing the renewal of life, the initiate assured himself of a blessed immortality that would allow him ("her" was usually ignored or seen as further evidence of "irrationality") to cross the boundaries of death. Sharing in the death and resurrection of mystery deities offered a ready comparison with Christianity, as a mystery religion through which the baptized, as in Pauline theology, die and rise with Christ and thus are assured of eschatological salvation. Indeed, much of the work on the mystery religions in this scholarship was governed by an assumption of a historical relation between the mysteries and Christian soteriology.[3]

The assumptions governing the study of mystery rites in late antique society have become far less certain in recent decades. Hopes for a blessed afterlife, along with good harvests, go back to the earliest records of the Eleusinian rites of the seventh century BCE. Plato in classical Athens laid the basis for hope for celestial immortality, perhaps drawing on Babylonian astrological theories formulated in the previous century. Hence, these ideas of eschatological hope appear early in Greek thought, not only in the later period. In addition, studies of the mystery rites up to the end of the empire show that these cults retained the expectation that initiation would bring worldly prosperity. A blessed life after death was certainly a hoped-for benefit, but it was far less central than has been assumed.[4] Although both state and family religions persisted to the end of the empire, the mystery religions also featured a new individualism, in which people began to turn to personal initiation as individuals rather than as members of families or communities.

A brief look at the rites of Cybele and Attis, as well as those of Isis, reveals this complexity. The worship of Cybele as the Great Mother, or Magna Mater, originated in Anatolia, where she had the character of a mistress of wild nature in the mountains, symbolized by carrying or being carried by lions (fig. 20). Her rites stood behind the power of kings, and she was served by castrated priests, although there is no evidence that originally her worship took the form of ecstatic rites in which these priests publicly castrated themselves.[5] In the sixth century BCE, the worship of Cybele had already traveled to Greece, where she was associated both with Demeter, as a grain Goddess, and with Dionysian ecstatic rites. In this Greek context (not from their original "oriental" heritage), the rites of Cybele took the form of nocturnal gatherings of women beating the tympanum and experiencing ecstatic possession.[6]

The association of Cybele with Attis, a young lover who castrated himself and

FIGURE 20
Magna Mater (Cybele) seated in her chariot, pulled by lions, second century CE. Statue.
(The Metropolitan Museum of Art, Gift of Henry G. Marquand, 1897 [97.22.24])

died under a pine tree, is found only in the Hellenistic period, not in the earlier traditions of Asia or Greece. There is a sharp debate among scholars over whether the
Greeks had earlier excluded this story because of its repugnant nature or whether
it was actually invented only in the Hellenistic setting.[7] In 204 BCE, the Romans imported the worship of Cybele to Rome during the Hannibalic wars. Here, Cybele
was linked with the myth of the Romans' descent from the Trojans and thus was
made to represent the ancient Goddess who blessed the ancestors of Rome. Cybele
was worshipped through public rites at her temple in Rome. Roman officials presided
over annual games, theatrical performances, and the washing of her statue in the
Almo. The aim of these rites was to shore up the well-being of Rome, its prosperity and political preeminence.[8]

In addition to these public rites, the Phrygian priests of Cybele developed annual rites, held from March 15 to March 28, that focused on the sufferings of Attis,
as a prototype of the Galli, the castrated priests of the cult (fig. 21). Part of the ritual
involved carrying in a pine tree, representing the tree under which Attis died. This
was followed by ecstatic rites on the Day of Blood, in which the priests beat and
gashed themselves. In a state of ecstatic possession, one dedicating himself to this

FIGURE 21

Meter (Cybele) and Attis, late second century BCE. Relief, provenance unknown. (Archaeological Museum, Venice)

priesthood might publicly castrate himself. The rites focused on mourning for the death of Attis.

Only in the third century CE do we have evidence of an additional day of the Hilaria (Day of Rejoicing) in which this mourning was followed by expressions of joy. But the story of Attis is not one of a resurrected god; rather, he dies and yet is preserved in death. We have little clear evidence that those who engaged in the rites believed that they were ensuring their own immortality by participating. It seems instead to have been an ecstatic experience of union with powerful divine forces that gave hope of general renewal of life here on earth.[9]

One ritual that came to be connected with Cybele was the taurobolium, the sacrifice of a bull for the welfare of the Roman state. Only in the second century CE did this develop into a blood "baptism," in which the initiate stood in a hollowed-out area beneath the platform on which the bull was sacrificed and was bathed with its blood. Such a rite was available only to the wealthy, who could afford to pay for the sacrifice of such an animal. Because the bull was an ancient symbol of powerful, virile life, the blood-drenched initiate emerged "purified" and renewed. Participants saw worldly prosperity and health as the primary benefits of this rite, rather than focusing on life after death. Indeed, the effects of the "baptism" were expected to last only twenty years and then to be in need of renewal.[10]

I pass over discussion of the cult of Mithra here because it is a severely male-identified religion, with no goddess figures and admitting only male initiates. In contrast, we can examine the Hellenistic cult of Isis. It seems that eschatology was always a central concept of the cult of Isis and Osiris. As chapter 2 explained, Osiris was the mummified pharaoh who reigned over the world of life after death. The route to such life was expensive, at first reserved for royalty and gradually extended to wealthier merchants and officials. With the Greek conquest of Egypt, the rites of Isis and Osiris were converted into a Hellenistic religion, reinterpreted through the influence of the Eleusinian mysteries.[11] Temples of Isis appeared throughout the Greco-Roman world, with a permanent priesthood that carried out daily public rituals from morning to night (fig. 22). Anyone could attend these public rites, but initiation was reserved for individuals with special dedication to the Goddess who could pay for the considerable expenses involved.

The primary firsthand account of this rite is found in a novel from the second century CE. The Golden Ass, by Apuleius, seems to reflect the author's own experience of becoming an initiate of Isis. The account of a man transformed into an ass and then liberated from this form was borrowed from earlier novels.[12] Apuleius uses it to tell the amusing story of Lucius Apuleius, a man of good family led astray by dabbling in magic. He is accidentally turned into an ass (a hairy animal representative of barbarian people) by the slave woman of a witch from whom he is seeking knowledge of magic powers. He undergoes various vicissitudes in this asinine form, until he is finally released by the Goddess Isis and becomes her worshipper. In the concluding chapters of the novel, we gain a dramatic glimpse both at the way Isis was pictured by a second-century Greek devotee and at the character of her rites.

Lucius, in his asinine form, escapes from a carnival, where he is about to be exhibited in a show of bestial intercourse with a woman. He gallops to a beach, where he falls asleep. He awakens to a vision of Isis rising from the sea. She is pictured as consummately beautiful, with symbols of her cosmic powers. She wears a chaplet woven with flowers, a mirror disk on her forehead upheld by vipers on each side, and ears of corn. Her robe shades from white to yellow to red, and she wears a black mantle glowing with stars and the moon. She carries a rattle in one hand and a boat-shaped dish in the other with an asp writhing on its handle. Her presence fills the air with perfume.

She speaks, identifying herself as the universal Goddess of nature who rules over

FIGURE 22

Ceremony performed by worshippers of Isis, first century CE. Wall painting, Herculaneum. (Museo Archeologico Nationale, Naples; photo: Erich Lessing / Art Resource, NY)

the heavenly world, the terrestrial world, and the underworld: "I am Nature, the universal Mother, the mistress of all the elements, primordial child of time, sovereign of all things spiritual, queen of the dead, queen also of the immortals, the single manifestation of all gods and goddesses that are. My nod governs the shining heights of Heaven, the wholesome sea breezes, the lamentable silences of the world below." The text declares that all the goddesses of the many peoples refer to her, but her true name, known only to the Egyptians, is Isis.[13]

This vision reflects the Hellenistic assumption that all deities are ultimately one and can be merged together in one universal cosmic vision. This idea of the Great Mother, which has been attributed to Paleolithic peoples by archaeologist Marija

FIGURE 23
Worshippers of Isis. Relief of a procession of priest and priestesses holding typical
sacred symbols, Roman period. (Vatican Museums, Vatican State; photo: Alinari /
Art Resource, NY)

Gimbutas, is, in fact, very much the product of Hellenistic universalism. It is an appealing vision, but, I suspect, one that could exist only as a by-product of cultural
imperialism, not in early scattered human communities. It is also primarily cosmic
and this-worldly rather than eschatological. The focus is on well-being throughout
all parts of the cosmos. The world of the dead is one part of the cosmos, located in
the underworld, over which Isis also reigns.

After Lucius's vision of Isis, he is directed to approach a procession of Isis worshippers (fig. 23) the next day as they carry a ritual boat to the sea to launch the season of navigation. The high priest will be carrying roses. Lucius is told to eat them,
which will transform him back into a human. He does so, recovers his human shape,
and is thereafter a firm devotee of Isis, in gratitude for his restoration. He then begins to attend the daily services of the Isis temple in Corinth and eventually asks to
be initiated. This requires many months of waiting, which include remaining sexually chaste and eating only plain food. Eventually, he receives a vision that allows
him to be initiated. After being bathed and sprinkled with holy water and fasting
for ten days, abstaining from meat and wine, he is led through a nocturnal initiation in the innermost sanctuary.

Although Lucius can speak only in code language about this initiation, it seems
to have taken the form of a cosmic journey to the underworld and then through the
celestial regions: "I approached the very gates of death and set one foot on Proser-

pine's threshold, yet was permitted to return, rapt through all the elements. At midnight I saw the sun shining as if it were noon; I entered the presence of the gods of the underworld and the gods of the upper world, stood near and worshipped them."[14] Emerging from this nocturnal journey through the cosmos, Lucius is then exhibited at dawn to the uninitiated worshippers in the robes of a transformed person, with twelve stoles around him, a linen outer garment with a border of flowers, an overgarment woven with sacred animals, a torch in his hand and a crown on his head imitating the rays of the sun. Lucius celebrates his day as his "birthday" with a banquet and, on the third day, after further ceremonies, a festive breakfast.

After his initiation, Lucius continues to worship at the temple for some days and then travels to Rome, where he associates himself with the daily services of Isis's temple in that city. There, he receives further revelations that he must go through two more initiations: one to the service of Osiris, and then a completion of his first Isaic initiation in Corinth. These initiations also demand days of fasting, rites, and banquets that cost considerable amounts of money. But their benefits are primarily this-worldly. Through the patronage of Isis, he is freed from his former "bad luck." In a world seen as governed by capricious fortune, a relationship to the Goddess protects one from such wavering fates and ensures steady good fortune. Lucius gains health, prosperity, and long life. His work as a barrister flourishes, and he becomes wealthy. Nothing is said of eschatological hopes. Presumably, he can expect a happy life in some Elysian field after death, but the focus is on protection from ill fortune and assurance of material success.[15]

Although eschatology seems less central to the experiences of initiation in these mysteries than earlier studies assumed, the impression of a turn to the eschatological in late antique society underlined by Gilbert Murray does not seem totally off-base. But this had more to do with the triumph of certain lines of Greek thought with a much earlier history, particularly in relation to the development of mystical Platonism and gnosticism in imperial culture, than with a univocal switch from this-worldly earlier culture to other-worldly later culture. Christianity absorbed and reshaped these movements and gave the coup de grâce to pagan rites that were more cheerfully focused on worldly well-being, of the sort that we see in Apuleius's account of his initiation.

Plato, in the fifth century BCE, had already reconceived the location and meaning of a blessed afterlife, and this view came to predominate in late antique thought. Ancient Greek, Hebrew, and Near Eastern religions had pictured the place of the dead as a gloomy underworld where the dead lived on as shades of their former selves. Homeric thought imagined a region of the Blessed Isles, situated at the end of the earth or in a special part of the underworld reserved for heroes.[16] Initiates to the mysteries evidently hoped to gain access to the Elysian fields also; this concept of a blessed afterlife in the underworld was still Apuleius's view in the second century CE.

It was Plato, probably influenced by Babylonian astrology, who conveyed a new location of the afterlife, situating it in the heavens.[17] The emergence of a Platonizing philosophical synthesis in the first century CE meant that this celestial view of the afterlife came to predominate in philosophy. The realm of the stars, far above this earth and its woes, came to be seen as the place of the coveted blessed afterlife of the soul. In Plato's creation story, the *Timaeus*, the soul is said to have been created out of the remnants of the world soul that animates the cosmos. The Demiurgos, or world creator, took the remnants of the world soul, divided it into pieces equal in number to the stars, and placed each piece in a star, where it might experience the "nature of the universe" and the "laws of destiny." Having thus gained a knowledge of cosmic reality prior to embodiment, the souls are incarnated in bodies on earth. There, they are to learn to master the passions that arise from the body and to live righteously.

If they succeed in doing so, they may shed the body at death and return to their "native star." But if they fail in this task, they will pass into a lower state, such as a woman or even an animal. They must then work their way up through successive reincarnations until they return to their "first and better state" and eventually win their way out of the cycle of rebirth to their original celestial existence.[18] This concept in Plato of the soul drama, tied to a doctrine of reincarnation, probably comes from the Pythagorean and Orphic groups.[19]

Popular religious philosophy translated this Platonic theory into a drama of the soul that could be liturgically experienced, thus ensuring, for the initiated, safe passage through the planetary spheres to its heavenly home. The cosmos was imagined as a series of concentric circles, with the earth at the center but also at the lowest point, ontologically and morally. Earth, the realm of finitude, and the passions that arose from the body imprisoned the soul in its lower forms of life. Between earth and the moon lay the region of demonic powers and wandering souls not yet released from the bonds of finitude.

Above the realm of the moon lay the sun and the five other planets through which the soul must travel to reach its starry home. These planets were believed to endow the soul with certain psychic qualities: sexual passion from Venus, covetousness from Mercury, aggression from Mars, lust for power from Jupiter, torpor from Saturn. Thus, the soul on its downward journey through the planetary spheres was corrupted by taking on these successive psychic "garments" from the planets, until it was encased in the final garment of corruption, the body. Salvation consisted in the successful liberation of the soul from these earthly and planetary encasements.

Celestial eschatology in much of Hellenistic philosophy was intracosmic. One ascended to one's "native star" in the upper regions within the cosmos. But some first-century religious philosophy began to expand Plato's cosmic hierarchy, to imagine a higher realm of "pure being" beyond the cosmos, and to view the soul as originating in this higher realm rather than within the cosmos. The goal of the soul, then, was to transcend the cosmos and to return to the higher spiritual realm, where God and the divine beings dwell. Salvation was to enter this transcendent realm and unite with God in divine community. Celestial redemption became anticosmic rather than intracosmic. Gnosticism expressed an extreme version of this dualism.

This view of the soul's ascent through the planetary spheres is explained in the final portion of the *Poimandres of Hermes Tresmegistus*, a hellenized Egyptian text of the first century CE:

First at the dissolution of the material body, you yield up to the demon your sensuous nature, now ineffective, and the bodily senses return each to its source among the elements. And thereafter man thrusts upward through the Harmony and to the first zone he surrenders the power to grow and to decrease, and to the second the machinations of evil cunning, now rendered powerless, and to the third the deceit of concupiscence, now rendered powerless, and to the fourth the arrogance of dominion, drained of its ambition, and to the fifth the impious audacity and rashness of impulsive deed and to the sixth the evil appetites of wealth and to the seventh zone the lying that ensnares. And then denuded of the effects of the Harmony, he enters the nature of the Ogdoas (the eighth sphere of the fixed stars), now in possession of his own power and with those already there exalts the Father; and those present with him rejoice with him at his presence, and having become like his companions, he hears also certain powers above the eighth sphere exalting God with a sweet voice. And then in procession they rise up toward the Father and give themselves up to the Powers and having become Powers themselves enter the Godhead. This is the good end of those who have attained gnosis: to become God.[20]

Members of the philosophical elite saw themselves as preparing for this cosmic journey through intellectual discipline. The philosopher learned to control his passions, purge himself of the demands of the flesh, and turn the eye of his soul heavenward through contemplative thought. But the ordinary seeker for immortality could not expect to follow this path of the leisured, educated class. For him (or her), the rites of the mysteries, with their temporary fasts, ordeals, and unveiling of the symbols of resurrected life, offered a more accessible path. In some Orphic sects, Pythagorean and Platonic speculations about the soul's celestial journey were identified with the benefits of initiation into the mysteries of Eleusis and Dionysus. The "Mystai" and "Bacchai" who underwent such ecstatic experiences were given secret information to guide them through the journey, enabling them to avoid wrong turns that might lead to reincarnation, to remember their higher heavenly home, and thereby to free them from the cycle of rebirth.

An Orphic sect of the second century BCE, for example, buried its dead with gold leaves containing such instructions. In these instructions, the realm of the moon, called Hades, is seen as a place of purification, and the soul must know the right path at this crucial point in the journey:

> You will find in the well-built dwelling of Hades, on the right, a spring near a white cypress. The souls of the dead go down there seeking refreshment, but do not on any account approach it. You will find another whose chill waters flow from the Lake of Mnemosyne. Before it stand guardians, who will ask you why you have come, searching the darkness of Hades. Say to them, "I am a child of the earth and of starry heaven: I am dried up from thirst and I perish, but give me quickly the cold water that flows from the Lake of Memory." And being servants of the King of the Underworld, they will have compassion for you and give you to drink of the Lake. And then you can follow on the sacred way the glorious procession of the other Mystai and Bacchai.[21]

ESCHATOLOGY IN HELLENISTIC JUDAISM

Earlier biblical Judaism shared with its Babylonian neighbors an acceptance of human finitude. Human life was bounded by temporal limits. There was a half-life of the shades in the underworld after death, but it did not carry hopes for a fuller life.[22] Prophetic Judaism developed a messianic futurism that located the fulfillment of justice and plentitude in an age to come, but this age was within history, and those who would enjoy it were mortal. In that age to come, finite life would reach its full limits. No child would die before its time, and every one would live to a healthy old age.[23] But this hope did not break beyond the limits of mortality.

During the end of the Hellenistic and early Roman eras, probably influenced by Zoroastrian eschatology transmitted to Jews during the Persian period, Judaism expanded this worldly futurism into an eschatology that transcended these mortal limits of finite hope.[24] In the apocalyptic writings, from the book of Daniel in Hebrew scripture to the book of Revelation in the New Testament and the intertestamental apocalypses in between, Jewish futurism became increasingly eschatological. The idea of the resurrection of the dead was inserted into messianic future hope, although this future was still seen as bounded by time. The dead will rise, each will receive his or her just punishment or reward—but all will, in due time, die.[25]

This limit was broken by imagining the future as a "two-stage" scenario. First will come the messianic age, when evil is bound and the blessed are rewarded, with or without the risen dead of past ages, during a limited time period (the millennium). Then will come the eternal age, in which this present cosmos is transformed into a spiritual and everlasting form, evil is finally bound, and the blessed enjoy eternal felicity, while the damned are eternally punished. This is the view found in the Christian book of Revelation (Rev. 17–22).

Here, we find the female counterpart to God reappearing in spiritually perfected form. God's bride, Jerusalem, will also enjoy this eschatological perfection; whereas God's enemy, the sea, will be finally defeated.[26] "I saw the new heaven and earth; for the first heaven and the first earth had passed away and the sea was no more. And I saw the holy city, new Jerusalem, coming down out of heaven from God, prepared as a bride adorned for her husband." In this new time of eternal perfection, God will be finally united with humans, and all possibility of sin and mortality will be overcome. "Death shall be no more" (Rev. 21:1–2, 4).

Hellenistic Jews also developed a second type of eschatology, drawn from Platonic religious philosophy, which looked to a celestial immortality of the soul rather than to a future transformation of history. Christianity would attempt to fuse both these eschatologies. The Hellenistic Jewish philosopher Philo (20 BCE–50 CE) testifies to this second type of eschatology. For Philo, drawing on the mystical Platonism of his time, eschatology is rooted in cosmogyny. God is understood as the transcendent One that is beyond the cosmos. From the One, there comes forth God's Word, or Logos, which is the noetic form of the mind of God, the archetype of the created world, and the instrument through which God created the world.[27]

In most of his writings, Philo absorbs divine Wisdom into the term "Logos" and thus masculinizes it. But in a couple of passages, he draws on the female symbolism of Wisdom from Proverbs 8:22–23. In these writings, God is seen as bringing forth Wisdom as the first of his creations. She is the noetic "Idea" of the universe through whom he generated the cosmos. She is both his offspring and his bride, and, through impregnating her, he brings forth their "only begotten son," the universe. Thus, we read in one treatise:

. . . the Creator of the universe is also the father of his creation and that the mother was the knowledge of the Creator with whom God uniting, not as a man unites, became the father of creation. And this knowledge, having received the seed of God, when the day of her travail arrive, brought forth her only and well-beloved son, perceptible by the external senses, namely this world. Accordingly wisdom is represented by some one of the beings of the divine company as speaking of herself in this manner: "God created me as the first of his works and before the beginning of time did he establish me." For it was necessary that all things which come under the head of the creation must be younger than the mother and nurse of the whole universe.[28]

Most of Philo's thought transfers the roles of female Wisdom to a male Logos as the noetic form of the universe, which is then, in turn, manifest in the perceptible universe. Humanity also begins as a noetic idea of "man," created in purely spiritual and nongendered form on the first day. This original "idea" of man is then expressed in embodied form on the sixth day of creation. But male and female are integrated into one androgynous being, with male intellect wholly controlling his "female side," the body. In Philo's view, the fall into sin and finitude takes place when the "female" side of the original androgyne revolts against its masculine "mind." Through this revolt, humanity is separated into male and female as distinct, gendered beings and must engage in degrading sexual intercourse to reproduce the species, having lost its original immortality.[29]

According to Philo, the eschatological remedy of this fall into gender, sex, sin, and death is through contemplative study. This remedy is accessible to both males and females, but both must put aside sexual intercourse in order to recover their original spiritual unity and communion with God. Philo describes what he sees as the optimum expression of this contemplative life in his treatise on a Jewish monastic community, the Therapeutae. Both men and women of this community put aside sexual relations, although this demand seems to have been more stringent for women than for men, given that women symbolized the lower self, or body. The men had earlier married and then, in a later time of life, having fulfilled their marital duties, turned to contemplative philosophy; whereas the women Therapeutae had grown old in chastity, never having "fallen" into sexual relations.

These philosophical adepts spent six days of the week in separate communities, contemplating the eternal ideas of the divine through allegorical reading of scripture. On the seventh day, they came together for a chaste celebration and banquet. By purging themselves of external passions and purifying their minds through philo-

sophical contemplation, the Therapeutae prepared themselves for the ultimate journey of the soul, as it drops off the body and its sexual differentiation and unites
itself with God.[30]

FEMALE SPIRITUAL POWERS IN GNOSTICISM

The gnostic treatises represented by the Nag Hammadi and Berlin Codices are surviving examples of a vast esoteric literature of the second to fourth centuries CE that
fused Jewish, Greek, and ancient Near Eastern mythologies. Many draw on these
mixtures to express a Christian message, while others place a Christian overlay on
a non-Christian original. The symbolism in these treatises mostly expresses a dualistic cosmology and seeks to convey redeeming knowledge (gnosis) to aid the escape of the entrapped soul-spirit from a corrupt lower cosmos into the eternal world
of light, from which the spirit came and to which it belongs.

Gnostic systems are extremely diverse. Some see marriage and reproduction as
lower expressions of what will be perfected on a higher level in the eternal world
above.[31] Female symbolism is also quite diverse and must be examined within each
treatise.[32] Sometimes different versions of the same treatise show shifts in gender
imagery and agency. Thus, the Nag Hammadi II version of the *Apocryphon of John*
assigns the revelatory speech to Adam and Eve from the Tree of Life and the final
hymn of salvation to Christ, whereas the Berlin Codex version assigns these to the
female power Epinoia. The Nag Hammadi version is also more misogynist, blaming women for sexual lust, whereas the Berlin version makes lust an evil plan that
the archonic rulers implanted in the male.[33] (Archons are cosmic rulers.)

This discussion focuses on the *Apocryphon of John*, with some comparison to parallel material in the *Hypostasis of the Archons* and the *Trimorphic Protennoia*, primarily to illustrate the role of female-identified transcendent powers in cosmogony,
revelation, and redemption. These female transcendent powers are known by various names—Pronoia, Ennoia, Epinoia, Barbelo, Sophia, and Zoe—but they are
seen as various levels and expressions of the same power of spiritual knowledge.
The idea of these female powers is indebted to the Jewish concept of Wisdom as
the female companion or agent of God in creation, revelation, and redemption,[34]
embedded within an esoteric exegesis of Genesis 1–6. These Wisdom figures have
counterparts in humanity: spiritual Eve and Norea.

The *Apocryphon of John* is framed within a revelation discourse given to the disciple John, son of Zebedee, in a heavenly vision revealed by "the one who is with
you forever," the Father, the Mother, the Son.[35] This revealer discloses the unfold-

ing of the heavenly pleroma (fullness) of spiritual beings, the origin of the fallen cosmos, and the hoped-for rescue of the spiritual elements from this fallen cosmos.

This story begins with the ultimate One, the Father of all, who exists as pure light, with "nothing above it," "prior to everything." This ultimate One brings forth from himself a female self-reflection, "his" Ennoia, the Pronoia of all, Barbelo, the "womb of everything."[36] This primal pair then ramifies into five androgynous aeons (emanations of the deity): thought, foreknowledge, indestructibility, eternal life, and truth. The Father then begets in Barbelo a "blessed likeness," the only begotten of the Mother-Father, one who does not equal him in greatness but is made perfect through anointing in the Spirit. This is the Perfect Man.[37]

The pleroma expands to include a community of heavenly beings, until the appearance of Sophia of the Epinoia.[38] It is through her "mistake" that the lower world will be generated; yet she will also mediate the rescue of the spiritual elements that fall into the lower world through her "deficiency." Sophia wishes to bring forth a being from herself without the "consent of the Spirit" or "her consort."[39] Since females by themselves are assumed to lack formative power, Sophia brings forth only a monstrous being, described as a "lion-faced serpent," named Yaltabaoth. A Mithraic image of the lion-faced Aion of Time, wrapped in serpents' coils, perhaps reflects the image suggested here (fig. 24).[40] Ashamed of this monster, Sophia casts it outside the heavenly world and hides it in a luminous cloud.

Yaltabaoth, though monstrous, nevertheless has some of the "power of the Mother" that belongs to the heavenly world. He proceeds to generate a demonic cosmos in imitation of the higher pleroma, with twelve powers, seven firmaments of heaven, five in the abyss below, and a multitude of angels numbering 365. In his impious madness, he claims to be the only God—"there is no other God beside me"—but this false claim only reveals his ignorance of the higher world.[41] Sophia then begins to move about in an agitated way. This agitated motion (reminiscent of the Spirit moving over the waters, from Genesis 1:2)[42] expresses her distraught repentance at the evil effects of her decision to bring forth a being without her consort. The pleroma takes pity on her, pours the Spirit on her, and raises her up to the ninth aeon, or level of being. But she will not be perfectly restored to her own aeon until the effects of her mistake are rectified.

Then unfolds the story of the creation of humans. A heavenly voice responds to Yaltabaoth's false boast by revealing the existence of the Perfect Man, the image of the invisible Father, and projecting his image on the waters below. The archonic powers (world rulers) seek to create a man in the image of this man. They collaborate on fashioning his psychic and material body, but their Adam is able to live only when

FIGURE 24
Lion-headed Aion of Time,
c. second or third century CE.
(Museo di Villa Albani, Rome;
photo: Alinari / Art Resource, NY)

Yaltabaoth is tricked into blowing into his face. This deprives the monster of the spiritual power he derived from his Mother and transfers this power to Adam. The archons then become jealous because they recognize that Adam is greater than they are, and they seek to imprison him in the abyss. But the heavenly powers have mercy on Adam and send down the female spiritual power, Epinoia, who is hidden within Adam, to teach him of his higher heavenly origins.

The archonic powers try to deaden the light within Adam by sinking his senses in luxury and deception. Seeking to take the spiritual power of Epinoia out of him, they make a woman (Eve) and draw this power into her. But when Adam sees this female companion, her spiritual counterpart, Epinoia (also Zoe, Life), is revealed to him, and the veil of ignorance is lifted from his mind. This is itself the redemptive work of Sophia. These combined female powers (Epinoia, Sophia, Zoe) then speak to the pair as an eagle from the Tree of Knowledge, to awaken them from their deception, and Adam and his companion recognize their nakedness (lack of knowledge).[43]

Seeking to keep control over the pair, the archons throw them out of paradise and plant sexual desire in their bodies. Pursuing Eve, to snatch the spiritual power out of her, they beget two sons, Yave and Eloim (Cain and Abel).

But Adam begets with Epinoia a third son, Seth, who represents a true likeness of the Heavenly, or Perfect, Man. The Heavenly Mother sent down her Spirit to perfect this spiritual son. He represents the true race of humanity that will be rescued from the fallen world when Sophia's "deficiency" is overcome and the pleroma once again becomes "holy and faultless." History unfolds in contests between the archonic powers, seeking to trap the spiritual power below, and the heavenly powers above, seeking to free it. The treatise ends with the expectation that this revelation, brought by John to the other disciples, will ensure that they will know themselves as that "immovable race" whose destiny lies in the world of light above.

The *Hypostasis of the Archons* covers much of the same territory as the *Apocryphon of John,* but with some interesting variations.[44] It starts with the archonic authorities already established as rulers over the fallen world and reveals their illegitimacy. The chief of these rulers is blind, arrogant, and ignorant of his true origins and the true spiritual world that transcends him—evidenced by his claim that "I am God; there is none apart from me." But a (female) voice comes down from the incorruptible world, correcting his mistake: "You are mistaken, Samael" (using a name for the God of the blind).[45] The gnostics use the Jewish proclamation of faith in the one God but invert its meaning, turning it into a statement of ignorance and impiety. This suggests that the Jewish creator God traditionally proclaimed by this statement is a fallen demonic power. By glimpsing the higher celestial world that transcends him, revealed through his mother, Sophia, his false nature is unmasked.

The treatise describes all the works of this archonic ruler as lacking real formative power. It is Pistis Sophia who gives form to his works, imitating the higher celestial world above. Her image, reflected in the waters below, inspires the archonic powers to try to seize it. But, possessing only psychic and not spiritual power, they are unable to do so. They try to attract the spiritual female power by creating a male, thereby seeking to draw her down into the man as her male counterpart. But these plans reveal their ignorance of the vast gap that separates the inferior terrestrial from the higher celestial power. This incitement of the powers to create a human is itself part of the redemptive plan of the celestial world to rescue the spiritual power that has gone out of it into the world below. But Adam can only crawl on the earth, because of the inferior psychic nature given him by the rulers. Only when the Spirit comes down to dwell in him does he become a "living Soul."

The rulers call the animals for Adam to name and then put him in the Garden to cultivate it. They order him not to eat from the Tree of Knowledge of Good and Evil, trying to keep him in ignorance of the true nature of reality. Telling him that he will die if he eats this fruit, they conceal the fact that only by knowing good and evil—that is, by knowing themselves as evil and the higher world above them as good—will he find true life. The archons also cause him to fall into the sleep of ignorance, opening his side and withdrawing the spiritual power from him into a female, so that he is endowed only with soul. But this causes him to see this female spiritual power face to face as his true source of life. She calls him to arise, and he replies, "It is you who have given me life; you will be called the Mother of the Living."[46]

When the rulers see this spiritual woman, they try to seduce her, but she flees from them, laughing, and becomes a tree, leaving only a shadow reflection of herself (Eve, or carnal woman), whom they defile. But the female spiritual power now comes as a snake, the instructor, and teaches the pair the truth, telling them that if they eat the fruit of the Tree of Knowledge of Good and Evil, they will not die; rather, their eyes will be opened, and they will be like gods. In an inversion of the Genesis story, it is the snake, manifesting the female spiritual power, that speaks the truth, while the fallen rulers lie. Carnal woman (as the counterpart of spiritual woman) initiates the act of liberation by eating the fruit and giving it to her husband. Because they are possessed only of soul, this act reveals to them their nakedness, their lack of spiritual power, and they seek to cover their loins with fig leaves.[47]

The rulers realize that Adam and Eve have discovered their deficiency. In order to prevent them from taking the next step and pursuing spiritual power, they expel them from the Garden. By throwing them into a life of toil and "distraction," the archons hope that "their mankind might be occupied by worldly affairs and might not have the opportunity of being devoted to the Holy Spirit." Eve now bears Cain and Abel. When God accepts Abel's gifts and not those of Cain, Cain pursues and kills his brother. Then Adam "knew" his female counterpart Eve and she bore Seth, as a replacement for Abel, and then a daughter, Norea. This daughter becomes the representative of the female spiritual power that was taken from Eve. Her mother,

Eve, proclaims that Norea is an "assistance for the many generations of mankind. She is the virgin whom the Forces did not defile."[48]

Seeing the reappearance of the female spiritual power in Norea, the rulers try to pursue and defile her, as they had done to her mother, Eve, not realizing that they had never defiled the spiritual woman, but only her carnal shadow. But Norea knows this and confronts them with the truth: "It is you who are the Rulers of the Darkness, you are accursed. And you did not know my mother; instead it was your female counterpart that you knew. For I have not come as your descendant, but rather it is from the World Above that I have come."[49] The rulers redouble their efforts to rape her, but Norea calls out to the true God of the celestial world to save her: "Rescue me from the Rulers of Unrighteousness and save me from their clutches."

The Great Angel, Eleleth, then comes down to help Norea. He reveals to her the higher celestial world and the fallen nature of the worldly rulers. He assures her that none of these rulers have any power over her, for "none of them can prevail against the root of Truth." The humanity rooted in truth will be preserved through the generations until its final delivery in the "final ages." The angel promises her that "these authorities will be restrained. And these Authorities cannot defile you and that generation, for your abode is in Incorruptibility where the Virgin Spirit dwells who is superior to the Authorities of Chaos and to their universe."

The angel then outlines for Norea the prehistory of the cosmos: how Pistis Sophia, dwelling in the incorruptible realm, desired to create something without her consort. Out of that desire, the veil between the world above and the realm below was breached. A shadow came into being beneath the veil, and this became matter. The aborted being produced by Sophia's desire then proceeded to organize this matter and to rule over it, proclaiming himself the only God. But it was Sophia above who introduced light into matter, while Zoe (Life), the daughter of Pistis Sophia, was the voice that revealed to the ignorant God Sakla (Yaltabaoth) his mistake.

Then follows a complicated section in which Sabaoth, the son of Yaltabaoth, repents of his father's mistake and praises Sophia and Zoe. They in turn draw him up and make him ruler over the universe, setting Zoe at his right hand so that he can be instructed in the higher world above, while placing the Angel of Wrath on his left hand, representing the unrighteousness of absolute power. Yaltabaoth in jealousy generates many demonic powers of death that rule the lower realms of the lower cosmos. The Great Angel completes his revelation to Norea by saying: "There I have taught you about the pattern of the Rulers and the Matter in which it was expressed and their parent and their universe."

Norea now wishes to know if she is from this matter. The angel assures her: "You, together with your offspring, are from the Primordial Father; from Above, out of the imperishable Light their souls are come. Thus the Authorities cannot approach them because of the Spirit of Truth present within them; and all who have become acquainted with this Way exist deathless in the midst of dying Mankind." Norea then asks the angel how much longer it will be before this deathless race is freed from its bondage in the world below. He tells her that this will continue "until that moment when the True Man, within modeled form, reveals the existence of the Spirit of Truth which the Father has sent."

Thus, the treatise ends with the prediction of the coming of the messianic True Man, who will teach the hidden descendants of Norea everything and "anoint them with the unction of Life eternal." Then they will be freed from blind thought, will trample underfoot death, which is from the authorities, and ascend to limitless light. "Then Authorities will relinquish their ages, and their angels will weep over their destruction and their demons will lament their death." The children of light will know "the Truth, and their Root and the Father of the Entirety and the Holy Spirit" and sing their praises forever.[50]

Female celestial power that represents the "Thought of God" finds additional dramatic expression in another treatise, the *Trimorphic Protennoia*.[51] Protennoia is Barbelo, the First Thought of the Father, seen as the female self-articulation of the original One, or monad. She is revealed through three descents, in the form of the Father, or Voice; the Mother, or Sound; and the Son, or Word. In each of these descents, Protennoia proclaims herself in the "I am" form. She begins:

I am Protennoia, the Thought that dwells in the light. I am the movement that dwells in the all, She in whom the All takes its stand among those who came to be, She who exists before the All . . . called by three names, although She exists alone, since She is perfect, I am invisible within the Thought of the Invisible One, I am revealed in the immeasurable ineffable things. I am intangible, dwelling in the intangible. I move in every creature.[52]

As Voice, Protennoia is the creative power of the Beginning, the source of life of all that has come to be, revealed in the likeness of "my masculinity." She is the true root that upholds all that exists, the power of life hidden in the work of the rulers that give it foundation. Then, as Mother, as Sound, Protennoia is the eschatological power of the End, the completion of all things. She descends in the last ages to reveal the transience of this lower world and its approaching time of disso-

lution. She reveals herself to the children of light to tell them that their time of deliverance is at hand: "Now I have come a second time in the likeness of a female and
have spoken with them. And I shall tell them of the coming end of this Aeon and
teach them of the beginning of the Aeon to come, the one without change."

At the sound of this Voice, the rulers of the lower cosmos are filled with terror
as they recognize that the universe they know is being shaken to its foundations.
They rise and go to the Archgenitor (Yaltabaoth) to challenge him in his boast that
he is the only and true God. The Voice that has come from the higher world is unknown to them, for they are ignorant of this higher world. They weep and mourn
as they realize that all they have thought to be real is but deceit and that the time of
their destruction is approaching. But Protennoia calls out to the true children of light
in the lower world to take heart, for the time of their redemption is at hand: "Listen to me, to the Sound of your Mother of Mercy, for you have become worthy of
the mystery hidden from the Aeons that you might be perfect. And the consummation of this Aeon and of the life of injustice has approached, and there dawns
the beginning of the Aeon to come which has no change forever."

Protennoia then reveals herself as androgynous, as Mother and Father, as able to
both beget and bring to birth from herself. "I am the womb that gives shape to the
All by giving birth to the Light that shines in splendor. I am the Aeon to Come. I am
the fulfillment of the All; that is, Meirothea, the glory of the Mother. I cast the sound
of the Voice into the ears of those who know me." She invites those who belong to
her to enter the "exalted perfect Light" and be glorified, to be enthroned, to receive
robes and baptism, to become glorious as they were in the beginning (before their
descent to the lower world, "the way you first were when you were Light").[53]

Third, Protennoia is revealed in a masculine form, the Word, himself springing
from the Voice of the Father and Sound of the Mother, to articulate the fullness of
light, "pouring forth living water from the invisible, unpolluted, immeasurable
spring, that is, the unreproducible Voice of the glory of the Mother, the glory of
the offspring of God." This third form of Protennoia, revealed in Jesus, has been
hidden in every creature until it would be revealed at the end of the ages and gather
up the children of light into the eternal kingdom.

What can be said about the meaning of divine female symbolism in these three
treatises? Clearly, there is much more here than simply a "gnostic myth of Sophia"
as a cosmic Eve, a weak female whose error brings about a fallen world and its evil
rulers.[54] Sophia is a celestial figure who exists on the margin of the pleroma, between the world above and the world below. But she herself is an expression of the
ultimate female "Thought" that comes forth from the Father and is in no way infe-

rior to "him." True, in these gnostic systems, the source of the whole celestial system is symbolized as male, as the Father. But this ultimate monad remains unarticulated without Pronoia, the first female Thought that comes forth from him and reflects him. Like the Logos in relation to the Father in orthodox Christian trinitarianism, Pronoia, God's female-identified Thought, is "second" to the Father, but in no way imperfect or less than him. Only through his Thought does God move from silence to speech, from rest to creativity. Through their joint creativity, the pleroma unfolds to express the fullness of the divine.

Sophia, as the "last" of these heavenly beings, is seen as precipitating the lower world through a "fault," through a desire to create as the primal One has created, out of him/herself, an androgynous being that both begets and brings forth from itself. But she is not able to bring forth in this way, "without her consort," although it is never made clear who her consort is. Although she herself is called androgynous, she is seen as somehow limited to the female aspect of procreation. In ancient medical theory, this means that she by herself lacks "seed" for formative power. Thus, what she brings forth from herself resembles an "aborted fetus," the product of her maternal menstrual blood but without the male formative power.[55]

This product is the first ruler, Yaltabaoth, who then shapes a fallen cosmos and claims primacy over it, ignorant of his lower origins and nature. But Sophia's act is never described as evil, nor is she ever seen as evil. Rather, she has erred, making a mistake from an excessive desire to imitate the creative work of the ultimate androgynous God/Pronoia, although she is unable to do so without her male aspect. She repents of her error and is restored by her fellow celestial beings to the inside edge of the pleroma, although not quite to her original place within it. Sophia's error begins the generation of the lower cosmic system, which culminates in the creation of Adam in imitation of either Sophia or Perfect Man, the offspring of God/Pronoia, reflected in the waters of chaos below.[56] Thus, her error is ultimately a felix culpa, a happy fault, necessary to create the human race that will be saved from the lower world by the redemptive incursions of spiritual power from above.

These redemptive incursions come from the female side, from Sophia, her daughter Zoe, and ultimately from the first Thought of God, Pronoia or Epinoia. These female expressions of the divine shore up and give substance to the lower world generated by Yaltabaoth. Yaltabaoth carries this spiritual power as a result of his maternal origins from above. This maternal spiritual power is, in turn, taken from him to endow Adam with life and is then taken from Adam to be expressed in the spiritual Eve, who reveals his true source of life to him. Finally, it finds expression in Norea, the true daughter of the spiritual Eve, who is the mother of the race of humanity to be redeemed.[57]

The female spiritual power is not passive, but active. She is where the divine acts, descends, empowers, and reveals the true nature of things. Most of all, it is through the female divine power that the false claims of the rulers are resisted. The female voice from above corrects the false claims of the deformed son. The female spiritual power continually flees, mocks, and escapes the efforts of the rulers to entrap her. This capacity of the female voice to be the "site of resistance" to the archonic powers becomes most dramatically manifest in Norea, who refuses their efforts to seduce her, crying out to the heavenly powers and receiving the redeeming revelation. Although the messianic expression of this true race is Jesus, the epitome of the True Human revealed in the end time, he is himself the child of Norea/spiritual woman/Sophia, the eschatological revelation of the primal "true human" who came forth at the beginning as the offspring of the primal Father-Mother. Thus, he completes the Sethian triad of divinity, which is Father-Mother-Son.

Why do we find this powerful role of feminine celestial spirit in these treatises? Too little is known about the sociology of the groups that produced and lived the message of the treatises to know whether these works reflect their own practice of egalitarian leadership, perhaps with particular roles for women as representatives of the female divine, although we have hints that this was the case for some groups.[58] Perhaps the emphasis on feminine spiritual power reflects yet another instance in which gnostic religious creativity expressed itself in dramatic reversals of social order and religious traditions. Just as the world ruler's claim of monarchical exclusivity is reversed by revealing it as an impious error, and the story of eating the apple in the primal paradise is reversed by seeing the snake as an instructor from the higher spiritual world, so gender order is reversed to express a higher spiritual female power capable of overthrowing the male-identified powers that rule over a false and fallen world.

Gender order is not totally reversed, to be sure. The higher celestial world is a complementarity of male and female aspects, crowned by the male-female God/ Pronoia. But in the redemptive work of the higher world counteracting the lower world, female spiritual power is often envisioned as subverting and overcoming male material/psychic power. This view also reflects the liminal role of Sophia, who not only represents the ultimate Pronoia/Epinoia but also stands on the upper margin between the higher and lower world. She precipitates the fall into the lower world, yet when she repents and is partly restored to the higher world, she is closer to the margin than before.

This liminal position between the two worlds also makes her the active agent in the rescue of the elements of life that have fallen below. Thus, the whole gnostic system of these treatises turns on Sophia. She is the redeemed redeemer who stands between the two worlds, ultimately reclaiming the offspring of light who have come from her error. Gnostics recognize in their own spiritual power the power of the Mother, through which they resist the rulers of this world.

FEMALE DISCIPLES IN SOME GNOSTIC GOSPELS

Norea is not only the human ancestress of the children of light; she is also the first disciple, the prototype of those who resist the archonic powers because they sense the "root of truth" within themselves and hear the revelation of redemptive gnosis. Do the gnostic Christian gospels correspondingly contain evidence of such exemplary female disciples of Jesus? In fact, the canonical gospels record a significant circle of female disciples, with Mary Magdalene as the leader, the "disciple to the disciples," who brings the good news of Christ's resurrection to the male disciples huddled in the upper room. But orthodox Christian tradition marginalized these female disciples. By the sixth century, Mary Magdalene had been stereotyped as a forgiven prostitute rather than treated as a leading disciple.[59] Yet a number of gnostic gospels see these female disciples as equal members of the circle to whom Jesus gave the leadership of his movement after his death, and a few see Mary Magdalene as playing a leading role that corrected and brought higher vision to the male disciples.

I will mention the role played by Mary Magdalene in seven gnostic writings: the Sophia of Jesus Christ, the Dialogue of the Savior, the First Apocalypse of James, the Gospel of Thomas, the Gospel of Philip, the Pistis Sophia, and the Gospel of Mary. Gnostic Christian treatises often take the form of a post-resurrection dialogue between leading disciples and the risen Lord, who gathers them together to receive higher esoteric instruction that goes beyond the teachings revealed to the multitude in his lifetime (known to the larger church through the canonical gospels). This format of Jesus teaching his disciples post-resurrection is the foundation of the gnostic Christian claim to have higher and fuller access to Jesus's teachings than that enjoyed by the larger church.

In these Christian gnostic writings, the roles played by the women disciples, as well as the gender symbolism of male and female, differ markedly. In the Sophia of Jesus Christ, a Christian revision of a pre-Christian cosmological treatise, the Eugnostos of the Blessed, twelve male disciples and seven female disciples are gathered with the risen Lord on a mountain in Galilee. The disciples question Jesus as a group. Five are mentioned by name: Philip, Matthew, Thomas, Bartholomew, and Mariamme (Mary Magdalene).[60] In this treatise, Mariamme belongs to an inner circle of disciples and is the key woman among them.[61]

In the Dialogue of the Savior, the disciples also question Jesus as a group. Three are identified by name: Judas (Jesus's brother, not Judas Iscariot), Matthew, and Mariam. These three ask a nearly equal number of questions, and Mariam is singled out as having a high level of understanding. Her answers are praised by the Lord with words such as, "This she spoke as a woman who knew the All," and "you reveal the greatness of the Revealer." Jesus takes the three aside and "set[s] his hand on them" so that they might see the "whole"—that is, so that they might become the privileged teachers of the esoteric knowledge he has disclosed.[62]

In the First Apocalypse of James, James (the Lord's brother) is the central figure to whom Jesus imparts secret teachings. James comforts and corrects the twelve male disciples through his special knowledge. James also confirms his teachings through the seven women disciples of Jesus, among them Salome, Miriam, Martha, and Arsinoe. These women disciples stand in a special relation to James, closer to him and above the twelve male disciples.[63]

In the Gospel of Thomas, by contrast, although Mary is in the inner circle of disciples, there is conflict over her presence. Thomas reflects a misogynist gender symbolism used among some gnostic Christians, in which the female represents the evil material world and is incapable of higher wisdom. This view is expressed in the confrontational words of Simon Peter to Christ, "Let Mary leave us, for women are not worthy of Life." Jesus is said to reject this misogynist view of woman, but only by partly confirming it. He replies, "I myself shall lead her in order to make her male, so that she too may become a living spirit resembling you males. For every woman who makes herself male will enter the Kingdom of Heaven." In the Gospel of Thomas, redemption necessitates the rejection of sexuality and reproduction. Because women are more identified with these aspects of life, they must engage in a double transformation. By rejecting sexuality and reproduction, they make themselves "male" and hence equal to their male colleagues. They must then undergo a second transformation, into a "living spirit."[64]

The Gospel of Philip, however, somewhat like the three treatises examined earlier, seems to see the female as representing the spiritual side of the soul-spirit hierarchy in humanity. The creation of woman drew this female spiritual power out of what was originally an androgynous male, Adam, leaving him with only soul power. This division of the original androgynous Adam into male and female brought death into the world. For the community of the Gospel of Philip, the sacrament of the "bridal chamber" could remedy this primal fall into gender duality and death. In this symbolic spiritual marriage, Valentinian gnostics believed that they reunified their male-female (psychic-spiritual) duality and thus ascended to redemptive wholeness.[65]

In this gospel, Mary Magdalene represents the female consort, or counterpart, of Christ. He is depicted as loving her more than the other disciples, "kissing her many times on the mouth." The male disciples are offended by this special relation of Mary to Jesus and protest: "Why do you love her more than us?" Jesus mocks their ignorance by saying, "Why do I not love you like her? When a blind man and one who sees are together in darkness, they are no different from one another. When the light comes, then he who sees will see the light, and who is blind will remain in darkness." By implication, Mary is one who possesses the capacity to see the light, while those who challenge her are blind.

In the Pistis Sophia, Mary is one of the most prominent among Jesus's disciples and often takes the lead in asking questions of the Lord. Peter is cast as the jealous, misogynist disciple who tries three times to silence her. In the first instance, Peter says, "My Lord, we are not able to suffer this woman who takes the opportunity from us and does not allow us to speak, but she speaks many times." Jesus then explains that anyone may speak whenever "the power of his Spirit has welled up so that she understands what I say." The implication is that Mary can speak often because she has this Spirit in abundance. On a second occasion, Mary declares that she has a perfect understanding and so believes that she should speak often, but she is afraid of Peter "because he threatens me and he hates our race [women]." On a third occasion, Peter complains, "My Lord, let the women cease to question that we also may question." Here, the Lord suggests to Mary and the other women that they give their brothers a chance to speak, too. This does not imply that the women should not keep silence, for they continue to talk, but simply that they should give the men the opportunity to speak as well.[66]

The most significant of these gnostic gospels that feature Mary's leadership in conflict with Peter's jealousy is the Gospel of Mary. It opens with a resurrection discourse from Jesus to the assembled male and female disciples. Only Peter, Mary, Andrew, and Levi are named. After this discourse, Jesus leaves them with the admonition that they are to cultivate inner peace among themselves and not lay down rules and laws to constrain the inspiration of the inner Spirit. With the Savior's departure, all the male disciples show that they lack this inner peace. They are grieving and fearful that if they go out to preach the Gospel of the Kingdom, they will be killed as the Savior was killed. Mary then stands up to address the disciples, showing that she is the only one who understands the spiritual nature of the Lord's message. She seeks to comfort them by assuring them that the grace of the Savior is within them and will protect them.[67]

Peter then turns to Mary and greets her as a "sister," who is recognized to have a special relation to the Lord, whom he loved "more than any other woman." Peter asks Mary to reveal to them the words of the Savior which he taught to her, but which the other disciples do not know. Mary then acknowledges that she has had a special vision from the Lord, and she begins to disclose the contents of this vision. This takes the form of a discourse on the ascent of the soul through the different planetary spheres, fending off the challenges of the rulers that command each sphere, until it obtains its final liberation.

Having mapped this path of the soul's journey upward to its true heavenly home, Mary falls silent, having reached the realm that transcends words. Andrew and then Peter challenge her testimony. Andrew expresses his disbelief in Mary's words because they differ from what he had heard from the Lord (a charge that the orthodox would also level at gnostic esoteric teaching). Peter then raises the gender question of Mary's role, objecting to the idea that the Lord would have taught a woman something he did not teach to the men. Mary becomes sorrowful that her male colleagues would doubt her spiritual integrity. Levi comes to her defense, challenging Peter's misogyny: "Peter, you have always been hot tempered. Now I see you contending against the woman like the adversaries. But if the Savior made her worthy, who are you indeed to reject her? Surely the Savior knew her very well. That is why he loved her more than us. Rather let us put on the Perfect Man and separate as he commanded us and preach the gospel, not laying down any other rule or law beyond what the Savior said."

With these words, Levi appeals to the better minds of the disciples, reminding them that it is not external rules (including those of gender) but the inner spirit within that represents "true humanity." The implication is that this true spiritual humanity is no different in women than in men, and it is this that they are to cultivate and preach. In this spirit, he calls the disciples to go forth and preach the gospel.[68]

These gnostic gospels give us a small glimpse into alternative circles of early Christians. They, like the more orthodox believers, struggled with the tension between sex and celibacy in relation to sin and redemption and were unclear how gender was related to body-spirit, earthly-heavenly dualities. Like the orthodox, they differed among themselves in how they answered these questions. But, in a more thoroughgoing manner than those who became the dominant church, they suggested solutions that included the women disciples equally with men as the apostolic foundation of the church. Some even suggested a gender reversal in which some females have special talents as representatives of the Spirit over against the oppressive powers of this world. They believed they had special insight into the Lord's teachings that made them privileged witnesses to the teachings of the Savior, whom the church must heed.

FIVE

· The Spiritual Feminine
in New Testament and
Patristic Christianity

The Christianity that grew to be the dominant, or orthodox, churches, whose scriptures were canonized in the New Testament, developed parallel to and often intertwined with the gnostic forms of Christianity discussed in the previous chapter.[1]
The anti-gnostic church fathers of the late second century, such as Irenaeus and Tertullian, made a forceful effort to separate from and eject gnostic Christians. They
also worked to canonize, as the original and true "deposit of faith," those early Christian writings that enshrined the views of what was then becoming the established
church. The feminine aspects of God, as well as the leadership of female disciples,
became greatly eclipsed in these dominant forms of Christianity, although significant
traces of female symbolism for God, the soul, and the church remained, ultimately
becoming channeled into Mariology. This chapter will trace the main lines of this
development.

WISDOM IN THE NEW TESTAMENT

The Christians who shaped the stories, hymns, and sayings of Jesus that lie behind
the canonical New Testament were reflecting on what for them was the decisive event
in salvation history: the life, death, and resurrection of Jesus. His teachings had
gripped and transformed their lives, but he had been rejected by the dominant forms
of Judaism and crucified by the Roman imperial powers as a dangerous popular
leader. Yet the disciples of Jesus felt themselves renewed in their faith by his resur-

rection, overcoming the power of death meted out by the rejecting authorities. In this renewed power, they were to continue to preach his name as redemptive.

What were the sources for reflecting on the theological meaning of Jesus? Two major complexes of Jewish tradition provided the sources for this reflection: apocalyptic messianism and Wisdom literature. These two traditions had already partly mingled in late Sapiential literature, such as the Wisdom of Solomon, and the writings of the Qumran community.[2] Sapiential literature provided these early Christians with the narrative of God's self-expression, Wisdom coming forth from God in the beginning, an agent with God in creating the cosmos, through whom the cosmos is sustained, providing the order of creation, and filling it with divine presence. Wisdom descends to earth, seeking disciples, and finds a home in God's elect people. Their teaching, the Torah, is the earthly manifestation of Wisdom. She offers spiritual nourishment, imaged as food and drink, to those who come to her; but she also is rejected, misunderstood by the wise and offered to the "simple." This was the mythic narrative of the Jewish teachers whose schools sought to shape young men in the exemplary life of the Jewish people.[3]

A second narrative pointed to the messianic events of a coming vindication of the Jewish people against their oppressive enemies, the empires and rulers of the Persian and Greco-Roman worlds. God would intervene through his elect son, the Messiah, who, with angelic powers, would overthrow the oppressive empires, which represented cosmic powers that had separated from and were hostile to God and God's people. The Messiah would be a new Son of David, who would reestablish on a final basis the salvific promise of the Davidic monarchy. Or, even more, there would come a Son of Man, an angelic expression of God's people, Israel, who would overcome not only evil but also finitude and would inaugurate a redeemed cosmos beyond both sin and death.[4]

The fusing of these two narratives into a unified story to reveal the secret identity of Jesus, the crucified teacher of the Christian movement, happened remarkably early, apparently within two decades after Jesus's death.[5] The early development of a cosmic Christology that fused Wisdom protology (theory of the "first things") and messianic futurism inspired some New Testament scholars to suspect that Jesus must have in some way identified himself both as the final prophet/ messianic envoy and as the expression of divine Wisdom.[6] Others question the validity of tracing these ideas to Jesus himself, given the unprecedented nature of this fusion, not to mention how unlikely it would have been for a Jewish teacher of the early first century CE to claim to represent either or both in his person.[7] What is unquestionable is that both narratives formed the matrix of the earliest Christian reflection on the theological identity of this teacher, who had been loved by his followers and who had been snatched from them by a cruel public death.

Cosmological Christology is represented in many fragments of hymns found in Pauline and Deutero-Pauline writings—for example, Philippians 2:6–11; Colossians 1:15–20; 1 Timothy 3:16; and Ephesians 2:14–16; as well as Hebrews 1:3; 1 Peter 1:20, 3:18, 3:22; and John 1:1–11. These hymnic fragments express elements of the cosmic-eschatological vision through which the life, death, and resurrection of Jesus are interpreted.[8]

Philippians 2:6–11 contains a full expression of this vision. Here, we start with protology; move through descent to earth and, finally, death; and then move to exaltation and enthronement as the heavenly Messiah who has subdued the cosmic powers. In this hymn, Christ Jesus is the one who originated in heaven, sharing the form of God but choosing to descend to earth, emptying himself of divine power to "take the form of a servant, being born in the likeness of men," humbling himself to the point of sharing the human condition of death. "Therefore God has highly exalted him, bestowing on him a name above every name, that at the name of Jesus every knee should bow in heaven, and on earth and under the earth, and every tongue confess that Jesus Christ is Lord, to the glory of God the Father."

Colossians 1:15–20 focuses on protology, alluding to the eschatological side briefly in elements that may have been added to what was originally a Wisdom hymn. Here, it is said that Christ "is the image of the Invisible God, the first born of all creation." In him, all cosmic powers in heaven and on earth were created; "all things were created through him and for him. He is before all things and in him all things hold together." The idea that he is the unifying power of the cosmos has been edited to make him the "head of the Church" and to identify the future reunification of the cosmos as having come about through the blood sacrifice of the cross:[9] "He is the beginning, the first born from the death, that in everything he might be preeminent. For in him all the fullness of God was pleased to dwell, and through him to reconcile all things to himself, whether on earth or in heaven, making peace through the blood of his cross."

Hebrews 1:1–4 intertwines protology and eschatology with quick strokes. It begins by positioning Jesus as part of the line of prophets through which God has spoken to his people in the past. But he is more than a prophet; he is the divine Son, who is both creator and redeemer. "In these last days he has spoken to us by a Son, whom he has appointed heir of all things, through whom also he created the world. He reflects the glory of God and bears the very stamp of his nature, upholding the universe by his word of Power. When he made purification for sins, he sat down at the right hand of majesty on high, having become as much superior to the angels as the name he has obtained is more excellent that theirs."

Cosmic Christology claims to deliver believers from the ruler of the demonic cosmic powers or to restore these cosmic powers to their proper place in submission to God. These ideas lie in apocalyptic thought, in which the oppressive empires on earth are seen as earthly manifestations of angelic powers that have revolted against God. Thus, Christ in his messianic work conquers these powers and restores the cosmos to its proper order and harmony. The claim that entering into the redeemed community and future restored cosmos, proleptically present in the church, liberates Christians from the domination of these hostile cosmic powers parallels the claim made in the Isis cult (see chapter 4) that Isis will free the initiate from the rule of fate.

Cosmic Christology is explicitly lacking in the synoptic gospels, which led an earlier generation of New Testament scholars to assume that it developed at a later period.[10] But its existence as tradition from which Paul draws indicates its early development. The Q tradition (Q stands for "source," which refers to common traditions in the synoptic gospels), from which Matthew and Luke draw, had already made a connection with Wisdom, seeing Jesus as a prophet-teacher of Wisdom.[11] Traces of the female personification of Wisdom are evident in several Q passages, in which Wisdom is said to have "sent prophets and apostles" whom the Jewish teachers have rejected and killed (Luke 11:49). Jesus weeps over Jerusalem as a "mother hen" who would "gather her brood under her wings" (Luke 13:34). Jesus's unconventional table fellowship with sinners is justified in Matthew 11:19 by identifying him as Wisdom herself: "Yet Wisdom is justified by her deeds."[12] Luke 7:35 probably preserves an earlier form of this saying, in which Jesus is portrayed as one of the children of Wisdom rather than as the unique incarnation of her: "Yet wisdom is justified by all her children."[13]

In the Gospel of John, we find the protological drama fused with the story of Jesus as teacher and revealer of the higher divine life, which his followers are invited to enter in order to share in the eternal life of God's presence.[14] John's prologue presents Jesus as the divine Word that was with God and was God "in the beginning." It then moves to reveal the Word as creator and sustainer of the universe, the source of life and knowledge for all creatures. He enters the world and is rejected by those to whom he came but is the source of eternal life for those who accept him:

All things were made through him and without him was not anything made that was made. In him was life and the life was the light of men. . . . He was in the world, and the world was made through him, yet the world knew him not. He came to his own home and his own people received him not. But to all who received him, who believed in his name he gave power to become children of God, born . . . of God. (John 1:3, 9–13)

This Johannine drama of the divine Logos as creator, revealer, and redeemer is then told through revelatory stories in the life and teachings of Jesus.[15] He teaches in paradoxical symbols that are misunderstood by those who have only material eyes, but that reveal him as the incarnation of redemptive life for those who receive them with the eyes of faith. Like Wisdom, he feeds and nourishes, gives saving bread and drink, offers the waters of eternal life, and speaks in the revelatory "I am" language with which Wisdom praises herself. Although rejected by those under the powers of darkness, he finds a home in a small embattled community of believers. These he makes "friends of God and prophets,"[16] through whom there is immortal life and to whom he sends the power of the Paraclete after he returns to his heavenly home above.

Yet the shift of language from Wisdom (*sophia*) to Word (*logos*) effectively eclipsed the female personification of this creator-revealer-redeemer. The roots of this masculinization of what in Jewish tradition was a female personification of God have been hotly debated in contemporary scholarship. Some view Philo, who insisted that Wisdom was female only as a subordinate expression of a male God but was masculine in the work of creation and was represented on earth in the Logos, as a key source of this shift in grammatical gender.[17] Another impetus may have come from the identification of Jesus not simply as child and prophet-teacher of Wisdom but as Wisdom incarnate—who, as a male, is he and not she.[18] Perhaps also his identification as Messiah, always a male figure in Judaism, impelled this change of language from *sophia* to *logos*, whose male grammatical gender is more in keeping with both the maleness of Jesus and the images of the Messiah.

In Elizabeth Schuessler Fiorenza's view, this combination of Logos and Jesus as divine-human son of God allows the dominance of the father-son language so evident in the Gospel of John in particular. The father-son relation readily encapsulates both the male hierarchical relation between the Father and Son aspects of God and the male hierarchical relation of God to the human Jesus as the incarnation of the divine Son. This lineage is then continued in the Christian "sons" born to God through baptism. Female mediation, such as that found in the Jewish Wisdom tradition and developed in gnosticism, is thus eliminated in this "orthodox" relation of father to son on the interdivine level, recapitulated on the divine-human level.[19]

FEMALE GOD LANGUAGE
IN THE WRITINGS OF CHURCH FATHERS

The identification of the roles of Wisdom with a masculine Logos-Christ largely repressed any development of a female personification of the divine, based on the figure of Wisdom, in the writings of church fathers. But the Wisdom literature of Hebrew scripture, including books such as the Wisdom of Jesus ben Sirach and the Wisdom of Solomon, was included in the Christian Bible. Patristic Christianity used the Greek Septuagint as the basis for its Old Testament, which included these later works.[20] Thus, a female-personified Wisdom remained scriptural for Christians. This figure would be elaborated in later developments in medieval Latin Christianity and Greek Orthodoxy.[21]

The father-son metaphor for the relation of God to the Word of God generally fixed the two poles of the Christian Trinity as male-male, but the Holy Spirit remained fluid. Imaged as a dove, it was not fixed in any gendered personification. An early stream of Aramaic-Syriac Christian tradition portrayed the Spirit as feminine. The Gospel of Philip sees the femaleness of the Spirit in a biological sense that precludes attributing Jesus's conception to the Spirit: "Some say Mary conceived by the Holy Spirit; they are mistaken; they do not realize what they say. When did a female ever conceive by a female? Mary is the virgin whom the forces did not defile."[22] It is not clear whether this view casts the Holy Spirit as a cosmic force alien to God, which would make such a conception a defilement of the virgin. In the Gospel of the Hebrews, the Holy Spirit is seen as Christ's mother and also the power that transports him to the mountain of his transfiguration. In this gospel, Christ says, "Even so did my mother, the Holy Spirit, take me by one of my hairs and carry me away unto the great Mountain, Tabor."[23]

The most lush development of female images for the Spirit is found in the second-century Syriac hymns the *Odes of Solomon*.[24] The language of these hymns is poetic, not philosophical, and explores a plurality of images for the believer's transformed life through communion with the divine. Feminine images cluster around the Spirit, as the Syriac word for spirit, *ruha'*, is itself feminine.[25] But the Father and the Word can also be imaged in feminine terms. Here, the source of the metaphors is not simply grammatical gender but the images themselves, such as milk and birth, that suggest the female activities of carrying a child in the womb, giving birth, and suckling.

God's Word as milk that a mother gives to a newly born child recalls Paul's use of this image in 1 Corinthians 3:1–2. But perhaps a more potent source for this image, which appears in the works of the Greek and Syriac fathers, is the baptismal practice of giving the newly baptized a cup of mingled milk and honey. This drink symbolizes not only the feeding of a newborn but also the image of paradise as a "land flowing with milk and honey," which the believer enters through baptism.[26]

The symbol of the Word as milk appears four times in the forty-two Odes. The image of being fed with milk fosters metaphoric development that images God as breasted and suckling us. Thus, Ode 8.14 has Christ, speaking as the Wisdom-Creator of humanity, say, "I fashioned their members and my own breasts I prepared for them that they might drink my holy milk and live by it." Ode 35.5 says of Christ, "And I was carried like a child by its mother, and He gave me milk, the dew of the Lord." In Ode 40, the writer declares, "As honey drips from the honeycomb of bees and milk flows from the woman who loves her children, so is my hope upon Thee, O my God."[27]

The most elaborate use of the milk metaphor is found in Ode 19:

A cup of milk was offered to me, and I drank it in the sweetness of the Lord's kindness. The Son is the cup and the Father is He who was milked and the Holy Spirit is She who milked Him. Because His breasts are full, and it was undesirable that His milk should be ineffectually released. The Spirit opened Her bosom and mixed the milk of the two breasts of the Father. Then she gave the mixture to the generation without their knowing and those who have received [it] are in the perfection of the right hand.

The Ode goes on to portray Mary receiving this divine milk and conceiving by it:

The womb of the Virgin took [it] and she received conception and gave birth. So the Virgin became a mother with great mercies. And she labored and bore the Son without pain because it did not occur without purpose. And she did not require a midwife because He caused her to give life. She brought forth like a strong man with desire and she bore according to the manifestation and acquired with great power.[28]

Such complex reversals of male and female images preclude taking these gender symbols literally. Mary can become a strong man in giving birth, while the Father has full breasts milked by the Spirit that gives life to believers and causes Mary to conceive.

The dove image of the Spirit also fosters metaphoric development. Thus, Ode

24 notes, "The dove fluttered over the head of our Lord Messiah, because He was her head, and she sang over Him and her voice was heard." Ode 28 imagines the dove fluttering over a nest to feed her nestlings. The image then changes from a nest to a womb, in which the believer is carried and leaps for joy, as Christ leapt in his mother's womb (Luke 1:41): "As the wings of doves over their nestlings, and the mouths of their nestlings toward their mouths, so the wings of the Spirit over my heart. My heart continually refreshes itself and leaps for joy, like a babe who leaps for joy in his mother's womb." The Spirit making music through us like a harp is also a favorite image, as in Ode 6: "As the wind moves through a harp and the strings speak, so the Spirit of the Lord speaks through my members and I speak through His love." The Holy Spirit as a harp through which we praise God also appears in Ode 14.8.[29]

Christ can also appear as Virgin Wisdom, who calls her sons and daughters to her, recalling the image of Wisdom in Proverbs. Ode 33 contains this call: "However the perfect Virgin stood who was preaching and summoning and saying, O you sons of men return, and you their daughters return and leave the ways of the Corrupter and approach me. And I will enter into you and bring you from destruction and make you wise in the ways of truth." The writer can speak of the Spirit as both giving rest and carrying him into the presence of God, where the sight of glory inspires these odes. Thus, in Ode 36: "I rested on the Spirit of the Lord and She lifted me up to heaven and caused me to stand on my feet in the Lord's high place before His perfection and His glory, where I continued glorifying [God] by the composition of Odes."[30]

Although more rare, female imagery also appeared in the writings of the second-century Greek church fathers, particularly related to the metaphor that describes God's Word as milk that feeds us spiritually and hence compares God or Christ to a nursing mother. Clement elaborates at length on how both Christ and God feed us with milk as a mother does, observing: "The Father's breasts of love supply milk." The medical idea of Clement's time that mother's milk was a curdled form of blood also leads him to a long disquisition on how Christ's redeeming blood is related to the milk by which he feeds us. Irenaeus also uses the milk-breast metaphor: "We being nourished as it were by the breasts of His flesh and having such a course of milk nourishment become accustomed to eat and drink the word of God."[31]

The Syriac and Greek fathers are clear, however, that gender imagery for God in no way makes God either male or female. Gender images, like all other images (such as bird, water, fire), are taken from our bodily experience and applied metaphorically to God. Ephrem, a fourth-century Syriac father, speaks of such metaphors as garments that God puts on and takes off to make God accessible to our imagination. "God puts one metaphor on when it is beneficial, then strips it off in exchange for another. The fact that He strips off and puts on all sorts of metaphors tells us that the metaphor does not apply to His true being because that Being is hidden, he has depicted it by means of what is visible."[32]

The fourth-century Greek church father Gregory Nyssa argues not only that God is neither male nor female but also that gender is ephemeral in humans. Our true nature is the spiritual nature by which we image God. This image exists equally in men and women and is not gendered. Gender is a temporary garb put on us in our historical existence, but it will be discarded in the resurrection. Women too can achieve the highest spiritual development and sometimes take the lead in relation to less developed male relatives. He occasionally speaks of God the creator as mother, while arguing that neither "mother" nor "father" refers to any literal gender in God. Thus, in his commentary on the Song of Songs, he writes:

No one can adequately grasp the terms pertaining to God. For example, "mother" is mentioned in place of "father" (Cant. 3.11). Both terms mean the same because the divine is neither male nor female (for how could such a thing be contemplated in divinity, when it does not remain intact permanently in us human beings either? But when all shall become one in Christ, we shall be divested of the signs of this distinction together with the whole of the old man). Therefore every name found [in Scripture] is equally able to indicate the ineffable nature, since the meaning of the undefiled is contaminated by neither female nor male.[33]

Gregory Nyssa understands the groom as Christ and the bride as the soul. The references to the mother of the bride he understands as God the creator: "All things have, as it were, one mother, the cause of their being."[34]

The view that gender terms for God are mere metaphor, since God is neither male nor female, is echoed by Gregory Nazianzus (another fourth-century Greek church father) and Jerome. Gregory Nazianzus mocks the Arians for their literalism in imagining that using the male grammatical gender for God makes God literally male: "God is not male although he is called father."[35] Jerome remarks that the word for the Spirit is "feminine in Hebrew, masculine in Latin and neuter in Greek, to teach us that God is without gender."[36] Yet the Greek and Latin fathers follow the cultural pattern of using "femininity" to symbolize the lower passions and bodily nature, and masculinity to symbolize the higher intellectual and spiritual nature. They argue that

FIGURE 25

Feminine Holy Spirit between the Father and the Son, fourteenth century.
Fresco in Church of St. Jakobus in Urschalling, southwest of Munich,
Germany.

both men and women have both capacities. Spiritually undeveloped men are womanlike, while spiritually developed women become "virile and strong."[37] But this interpretation of masculine and feminine suggests that male images are appropriate for God, while female images are not.

Augustine follows this tradition in identifying *sapientia*, or wisdom, as the higher or male part of the mind and *scientia*, or sense knowledge, as the female lower part of the mind through which the goods of the earth are administered. He uses this hierarchical gender symbolism to argue that divine Wisdom, although grammatically feminine and imaged as feminine in the Wisdom literature, is male. Male wisdom, not female sense knowledge, is the true image of God in humanity. This image of God is shared by both men and women, although women in their bodily nature image the lower nondivine reality. This insistence that masculinity images the incorporeal divine nature and femininity the bodily appetites means that, for Augustine, gender imagery cannot be used interchangeably for God. God has no "taint" of the feminine, and hence only male, never female, images are appropriate for God.[38]

This view seems to have had a determinative effect on the language used to describe God by the Latin and Greek church fathers after 400 CE, as the church councils hammered out the orthodox definition of the trinitarian God. At this time, feminine language in reference to God disappeared from the Syriac tradition.[39] The lush treatment of the divine as a plurality of male and female beings in gnosticism had been rejected by orthodoxy since the late second century. Even occasional metaphorical use of mothering language for God, on the grounds that God was nongendered and all metaphors were partial, faded. Metaphorical masculinity became tied to intellect and divinity, while metaphorical femininity was linked to the nondivine world of sense knowledge and bodily nature. Nonetheless, medieval art occasionally portrayed the Spirit as female (fig. 25)

FEMININE SYMBOLS FOR HUMANITY: ECCLESIA AND *ANIMA*

Hebrew scriptures had depicted the relation of God and Israel as a troubled one, between a wooing and punishing husband and a rebellious wife. These writings had also imagined a time of redemption, when this relationship would become one of idyllic love. The rabbis had allowed the Song of Songs to be included in the canon as an allegory of this future time of perfected bliss. The Christian church inherited this nuptial metaphor and transferred it to the relation of Christ and Ecclesia (the church). For Christians, the church was the beginning of that eschatological bride in whom all sin has been banished. Christians were the children of the free woman, the heavenly Jerusalem; the Jews were the children of the slave woman, Hagar, whose children are to be cast out (Gal. 4:21–31). In 2 Corinthians 11:2, Paul speaks of the church he has gathered as a "pure bride," whom he has betrothed to Christ and whom he does not want to be corrupted by heresy.

Bridegroom language for Christ is found in the gospels. In a question about fasting, the followers of Jesus who share common meals with him are referred to as the wedding guests who do not fast "as long as the bridegroom is with them." When the bridegroom is taken from them, "then they will fast" (Matt. 9:15; also Mark 2:19, Luke 5:34–35). In the Gospel of John, John the Baptist is the friend who rejoices to hear the voice of the bridegroom, to whom the bride belongs: "He who has the bride is the bridegroom" (John 3:29). Such language also appears in Matthew: in the Kingdom of Heaven, ten maidens await the coming of the bridegroom, but only five keep their lamps supplied with oil and hence are ready to go in with him to the marriage feast when he comes (Matt. 25:1–10).

For the author of the Epistle to the Ephesians, the church is Christ's bride, redeemed by his sacrificial love "that he might sanctify her, having cleansed her by the washing of water with the word that the church might be presented before him without spot or wrinkle or any such thing that she might be holy and without blemish" (Eph. 5:26–27). Rather improbably, this sanctified relationship is then made a model for the relation of husbands and wives. In Revelation, the vision of a woman clothed with the sun, the moon under her feet, and a crown of twelve stars on her head (fig. 26), who labors and brings forth a "man-child" and flees into the wilderness to take refuge against the dragon (Rev. 12:1–6), is the new Israel, the church who births a messianic humanity. When all evil has been conquered by Christ, the heavenly Jerusalem is pictured as "coming down out of heaven from God, prepared as a bride adorned for her husband" (Rev. 21:2).[40]

Drawing on these New Testament interpretations of the marriage metaphor, Christians early began to write commentaries on the Song of Songs as an allegory of the nuptials of Christ and his redeemed bride, the church. Hippolytus of Rome developed the ecclesial meaning of the Song of Songs in his commentary in the second century.[41] But it was the voluminous commentary by the third-century Alexandrian father Origen that would have the most lasting influence. For Origen, the Song of Songs points through the veil of allegory to two different aspects of the wedding between God and humanity: the wedding between Christ and Ecclesia (the

FIGURE 26
Mary as the woman clothed with the sun, early fourteenth century. Monastery of
Katharinental, Switzerland. (From Kyra Belán, *Madonna: From Medieval to Modern*
[New York, NY: Parkstone Press, 2001])

church), and that between Christ and *anima* (the soul). Origen's commentary
differentiates and parallels these two dimensions of meaning—the collective, historical meaning and the individual, personal meaning.[42]

Origen begins his commentary by seeking to banish from the reader's mind any
attention to the lush eroticism of the actual text of the Song. For Origen, this sexual language is a mere external veil that conceals the true spiritual meaning. Only
the spiritually mature who have overcome all sexual lust dare approach this text;

those whose sexual appetites might be aroused by its language are not fit to read it. The love referred to in the Song is not bodily but spiritual. It is that higher Eros by which the soul is led upward to its communion with God.[43]

Origen then proceeds to extract a spiritual meaning for each phrase of the Song through a concatenation of texts from Hebrew scripture and the New Testament, read allegorically in the manner that had been established by the Jewish Hellenistic exegete Philo. Through this method, the poetry of the Song becomes a series of symbols pointing to the story of the church in her historical journey and eschatological fulfillment and also the journey of the soul to restored spiritual perfection. The bridal relation of Christ and the church does not begin with the historical Jesus; rather, it originates in the first calling of God's people, Israel. The story of the soul begins in heaven, before the fallen, bodily world.

God's choosing of Israel is described in Origen's commentary as the betrothal of an immature girl who is not yet ready for marriage. She receives from God the betrothal gifts of the Law and the Prophets to prepare her for her future groom, while she longs for his coming and their wedded bliss. In Christ, the bridegroom has come, but the full consummation of their love is still in the future. Then a new bride of Christ is brought in from among the Gentiles. She lacks these earlier betrothal gifts, and hence is more sinful, but now has become transformed and supersedes the unbelieving Israel (Origen's interpretation of the description of the bride as "black but beautiful"). Yet the redeemed bride of Christ is still harassed by demonic powers and surrounded by heretics who have distorted the faith. But very soon the returning Christ will overcome these enemies, and the church's communion with Christ will be fulfilled.[44]

The journey of the soul (anima) runs parallel to that of the church (Ecclesia), but in an individual and vertical trajectory. Although Origen did not develop this idea in his commentary, we know from his treatise De Principiis (On First Things) that he believed that souls were originally created as luminous intellectual spirits (logikoi) that imaged the divine Logos and formed the original divine pleroma with the trinitarian God. But these intellectual spirits turned away from God and fell into various levels of alienation from him. These levels of alienation were then organized into a hierarchically ordered cosmos, with some becoming planetary angels, others human souls, and others demons. The level of "fallenness" is expressed through various types of bodies, with the angels taking on fiery bodies; the humans gross, material bodies; and the demons dark, shadowy bodies.[45]

For Origen, the journey of the soul is a process of moral, intellectual, and spiritual learning, by which she gradually recovers her original spiritual nature and sheds the material body into which she has fallen. Origen sees his own catechetical school as an epitome of this journey. In such schools, the souls learn moral and natural philosophy, preparing them for higher mystical insights.[46] These preliminary stages of education correspond to the Law and the Prophets in Israel's history as "betrothal gifts," given in preparation for the wedding of the soul with her bridegroom, the heavenly Logos. This preparation includes moral discipline. The soul must learn to repress bodily appetites and free her true self from the lower world of the senses. As she achieves this spiritual maturity, she then is ready for the coming of the bridegroom—that is, the illumination of the soul by the divine Logos and its restoration to its original spiritual nature.[47]

In this account of the soul's journey, Origen follows a typical pattern of Platonic mysticism. The journey involves moral *ascesis,* or disciplining of the appetites and intellectual purification of the mind from sense knowledge, leading to intellectual illumination.[48] There is no place for erotic feelings, even in a sublimated form such as we find in medieval mysticism (see chapter 6).[49] The feminine imagery of the church and the soul as bride is employed only as a symbolic pointer to a nongendered, spiritual meaning.

For Origen, gender, like the body itself, is a secondary acquisition, taken on through the fall, but it will be discarded as the soul is restored to its true nature. Therefore, neither feminine imagery for the church and the soul nor masculine imagery for Christ as bridegroom has any counterpart in the spiritual world. They are conventions of human language but have no spiritual meaning. God, the Word of God, the church, and the soul are in their essential spiritual nature "neither male nor female."[50]

Gregory Nyssa's commentary on the Song of Songs, written a century and a half after that of Origen, concentrates more exclusively on interpreting the text as an allegory of the soul's journey to God, although it also makes reference to the nuptials of the church with Christ. For Nyssa, neither God nor the soul has gender; the feminine image of the soul as bride and the masculine image of Christ as bridegroom are simply poetic forms adapted to our present finite life. Indeed, the young man exhorted to seek Wisdom in Proverbs is in the Song changed into a bride; while Wisdom, feminine in Proverbs, is the bridegroom—indicating the nonessential nature of gender imagery.[51]

For Nyssa, the soul made in the image of God is genderless, like God. Gender is acquired as part of the soul's fall into sin, taking on "coats of skin," that is, the mortal body. But as the soul grows in spiritual life, it regains its original nature in union with God. At the resurrection, gender differences will be discarded; and the soul, united with a nongendered spiritual body, will grow "from glory to glory" in infinite imitation of the eternal nature of God, drawn by the power of love. In Nyssa's view, the erotic, gendered imagery of the Song is to be ignored. Its true meaning points to the journey of a nongendered soul to a nongendered God.[52]

Jerome, as noted earlier in this chapter, shares this view of God as neither male nor female. In his long letter to Eustochium, the teenaged daughter of his spiritual companion, Paula, Jerome vividly exploits the erotic language of the Song, all the while exhorting the young girl to guard herself not only from the presence of worldly companions but even from all thoughts that might awaken her bodily desires. Her relation to Christ as her true bridegroom must be guarded from any temptation to fall into physical relations with an actual man. The love language of the Song is transferred to the spiritual relation Eustochium should imagine herself to be having with Christ:

> Let the secret retreat of your bedchamber ever guard you. Ever let the Bridegroom hold converse with you within. When you pray, you are speaking to your Spouse. When you read, He is talking to you, and when sleep comes upon you, He will come behind the wall and He "will put His hand through the opening and will touch your body"(Cant. 5.4). You will arise trembling and will say, "I languish with love" (Cant. 5.8). And again you will hear His reply: "My sister, my spouse, is a garden enclosed, a fountain sealed up" (Cant. 4.12).[53]

A late third-century treatise, the *Symposium*, also depicts female Christian virgins as the ideal type for this spousal relation to Christ. Drawing on Plato's *Symposium*, Methodius, the author, imagines a banquet in a paradisal setting, in which ten Christian women discourse on the superiority of virginity over marriage (although one of them warns that faithful marriage has not been ruled out in Christian times).[54] Although Methodius uses this gathering of women to exemplify the highest Christian life, he shares a low estimate of "femaleness" itself. For him, maleness represents the rational part of the soul, whereas femaleness represents carnal sensuality. Women are prone to weakness, silliness, and fatuous conversation.[55] Yet all these characteristics are belied by these Christian virgins, who have put off female weakness and have been transformed through chastity into types of spiritual purity and power.

For Methodius, sexual reproduction and even polygamy were allowed during the earlier era of human history when humans were spiritually immature. But virginity is now the ideal state of life, which points toward the redemptive era of incorruptibility that is dawning. In imagery drawn from Plato's *Phaedo*, chastity guides the chariot of the soul as it soars aloft into the heavens and glimpses the celestial world of immortality.[56] Chastity both restores humanity to its original paradisal state before the fall and anticipates its restoration to this heavenly state.

Methodius also explores the church's virginal nuptials with Christ. The church is imaged as the true Eve, who is born from the side of Christ, the true Adam, as Eve was born from the side of the old Adam, an image also found in Tertullian's *De Anima*.[57] Christ's passion on the cross is imagined as a spiritual counterpart to sexual ejaculation, through which Christ inseminates his spouse, the church. The church, in turn, bears many children to immortality in baptism:

So too the word "increase and multiply" is duly fulfilled as the Church grows day by day in size and in beauty and in numbers, thanks to the intimate union between her and the Word, coming down to us even now and continuing his ecstasy in the memorial of his Passion. For otherwise the Church could not conceive and bring forth the faithful "by the laver of regeneration" unless Christ emptied Himself for them too for their conception of Him, as I have said, in the recapitulation of his Passion, and came down from heaven to die again and clung to his Spouse the Church, allowing to be removed from His side a power by which all may grow strong who are built upon Him, who have been born of the laver and receive His flesh and bone, that is, of his holiness and glory.[58]

A different image of the church is explored in the second-century treatise the *Shepherd of Hermas*. Here, the church is portrayed more in the lineaments of Wisdom, as teacher, an image that would be carried over into medieval art (fig. 27). In a vision, the church appears to Hermas as an older woman in a shining robe with a book in her hand, who seats herself on a large white chair. Reading from her book, she reveals that the world was created from the beginning by God for the sake of the church.[59] The church is the foundation and fulfillment of God's plan for creation (although the church is not credited, as Wisdom was, with being an agent in the creation). The church is a revealer of visions, a teacher of the right understanding of ethical discipline, which includes the possibility of a second forgiveness after baptism. The woman in the vision dictates messages to the leaders of the church, which Hermas is directed to deliver.

In a third vision, an angelic young man discloses the identity of the heavenly woman to Hermas, who at first mistakes her for the Sybil: "'Then who is she?' I asked.

FIGURE 27

Mary as Wisdom, on the lion throne, c. 1150. Eynsham Abbey, Oxfordshire. (From Kyra Belán, *Madonna: From Medieval to Modern* [New York, NY: Parkstone Press, 2001])

'The church,' he said. 'Then why is she elderly?' 'Because,' he said, 'she was created before everything. That is why she is elderly, and for her the world was established.'"[60]

Although the church is preexistent and heavenly, she is also an imperfect community being built up through history. She is portrayed as a tower being built by angels, who are selecting the "stones" (believers) that have true faith and those with true repentance and discarding those who have fallen away and failed to repent. Lady Church then reveals to Hermas seven daughters. The first is Faith, and the other six— Restraint, Simplicity, Knowledge, Innocence, Reverence, and Love—are each in turn the daughter of the previous child. Through them, the tower church is being built. When Hermas asks Lady Church how soon the building of the tower will be completed, she fiercely rebukes him, for when the tower is completed, this will be the end of history.[61] This time is soon, but it is not yet come and cannot be known at this time.

In language drawn from the Wisdom treatises, Lady Church then addresses Christians as "children," who were raised to be "justified and sanctified from all evil" but who have fallen into quarrelsome and sensual habits. She singles out the leaders of the church, declaring that they cannot discipline others if they do not discipline themselves. Lady Church gives them a short time to rectify their ways before she prepares a final accounting to God.[62]

In a final vision of Lady Church, the meaning of her various "ages" is revealed. When first seen, she was old and seated in a chair; in successive visions, she becomes younger and more beautiful. This growing youth represents her ongoing rejuvenation through the coming of Christ and new converts reborn in Christ. Her youth also anticipates her final transformation in the renovation of the world.[63] Thus, for Hermas, Lady Church is both a heavenly reality, the original purpose of Creation and its eschatological fulfillment, and also an earthly reality being built up day by day as a community of faith. This process is drawing to a close but has not yet reached its final point; Christians, then, still have a chance to reform their lives and be incorporated into its secure edifice.

Although the idea that the church is the spouse of Christ, impregnated through his passion to bear children in baptism, implies that the church is our mother, this image was rarely used in the second century.[64] It became central in the middle of the third century in the theology of the African bishop Cyprian, who used it to distinguish the true children of God from schismatics who had separated from the one faithful spouse of Christ, the true apostolic church.

Although the church "spreads her branches in generous growth over the whole earth," yet there is one source of this fecundity, "one mother who is prolific in her offspring, generation after generation. Of her womb we are born, of her milk we are fed, of her Spirit our souls draw their life breath." Since this true mother is the undefiled spouse of Christ, she "is faithful to only one couch." Anyone who breaks with this one apostolic church and joins a sectarian church thus enters an adulterous household. Baptism in such churches is null, lacking true power of regeneration. Such a person has no true relation to God. In a phrase that would be reiterated in his writings, Cyprian insists, "You cannot have God for your father if you have not the church as your mother."[65]

This image of the church as virginal mother is more fully developed in Augustine, who applies it directly to his own spiritual journey as well as to all Christians reborn in the waters of baptism. Although Monica is for Augustine in some sense a model for Mother Church, who elects him from her womb, pursues him, and will not tire until she sees him safely incorporated into the one true Catholic Church, the motherhood of the church also supersedes human motherhood. The birth we receive from our mothers is one from which we die, in the sin transmitted by sexual reproduction. We receive true birth, the birth from which we will not die but have immortal life, only in the womb of Mother Church, in the waters of baptism. The milk of the catechumenate gives us true nourishment, while only mortal life flows from the breasts of our mothers. Thus, for Augustine, the motherhood of the church is contrasted with the inferior birthgiving and nurturance of actual mothers,[66] as true life to spiritual death, purity to impurity.

MARY IN THE NEW TESTAMENT
AND PATRISTIC THEOLOGY

Much of this feminine imagery of the church as Wisdom, bride, and mother would be absorbed into Mariology by the later church fathers and during the Middle Ages. Already in the late fourth century, Ambrose and Augustine had identified Mary as the "type" of the church.[67] Standing with her cloak sheltering the Christian people, the Madonna of the Misericordia is the protecting Mother Church (fig. 28). Yet, in the New Testament, Mary is a minor figure. She is never mentioned by name outside the Gospels and the Book of Acts. Paul speaks only once of Jesus's mother and then simply to assert the human status of Jesus: "when the time had fully come, God sent forth his Son, born of woman, born under the law to redeem those who were under the law" (Gal. 4:4).

The few references to Jesus's mother in the synoptic gospels, aside from the infancy narratives of Matthew and Luke, seem to reflect a tradition that positions Mary and Jesus's brothers as unbelievers, linked to a hostile hometown community of

FIGURE 28

Madonna of the Misericordia, by Piero della Francesca, 1445–62.
Centerpiece of polyptych. (Pinacoteca Communale, Sansepolcro;
photo: Erich Lessing /Art Resource, NY)

Nazareth and not to the church. Mark describes this local community as seeking
to seize Jesus, believing him to be mad. Jesus's mother and brothers then come
and, standing outside, ask to speak to him. But Jesus repudiates them, identifying
his followers—and not his family—as his "brother, sister and mother" (Mark 3:21,
31–35). Matthew 12:45–50 and Luke 8:19–21 repeat the same story with variations.

The two references to Jesus's mother in the Gospel of John also seem to locate her as part of the old Israel, although a part that is open to the new. In John 2, she intervenes at the marriage feast at Cana to ask Jesus to perform a miracle to supply wine. Jesus addresses her harshly: "Woman, what have you to do with me? My hour is not yet come." The stone water jars that his mother asks him to use to produce the wine are then identified as part of the Jewish rites of purification. Jesus is the new wine that will supersede these old, inefficacious rites. Mary, Jesus's mother, reappears at the foot of the cross, along with several women disciples. Jesus entrusts her to the care of the "disciple" (John). Here, she is that part of the old Israel that is transferred to the care of the new (John 19:25–27).[68]

Significantly, none of the synoptic gospels place Mary either at the cross or at the empty tomb as witness to the resurrection. In these instances, the women disciples of Jesus, led by Mary Magdalene, are the chief actors and representatives of the believing remnant of the church. Mary Magdalene is also the first witness to the resurrection in John; Jesus's mother is not mentioned. These absences seem to reflect an early view that Mary was not part of the community of believers in Jesus's lifetime. However, in Acts, the believing community in Jerusalem, which awaits the coming of the Holy Spirit at Pentecost, includes the eleven male disciples, with the "women" (disciples) and "Mary the mother of Jesus and with his brothers"(Acts 1:13–14). Although Mary is not mentioned thereafter, Jesus's brother James plays a key role as a leader of Jewish Christianity in Jerusalem (Acts 15:13; Gal. 2:9).

The tradition of Mary's virginal conception of Jesus appears in the infancy narratives added to the Gospels of Matthew and Luke.[69] Yet Mary plays very different roles in these two narratives. In Matthew, Joseph is the central figure. He at first takes Mary's pregnancy prior to their marriage as evidence of her wrongdoing and resolves to divorce her, until he is told by an angel in a dream that the child was conceived by the Holy Spirit. He then accepts her as his wife. Two further angelic visits in dreams tell Joseph to take Mary and Jesus to Egypt and then bring them back again when Herod has died. Mary remains a passive figure in this drama (Matt. 1:18–2:21).

In Luke's infancy narrative, by contrast, Mary is an active agent in the miraculous conception. She is the one who receives the angelic visit announcing God's plan and accepts it: "Behold I am the handmaiden of the Lord. Let it be done to me according to thy word" (Luke 1:38). This scene would become a favorite in art (fig. 29). In a visit to her cousin Elizabeth, Mary greets her with a song that identifies herself as the prototype of the messianic community through whom the wrongs of history will be righted. Mary stays with Elizabeth three months and never consults Joseph through any of these events. She is the central player in Jesus's birth, although

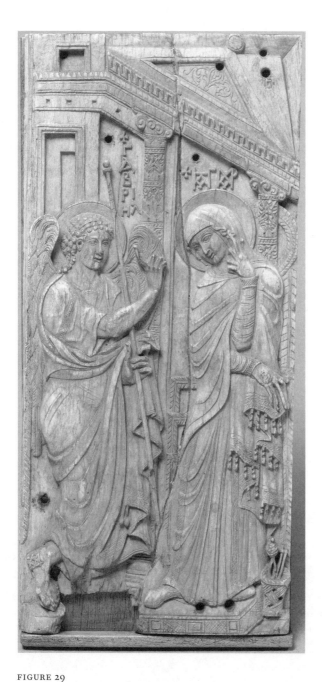

FIGURE 29

The Annunciation, c. 700. Ivory relief. The wool blanket at the
virgin's feet alludes to the legend of her upbringing in the temple
of Jerusalem, where she spun and made robes for the priests.
(Castello Sforzesco, Milan; photo: Scala/Art Resource, NY)

Joseph is at her side. Clearly, it is the Mary of Luke's infancy narrative who is the font of Christian Mariology. From these modest seeds, a mighty thicket would grow over the following centuries.

The second century saw the first major elaboration of Mary's redemptive role, building on Luke's infancy narrative. Drawing on Paul's theme of Christ as the new Adam (Rom. 5:12–21), several second-century church fathers created a parallel role for Mary as the new Eve.[70] This theme was enunciated in the middle of this century by Justin Martyr. Here, the disobedience of the virgin Eve at the behest of the serpent, through which death comes, is paralleled and reversed by the obedience of the virgin Mary to the good tidings of the angel Gabriel. Her obedience brings about the birth of the Son of God, through whom death and the serpent are destroyed.[71]

A generation later, Irenaeus elaborated this parallel. The virgin Eve's disobedience brings death for herself and for the whole human race, whereas the obedience of the virgin Mary is the cause of salvation for herself and for the whole human race.[72] Irenaeus returned to this theme in his fifth book: "And if the former did disobey God, yet the latter was persuaded to be obedient to God, in order that the Virgin Mary might become the patroness of the virgin Eve. And thus as the human race fell into bondage by means of a virgin, so it is rescued by the virgin; virginal disobedience having been balanced in the opposite scale by virginal obedience."[73]

Irenaeus assumes that Eve and Mary, like Adam and Christ, are corporate personalities. Eve's disobedience and Mary's obedience affect all of humanity, the one bringing death to all and the other making eternal life available to all. Mary is thus assigned an essential role in the history of salvation. Although her son is the one who redeems us, he would not have existed without his mother's "fiat" to the angel. Her redemptive obedience precedes and makes possible his redemptive work.

The notion of the virginal conception of Jesus, developed in the infancy narratives of the gospels, signified an understanding of Jesus as God's elect from his mother's womb—that is, his coming was through divine and not human agency. Yet Matthew's tracing of Jesus's genealogy from Abraham and David to Joseph was constructed by a writer who assumed Joseph's paternity (1:2–16). Matthew's infancy narrative, although claiming a virginal conception for Jesus, takes for granted that Mary and Joseph had sexual relations after Jesus's birth: "He took his wife, but knew her not until she had borne a son, and he called his name Jesus" (1:24–5). Mark speaks of Jesus as "the carpenter, the son of Mary, and brother of James, and Joses, and Judas and Simon, and are not his sisters with us?" (Mark 6:3).[74] Joseph is absent in this account (although he is inserted in Matthew 13:56, where Jesus is called "the carpenter's son"). These references seem to assume that the brothers and sisters of Jesus are Mary's children.

But the developing asceticism of early Christianity soon made these assumptions unacceptable. For ascetics, virginity is the purest state of life, while sexual marriage is less pure. Those who would anticipate the kingdom of heaven, where there is no marrying, give up marriage and sexual relations (Luke 20:35). This ascetic interest shifted the focus from the virginal conception of Jesus, as an expression of his divine election, to Mary's virginity as an expression of her purity. As the epitome of the eschatological ethic of virginity, she cannot be imagined to have "fallen back" into the lower state of marriage and sexual reproduction. Hence, her subsequent sexual relations with Joseph and her maternity of Jesus's brothers and sisters must be denied.

An early expression of this view is found in the Proevangelium of James, an apocryphal gospel from the middle of the second century.[75] This book purports to have been written by Jesus's brother James. It begins with the story of Mary's parents, Joachim and Anna, a rich and pious couple who are childless. After prayer and supplications, both receive angelic revelations that they will have a child. They vow to dedicate the coming child to service in the temple. When Mary is born, she quickly shows a precocious piety and is duly dedicated as a perpetual virgin. When she is twelve, the temple priests decide that Mary must be put under the guardianship of a widower, lest her menses pollute the temple. They announce a contest of widowers. Joseph, an old man with grown children, is selected through a divine sign (a dove that flies out of his staff).

Mingling the infancy narratives of Matthew and Luke, the Proevangelium then describes how Mary receives the angelic visitation and becomes pregnant. She stays three months with her cousin Elizabeth while Joseph is away on a building contract. He returns when she is six months pregnant. He assumes that she has sinned but is informed otherwise by an angel. Both Joseph and Mary are accused of sin by the priests, but they are vindicated through an ordeal. The Proevangelium then goes on to recount the miraculous birth of Jesus, which does not violate Mary's virginity.

As Mary and Joseph travel to Bethlehem, Mary's time for delivery comes. Joseph leaves her in a cave and goes to fetch a midwife. The midwife returns with him and is an eyewitness to the miraculous birth, in which the cave is flooded with light and the infant, like a beam of light, passes through Mary's hymen without breaking it. The midwife then runs and encounters a second midwife, Salome, to whom she tells the story of the miraculous birth. Salome plays the role of doubting Thomas, insisting that she will not believe that a virgin has brought forth unless she can test this with her own finger. She then enters the cave and demands that Mary show her genitals. Probing them with her finger, she verifies that Mary's hymen is indeed unbroken, but Salome's hand is immediately withered by fire. Only when she repents and is entrusted to embrace the child herself is her hand healed.[76]

This pious tale would deeply shape subsequent Christian imagination of Mary's infancy and the virgin birth, but it was not quickly accepted by leading church fathers. Tertullian expressed the established view of his time, which held that Mary, although a virgin at the conception of Jesus, subsequently was the faithful wife of Joseph. Tertullian took her to be a representative of the blessedness of both states of life, virginity and faithful monogamy.[77] He did not discuss the issue of whether the brothers and sisters of Jesus were the children of Mary, but the view that they were half-siblings, children of an earlier marriage of Joseph, was gaining currency and was embraced by the Alexandrian father Origen.[78]

By the late fourth century, Tertullian's view had become unacceptable. About 382 CE, Helvidius, a Latin cleric, defended the equal status of virginity and marriage by pointing to Mary as an exemplar of both states. Although she had been a virgin at Jesus's birth, he pointed out, she subsequently had sexual relations with Joseph and bore the children referred to in the gospels as brothers and sisters of Jesus. Jerome responded with great outrage at the thought that Mary, having once been a pure virgin, could have regressed to the inferior status of wife. In a convoluted exegesis, he insisted that the brothers and sisters of Jesus were actually cousins, children of a sister of Mary (also called Mary), and that both she and Joseph were perpetual virgins.[79]

A monk, Jovinian, then challenged Jerome, labeling him a Manichean. Jovinian declared that both marriage and virginity were equally blessed and attacked the view that virgins would have a higher place in heaven than the faithfully married. This attack gave Jerome the opportunity to defend his insistence that virginity was indeed a higher state of life than marriage. Although marriage was still allowed in Christian times, he argued, a vowed virgin who "fell" into the inferior state of marriage was to be condemned.[80] This view was endorsed by Ambrose and Augustine and became the accepted orthodoxy, while Jovinian was condemned at several church councils.[81] Thus, the doctrine of Mary's perpetual virginity became enshrined in church teaching as an expression of the superiority of virginity to marriage.

The next major controversy in relation to Mary arose in the Eastern church over the increasing use of the title Mother of God (Theotokos) for her. At its heart, this is a Christological rather than a Mariological issue. It has to do with how one defines the two natures of Christ, divine and human. Are they to be kept clearly separate, so that Mary can be spoken of only as mother of Jesus's humanity? Or are the two natures so commingled—that is, the human one she bore is also God—that she can be spoken of as Godbearer?[82]

Antiochene theologians, such as Theodore of Mopsuestia and his disciple Nestorius, bishop of Constantinople in 428 CE, favored a clear separation of the two natures, seeing them as united in Christ by Jesus's act of will in obeying God rather than by an ontological union. In contrast, the theologians of the Alexandrian church argued that the incarnation of Christ brought together the two natures into one divine-human union, ending any separation. This view of Christ was foundational to their concept of salvation as a divinization, in which humans are transformed through Christ into a share in his divine-human nature. In this view, Mary can appropriately be called Theotokos.

After violent clashes at various church councils, the matter was officially resolved in the Council of Chalcedon in 451 CE. Aided by an intervention from the Roman Pope Leo, this council defined the two natures of Christ as both distinct and whole each in themselves and yet united in such a way that it is possible to speak of Mary as Godbearer.[83] This is not because Mary is literally God's mother, but because, in bearing Christ's humanity, she also bore one who was God.

These careful distinctions satisfied Catholic orthodoxy, but not Alexandrian Monophysites or Antiochene Nestorians, both of whom refused to accept the formula of Chalcedon and split into separate churches. But such distinctions hardly account for the passion with which Mary's title of Theotokos was defended by its partisans. When this title was vindicated at the Council of Ephesus in 431 CE, the people of Ephesus danced in the streets.[84] The people of this city, formerly devoted to Artemis, clearly saw Mary as Mother of God in a fuller sense. She was a divine mother who bore within herself the mystery of the universe and could be venerated as a continuation of that Magna Mater and mother of the gods long worshipped by Mediterranean people as a guarantor of good fortune. The orthodox icon of Mary Panagia gives us one powerful image of the Theotokos (fig. 30).

Something of this veneration of Mary as Godbearer is captured in a section of the apocryphal Gospel of Bartholomew, a Coptic collection of the fifth century. In this text, the resurrected Christ teaches the apostles the mysteries of redemption and then vanishes. Mary is with the apostles, and they decide to ask her "how she conceived the incomprehensible or how she carried him who cannot be carried or how she bore so much greatness." She warns them that she cannot describe this mystery: "For if I begin to tell you, fire will come out of my mouth and consume the whole earth."[85]

But the apostles continue to entreat her to describe the conception of God. She then calls them to pray. She spreads her hands to the heavens and prays to God as the

FIGURE 30

The Virgin of the Great Panagia (also known as the *Virgin Orant of Jaroslav*), c. 1224.
(Tretyakov Gallery, Moscow; photo: Scala /Art Resource, NY)

FIGURE 31

Vierge ouvrante, c. 1400. (Musée du Moyen Age [Cluny], Paris; photo: Réunion des Musées Nationaux /Art Resource, NY)

creator of the cosmos, who ordered the vault of the heavens and separated darkness from light: "The seven heavens could hardly contain thee, but thou wast pleased to be contained in me, without causing me pain, thou who art the perfect Word of the Father through whom everything was created." Mary then calls the apostles to be seated around her, each holding a part of her body, lest her limbs might be loosened when she describes the mystery of her conception of the Creator. She begins to tell the story of the appearance of the angel who announced the impending conception. "As she was saying this, fire came from her mouth and the world was on the point of being burned up. Then came Jesus quickly and said to Mary, say no more or today my whole creation will come to an end."[86] Clearly, in the imagination of this writer, the mystery that was contained in Mary's womb was not simply a humble human who was also God but was in fact the Almighty, the Creator of the whole cosmos. The thirteenth-century image of the *Vierge ouvrante* is a striking expression of this view of Mary as containing the entire Trinity and cosmos (fig. 31).

Although the title Theotokos allowed Christians to venerate Mary as one who had contained and borne God, controversy remained about the status of her own conception and her death. These questions were closely related in the thought of the time. Humans were believed to have been originally created with sinless and undying bodies. Disobedience caused them to fall into mortal bodies, which then necessitated sexual reproduction. But at the resurrection, believers were to be restored to their original spiritual and immortal bodies. If Mary had been conceived sexually, presumably she shared in this same sinful mortality. She too, then, would have died, and her body would have fallen into corruption, like all other humans. Her soul would thus have to await the future resurrection of the dead, when her risen body would be joined to her soul.

But other Christians were convinced that Mary must have been purified from any actual sin and thus that her body would not have been corrupted. Two different apocryphal texts of the late fifth century seek to answer these questions of Mary's death. In one, Pseudo-John "Concerning the Falling Asleep of Mary," Mary dies surrounded by the apostles and is laid in a tomb. After three days, her body is transported to paradise, where she joins other saints and awaits the resurrection of the dead.[87] But in Pseudo-Melito "On the Passing of Mary," Mary's dead body shines with heavenly light, revealing its immunity to corruption. The apostles then carry her to her tomb. Jesus appears and asks the apostles what they think should happen to Mary. They express the view that she should share immediately in Christ's resurrection and not suffer the corruption of death: "Thou having vanquished death reigns in glory, so raising up the body of thy mother, thus should take her with thee into heaven" (fig 32). Jesus agrees and orders the archangel Michael to bring Mary's soul and to roll back the stone from the door of the tomb. Jesus summons Mary to arise: "Arise my beloved and my nearest, Thou who hast not put on corruption with man, suffer not the destruction of the body in the sepulchre." Mary arises and is carried by angels bodily into heaven, along with Jesus.[88] The first view does not give Mary a greater status than other great saints, who also await in some celestial realm the future joining of soul and body in the resurrection. The second view sees Mary as already sharing with Christ in the bodily resurrection and locates her with him in heaven.

It was assumed that Mary had never been tainted by actual sin and thus was preserved from mortal corruption. But Christian tradition did not see her own conception as virginal, even though some versions of the Proevangelium of James suggest that this was the case (by having Anna already pregnant through an angelic vision when her husband, Joachim, returns from his retreat to the desert to pray for

FIGURE 32

The day of Mary's death and resurrection is August 15, known as the Assumption. The page shown here is from the feast-day gospel with tablets of the canon from the school of Reichenau, c. 1030. (From Caroline H. Ebertshauser et al., *Mary: Art, Culture, and Religion through the Ages* [New York: Crossroads Publishing, 1997]) a child).[89] This issue became more controversial in the Western church, with the victory of the Augustinian view that original sin, from which we all die, is transmitted by the sexual act of our parents. Although Augustine believed that Mary had been cleansed in the womb from the effects of original sin and hence never fell into actual sin, he does not exempt her from an initial transmission of original sin, which was the necessary result of her sexual generation.[90] Only Christ was conceived virginally and hence was exempt from original sin. Mary, then, shares with us the general human condition of children of the fall.

This problem of Mary's sinlessness would continue to be debated, even among medieval theologians. It was eventually resolved by the doctrine of the Immaculate Conception, which defined Mary as cleansed from the effects of original sin in the very act of being conceived and thus free from sin from the moment of conception.

Although the details of Marian theology, as well as practices of devotion to Mary, would greatly expand in the Latin Middle Ages, the main outlines of Mariology were largely in place by the end of the fifth century. A sinless virginal mother, the epitome of Christian virtue, had been installed in heaven side by side with Christ, there to be available as benefactress who would hear our prayers and come to our assistance in distress. Despite the quibbles of theologians about the distinctions between *hyperdulia* (high veneration) owed to Mary and *latria* (worship) owed to God alone,[91] Christians now had a divine mother in heaven to whom they could turn when the male God and his Son appeared impervious to their needs.

SIX · Feminine Symbols in
Medieval Religious Literature

MARIOLOGY

The Middle Ages would see a great flowering of devotion to Mary. Her feast days proliferated, hundreds of churches were dedicated to her, and the Mary altar became a standard part of every church. Relics of her hair, milk, clothing, and house multiplied in numerous shrines. Private devotions, such as the rosary, were created so that worshippers could pray to her daily. Contemplative men and women saw her in visions and dedicated their lives to her service. Hymns, paintings, and sculpture celebrated all aspects of her life, from her own conception and the birth of Jesus to her Assumption and crowning as queen of heaven. Theologians debated the expansion of her titles and special privileges.[1]

Eastern and Western Christians agreed that, because of her virginal purity, her body at death did not suffer corruption. But the question of whether this body was preserved in some paradise to be united with her soul at the general resurrection or whether she had been resurrected and assumed bodily into heaven immediately after her death remained open. In the eighth century, shocked by the expansion of Islam and its conquest of the holy city of Jerusalem, several Greek church fathers—Germanus (d. 732), patriarch of Constantinople; Andrew of Crete (d. 740) and John Damascene (d. c. 749), both monks in Jerusalem—appealed to the apocryphal stories of her Dormition ("falling asleep" in death) in Jerusalem as official church teaching. John Damascene argued for the Assumption through analogy to Christ's Ascension: "Rather, just as the holy and incorrupt body that had been born of her, the body that was united hypostatically to God the Word, rose from the tomb on the third day, so she too should be snatched from the grave and the Mother restored to her Son; and, as He has descended to her, so she should be carried up . . . to heaven."[2]

In 600 CE, the emperor Maurice ordered that the Dormition of Mary should be celebrated on the fifteenth of August.[3] This date was accepted in the West as the feast of the Assumption. In the mid-ninth century, Pope Nicolas I put this feast on a par with Christmas and Easter.[4] The German visionary Elizabeth of Schönau (d. 1164) saw Mary rising bodily into the heavens and crowned queen of heaven.[5] The circulation of these visions, which were transcribed by Elizabeth's brother Ekbert, the abbot of Schönau, further disposed the Western church to believe in Mary's bodily assumption, although the doctrine was not officially declared until 1950, by Pope Pius XII. By that time, images of Mary bodily ascending into heaven had become a favorite theme for church paintings, familiar to all Catholics, and hence appeared to support an established "fact" (fig. 33).

The corollary belief, suggested by Augustine, that Mary had been sanctified in her mother's womb and therefore preserved from all actual sin from birth was also generally accepted in the West. But the hint found in the Proevangelium of James that she had been conceived without her parents actually having sexual intercourse was not acceptable. Only Christ had the special privilege of being conceived virginally and therefore being untainted by original sin. The view that Mary had been conceived sexually—and thus that original sin had been transmitted to her—was intrinsic to the affirmation that she was a part of fallen humanity, saved like all other humans through her son.

Sanctification in the womb could not be pushed back to coincide with her conception, which would have exempted her from the common human condition of original sin and therefore from the need for salvation by Christ. Defense of this principle caused the major theologians of the twelfth and thirteenth centuries—Bernard of Clairvaux, Thomas Aquinas, and Bonaventure—to reject the concept of Mary's Immaculate Conception. Some interval between her conception in original sin and her sanctification, when Christ's grace was applied to her to remedy the effects of sin, must be maintained, they argued.

In 1140, Bernard of Clairvaux penned a horrified letter of protest to certain canons of Lyon who had instituted a festival of the Immaculate Conception. Although Bernard affirmed that Mary had been sanctified in the womb, he declared that her conception had nevertheless been sexual and that she shared the human condition of original sin. Her sanctification itself presumed a prior sin in need of remedy: "If then she could not be sanctified before her conception, because she did not exist, neither

FIGURE 33

The Assumption of Mary, by Titian, sixteenth century. Oil on canvas. (S. Maria Gloriosa dei Frari, Venice; photo: Erich Lessing / Art Resource, NY)

in her conception itself, by reason of the sin that was there, it remains that we believe that already conceived and existing in her mother's womb she received sanctification which, taking away the sin, made her birth holy but not her conception."[6]

For Thomas Aquinas, the concept of the Immaculate Conception defied his understanding of human gestation. In his view, since the soul is the form of the body, ensoulment must take place some months after conception, when the body of the fetus assumes its human form. Thus, sanctification in the womb can take place only after ensoulment, not at conception. This position was necessary for two reasons: first, to affirm that Mary shared the human condition of sin and hence was dependent on Christ for her salvation; and, second, because there cannot be a purification of a human before she is fully human—that is, before soul and body are joined.[7]

This topic was hotly debated in the fourteenth and fifteenth centuries, with the Franciscans pushing for the Immaculate Conception and the Dominicans following Aquinas's position, which acknowledged an interval in which Mary existed in original sin. The fourteenth-century theologian Duns Scotus attempted a bold resolution of the conflict. Arguing that it was a higher honor to be preserved from damage than to remedy it after it has taken place, Scotus suggested a backdating of Mary's sanctification to the moment of her conception. Although her conception was sexual and thus carried with it in theory the penalty of original sin, by a special grace Christ prevented original sin from actually being transmitted along with the seed by which Mary was conceived. Thus, Mary was still redeemed by Christ's grace, without having ever suffered even a moment of existence in original sin.[8] This theory also eliminated the interval between conception and ensoulment, which was part of the generally accepted medieval view of gestation, derived from Aristotle. As a result, Catholic thought came to argue that the soul is transmitted to the zygote from the moment of conception, not at a later stage of fetal formation. Although this view became normative only in the nineteenth century, current Catholic opposition to abortion from the first moment of conception assumes this view of gestation.[9]

Scotus's solution to the problem of the Immaculate Conception did not immediately win the day. The Council of Basel declared it a doctrine in 1439, but the council's decision was not taken as valid by the Curia. In 1426, Franciscan Pope Sixtus IV granted special indulgences to those celebrating the feast of the Immaculate Conception. Nevertheless, debate continued with such acrimony that further discussion was forbidden in 1482 on pain of excommunication. This command did not silence the argument and had to be repeated in 1483 and 1503.[10]

The Council of Trent did not rule definitely on the issue, even though the major Counter-Reformation order, the Jesuits, enthusiastically backed the notion of

FIGURE 34
The Virgin of the Immaculate Conception, c. 1638. Spain.
(Courtesy National Gallery of Ireland)

the Immaculate Conception. Its declaration as a doctrine in 1854 by the anti-modern Pope Pius IX appeared to be a deliberate defiance of modern enlightenment and a test case for the pope's subsequent declaration of papal infallibility in 1870.[11] As early as the sixteenth century, artistic representations of Mary as the Immaculate Conception had become popular, using elements of Revelation 12 to picture her as a virginal girl standing on the moon or on clouds in a heavenly space (fig. 34).

These two doctrines, Mary's preservation from original sin and her bodily as-sumption into heaven, which were still under some debate at the end of the Middle Ages, nevertheless drew on what was already an established stream of popular piety, always ahead of official doctrine. Popular devotion had long visualized Mary not only as bodily assumed into heaven but also as crowned by Christ and reigning on his right hand as queen of heaven (fig. 35). She was understood to be uniquely influential with Christ. From the twelfth century, the sermons of St. Bernard de-scribed Jesus and Mary as dividing the kingdom of heaven, with Jesus representing strict justice, while she moderated his judgments on sinners through her mercy.[12] This gendered dualism of justice and mercy made Mary the hope of sinners, the mediatrix to Christ, who was the mediator with the Father.

Popular piety spun endless stories of feckless sinners, deserving of hell or at least a long time in purgatory, who, through their devotion to Mary, were rescued at the last minute, allowed to repent, and thus saved. In one popular story, a wayward girl was decapitated and her head thrown in a well. Because of the girl's devotion to the rosary, Mary intervened to keep the head alive. The head was brought up at the com-mand of St. Dominic and allowed to confess and receive communion, sparing the girl's soul.[13] Through such tales, Christians' fear of strict juridical justice was as-suaged. They were assured that they had a mother in heaven and that, like all moth-ers, she had a soft heart for her children. If they only continued to love her, she would intercede for them with her son, who could refuse his mother nothing.

This splitting of the heavenly realm between justice and mercy positioned Mary as the representative of the purely human, in a way that identified the feminine with the human, the masculine with the divine. Jesus too is human, but as his humanity is hypostatically united with his Godhead, he belongs more to the God side of the human-divine dichotomy. Mary as feminine, and purely human, is more in touch with human feelings and failings.

Mary's sinlessness, even without a clear doctrine of the Immaculate Conception, allowed medieval piety to see her as representing the innocent humanity that had ex-isted before the fall. Adam and Eve, though originally good, had the freedom and capacity to sin; Mary alone preserved our original goodness, although more perfectly, since she was not able to sin. Representing that goodness, she assured Christians that this good nature was still available to them, despite its disfigurement in sin.

The Assumption of Mary ratified her uncorrupted goodness and so held out to believers the hope that they too could look for such an eventual unification of re-deemed soul and uncorrupted body in a heavenly world to come. Mary thus took over theological functions that once had been served by Jesus's humanity, resurrection,

FIGURE 35

The Coronation of Mary, by Jacopo Torriti, 1292–95. (S. Maria Maggiore, Rome; photo: Scala / Art Resource, NY)

and ascension. As the developing understanding of his God-manhood came to make him too removed from the human condition, Mary became the guarantor of these human hopes, as one who was "purely" human, in both senses of the word "pure."[14]

Some medieval speculation pushed Mary even beyond this status as representative of our original good nature. Gabriel Biel, fifteenth-century theologian and member of the Brethren of the Common Life, adhered to a belief in the preexistence of Mary's soul. As an advocate of the Immaculate Conception, Biel located this not only in her purification at the moment of conception but in her creation in sanctifying grace before Creation itself. Here, Mary takes on the lineaments of divine Wisdom, created at the beginning, sharing with God in the creation of the world.[15] But this perfection of her unfallen soul, breathed into her body at her conception, does not take her beyond the creaturely into being part of the Trinity. Rather, it reflects a view of the soul itself as God's perfect icon, for which the world was created. Mary's soul exemplifies the original and true nature of the soul.

Mary, then, is the pure virgin at her conception and at the birth of Jesus as well as the exalted queen of heaven. But she is also the sorrowful mother. She understands and is with us in our suffering. More fundamentally, she shared fully in her son's suffering, having foreknowledge of his crucifixion from his birth. She stood at the cross, joined with him in his pain, and also offered his suffering to God for the redemption of the world. These ideas suggest that Mary is co-redemptrix, although they stop short of the obvious conclusion that she represents the priest at the cross.[16]

Only through Mary's fiat was Christ born, and only with her consent was he offered up for our sins. This view suggests the importance of human consent to God's grace. God saves us only through our cooperation with his grace, not against our will. This theme also identifies Mary with the theology of the church. She is the exemplar of Mother Church, who, through the priest, offers Christ to the Father at Mass and who distributes Christ's saving grace to the fallen world. As in Cyprian of Carthage's ecclesiology of Mother Church, no grace comes to us save through the (true) Mother Church. This theme of co-redemptrix has yet to be declared a doctrine of the Catholic Church, although Pope John Paul II has indicated his wish to do so.[17]

HILDEGARD OF BINGEN:
A PANOPLY OF FEMININE SYMBOLISM

Feminine symbolism is also central to the work of several key medieval mystical writers. One in particular, Hildegard of Bingen, was the abbess of the Benedictine community in Rupertsberg, near the modern German town of Bingen. Hildegard was one of the most extraordinary and prolific writers of the twelfth century (1098–1179). She produced three major visionary writings that combine cosmology, theology, and ethics: *Scivias* (*Know the Ways*), written over ten years, from her early forties to early fifties; *The Book of the Rewards of Life* (*Liber Vitae Meritorum*), a compendium of virtues and vices, rewards and punishments, written in her early sixties; and *The Book of Divine Works* (*De Operatione Dei*), a reworking of her theology in a cosmological context, written in her late sixties and seventies.[18] In addition, Hildegard wrote two treatises on natural science and medicine (*Physica* and *Causae et Curae*), two saints' lives, a compendium of answers to theological and scriptural questions, an explanation of the Benedictine rule, a morality play, a cycle of songs set to music (*Symphonia Armonie Celestium Revelationem*), various other occasional writings, and hundred of letters to people of all social strata.[19]

Hildegard was not a contemplative mystic in the sense of one charting her soul's personal journey to God. Her visions take the form of vast images covering the whole sweep of cosmological relations between God, the cosmos, and humanity. They encompass salvation history from creation, the fall of Lucifer and the primal parents, the preparation for Christ in the history of Israel, the birth of Christ from Mary's virginal womb, the struggle to build the church, the anticipation of the coming Anti-Christ, and the consummation of world history. These visions appear in vivid pictorial representations, which Hildegard both explicated in words and had painted in symbolic colors, probably by women of her monastery.[20]

One of the most striking aspects of Hildegard's visions of cosmology and salvation history is the panoply of interconnected feminine symbols by which she depicts this story. Hildegard synthesized in a unified theological system of relationships an entire range of feminine symbols from the scriptures and Christian tradition, including Wisdom, Eve, Mary, and the church.

In Hildegard's work, the foundational feminine figure present with God from the beginning, the link between God and creation and the means of God's creation of the world, is Wisdom (Sapientia), also called Love (Caritas). The roots of this image lie in the Wisdom literature of Hebrew scripture, which continued to be read as an integral part of the Bible of the medieval church. Although the New Testament and the early church identified (and masculinized) Wisdom as Christ, Hildegard reclaimed and developed this figure in her feminine personification. Hildegard followed a Platonic, exemplarist cosmology that saw all things that are to be created existing originally in the mind of God. Wisdom is present in and as God from all eternity, as the mind of God and the collective preexistence of all that is to be created.[21]

Wisdom is the means by which God brings all preexistent ideas to be manifest in material form. In this role, Wisdom can be spoken of as the Alpha and Omega, the beginning and end of all things, who orders the whole creation. "She has invoked no one's help and needs no help, because she is the First and the Last . . . she who is the First has arranged the order of all things. Out of her own being and by herself she has formed all things in love and tenderness. . . . For she oversaw completely and fully the beginning and end of her deeds because she formed everything completely, just as everything is under her guidance." Hildegard speaks of the whole creation as "Wisdom's garment."[22]

Wisdom is the energy—or, in Hildegard's favorite metaphor, the "greening power" (*veriditas*)—that gives life to all things, subsisting in God as the source of life. All creatures are "sparks from the radiation of God's brilliance."[23] In a hymn to Wisdom, *O Virtus Sapientie*, Hildegard exclaims, "Oh energy of Wisdom, you circle circling, encompassing all things in one path possessed of life. Three wings you have, one of them soars on high, the second exudes from the earth and the third flies everywhere. Praise to you, as befits you, O Wisdom."[24] The creation is not so much an object outside of God as encompassed by God. Like a timeless wheel, "the Holy Godhead enclose[s] everything within itself."[25]

This encompassing of the creation by God is imaged as a cosmic circle with the outer rings of the stars, planets, and elements. The earth lies in the center, in which the human being stands as microcosm to macrocosm. The whole cosmic circle is encompassed by the feminine figure of Wisdom, or Love, who embraces it as her body.[26] Wisdom is thus the *anima mundi*, the world soul whose life-giving immanence causes the whole cosmos to live (fig. 36). Wisdom is also *materia*, the matter that founds all bodily existence.[27] Wisdom interconnects the divine and the creaturely. She is both the creator's self-manifestation and the creature's loving, exultant response to its creator, the mutual in-dwelling of God and creatures.

The relation of God and Wisdom (or Love) is also described erotically. Wisdom is God's bride, "united with him in most tender embrace in a dance of blazing love."[28] Wisdom is a "most loving friend full of love" for God. "She will remain with God since she is always with him and will always remain with him."[29] At the same time, she is providence who rules the world. "Wisdom is the eye of God which foresees and contemplates all things." Like a good wife, she performs the heavenly works through which humans clothe themselves. Like a mother, she teaches her children how to work. Encompassing both the physical and the ethical/spiritual aspects of this "work," Wisdom clothes and teaches her offspring to clothe themselves in virtues, like a wife who weaves wool and flax to cover the nakedness of her family.[30]

Wisdom speaks through human sciences to understand the natural world. She is also the Wisdom of the philosophers. But, more, she is the source of the revelatory and redeeming knowledge that brings the fallen world back to God. Like streams of living water, she speaks through the prophets in Israel's history. She brings to fruition the central act of God's redeeming work, in the incarnation of Christ in Mary's virginal womb. She speaks through the evangelists. The theological knowledge of the church springs from her. Like Wisdom in Proverbs, she stands on the seven-pillared "house of Wisdom," understood to be the church.[31] Through Wisdom, salvation history is brought to its culmination, and creation attains its final communion with God.

Last but not least, Wisdom speaks through Hildegard herself, both in her knowledge of natural sciences and in revelatory visions. "Wisdom considers her own achievement, which she has arranged in the shadow of living water in accord with just decision. She did so by revealing through the untutored woman [Hildegard] mentioned above certain natural powers of various things, as well as writing about the meritorious life and certain other deep secrets which that woman beheld in a true vision and which exhausted her"[32] (fig. 37).

FIGURE 36

The cosmic wheel, the universe as an egg. Drawing by Hildegard of Bingen, eleventh century. (Photo: Erich Lessing/Art Resource, NY)

For Hildegard, the creation of the human being was preordained before creation in God's Wisdom. God also preordained and created the angels as luminous spirits to endlessly praise him. But God intended that the human would be the capstone of creation. This enraged Lucifer, who saw the human created from clay as inferior to his immortal body of light. Rebelling against God, Lucifer fell, with his angelic followers, and took on a dark, bestial body. Located in the gloomy, frozen, northern region of earth, he plots against God and God's favorite, the human being. Human history is defined by this struggle between God and Lucifer, to be overcome only at the end of history.[33]

Thus, Hildegard mitigates Adam and Eve's guilt for the fall by transferring much of its onus to the jealous rage of Lucifer. Adam was originally born with a shining, uncorrupted body taken from virgin earth and a beautiful singing voice that expressed the music of paradise. In a virginal birth, Eve arose from Adam's side, containing in herself the seeds of all the human offspring who would be born to fill up the intended community of the redeemed (the church). Originally, Adam and Eve would have lain together in a sweet embrace of pleasure that would have transmitted fructifying power between them like perfume. Their children would have been born from Eve's side, as she was born from Adam's side, without debasing lust or the rupture of her virginity.[34]

But Lucifer sought to destroy humanity by approaching Eve, as the mother of the coming humanity, and offering her a poisoned apple. She took it naively and also gave it to Adam, thereby corrupting their future sexual relations and offspring with sin. But, unlike Lucifer, humans never lose the image of God within and their longing for God. They sin by bending toward the pleasures of their bodies apart from God, but these errors themselves awake in humans a desire for repentance. The love of God subsists in them as their true nature and stirs up remorse.[35] Though partially distorted, the harmonies of the cosmos and the body-soul relations remain, to remind humans of their true nature and destiny.

Though Hildegard can speak in terms of ethical dualism, in which body and soul war, the mutual interdependency of body and soul persists. The soul vivifies the body, giving it life, or "greening power," and the body manifests the work of the soul in it. Hildegard's ethics are based on a balance of forces rather than extremes of body negation for the sake of spiritual perfection. Indeed, she suggests that too much abstemiousness awakens both lust and exhaustion.[36] What is needed is to reestablish the harmonious interplay of soul and body.

The relation of Adam and Eve itself images this bond and the intended union of soul and body. While Adam images God, Eve images the humanity of God's son.

FIGURE 37
Hildegard of Bingen receiving revelations from God's
Holy Spirit. Drawing by Hildegard of Bingen, eleventh
century. (Photo: Erich Lessing /Art Resource, NY)

She represents the body of the coming God-man.[37] Eve gives the garment of flesh
to every soul, without which it cannot live. Ultimately, she prefigures Mary (or,
rather, Mary is Eve's original nature restored), who clothes the Word of God in sinless flesh harmoniously united to God's Word, in whose image the soul is made.

Hildegard often uses the traditional Christian language that contrasts Eve and
Mary, casting Eve as the woman whose disobedience is reversed by the obedience
of the Second Eve. To Hildegard, Mary is the restoration and perfection of the good
nature of humanity, which Eve originally possessed and would have transmitted to
her offspring through virginal childbearing. Hildegard's Mariology reflects a patristic and Carolingian tradition. She does not mention the doctrines that exercised

the later medieval church, the Assumption and Immaculate Conception, nor does she have personal revelations of Mary.[38]

For Hildegard, Mary remains a majestic and somewhat abstract figure, representative of the Seat of Wisdom with the child Christ enthroned in her lap, an iconography derived from the Isis-Horus tradition and a favorite of the Carolingian church. The intimate Mary of later Franciscan spirituality, who sits on the ground with bare feet and a fat, naked babe at her breast, would have been distasteful to Hildegard. Mary's central role is to be the vehicle of the incarnation, the restoration of humanity through giving birth to the Word of God in sinless flesh. Through her virginal body, untouched by sin, she provides the incarnate Word with the garment of uncorrupted flesh that restores the original harmony of God and humanity, of soul and body, of the first parents.

As Eve restored, Mary conceives without sex and gives birth through her side, without rupturing her virginity.[39] In her, the original harmony of creation with God is restored, and sin and death are overcome. As Hildegard puts it, in a short praise verse for the Virgin, "Alleluia, O branch mediatrix, your holy body overcame death and your womb illuminated all creatures with the beautiful flower born from the sweetest integrity, the modesty of your closed garden."[40] Mary renews the union of God and *materia*. In her, divine light streams through the body as it would through a clear glass. In a hymn that encapsulates the drama of original creation disrupted and renewed, Hildegard writes:

> O resplendent jewel and unclouded beauty of the sun poured into you, a fountain springing from the Father's heart. This is his only Word by which he created the primal matter of this world, which Eve threw into chaos. For you, the Father fashioned this Word into a man. So you are that luminous matter through which the Word breathed forth all Virtues, as in the primal matter he brought forth all creatures.[41]

The ultimate theophany of the divine feminine in Hildegard's symbol system is Ecclesia, the church. A much more complex and human symbol than Mary, Ecclesia is both Christ's mother and bride, but she is also the struggling community of Christians in history (fig. 38). In an echo of the *Shepherd of Hermas*, Hildegard sees the church as preexistent and foreordained before the foundation of the world and yet also being built in the last age of world history as the reborn race of humans who issue from the font of baptism, sharing in Christ's redemptive God-manhood born from Mary.[42]

FIGURE 38
Hildegard of Bingen's image of Wisdom, the Mother
Church. Drawing by Hildegard of Bingen, eleventh century.
(Photo: Erich Lessing/Art Resource, NY)

As in the *Shepherd of Hermas,* it is the Virtues, whom Hildegard personifies as
female, who build the tower of the church.[43] The Virtues represent the synergies of
divine and human energy, of divine life meeting human response. The Virtues bring
the living stones of new members of the church to build the city of New Jerusalem
in history. Hildegard depicts Synagoga, the Jewish people, as a disconsolate bride
who has lost her election as God's spouse through failure to believe. Synagoga is
something like a communal Eve, but she will be saved through Ecclesia. She will
finally repent and be incorporated into the edifice of redemptive humanity at the
end of history.[44]

Echoing a patristic metaphor from Methodius, the church is the bride of Christ,
born from his side. She receives as her dowry the blood and water that flowed from

his wounded side on the cross. Through her fertile womb, those who inherit the sin of Adam through their mothers, the daughters of Eve, receive rebirth into the redeemed humanity of Christ.[45] In a striking image of baptism as womb of rebirth, Hildegard images black babies swimming toward the church, being drawn into her womb like fish gathered into a net. Reborn in the font of her womb, they reappear from her mouth, through which they are instructed in the Word. Their black skins are peeled off, and they are given luminous white baptismal garb.[46]

To the image of the church as bride of Christ and mother of Christians in baptism, Hildegard adds imagery from the Eucharistic spirituality so central to medieval Christianity. Ecclesia is a priest who receives the dowry of water and blood from Christ's side in a chalice (fig. 39).[47] Offering the bread and wine of Christ's body at the altar, she continually gives birth to God's body as food for reborn Christians.

But the church in history is also the sorrowful mother, weeping for the lost children who have cut themselves off from her by their heresy. She is assaulted by corrupt prelates, who prefer sinful pleasure to virile virtue and fail to protect Christ's bride and their mother. In a striking image, Hildegard pictures the church corrupted by these prelates as a ravished woman from whose vagina emerges a bestial figure with donkey's ears, like an erect penis (fig. 40).[48] In a striking reversal of male-female stereotypes, Hildegard typically speaks of the corruption of these male prelates as a fall of the church into "womanish times" (*muliebre tempus*).[49]

Although Hildegard accepts the class and gender hierarchies of her society, she subverts their biological literalism. Because the male clergy have succumbed to "effeminate" vices, God has raised a woman prophet (Hildegard) to be God's woman warrior (*bellatrix*) and to call the church to repentance.[50] Hildegard uses the metaphor of effeminacy for male vice but does not portray the vices themselves as female. Rather, vices and the devil are pictured as having human elements combined with animals. They are typically dark, ugly, and bestial; the virtues are feminine, beautiful, and shining with light. While vice-ridden men are "effeminate," God can raise up weak women to become virile and manly, paragons of divine power and teachers of virtue.

The final crisis of the church in world history is still to come, Hildegard declares, though it is anticipated in these corrupt, "womanish" times. The final paroxysm of world history will take place with the birth of the Anti-Christ. In a reversal of Mary's role, he will be born from a harlot but feign a virgin birth in a diabolic parody of Christ.[51] Although he will lead many astray, his downfall is sure. When he is defeated by the returning victorious Christ, the church and Christ will finally be united in loving communion. This can happen only when the full number of humans preordained from the beginning of the world are born and reborn in baptism.

FIGURE 39
The crucifixion of Christ and
the sacraments. Drawing by
Hildegard of Bingen, eleventh
century. (Photo: Erich Lessing /
Art Resource, NY)

FIGURE 40

The struggle against evil within the church. Drawing by Hildegard of Bingen, eleventh century. (Photo: Erich Lessing/Art Resource, NY)

In the final salvation in the heavenly new creation, the soul will receive back its beloved body, without which it cannot function. Then the final cosmic harmony of God and *materia* will be completed.[52] Although this time is still in the future, it is prefigured now in the communities of virgins, such as the one in Hildegard's own abbey. Clad in shining white garments and crowned with golden crowns, their sweet voices are raised in songs of praise that prefigure the community of paradise restored and perfected in the heavenly new creation.[53]

FEMININE SYMBOLS IN CISTERCIAN AND BEGUINE LOVE MYSTICISM

Although Hildegard did not focus on the bridal relation of the soul to Christ, a major stream of contemplative mysticism made this central, using the Song of Songs as its primary text. Specifically, Bernard of Clairvaux's commentary on this text serves as a foundational exposition of Cistercian mysticism. It is then useful to compare his work with the bridal mysticism of three female mystics of the thirteenth to early fourteenth centuries, Mechthild of Magdeburg (1208–1294?), Hadewijch (c. 1250), and Marguerite Porete (d. 1310). All three were Beguines, members of new, informal women's communities, often suspected of heresy (Marguerite Porete was burned as a heretic) and thus far removed from the established Cistercian world of Bernard, who lived and wrote more than a century earlier.

BERNARD OF CLAIRVAUX AND BRIDAL MYSTICISM

Bernard of Clairvaux's bridal mysticism is distinguished from the Neoplatonic allegorical exegesis of Origen and Gregory Nyssa (see chapter 5) by its much greater appeal to the emotions as a positive aspect of the soul that draws it to God. Although Bernard alludes to both the church and the Virgin Mary as brides of Christ, the soul is the primary reference for understanding the bridal relationship of humans to God. For Bernard, the Song of Songs so perfectly describes the relation of the soul to God that he speaks of it as the "book of our own experience."[54] The soul, made in the image of the Word of God, has a natural affinity for the second person of God. Bernard can even speak of the soul and the Word as sister and brother under God the Father, as well as bride and bridegroom.[55]

The soul has been alienated from the Word through sin, but it has not lost this natural affinity, which is its created nature.[56] Yet, in its alienated state, it cannot turn back to God of its own will. Rather, it is God's love that awakens the love of the soul for God. The initiative for our journey to God always remains with God. But this is more an awakening of a potential that is still present than a new creation of what has been lost.

> She who loves is herself loved. . . . The love of God gives birth to the love of
> the soul for God and his surpassing affection fills the soul with affection and his
> concern evokes concern. For when the soul can once perceive the glory of God
> without a veil, it is compelled by some affinity of nature to be conformed to it
> and be transformed to its very image.[57]

Central to Bernard's understanding of psychology is the need to integrate love and knowledge. Without love, knowledge is dry and mere external theory. But love without knowledge is heat without light. Only when knowledge and love are united and mutually transformed is there true knowledge, a real possession of and participation in the thing known.[58] This union of knowledge and love is true of our relation to others as well as our relation to God. In the favorite text of 1 John 4:16, "God is love," there is no knowledge of God without love of neighbor.

This emphasis on love of neighbor as well as love of God leads Bernard to a partial reversal of the hierarchical relation of action and contemplation in monastic life. Bernard does not see action as the inferior sister of contemplation, as in the traditional imagery that compared Martha, as a symbol of the active life, to Mary, as a representative of the contemplative life. Nor does he see the active life only as *ascesis*, or purgation, in preparation for *theoria*, or contemplation. Rather, Bernard creates a trilogy of Lazarus, Mary, and Martha and insists that they all must live in mutual interaction in one household. Lazarus is the ascetic purgation of vice, and Mary is contemplation of God, while Martha is active love, expressed in service to others.[59]

Again and again, Bernard insists that, much as monks might like to spend their time in contemplative ease, they must break this off in order to engage in active service to others. Bernard has many kinds of service in mind—for example, interrupting a sermon to serve guests who have come to the monastery.[60] Service can also mean care of the souls of other monks within the monastery. It is the work of preaching, an activity that was becoming more important in the twelfth century.[61] It also includes works of mercy to the poor, even love for enemies. Love of God is expressed both in the transformed self seeking union with God and in the gifts of outer service to others. Both are expressions of the work of the Holy Spirit. The second cannot be neglected for the sake of the first.[62]

In an extraordinary image, Bernard exegetes the opening phrase of the Song of Songs, "Let him kiss me with the kisses of his mouth," as both the bridal embrace of soul and Word and also the bride's impregnation, which makes her a mother, filling her breasts with milk to feed her children. He continually directs abbots, preachers, and administrators to be mothers of their flocks and not tyrants. He interprets the work of caring for others as motherly nurture, feeding them an overflowing milk from the breasts of those who have been kissed by the embrace of the Word: "The filling of the breasts is proof of this. For so great is the potency of this holy kiss, that no sooner has the bride received it than she conceives and her breasts grow rounded with the fruitfulness of conception, bearing witness, as it were, with this milky abundance." This "milky abundance" testifies to the presence of God as an infusion of grace, which takes place when prayer is transformed from dry routine to an experience of overflowing love. But it must be expressed in service to others, not merely in cherishing one's own inward experiences: "Far better the profit in the breasts you extend to others than in the embraces that you enjoy in private."[63]

While Bernard exhorts male church leaders to be mothers in relation to those under their charge, his language is not without misogyny toward women and what they represent. Although the bride is spoken of as "fairest of women," her femaleness indicates that she belongs to the sin-prone body: "For I think that in this passage, under the name of 'women,' He speaks of carnal and worldly souls, which have in them no manly force, displaying nothing constant or generous in their actions, but of which the whole life and character is soft, remiss and, in a word, womanish."[64]

Interestingly enough, he also characterizes monks as soft and womanish and warns them against criticizing bishops, who live a far laxer life in respect to the pleasures of the body. Bishops, Bernard scolds, actually live a harsher life and must shoulder difficult responsibilities in society, which are beyond the capacities of weak monks:

> Let us admit that our powers are unequal to the task, that our soft effeminate shoulders cannot be happy in supporting burdens made for men. It is not for us to pry into their business but to pay them respect. For it is surely churlish to censure their doings if you shun their responsibilities; you are no better than the woman at home spinning, who foolishly reprimands her husband returning from the battle.[65]

Bernard reminds his monks of the scriptural passage, "Better the wickedness of a man than a woman doing good" (Wisdom of Jesus ben Sirach 42:14),[66] to put their womanish virtues in their proper place in relation to the superior virility of bishops.

Such passages remind us of the deep ambivalence toward the feminine in Bernard's monastic cultural symbolism. The male monk may imagine himself a beloved maiden whose breasts fill with milk when kissed by a handsome bridegroom and may see his pastoral responsibilities as analogous to those of nursing mothers. But females nonetheless symbolize a carnality linked to vice and a weak softness that should abase itself before virile manliness, even in the male-male relation of monk to bishop.

Such imagery suggests that we should exercise some care in assimilating twelfth-century male monastic understanding of the bridal soul into modern Jungian valuing of the feminine *anima*. Ultimately, for Bernard, bodily images for God, such as feet, hands, and mouth, are figures of speech;[67] and probably, for him, the notion of the soul as female would have fallen in the same category. It is appropriate as an expression of the dependency of creature upon creator, however much their love may be hymned as mutual. But this does not easily translate into a general valuing of the feminine as a distinct aspect of the soul.[68]

The three Beguine mystics discussed here drew on the male tradition of bridal mysticism based on the Song of Songs, but they transformed it by fusing it with the secular tradition of courtly love. This created a new genre of mystical love that Barbara Newman has called *mystique courteoise*.[69] In theory, the two kinds of love were incompatible. Christian ascetics since Origen had labored to distinguish the spiritual love of God from sexual passion. But, from the twelfth century, the two had begun to flow into each other. Poets of secular love had adopted elements of religious language, while contemplative writers, such as Richard of St. Victor, recognized that sexual passion and spiritual love passion, though morally opposite, were psychologically similar.[70]

The union of the two genres in *mystique courteoise*, as exemplified in the works of the three Beguine mystics, created more vivid erotic language, more violent paradoxes of love and despairing longing unto death, and a gender fluidity for both lovers, God and the soul. The soul was pictured as the bride longing for and entering into a love union with her lord but also as the warrior-knight in quest of the distant lady. God was pictured in traditional male language as father, son, and spirit but also as lady love, enthroned as queen of heaven.

While male mystics such as Bernard pictured themselves as brides and impregnated mothers, with full breasts nursing those in their care, female mystics could see themselves not only as female brides but as male lovers tormented by the disdainful queen. Significantly, Bernard's image of pregnant, nursing mothers is absent in the writings of the women. The three female mystics did venerate the Virgin Mary as a key theological symbol. Hadewijch, for example, imagined herself becoming Mary, giving birth to Christ, and imitating her suffering motherhood; but she does not connect this with mothering her young Beguines.[71] Moreover, it is Mary Magdalene who appears as the role model for the love relation of the spousal soul and Christ.[72]

Mechthild of Magdeburg For Mechthild of Magdeburg, the creation of the soul by God the Trinity was the primal work of God's love at the beginning of creation. Contrary to the orthodox image of God the Trinity as self-sufficient, God is incomplete without the soul as beloved and bursts forth to create and give himself to her: "In the Jubilus of the Holy Trinity, when God could no longer contain Himself, he created the soul and in his immense love gave himself to her as her own."[73]

Mechthild imagines the Trinity engaging in conversation after the creation of the angels. The Son longs to create man in his image, even though he foresees tragedy in this act of love. The Father agrees, desiring one who will love them in return:

> The Father said, "Son, a powerful desire stirs in my divine breast as well, and I swell in love alone. We shall become fruitful so that we shall be loved in return. . . . I shall make a bride for myself who will greet me with her mouth and wound me with her beauty. Only then does love begin." Then the Holy Spirit spoke to the Father: "Yes, dear Father, I shall deliver the bride to your bed."[74]

The fall of the soul through the disobedience of the primal parents deprived the Father of his bride, but his anger was curbed by Eternal Wisdom, together with Mary. Mechthild sees Mary as the one unfallen soul, who becomes God's bride during the long ages between the fall and the incarnation: "The Father chose me for his bride, that he might have something to love, for his darling bride, the soul, was dead. The Son chose me as his mother." Mary is viewed as the preexistent church, who nurtured God's people through the ages and comes to fruition as mother of the Son's humanity. Through the incarnation, the soul can be restored as God's bride. Mary is both the unfallen counterpart of the bridal soul and Mater Ecclesia, whose full breasts suckle both the prophets and the Christian people.[75]

The soul is called the Father's daughter, the Son's sister, and the Holy Spirit's friend, bride of the whole Trinity. God's love for the soul is depicted with explicit eroticism. The bride clothes herself in virtues in preparation for the love dance. But when she enters the bridal chamber, her divine lover bids her strip off her clothes. When the soul becomes "naked," perfectly conformed to God, external practices of virtues need no longer come between God and the soul. "He surrenders himself to her and she surrenders herself to him," a love union that anticipates their "shared lot" in eternal life without death.[76]

In the manner of a courtly lover, God is depicted bending his knee to Lady Soul. God "surrenders himself to her power." After their union, God is still as lovesick for her as he always was (unlike human love, which becomes exhausted in union). The soul tears her heart in two to put God in it and thereby becomes a soothing balm for God's desire for her.[77]

Yet the love relation with God is not all sweet ecstasy, for Mechthild. Mostly it is pain and suffering, a suffering in estrangement from God, which expresses the finite, bodily condition and also the persecutions of those who do not understand her way of life. But by willingly accepting Lady Pain, Mechthild also participates in the sufferings of Christ and herself becomes Christ. Like Christ, her head is struck with a reed; she is forced to drink vinegar rather than wine; she is hung on high and descends into hell, consoling dejected souls; she is buried, "enjoying a lament of love with her Lover on the narrow bridal-bed"; rises on Easter day; passes through the shut doors to her disciples; and finally ascends to heaven.[78] As sharer in the sufferings of Christ's humanity, the soul becomes co-redeemer with Christ.

Hadewijch   We turn now to Hadewijch, a Flemish Beguine who was a contemporary of Mechthild.[79] Hadewijch uses several voices in her exploration of her love relation to God. In her Poems in Stanzas, she is the knight errant engaged in high adventures and difficult trials in order to win the favor of Lady Love. In these poems, she assumes all the affects of the male courtly lover seeking to conquer the distant lady. She lays siege to the lady's castle. She complains of the lady's fickleness and cruelty. She even accuses the lady of treachery, of cheating in duels and at cards, and threatens to abandon her. But she returns again to pursue her "suit." She imagines herself riding a proud steed, only be unhorsed.[80] She speaks even of love's madness, of going mad with love. She sighs and proclaims her sufferings for the sake of love, speaking of this contest in the courtly language of a "school of love."[81]

But she ever returns to her proclamation of fidelity and longing to be one with the lady, imagining their final union in which they "flow through each other": "Let your whole life be holy affliction until you are master of your beloved. . . . You shall row through all storms until you come to that luxuriant land where Beloved and loved one shall wholly flow through each other, of that, noble fidelity is your pledge here on earth."[82]

In her visions (written before the lyrics, when she was young), Hadewijch primarily speaks of herself as a bridal soul, who longs for her beloved and imagines herself being led to the apocalyptic wedding with him in the New Jerusalem. Here, the identity of the bridal soul merges with that of the church, through whom the whole community of heaven lives:

> Then I heard a Voice loudly crying, "New Peace be to all of you and new Joy! Behold this is my bride, who has passed through all your honors with perfect love and whose love is so strong that, through it, all attain growth!" And then he said: "Behold, Bride and Mother, you like no other have been able to love me as God and Man! . . . Now enjoy fruition of me, what I am,

with the strength of your victory, and they shall live eternally contented through you."[83]

In another vision, Hadewijch sees herself adorned with all virtues, escorted through the heavenly city to union with the divine Countenance, enthroned on the disk of the unfathomable unity of divine Being. Through her virtues, she has conformed to and been assimilated into the perfect humanity of Christ, and now she comes into her heavenly kingdom as God's bride. The eagle (of her revelation) cries out: "'Now see through the Countenance and become the veritable bride of the great bridegroom and behold yourself in this state.' And in that very instant I saw myself received in union with the One who sat there in the abyss upon the circling disk and there I become one with him in the certainty of unity." In this vision, Hadewijch, as bridal soul, is "swallowed up" into God. "Then I received the certainty of being received, in this form, in my Beloved and my Beloved in me."[84]

In her poems and visions, Hadewijch personifies Love as female in a way that merges Christian *caritas*, the love nature of God as described in 1 John 4:16 ("God is love"), with Frau Minne, the *eros* of courtly love. Personified Love is simultaneously the subjective experience of love of God in the soul and the object of this love, God. Or, one might say, Love is the meeting point and merger of the two, the soul's experience of love and God's Being as love. For Hadewijch, Love is not only the circulating energy that unites the three persons of the Trinity and takes the soul into its inner circle of love; it is also the unity or essence of Being in which the three persons of God subsist.

Love can thus be imagined as a goddess enthroned upon the being of God:

I saw in the eyes of the Countenance a seat. Upon it sat Love, richly arrayed, in the form of a queen. The crown upon her head was adorned with the high works of the humble. . . . From Love's eyes proceeded swords full of fiery flames. From her mouth proceeded lightning. Her countenance was transparent, so that through it one could see all the wonderful works Love has ever done and can do. . . . She had opened her arms and held embraced in them all the services that anyone has ever done through her. Her right side was full of perfect kisses without farewell.[85]

Barbara Newman speaks of this vision of Love as "the verbal icon of God as female."[86] But enthroned Love here stands for more than God in God's original being prior to creation. Love is the ultimate apocalyptic completion of God's relation to creation in its redemptive union, when God shall be "all in all" (1 Cor. 15:28). Hadewijch sees in a lightning flash this ultimate nature of Love, God "all in all" in union with creation. In this revelation, Love herself cries out, "I am the one who holds you in my embrace! This is I. I am the all! I give the all!"[87]

Marguerite Porete   In Marguerite Porete, we find the paradoxes of Beguine mysticism pushed to a radical extreme in a way that became intolerable to the official church of the fourteenth century. Marguerite wrote her book *The Mirror of Simple Souls* between 1296 and 1306. She was arrested several times on suspicion of harboring the heresy of the "free spirit,"[88] and her book was burned by the Inquisition. But she continued to circulate it and sent it to three noted scholars, all of whom approved it.[89] She was arrested again in 1309 and held in prison for a year and a half, during which she refused to give any testimony. The Dominican Inquisitor extracted a list of articles from her book, out of context, and sent them to the theological regents of the University of Paris, who condemned them. She was executed in the Place de Grève on June 1, 1310. But her text continued to circulate in Old French, as well as in Latin, Italian, and Middle English translations, under the cover either of anonymity or the names of more established male mystical writers.[90]

Toward the end of her book, Marguerite lays out her theory of seven stages of spiritual ascent, which she has presupposed throughout the text. In the first stage, the soul is touched by the power of God's grace. Stripped of the power to commit sin, she vows to observe all the commandments for the rest of her life. In the second stage, the soul goes beyond the commandments and mortifies nature, observing the counsels of evangelical perfection exemplified by the life of Jesus Christ. In the third stage, the soul's spirit is sharpened "through a boiling desire of love" and seeks to kill her own will in order to live only by the will of God. In the fourth stage, the soul experiences an ecstasy of absorption in divine love, relinquishing "all exterior labors and obedience." In the fifth stage, the soul falls into total wretchedness, experiencing the nothingness from which she was created, in order to annihilate any self separate from God and thus to live love, not as herself but as God living and willing in her. In the sixth stage, the soul becomes totally transparent to God with no impediment of a separate self separating her from God. The seventh stage is unknown. It is the ultimate state that "love keeps within herself in order to give us eternal glory of which we have no understanding until our soul has left our body."[91]

Marguerite speaks of these stages of spiritual ascent as entailing three deaths— a death to sin, a death to nature, and finally a death to spirit itself as a separate existence from God's spirit.[92] The *Mirror* is written as a dialogue among Reason, Love, and the Soul, all personified as female. Love declaims the revelations of the higher stages of life, while Reason represents conventional virtues and the rationality of the official church, who is constantly amazed by the daring teachings of Love. The Soul speaks by questioning Love about the meaning of her teaching and about what new heights of spiritual ascent she should scale.

For Marguerite, Reason is spiritually inferior to Love and represents the first and second stages of the life of established morality and monastic piety. Reason is spoken of as "one-eyed," being incapable of understanding the higher reaches of ecstatic union and annihilation of the soul in God. She is scandalized by talk of these higher stages of spiritual ascent, which threaten her institutional system.[93]

Reason is particularly horrified by Love's talk of leaving behind the virtues, discarding the external props of the institutional church: Masses, sermons, fasts, and prayers. The Soul declares that she was once servant of these virtues but now is freed of their dominion:

> Virtues, I take leave of you forever. I will possess a heart most free and gay. . . .
> I was once a slave to you, but now am delivered from it. I had placed my heart
> completely in you, you know well. Thus I lived a while in great distress. I
> suffered many grave torments, many pains endured. Miracle it is that I have
> somehow escaped alive. This being so, I no longer care. I am parted from you.
> For which I thank God, good for me this day. I am parted from your domin-
> ions, which so vexed me. I was never more free, except as departed from you.
> I am parted from your dominions, in peace I rest.[94]

This inferiority of Reason and the virtues signals the foundational hierarchy of Marguerite's system of spirituality, the hierarchy of Holy Church the Great over Holy Church the Little. Holy Church the Little lives by reason, the virtues, and external observances. Those who live at this level will be saved through God's gracious incarnation in Christ, so they are not excluded from paradise in the end. But they are incapable of understanding or instructing the elite of the "free souls," of Holy Church the Great, who have passed on to the higher stages of spiritual life. Rather, the "free souls" mediate this knowledge to Holy Church the Little, who should submit to their instructions.[95]

Marguerite speaks of two kinds of souls who fall into the lower levels of spiritual life and have not attained the state of the "unencumbered soul." These are the "lost souls" and the "sad souls." The lost souls have no clue about the higher life and are hostile to any intimation of its existence, whereas the sad souls know that there is a higher stage of life but do not know how to attain it. Marguerite admits that she was long one of these "sad souls."[96] Clearly, it is precisely this doctrine of the spiritual aristocracy of "free souls" above "Holy Church the Little" in which Marguerite pushed the limits of the church's acceptance of mysticism.

Mystical thought always presented the danger of transcending the church's institutional means of grace in favor of an independent, direct relation with God. Marguerite not only hinted at but flaunted this transcendence of the institutional church. Hildegard of Bingen, Mechthild, Hadewijch, and many other mystics denounced the corruption of the clergy and criticized clerical inability to understand their pursuit of a higher spiritual life. But Marguerite goes beyond such critiques of corrupt or blind clergy to a systematic characterization of the institutional church as inferior, while the others were always careful to at least pay lip service to its authority.

Marguerite's confidence in the possibility of the soul's transcendence of its own separate self to live "no longer as I, but God living in me" (reinterpreting Paul, Gal. 2:20) lies in her ontology of the Being of God in relation to creation. Marguerite builds on the longstanding Christian view that creation itself has no independent substantive existence apart from God's Being.[97] Apart from God's Being, creation is Nothing. Creation was taken from this Nothing to become "something" through God's creative act. Becoming an "annihilated soul" is literally a return to that Nothing, which is the soul's reality apart from God's Being. In that leap into Nothingness, the soul also ceases to have a separate existence and is united with the Divine Being, the only Being that truly is.

This understanding of Nothingness as the reality of creatures apart from the All of Divine Being underlies Marguerite's constant paradoxes, in which the Soul, denying her will and finally her separate existence, becomes Nothing, thus becoming All. She no longer lives, loves, or wills of herself; but God lives, wills, and loves in her and as her, "without her." This fall into the abyss of Nothingness, in which the Soul becomes All, while always aware of being Nothing, is paradoxically the final act of the self. But it can never happen as long as the Soul has a self that wills apart from God. Thus Love says to the Soul: "If you understand perfectly your nothingness you will do nothing and this nothingness will give you everything. . . . As God has transformed you into Himself, so also you must not forget your nothingness. That is, you must not forget who you were when He first created you."[98] This loss of will and separate existence cannot happen through an act of will of the self. It is purely a gift of grace, in which God transforms us into himself. Marguerite's mystical theology is one of divine grace without any human "works."

Yet Marguerite is acutely aware that all "talking about" this transformation, including the words of her own book, falls on the side of a separate self that still acts as a self, and not as God working and willing in her. Thus, compared to the actuality of being in God, all the words of her book are "lies." They talk about something that she has not yet accomplished or, rather, that has not yet happened in her. She is still a "sad soul," who knows of a higher life but has not yet been transformed into it. The name of this God that she glimpses from a distance is poignantly called "ravishing Farnearness,"[99] a deity that is infinitely distant, while being closer to oneself than one is to oneself.

In the first chapter of her book, Marguerite speaks of herself as a "maiden, the daughter of a king," who falls in love with a noble king, Alexander, whom she had never seen but could only imagine. She has an image painted of this beloved, which represents both her love and the object of her love, and she contents herself with loving this portrait, in the absence of the reality of her beloved.[100] Marguerite's *Mirror of Simple Souls* is her portrait of the imagined king that mirrors but is not the reality of the loved one.

Marguerite's acute sense that her words "about" or her portrait "of" this beloved one ever fall on the creaturely side of the separate self, a self that is not yet "annihilated," perhaps explains her behavior in the hands of the Inquisition. She refused to give any answer to their inquiries, maintaining a silent, noble resolve to the end, which brought tears to the eyes of the spectators as she went to her fiery death. In willing her own annihilation, she also testified to her faith in her ultimate transformation, in which she would become, finally and really, no longer "I, but God living in me." The Inquisition's act of annihilating her was perhaps, for her, her final perfection in Love in and as God.

MOTHER WISDOM AS THE SECOND PERSON OF THE TRINITY: JULIAN OF NORWICH

From Marguerite Porete's quest to become an "annihilated soul," culminating in her bodily destruction, we turn with some relief to the "homier" views of a fourteenth-century recluse, Julian of Norwich. Yet Julian began her spiritual path with a wish to share Christ's crucifixion to the point of death. As a young woman, she prayed for three gifts—to see Christ's dying on the cross, to experience a sickness to the point of death, and to experience three wounds: contribution, compassion, and complete longing for God. Starting on May 8, 1373, when she was thirty and a half years old, Julian's prayers were answered. She lay at death's door for seven days, culminating in sixteen visions of Christ dying on the cross. At the point of death (his death and also hers), Christ was suddenly transformed to risen life, and she too was restored to health.[101] Julian spent the rest of her life meditating on the meaning of these visions. It was probably at this time that she decided to begin the life of an anchoress (a solitary recluse enclosed in a room attached to a church, where she could both hear Mass through a window and counsel others).[102]

Julian uses neither bridal mysticism nor the language of courtly love. She does not describe the soul as a bride or personify it as a female, nor does she describe God as a lover. There is no appeal to personified Love. Rather, her language for the relation of God to humans is more familial, paternal and maternal. The self is a beloved child or servant of a kindly lord. Julian's major theological problem is theodicy, reconciling her understanding of God as loving and forgiving with the church's teaching on the final damnation of unrepentant sinners. She also seeks to understand how God can allow the prevalence of evil and violence, such as she saw around her in her society.

Julian addresses this problem by a reinterpretation of sin and God's response to sin. Following a well-trodden path from Augustine, Julian sees sin or evil as having no real substance. Rather, it is absence or privation. God is pure goodness. Since humans have their source in God and are God's image, in their true created nature, or "substance," they too are completely good. But in their actual existence, or what Julian calls their "sensuality," they become separated from God. This separation is experienced by fallen humans as both pain and shame. They become enclosed in their fear and guilt and are convinced that God is angry at them. They become entrapped in this fear of God's anger and are unable to rise and realize that God is not angry at them but continues to love them and wish them well.[103]

Christ takes on human "sensuality" in the incarnation, thus becoming humanity's substitute "servant" and bearing all human distresses. Standing before God as our representative, Christ carries all the fallen servants with him and enables us to see that we are still loved by God, despite our mistakes. For Julian, the fallen condition is itself painful and distressing, rather than pleasurable, and thus serves as "medicines" that stir us up to seek to overcome this condition.[104] But this solution to fallenness still maintains the possibility that many will not accept their redemption and will not open their eyes to God's enduring love, and so will be damned eternally. Julian cannot openly deny the church's teachings about hell, but she has a guarded hope that, in the end, no souls will actually be found there. God will work the ultimate miracle of grace, and all souls will be saved. In the end, "all will be well, all will be very well."[105]

This faith in God's enduring love and kindness is expressed in her combined fathering and mothering language for God: "Thus in our making God almighty is our kindly Father, and God all-Wisdom is our kindly Mother, with the love and goodness of the Holy Spirit, which is all one God, one lord."[106] Julian brings mothering language into the Trinity by a recovery of female-personified Wisdom, identified with the second person of the Trinity as mother. Wisdom is our mother as agent and means of creation and hence as the one through whom we are created "substantially" as children of God. As incarnate Christ, the second person is also our mother as the one who takes on our body and redeems us, bringing us to reborn life. The incarnate Christ, in whom we are birthed anew and fed in the Eucharist, is then our mother "sensually." Julian draws on Christ's work in birthing anew and feeding us, not to image the church but rather to image Christ as mother. Thus, Julian says:

> Furthermore I saw that the second Person who is our mother substantially, the same dear person is now become our Mother sensually. For of God's making we are double; that is to say, substantial and sensual. Our substance is that higher part which we have of our Father, God almighty. And the second Person of the Trinity is our Mother in kind, in our substantial making—in whom we are grounded and rooted, and He is our Mother of mercy in taking our sensuality. Thus our Mother means for us different manners of his working, in whom our parts are kept unseparated. For in our Mother Christ we have profit and increase; and in mercy he reforms and restores us, and by the power of our passion, his death and his uprising, oned us to our substance. Thus our Mother in mercy works to all his beloved children who are docile and obedient to him. . . . Thus Jesus Christ who does good against evil is our very Mother. We have our being of him, where every ground of Motherhood begins, with all the sweet keeping of love that endlessly follows. As truly as God is our Father so truly is God our Mother.[107]

With these famous lines, Julian restored mothering language to the nature of God, language that had largely disappeared for Christians with the New Testament masculinization of Wisdom as Christ the "Son" and the repression of early Christian images of God as father, mother, child (see chapter 5). Here, Mother Wisdom is identified as the second person of the Trinity and incarnate Christ, who is our mother both as creator and as re-creator of our humanity.

SEVEN

Tonantzin-Guadalupe

The Meeting of Aztec and Christian
Female Symbols in Mexico

In 1492, the expansion of western European powers began with the voyage of Cristobal Colón, whose last name suggests the word "colonialism" (from *colonia*). The first wave of Western colonialism came from Catholic Spain and Portugal. Both countries saw the task of converting the natives to Christianity as integral to their self-justification for conquering hitherto unknown peoples and lands. The Spanish conquered in the name of Christ and the king of Spain, as a nation that saw itself chosen by God to counteract infidels and spread the true faith. They also carried with them the veneration of the Virgin Mary, in many local Spanish expressions, and planted these in the New World.

This chapter examines the violent meeting between an aggressive Catholic Christianity with strong Marian devotion and indigenous Mesoamerican cultures with highly developed religious systems that paired male and female divinities. The Spanish construed indigenous religion as "idolatry" and indigenous gods as "demons," expressions of the devil. They set themselves the task of wiping out all traces of native religion and replacing it with Spanish Catholicism. To this end, they demolished all the temples they found, destroyed images, and burned the codices that enshrined local wisdom. They also effected a near-genocide of the indigenous people, reducing the population of Mesoamerica from an estimated twenty-five million in 1519 to one million by 1592, partly through warfare and exploitation of labor and partly through the inadvertent transmission of diseases from Europe to which indigenous peoples lacked immunity.[1]

Ironically, the first Spanish missionaries, particularly the Franciscans, are also a main source for what we know of native religion, society, and culture. A small number of Franciscans believed that in order to evangelize the Nahuatl peoples of Mesoamerica, they must learn their language and strive to understand and carefully record their culture. Only in this way could they communicate the true faith effectively and free the "Indios" from their idolatry. The Franciscans did not intend to create a syncretism between Christianity and the religions of the Nahuas, but they nevertheless helped to do so by creating a linguistic and cultural bridge over which the Nahuas could cross into Christianity while preserving much of their own worldview under the surface. In the process, the Franciscans left us major ethnographic studies of Nahuatl culture and society, such as Andres de Olmos's (1491–1570) Codex Tudela and Bernadino de Sahagún's (1499–1590) twelve-volume *Historia general de las cosas de Nueva España (General History of the Things of New Spain).*[2]

That modern study of Nahua and Mexica (Aztec) religions relies on documents created for the purpose of eliminating these religions raises serious problems. Can we really free the content of these documents from their interpretive bias and accurately hear the voices of the indigenous culture? Generally, scholars of Nahuatl culture argue that we have no choice but to use these documents. Moreover, the Franciscan methodology of training indigenous youth to be trilingual (Nahuatl, Spanish, and Latin) and then using these literate youth as go-betweens to interview the elders of Nahuatl culture about their traditions has provided us with invaluable source material. By considering this material in combination with surviving preconquest codices, archaeological studies of preconquest sites, and anthropological study of contemporary Nahuatl people, most scholars believe that a reasonably accurate picture of preconquest culture can emerge.[3]

This chapter presents a brief sketch of female divinities among the Mexicas shortly before and after the Spanish conquest. It then examines the current state of knowledge about the emergence of the veneration of the Virgin of Guadalupe at the hill of Tepeyac, near Mexico City. I also attempt to evaluate the extent to which this veneration of Guadalupe represents a syncretism of the Catholic Mary and a pre-Columbian veneration of a Mother Goddess, Tonantzin. In the context of this book, this chapter provides a case study of how the Catholic veneration of Mary, with its own roots in ancient Near Eastern goddess worship, was and continues to be a vehicle for the assimilation of goddess worship into Christianity from the conquest period to today.

NAHUA VIEWS OF FEMALE DEITY

The Aztecs built their understanding of the divine on many layers of earlier Mesoamerican culture. Given the nature of the sources, tracing these different stages of development is too difficult to be attempted here. Suffice it to say that the views of the divine found in the fifteenth- and sixteenth-century codices and documents represent a long process of cultural growth going back thousands of years to classical and preclassical Mesoamerican village and urban cultures.[4] The developed Aztec understanding of the gods reflects a view of a sacred cosmos with many levels. At the deepest level, unmanifest divinity is seen as existing in the ultimate, or thirteenth, heaven. This divinity underlies all life but never appears in human affairs. Rather, it is manifest in a multiplicity of deities that come forth from this ultimate divinity and in turn generate and are present in the visible cosmos.

This ultimate divinity is understood as both unitary and dual, male and female: Ometéotl, the giver of life, or master of duality, whose dual male-female nature is represented by the pair Ometecuhtli and Omecíhuatl, the lord and lady of duality. The following outline by Miguel León-Portilla illustrates the observation of the sixteenth-century Spanish Franciscan chronicler Juan de Torquemada "that these Indians wanted the Divine Nature shared by two gods, man and wife."

Ometecuhtli-Omecíhuatl, the Lord and Lady of Duality
Tonacatecuhtli-Tonacacíhuatl, the Lord and Lady of our maintenance,
In teteuinan, in teteu ita, Huehuetéotl,
the mother and father of the gods, the old god.
Xiuhtecuhtli is at the same time the god of fire,
who dwells in the navel of fire, tle-xic-co
Tezcatlanextía-Tezcatlipoca, the mirror of day and night,
Citlallatónac-Citlalinicue, the star that illumines all things,
the lady of the shining shirt of stars,
In Tonan, In Tota, our mother, our father,
Above all, he is Ometéotl, who dwells in the place of duality, Omeyocan.[5]

This unity in duality allows all the plurality and contradictory forces of the universe to emerge from the primary source of life and to be held together as an ultimate unity. In Nahua mythology, a dual male-female deity emerges from Ometéotl, who rules over the visible world. The pair is made up of Tezcatlipoca (smoking mirror), who represents night, and his female counterpart, Tezcatlanextía (illuminating mirror), who represents day.[6] This female aspect of Tezcatlipoca exists side by side with the fourfold expressions of Tezcatlipoca, the four sons of the primal parents, who represent the four directions of the horizontal spatial world. These four directions are signified by the four colors of Tezcatlipoca—red, white, blue, and black. Quetzalcóatl, a beneficent deity that created humans and provided them with corn, is identified as one of these sons, while the Aztecs identified the blue Tezcatlipoca with their warrior God Huitzilopochtli.[7]

Tezcatlipoca, the "Lord of the Near, the Close" (*tloque nahuaque*), came to be seen as the primary sovereign deity of the universe. He is all-powerful but also arbitrary and capricious, even sinister, subjugating humans to a power they cannot control or count on as beneficent and to whom they can only plead for favor. In words recorded by the Franciscan Andres de Olmos, "Tezcatlipoca was everywhere and knew the hearts and minds of others, so they called him Moyocoya, or the all powerful and unequaled."[8] Prayers addressed to Tezcatlipoca often include an address to "our mother, our father," such as the following dedication of a child to the priesthood shortly after birth:

Our Lord, Lord of the Near and the Close, [this child] is your property, he is your venerable child. We place him under your power, your protection with other venerable children, because you will teach him, educate him, because you will make eagles, make ocelots of them [the two orders of Aztec warriors], because you educate him for our mother, our father, Tlaltecuhtli, Tonatiuh [the earth Goddess and the God of the fifth sun of the present era].[9]

This male-female duality of the Nahua cosmic system does not seem to be a hierarchy of value. Maleness does not represent a superior principle and femaleness an inferior principle, as they did in the Greek dualistic hierarchy of spirit and matter. Aztec society was strongly gender differentiated and socially stratified, with male elites dominating the powerful public military, priestly, and political roles, while women were located primarily in the domestic sphere. But women's work roles of food preparation and weaving, as well as their participation in public areas such as marketing, medicine, and priestly functions, were vital for both family and corporate life.[10] Gender differentiation does not seem to have been abstracted as a moral or ontological hierarchy.[11] Nor does cosmic gender duality appear to have been organized in terms of complementary opposites, such as light-darkness and active-passive, although one leading scholar of Nahua culture has construed it in this mold.[12]

Rather, male-female dualism appears to operate more as a dynamic parallelism that pervades the cosmic system. The Aztecs conceived of the cosmos as spatially organized into thirteen upper heavens and nine levels of the underworld, with the surface of the earth lying between the two. There are male and female deities at every level of this cosmos. Just as the ultimate deity of the thirteenth heaven is a male-female duality, so the deepest (ninth) level of the underworld is ruled by a male-female pair, Miclantecuhtli and Mictecihuatl, the lord and lady of Mictlan, the underworld where ordinary people went when they died. Male and female deities also represent fertility, rain, fire, and other such cosmic forces.

Many deities are described as androgynous or coupled. The old deity of fire, Huehuetéotl, for example, is sometimes seen as androgynous and sometimes as linked to the Goddess Teteo Innan, "mother of the gods," or Toci, "our grandmother." Sahagún speaks of this Goddess as strongly related to healing:

> She is the mother of the gods. Her devotees were physicians, leeches, those who cured sickness of the intestines, those who purged people, eye-doctors. Also women, midwives, those who brought about abortions, who read the future, who cast auguries by looking upon water or by casting grains of corn, who read fortunes by use of knotted cords, who cured sickness by removing stones or obsidian knives from the body, who removed worms from the teeth, who removed worms from the eyes. Likewise the owners of sweat-houses prayed to her; wherefore they caused her image to be placed in front of the sweat-house. They called her the "grandmother of the baths."[13]

The main festival dedicated to Toci or Teteo Innan was the harvest festival of Ochpaniztli, which celebrated both the gathering of the harvest and the return of the dead stalks to the earth for the renewal of life in the spring. For this festival, a woman was chosen to represent Toci. She was garbed, named, and treated with greatest honor and veneration as the Goddess. She danced and rejoiced "so all could see her and worship her as a divinity." At the culmination of this time of veneration, she was sacrificed and the skin removed from her body. The skin was donned by a man, who was then venerated as the Goddess. In this way, the role of the Goddess was taken primarily by a female and then secondarily by a male. Finally, the skin was placed on a straw figure to represent the final incarnation of the Goddess into the maize stalks. Each transformation represents a stage in the cycle of the ripened corn turned into the human being and then back to the earth.[14]

Women played key roles in the priesthood. A girl baby destined for the priesthood was dedicated at birth. At fifteen, she was taken to be trained as a woman priest, or *cihuatlamacazqui*. Women priests remained celibate during their time of service but could later marry. The Ochpaniztli festival, dedicated to the Mother Goddess Toci, was directed by a woman priest with a woman assistant, a "white woman" (painted white) responsible for the decorations, the preparation of the ritual, the sweeping of the site, and the lighting and extinguishing of the ritual fires. Women priests were specially garbed and led ecstatic dancing during rituals. "When they danced, they unbound their hair, their hair just covered each one of them like a garment."[15]

During the maize festival of Quecholli, young priestesses dedicated to the Goddess of corn carried seven ears of corn wrapped in cloth in a procession. They wore feathers on their arms and legs, and their faces were painted to represent the Goddess. They sang and tossed handfuls of corn of different colors and pumpkin seeds to the crowds that lined the processional way. The people scrambled to gather up the corn kernels and seeds as a token of the good harvest of the coming year.[16]

Other deities, such as Xochipilli, lord and lady of flowers and festivals, and Tlaltecuhtli, the earth serpent, are also androgynous, although primarily seen as female. Gods and goddesses are often portrayed as couples, such as Tlaloc, the God of rain that waters the earth, and Chalchiuhlicue, associated with underground springs and waters. The Tlalocs are also seen as plural, and Chalchiuhlicue is called their "older sister."[17] Quetzalcóatl, the plumed serpent, is himself dual, combining bird and reptile. He is paired with various goddesses—Tonantzin (our precious mother), Cihuacóatl (female serpent), Yaocihuatl (warrior woman), and Coatlicue (serpent skirt).[18] Some of these male and female deities probably existed independently, and priestly thinkers have sought to systematize them into pairs. But the pairing often shifts, and the goddesses remain definite personalities in their own right.

One interesting Goddess is Tlazolteotl, "the filth eater." She is described by Sahagún's informants as both condoning and purging debauchery and moral evils of all kinds: "One placed before her all vanities, one told, one spread before her all [one's] unclean works—however ugly, however grave, avoiding nothing because of shame. One exposed all before her [and] made one's confession in her presence." For Sahagún, such a dual role was morally incomprehensible; but for the Aztecs, ordure and other wastes were both the symbols of debauchery and also recycled fertilizer, so it was comprehensible to see the Goddess of "filth" as also purging it.[19] Sahagún goes on to quote a penitential prayer to this Goddess and to all the gods: "Mother of the gods, father of the gods, old god, here hath come a man of low estate. He cometh here weeping and anguished. Perhaps he has sinned, perhaps he has erred, perhaps he has lived in filth. He cometh heavy-hearted; he is sorrowful. Master, our Lord, protector of all, also take away, pacify, the torment of this man."[20]

Central to Aztec cosmology and culture is a sense of a dynamic twoness or plurality that interacts along various axes to sustain life. In the sacred center of the capital city of Tenochtitlán, the great pyramid is unified at the base and separates into two, one dedicated to the sun and war God, Huitzilopochtli, and the other to the God of rain and fertility, Tlaloc. Authority in the Aztec state was also dual, represented by the Tlatoani, or speaker, and Cihuacóatl, the Mother Goddess, both roles taken by males.[21] The two elite warrior groups whose compounds are on either side of the great temple are identified as jaguars (ocelots) and eagles, thus pairing two powerful land and sky animals. The human body itself combines the energies of the head, identified with the sun and the destiny of the individual (controlled by the calendar); the heart, linked to divine fire; and the liver, linked to breath and health. The body is literally the meeting place of these many cosmic forces.[22]

Aztec rhetoric, or elegant language, typically takes the form of a double phrasing, describing everything in two ways that are parallel and mutually reinforcing. Only by looking in two different ways does one hit at the deeper meaning that connects the two descriptions. Thus, for example, in an address to a newly born girl child, the father says to her: "Here you are, my little daughter, my precious necklace, my precious quetzal feather, my human creation, my offspring. You are my blood, my color, in you is my image. Now grasp, listen; you were born, sent to earth by our Lord, Possessor of the Near and the Close, maker of humankind, creator of people."[23]

Although rooted in ultimate oneness in duality, the manifest universe is seen as ephemeral, besieged by conflicting forces that tend toward collapse and destruction, and maintained only by self-sacrificing efforts on the part of gods and humans. The Aztecs told the story of cosmic history as a succession of four "suns," or ages, each of which was eventually destroyed and swept away. The first age, or sun, began three thousand years ago. The gods battled for ascendancy, with Tezcatlipoca predominating. This age was populated by acorn-eating giants, who were finally devoured by jaguars. Quetzalcóatl presided over the second sun, which was populated by piñon nut eaters and ended with a devastating hurricane that transformed the survivors into monkeys. The third sun was associated with Tlaloc, inhabited by aquatic seed eaters, and destroyed by a fiery rain that transformed the survivors into dogs, turkeys, and butterflies. Chalchiuhtlicue, Goddess of waters, presided over the fourth sun, which was populated by wild seed eaters. They were victims of a great flood, and the survivors were turned into fish. At the end of each age, the sun was destroyed, and the world plunged into darkness.[24]

After the end of the fourth sun, the gods gathered at Teotihuacán (the great sacred city of the classical era, 200–800 CE, which was in ruins when the Aztecs arrived in the Valley of Mexico). There, the gods sacrificed themselves to create the fifth sun. They kindled a great fire and invited the brave young warrior God Tecuciztecatli to sacrifice himself by hurling his body into the fire. He tried four times but drew back each time in fear. Finally, an old, sickly God, Nanahuatzin, threw himself into the flames and was transformed into the sun. Then Tecuciztecatli gained courage and also jumped into the flames, becoming a second sun. In order to avoid having two equal suns, the gods threw a rabbit at the second sun, darkening it to become the moon.

But when the sun rose in the east, it did not move but "swayed from side to side." All the gods then decided to sacrifice themselves in order to empower the sun to move through the sky. But even then the sun did not move, until one remaining God, Ehecatl, the wind God, "exerted himself fiercely and violently as he blew," setting the sun moving in an orderly way across the sky.[25] But this sun too will eventually fail and be destroyed. "As the elders continue to say, under this sun there will be earthquakes and hunger and then our end will come."[26] Thus, the Aztecs lived with a pessimistic worldview, in which joys were fleeting and eventual destruction sure, staved off only by tremendous effort.

Just as the gods sacrificed themselves to create and empower this sun, so humans must sacrifice, both by bleeding themselves and by sacrificing the flower of their men and women to feed the sun in its threatened daily course. This worldview was the foundation of the Aztec sacrificial system. The elites, kings, and priests—and at times the whole community—pierced their bodies with thorns to offer their blood. They sacrificed the elite of warriors taken in battle, and also women and children, to offer their blood to sustain the energies of the sun and the earth. Those sacrificed, the heroes who died in battle and the women who died in childbirth, became gods and went to the house of the sun, where they accompanied and aided the sun in its daily course across the sky.

After the fifth sun was secured, the land surface of the earth and its vegetation were created by Tezcatlipoca and Quetzalcóatl by bringing the Goddess of earth from the heavens. The Goddess floated down on the existing waters. The two Gods changed themselves into huge snakes and took hold of the two ends of the Goddess and broke her in half. They made the earth from her front half and took the other half back to the heavens. But the Goddess was angry, and the other gods consoled her, ordering that all the fruits necessary for the life of humans would be made from her. They made from her hair the trees, flowers, and grasses; from her skin, the fine grass and flowers; from her eyes, the wells and springs; from her mouth, the great rivers and caverns; from her nose, the valleys; and from her shoulders, the mountains. But the Goddess continued to weep and would not be quiet or bear fruit until she was watered with the blood of humans.[27] Again, the sacrifice of the gods must be compensated by humans sacrificing themselves.

Two other important stories are told of Quetzalcóatl, the wise, beneficent God, as creator of humans and giver of corn, the food that sustains humans of the present sun. Quetzalcóatl went to the region of the dead, appearing before the lord and lady of Mictlan, to fetch the bones of those who died, in order to create from them a new generation of humans. But, before he would release the bones, the lord of Mictlan set Quetzalcóatl the seemingly impossible task of blowing on a conch shell with no holes. With the aid of worms that made holes and bees and hornets that filled the shell, Quetzalcóatl accomplished this task. But when he tried to leave with the bundle of bones, he fell down into a pit, scattering the bones, which were nibbled by quail. When he revived, Quetzalcóatl gathered what was left of the bones and took them to the paradisal realm of Tamoanchán. There, he gave them to the Goddess Cihuacóatl, who ground them in her jade bowl. Quetzalcóatl then bled his penis over the bones, and, from this combination of ground bones of the dead and divine blood, the new race of humans was made.[28]

Then, to provide food for the humans, Quetzalcóatl changed himself into an ant and followed a red ant into a mountain where corn was stored. He carried it to Tamoanchán, where he gave it to the first human pair, Oxomoco and Cipactónal. There, the gods ate of the corn and "fed it to us to nourish and strengthen us."[29] Corn was the basis of human nourishment, and humans themselves were seen as "corn-beings." This view that corn and human flesh were the same substance seems to be reflected in the Aztec practice of eating small pieces of the flesh of sacrificed victims, which were placed on the corn stew in a ritual meal in the homes of those who contributed the sacrificed captive.[30] In effect, corn and human flesh were seen as "consubstantial."

Significantly, the human counterpart of the God Quetzalcóatl, the wise priest-king of Tollan, was remembered as opposing human sacrifice. He practiced self-bleeding for his people and called only for the sacrifice of flowers and butterflies in the temple. But he was defeated by a number of tricks perpetrated by the sorcerer Titlacauan. In another version, this sorcerer was Tezcatlipoca, who revealed Quetzalcóatl's vulnerability to him by showing him his old age in a mirror and seducing him into drunkenness and sexual impropriety. This caused Quetzalcóatl to flee his city in shame, and it fell into ruins. In one version, he fashioned a raft and set forth into the sea to the east. In another, he sacrificed himself on the shore of the sea and was transformed into the morning star.[31] Quetzalcóatl and his city of Tollan were remembered as the prototypes of the ideal city and ruler, but they were seen as too idealistic and so bound to fail.[32]

Yet it was believed that Quetzalcóatl would return, as a white-skinned bearded man coming from the eastern sea (the Atlantic). Ironically, the demise of the Aztecs was partly a result of their willingness to entertain the belief that the Spanish conqueror Hernán Cortés, who arrived in ships in 1519, might be Quetzalcóatl returned. By a striking coincidence, Cortés landed on the very day of I Reed (a year in the Aztec calendar of fifty-two-year cycles) when it was believed that Quetzalcóatl had departed and would return.[33]

The Aztecs also had stories specific to their own group, depicting themselves as a people destined for empire. They told of their migration from their original place of origin—a "white place," Aztlan, in the north—as poor and despised people and their arrival in the Valley of Mexico. They battled with other established groups in the region and were banished to the swampy region of the lakes. There, they saw the prophetic sign of the eagle perched on a cactus eating a snake (the image on today's flag of Mexico) that signaled the place where they were to build their great city.

Two Aztec origin stories strikingly feature conflict with rival sisters of the warrior God Huitzilopochtli. One has to do with the birth of Huitzilopochtli. His mother, the earth Goddess Coatlicue (fig. 41), was doing penance by sweeping in a temple on the mountain of the serpent, Coatepec, when a ball of feathers fell down on her. Placing these in her bosom, she became pregnant. Her daughter, Coyolxauhqui, became enraged at what she saw as her mother's disgrace and summoned her four hundred brothers, the gods of the south, to come and kill their mother. But one of the brothers warned the mother of the coming assault. When Coyolxauhqui led her brothers up the hill, Huitzilopochtli was born fully armed and struck his sister, cutting off her head and sending her body rolling down the hill to break in pieces.[34]

In 1978, workers in Mexico City discovered a huge circular stone in the area of the plaza behind the national cathedral, which is built on the Aztec sacred temple precinct. The stone carried a carving of the dismembered body of Coyolxauhqui, dressed in the feathered helmet and arm and leg armor of a warrior but with bare torso. This area has since been excavated, and it has become evident that this image of the shattered body of Coyolxauhqui once lay at the foot of the great temple of Huitzilopochtli. At the top of the temple, victims were sacrificed, their chests split open and their hearts offered to the gods to sustain the sun, while their bodies were sent tumbling down the stairs to land in the area of the dismembered body of the

FIGURE 41
The Aztec Earth Goddess Coatlicue,
fifteenth or sixteenth century. (Museo
Nacional de Antropologia, Mexico
City; photo: Werner Forman /
Art Resource, NY)

conquered sister. In effect, the temple itself represented the serpent hill, Coatepec, and each sacrifice reenacted the defeat of the enemy sister (fig. 42).[35]

The second story took place in the migration period. On their way to discovering the place of their capital, Tenochtitlán, Huitzilopochtli abandoned his Goddess sister Malinalxoch, described as an evil sorceress, while she was sleeping. When she woke up and found herself abandoned by her brother, Malinalxoch led her followers to the mountain Texcaltepetl, where they established themselves. She bore a child named Copil to the king of Malinalco and thus became the founder of a rival city-state.[36]

What do these stories of the conquered or abandoned divine sister mean for Aztec gender relations? On one level, the story of the defeat of Coyolxauhqui and the four hundred brothers is a cosmological story of the daily defeat of the stars by the rising sun. But it also seems to reflect wars with rival cities that the Aztecs subdued to build an empire in Mesoamerica. Some of these cities may have had powerful female rulers, but it may also be that the Aztecs represented conquered cities as rival, conquered sisters.[37] Recent excavation of the temple center at Xochitecatl, a sacred site that flourished between 650 and 850 CE, resulted in the discovery of a large group of figurines, mostly female. The figurines express the female life cycle, from pregnant

FIGURE 42

The dismembered Goddess Coyolxauhqui, fifteenth or sixteenth century. (Museo del Templo Mayor, Mexico City; from Esther Pasztory, *Aztec Art*, published by Harry N. Abrams, Inc., New York; all rights reserved)

women and women with children in their arms and babies in cradles, to young women orantes and priestesses, to elderly women. At the center of this group of females is the stunning figure of a priestess warrior seated on a throne or palanquin, wearing a helmet and holding a scepter and shield of her office as governor (fig. 43).[38]

The story of Quetzalcóatl speaks of such a female priestess-ruler: "The Lady Xiuhtlacuiloxochitzin was installed as Speaker. Her grass dwelling stood at the side of the market plaza where Tepextitenco is today. The city of Cuauhtitlán passed to her since she was the wife of Huactli, it is said, and because she spoke often to the [*sic*] devil Itzpapalotl" (the Goddess Obsidian Butterfly—in keeping with the Spaniards' demonization of Aztec deities, the Spanish chronicler calls her a devil).[39] Perhaps when the Aztecs arrived in the region, there were some powerful women

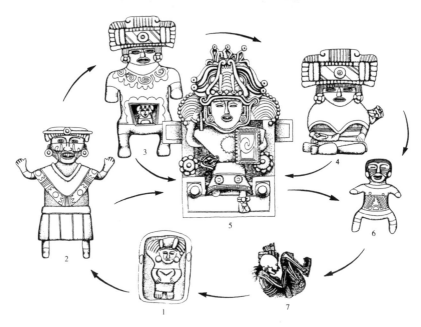

FIGURE 43

From top left, clockwise: Praying woman figurine, temple of Xochitecatl; pregnant woman figurine, temple of Xochitecatl; group of women figurines expressing the life cycle, twelfth century, pyramid of Xochitecatl. (From *Arqueología Mexicana* 5, no. 29 [January–February 1998]) rulers of cities who opposed their rise to power, and the defeat of the priestess-warrior sisters symbolized the subjugation of these rival peoples.

THE NAHUAS AFTER THE CONQUEST AND
THE EMERGENCE OF THE CULT OF GUADALUPE

The history of Spanish-native relations in sixteenth-century Mexico has been portrayed as complete devastation of the indigenous peoples. Their ceremonial sites were destroyed, their codices burned; nearly 90 percent died from disease. The Spanish appeared to have wiped out native culture, creating a blank slate on which they imposed Spanish Catholicism and an administrative system controlled from Spain. Insofar as native culture survived, most believed, it did so in isolated pockets removed from Spanish control. But this picture is misleading. In fact, recent study of documents of daily life written in Nahuatl by Nahua peoples themselves, in the alphabetic script devised by the friars, reveals a different picture. Although Aztec power was destroyed and replaced by the Spanish central authority, many of the deeper structures of Nahua social organization and culture continued, under a surface appearance of Christianization and Hispanicization.

The rapid victory of the conquerors actually owed less to Spanish military capacity than to the rebellion of groups subject to Aztec rule who became allies of the Spanish, seeing Spain as the new imperial power. The Nahuas, by custom, accepted the god of the new rulers as the overlord, but expected that the traditional gods of the local areas would continue to be worshipped. In the *Colloquies* between the Spanish friars and the native priests—written by Sahagún in 1560 but also representing dialogues that took place when the first twelve Franciscan missionaries arrived in 1519—the Nahua view is evident. The friars argue that the Nahuatl gods are false and demonic and that the Nahuas must cease to worship them and must be converted to the one true god. The native priests do not object to the advent of the Christian God, but they insist that worship of their own gods should continue, gods "who from time immemorial have provided the spiritual and material means through which they and their forebears have sustained life."[40]

Long before Aztec imperial rule, Mesoamerica had been organized into *altepetl*, or independent self-governing territories, occupied by peoples who each had their own identity, religious centers, markets, and myths (either of migration or of being descended from the breakup of the Toltec empire). The Aztecs did not change this system; rather, they simply turned many of these *altepetl* into tribute-paying subject peoples. Others, such as the Tlaxcalans, remained fiercely independent and were never subdued by the Aztecs. The Tlaxcalans were among those who were first conquered by the Spanish and then became their allies against the Aztecs. When the Aztec empire was destroyed, these *altepetl* communities remained and became the basis of Spanish administrative rule.

This situation explains the apparent rapidity of the spread of Spanish rule and Catholicism among the native peoples in the first decades after the conquest. In effect, the conquerors simply gave a Spanish veneer to what continued to be the organizational and cultural structure of the existing ethnic communities. The *encomiendas* (territories given to Spanish leaders for agricultural production and evangelization), the parishes, and the municipalities were all formed based on the existing *altepetl* communities.[41] Religious life also followed this structure. Local leaders became both the heads of municipalities and the leading laity of the parishes, who often owned the land on which the church was built. The temple that had represented the local community and its god was replaced as the center of worship by the parish church, often built on or near the existing site and with the same stones as the earlier temple.

The *altepetl* were themselves divided into constituent subcommunities (*calpolli*), each with its own leadership and religious center. These in turn were divided into neighborhoods or households. These subcommunities were accustomed to rotating the leadership of the *altepetl*. This structure continued to be the basis of parish and government administration under the Spanish. Parish lay sodalities, or *cofradias,* dedicated to specific patron saints, were based on these traditional units. The Nahuas adapted the Spanish concept of saints to their own understanding of local patron gods, often picking a saint who had similar characteristics and whose feast day was near that of their traditional god.[42]

Many traditional religious practices continued, now directed to the Christian God and saints: the burning of copal incense, dancing and singing, marching in processions, offering flowers and ears of corn, engaging in divination and healing, and pricking with thorns to draw blood. Although they expressed very different worldviews, many Spanish Catholic practices were, on the surface, similar to Nahuatl practices, which aided this transition. Healing could now be understood as receiving miraculous favors from a saint, often manifest in a revered image. The Spanish practice of penitential self-abuse, beating with whips and wearing spiked chains, bore some resemblance to Nahuatl self-bleeding. For the Spanish, such self-abuse expressed the subduing of the sinful body; for the Nahuas, blood was the sacred fluid of life, which one returned to the gods, who had themselves given their lives to create the cosmos and humanity. This self-sacrifice of the Nahuatl gods seemingly was not far removed from the idea that Jesus Christ shed his blood, dying on the cross to redeem human beings. The image of a bloody Christ with a crown of thorns on his head and nails in his hand and feet might appear similar to the Nahuatl gods and priests who pricked themselves with thorns, shedding blood to create and sustain life.

The decision of the Spanish friars to evangelize the indigenous peoples in the Nahuatl language, creating dictionaries and grammars and an alphabetic spelling, allowed the Nahuas to express Christian ideas in language that recalled the traditional divinities. Just as Ometéotl was far away and did not appear directly in human life, but was instead represented by many second-rank deities, so the Christian God could be similarly far away, represented by the saints, who were the effective local expressions of God connected to particular local communities and territories. The different Marian cults of various local communities in Spain, each manifest in distinct miraculous images, such as the Virgin of Guadalupe de Extremadura and the Virgin de los Remedios, were to appear in miraculous stories and images of Mary in New Spain and were adopted by different indigenous communities.

The word for Mary as mother of God was translated as Totlaconantzin (our precious mother), a familiar term for the Nahuatl mother of the gods. This term for Mary paralleled the Nahuatl word used for God the father, Totlacotatzin (our precious father). The pairing of the two titles was reminiscent of the paired male and female expressions of the Nahuatl high God Ometéotl. By using these words, the Nahuas implicitly saw Mary as the female expression of God. Many Nahuatl words traditionally used for Tezcatlipoca, such as "Lord of the Near, the Close," were used for God or Christ.

The friars were well aware of the dangers of referring to the Christian God and saints with Nahuatl words that had been used for Nahuatl deities, and they tried to substitute Spanish terms, such as *dios*. Spanish translations of the Nahuatl documents typically use Spanish Catholic terms, but examining the Nahuatl documents themselves reveals the extent to which familiar words from preconquest Nahuatl religion became the terms used for Christian concepts, thus translating these Christian concepts into the Nahua worldview.[43]

The first generation of Franciscans, who did the pioneering study of Nahuatl culture and language, were very concerned about indigenous "idolatry" hiding under superficial Catholicism. From Spanish Christian humanism (Erasmianism), they had developed a vision of a pure, apostolic Christianity planted in the New World that would replace the corrupt Christianity of Europe. But by the middle of the sixteenth century, these Franciscans were being replaced by nonorder bishops and Creole (American-born Spanish) clergy. The influence of the Counter-Reformation and the Jesuits, who arrived in 1572, was hostile to such "apostolic purity" and less concerned with possible syncretism. It was in this environment that the cult of the Virgin of Guadalupe, infused with indigenous elements, would develop on the hill of Tepeyac.

The history of the cult of the Virgin of Guadalupe is heavily contested, particularly in regard to the cult's early development in the sixteenth century. Fierce disputes have raged between those who believe that a humble Indian, Juan Diego, saw the apparitions in 1531 and had the image of the Virgin miraculously implanted on his cloak and those who see this whole story as a pious fiction of the seventeenth century, arguing that the image was painted by a skilled Indian artist trained by the Spanish. The following account details what I have come to regard as the likely history of the origins and early development of this cult, but it focuses primarily on the meaning of the Virgin of Guadalupe for Mexican religious and national identity. It is here that we see the extraordinary variety of interpretations that have been and are being attached to this Marian symbol.

It is possible that a small shrine to the Virgin of Guadalupe of Extremadura was connected with Tepeyac (Tepeyacac, in Nahuatl) sometime before 1550, although there is no way to know how long before. Part of Cortés's army camped on this hill (which lies northeast of what was the lake area in which Tenochtitlán was built) in preparation for the siege of the Aztec capital in 1521.[44] Cortés and many of his men came from the Spanish region of Extremadura and brought a devotion to the Virgin of Guadalupe of Extremadura with them to New Spain. When they returned to Spain, they visited this shrine and offered donations in thanks for their victories. The region of Extremadura and the image of the Virgin found there (named Guadalupe for the river of that name nearby) were themselves connected with the history of the Spanish struggle against the Moors.

According to the legendary account, the small wooden statue of the Virgin of Guadalupe at Extremadura was carved by Saint Luke. It eventually found its way to Spain, as a gift from Pope Gregory the Great to San Leandro, the archbishop of Seville, in the seventh century. The statue, of Byzantine style, pictured a seated and dark-complexioned Mary with the Christ child in her arms. When the city of Seville was captured by the Moors in the eighth century, a group of priests escaped with the statue and buried it in the hill of Extremadura, near the river of Guadalupe. In the early fourteenth century, the Virgin Mary was believed to have appeared to a poor herdsman who had lost his cow. She told him to tell priests to come and dig at the place where she appeared. They came, discovered the old statue, and built a chapel to house it.

The statue soon became an object of pilgrimage for those who believed in its miraculous healing powers. The shrine was entrusted to the Hieronymite order, which had close ties to the royal dynasty of Castile. Veneration of the Virgin of Guadalupe proliferated, and many subsidiary shrines were created with copies of the statue.[45] It is possible that one of Cortés's men carried a print or small statue of the Virgin of Guadalupe at Extremadura, which might have become the model for the painting of the Virgin on Juan Diego's cloak. Although the statue revered at Extremadura was of a seated woman with a child in her arms, and hence did not resemble the painting, the shrine at Extremadura contained a second image of Our Lady over the oratory, surrounded by a sunburst with thirty-three rays and standing on an upturned moon. Some copy of this—the typically European image of Mary as the woman of Revelation 12 and as the Immaculata—could have been the model for the Mexican painting.[46] It is likely, then, that the name "Virgin of Guadalupe" was derived from a connection to the Virgin of Extremadura.

Some time before 1556, an Indian painter trained by the Spanish to decorate churches probably painted an image of the Virgin on maguey cloth, the cloth woven from the maguey cactus plant that was used for rough Indian cloaks. Such Indian painters were well known for their skill (fig. 44). The painting associated with the shrine of the Virgin of Guadalupe at Tepeyac began to draw pilgrims to the shrine, based on a belief in its miraculous healing powers. In 1556, we find the first definite reference to veneration of the Virgin of Guadalupe at Tepeyac. In that year, a dispute broke out between the bishop of Mexico City, Alonzo de Montúfar, and the Franciscan provincial, Francisco de Bustamante, over the archbishop's sermon of September 6 encouraging devotion to the Virgin of Guadalupe.

In a counter-sermon on September 8, 1556, Bustamante protested the promotion of this devotion. The archbishop then ordered an investigation, whose records were kept, although not published until 1888–1890, hence becoming the center of modern criticism of the historicity of the apparitions.[47] At the time, this dispute reflected the struggle to replace the "purist" hopes of the Franciscans for a repristinated apostolic Christianity with a Counter-Reformation baroque devotionalism that focused on visual images. Underlying the dispute was also the effort of bishops from the diocesan clergy to wrest power from the orders, especially the Franciscans.

In his protest, Bustamante described the devotion to Guadalupe as without historical foundation, based on a painting done by an Indian and encouraging the very idolatry that the Franciscans had sought to overcome in their missionary philosophy:

> Nothing is better calculated to keep the Indians from becoming good Christians than the cult of Our Lady of Guadalupe. Ever since their conversion

FIGURE 44
Virgin of Guadalupe, c. seventeenth
century. Painting on maguey cloth
cloak, exhibited in the shrine of the
Virgin of Guadalupe, Mexico City.

they have been told they should not believe in idols, but only in God and our
Lady. . . . To tell them now that an image painted by an Indian could work
miracles will utterly confuse them and tear up the vine that has been planted.
Other cults like that of Our Lady of Loreto have great foundations, so it is
astounding to see the cult of Guadalupe without the least foundation.[48]

In this protest, Bustamante clearly had never heard of apparitions of Mary appearing to Juan Diego, disclosed to the first bishop of Mexico City, the Franciscan Juan
de Zumárraga. Bustamente also believed that the image had been painted by an Indian. He protested the cult arising around this image, but the image itself was not
understood to have been miraculously produced.

The growing cult of Guadalupe was also of concern to the Franciscan pioneer
of Nahuatl studies Bernadino de Sahagún. In his *General History of the Things of
New Spain*, completed in 1576–1577, Sahagún expressed his reservations about the

growing veneration of the Virgin of Guadalupe under the name of the ancient Mother Goddess Tonantzin. He noted that the hill of Tepeyac had long been the site of veneration of the Aztec Goddess; Indians came there from distant areas to offer sacrifices at the temple to Tonantzin. "And now that there is a church of Our Lady of Guadalupe, they call her Tonantzin, taking advantage that the preachers call Our Lady, the Mother of God, Tonantzin." Sahagún protested the translation of Mary's title as Mother of God into the Nahuatl word Tonantzin, saying that it should instead be translated as Diosinantzin. He was alarmed that, because the title Tonantzin was being used for Mary, the Indians were coming from distant lands to worship Guadalupe, understanding her to be the continuation of the old Aztec Mother Goddess. "It appears a satanic invention to palliate idolatry under the equivocation of this name Tonantzin."[49]

Clearly, Sahagún knew of no tradition of apparitions or miraculous production of the image of Guadalupe. His only concern was that the Indians flocking to the church of Guadalupe at Tepeyac might understand Guadalupe Tonantzin as a Goddess, the representative of the Nahuatl Mother Goddess and the female side of a dual God in new form. Sahagún's protests have been understood in modern times to mean that an Aztec Goddess named Tonantzin had a temple on the hill of Tepeyac, but this has been questioned. Tonantzin was a title for the maternal aspect of any Aztec goddess, not the name of a particular goddess. When it was used as a title for Mary, the maternal aspect of the Aztec Goddess could be read into the Spanish Marian cult by Nahua Christians. This seems to be what happened, rather than the cult of Guadalupe intentionally replacing an earlier temple or cult of an Aztec Mother Goddess at this particular site.[50]

Despite these Franciscan protests, devotion to the Virgin of Guadalupe continued to grow, and the first church was built in 1555 or 1556 by Montúfar.[51] Apparently, both Indians and Spaniards came to the site, although Guadalupe was never the patron of an indigenous *altepetl* but was always associated with the Mexico City region generally.[52] In 1566, Alonso de Villaseca, a wealthy mine owner, donated a life-size silver and copper statue of the Virgin, which became an object of devotion, although we do not know what it looked like. It was melted down for candlesticks at the end of the seventeenth century, when the painted image was firmly established as the cult object of the shrine.[53] By the seventeenth century, the church had grown too small, and a second one was built in 1622.

There was a growing belief in the power of the Guadalupe painting to work miracles, not only for individuals but also for the community as a whole. In 1629, the archbishop of Mexico City brought the Guadalupe painting to the national cathedral to implore the Virgin's help in abating the flood waters that had covered the city. When the floods receded, the painted cloak was returned to the church at Tepeyac, escorted by both the viceroy and the archbishop and carried through the decorated streets accompanied by music and fireworks. In this role, Guadalupe paralleled the cult of the Virgin de los Remedios, whose image was similarly brought to the national cathedral in times of drought, in hopes of bringing rain.[54]

Despite this growing devotion, no document or account of the period mentions apparitions or the miraculous origin of the image until the middle of the seventeenth century. In 1648, Miguel Sánchez, a well-known preacher, published *The Image of the Virgin Mary, Mother of God, of Guadalupe, Miraculously Appeared in the City of Mexico, Celebrated in Her History by the Prophecy of Chapter Twelve of Revelation.*[55] In this book, Sánchez tells what would become the established story of the appearances of Mary to the Indian Juan Diego. Mary demands that Juan Diego tell the archbishop to build a church to her at the place of her appearance on Tepeyac. The bishop is skeptical and demands a "sign." Mary responds by instructing Juan Diego to pick flowers that miraculously appear on the hill (out of season, for it is December) and take them to the archbishop in his cloak. When Juan Diego opens the cloak to release the flowers in the presence of the archbishop, the image of the Virgin is found miraculously printed on the cloak. As further proof of the miraculous powers of this Virgin, Juan Diego's uncle, who had been on the point of death, is cured, at the very moment when the Virgin promised Juan Diego that this would happen.

This account follows the lines of a typical European apparition story. Sánchez's narrative is interspersed with biblical interpretations. He claims that the image that appeared on Juan Diego's cloak was the "true image" of Mary herself. This image had appeared in the mind of God from all eternity and was the very image that the apostle John had seen in his vision of the woman "clothed with the sun, and the moon under her feet, and upon her head the crown of stars," recorded in Revelation 12. Following a long-established exegesis of this passage from Revelation, Sánchez understands the image to represent both Mary and the church.

After each segment of the story of the apparitions, Sánchez makes biblical digressions. He compares Juan Diego to Mary Magdalene and the bishop to the apostles who did not at first believe her when she told them of Christ's resurrection. They doubted because she was a woman of bad reputation, a recent convert, like the Indians, who have been possessed by the "seven devils of idolatry." Tepeyac is called the new Mount Tabor, Juan Diego the new Moses, and Mexico the Promised Land. The first pilgrims who hasten to the shrine are compared to the shepherds that hastened to see the baby Jesus and his mother in Bethlehem. These comparisons situate the apparitions in the context of biblical typologies and their reenactment in Mexico.

The following year, a second account of the apparitions appeared in the Nahuatl language, written by Luis Laso de la Vega, the vicar of the shrine of Guadalupe. This account lacks the biblical digressions of Sánchez's narrative. The story is told in an elegant Nahuatl that recalls many of the forms of Aztec rhetoric. Mary addresses Juan Diego as "my dear little son," "my youngest child," while Juan Diego addresses Mary as "my patron, personage, Lady, my youngest child, my daughter." But other than the use of these polite forms of address, de la Vega's account follows the general lines and often the wording of the Sánchez book, although in Nahuatl.[56]

Several key questions arise. Did Sánchez make up the story of the apparitions out of whole cloth, or was he dependent on earlier traditions for which we have no historical records? Was de la Vega's account copied from Sánchez, or was he using an earlier account written shortly after the apparitions by an Indian skilled in Nahuatl, an Indian trained in the college of Sahagún to be trilingual in Latin, Spanish, and Nahuatl? The structure of Sánchez's book, which takes the form of biblical commentary on each segment of the story of the apparitions, suggests that he had at least some source for it. He claimed that there was no written source but that he had followed an unwritten tradition. He had set himself the tasks of making a written version of this story and unveiling its deeper meaning in the light of biblical typologies.[57]

But the archives of Archbishop Juan de Zumárraga, the supposed recipient of the miraculous image, contain no records of the apparitions. Zumárraga was a Franciscan, who would have shared the order's hostility to images. He was reputed to have gathered up and burned the Aztec codices of the archives of Tlatelolco.[58] Discussions of the shrine of Guadalupe in the sixteenth century and the first half of the seventeenth century also reflect no knowledge of such apparitions. It is likely that the story of the apparitions and the miraculous appearance of the image began to develop in oral tradition in the late sixteenth or early seventeenth century. There are two brief accounts in Nahuatl that seem to reflect this earlier oral tradition, but the tale was only locally known, as one apparition story among others, and not taken seriously.[59] It was this oral tradition that Sánchez drew upon to write the story and elaborate his biblical commentary.

From the late seventeenth century into the twentieth century, the tradition grew that de la Vega's story of the apparitions was independent of Sánchez's book, that it had not been written by de la Vega himself but had been copied from an earlier account written by an Indian trained by Sahagún at a time shortly after the apparitions were seen. This Indian was later identified with Antonio Valeriano (d. 1605), a noted native Nahuatl scholar and governor.[60] In a recent study of the similarities between Sánchez's Spanish account and de la Vega's Nahuatl account, three contemporary Nahuatl scholars—Lisa Sousa, Stafford Poole, and James Lockhart—concluded that de la Vega's story of the apparitions was dependent on Sánchez. There was no earlier Nahuatl account written by an Indian hand, although de la Vega may have used skilled Indian writers to polish the Nahuatl language of his version.[61]

De la Vega himself addressed a letter to Sánchez after reading his book, in which he said, "All the while my predecessors and I have been slumbering Adams, though ·all the while we possessed this New Eve in the paradise of her Mexican Guadalupe."[62] This might mean that de la Vega had never known of the apparition stories before he read Sánchez's book, even though he was the vicar of the Guadalupe shrine. In his letter, he also refers to himself as "entrusted with the sovereign relic of the miraculous image of the Virgin Mary, whom the angels alone merit to have for their companion." This statement could simply mean that the image was known to produce miracles, rather than implying that the image itself had been produced by a miracle. At the least, de la Vega testifies that he had not understood the deep theological significance of the image before reading Sánchez, whether or not he had heard of the apparition story earlier.[63]

The year 1663 saw the beginning of a long campaign by the cathedral chapter of Mexico City to persuade the Vatican to accept the Mexican Virgin of Guadalupe, based on revelations of Mary in Mexico, and to give the cult its own feast day of December 12. Until then, the feast of Our Lady of Guadalupe had been associated with the general feast of the nativity of Mary on September 8. Occasionally, the Hieronymite order that controlled the cult of Mary of Extremadura in Spain sought to claim the alms from the Mexican shrine on the grounds that it was an extension of their own.[64] There had already appeared in 1660 a version of Sánchez's account of the apparitions, but without the biblical exegesis by the Spanish Jesuit Mateo de la Cruz. He used old church calendars to establish the date on which the miraculous image was revealed to Archbishop Zumárraga as December 12, 1531. In 1663, the cathedral chapter in Mexico City asked the pope to recognize December 12 as the feast day of the Mexican Virgin of Guadalupe, thus clearly severing her cult from that of Mary of Extremadura in Spain.

At issue was the establishment of a unique revelation of Mary in Mexico. Mary could be seen in some sense as the founder and patron of the Mexican church. By appearing in Mexico, she established an independent basis for her (and God's) relation to Mexican Christianity, not simply dependent on Spain. Creole Mexicans could see Mary as one of them, a Mary birthed in Mexico. In order to prove their case to the Vatican, historical records of the apparitions going back to 1531 were necessary. But none were to be had. The search of the archives of Archbishop Zumárraga yielded no evidence that he had known of the apparitions or the miraculously produced image.

Lacking records, the Mexican church elicited signed testimonies from elderly Mexicans, both Spanish and Indian, that they had known of the apparitions from their youth and had heard of them from their parents and grandparents. In this way, church officials hoped to provide evidence of an oral tradition going back to 1531. These testimonies, from twenty people, Indian and Spanish, were obtained through a set of questions that itself contained an account of the apparitions and tended to elicit the very answers that were sought.[65] The petition from the cathedral chapter, supported by the Jesuits and other religious orders, was sent to Seville in 1666 to present the case to Rome, along with a direct letter to Pope Alexander VII. But this petition did not find favor in Rome, where the Vatican feared an excessive proliferation of miraculous images.

With the 1666 petition, there was also an account of the apparitions, drawn mainly from de la Cruz, by one Luis Becerra Tanco, who produced a readable version of Sánchez's story without the biblical digressions. But this account was complicated by Tanco's claim that the Indians not only had preserved an unbroken oral tradition concerning the apparitions but also had painted scenes of the story and produced a narrative in Nahuatl. This was the first effort to claim the existence of a document contemporaneous with the apparitions written by an Indian, although this document was not yet identified with Valeriano.[66]

The Holy See did not accept December 12 as the feast of the Mexican Virgin of Guadalupe until 1754. Nonetheless, from the late seventeenth century, Mexican theologians and preachers grew ever more daring in their eulogies of the Virgin's miraculous image. Preachers such as José Vidal de Figueroa expounded on Sánchez's idea that the image of the Virgin represented the exact representation of Mary in the mind of God for all eternity.[67] The light around the image of Mary was said to represent Christ's divinity, while Mary herself incarnated Christ's humanity. The Jesuit chronicler Francisco de Florencia even claimed that the very image of Guadalupe made Mary physically present, just as Christ was physically present in the Eucharist. This line of eulogy became common in Mexican theologizing on Guadalupe during the late seventeenth and eighteenth centuries.[68]

In 1709, a new and enlarged basilica was erected at Tepeyac to replace the 1622 church. In 1739, the Virgin of Guadalupe was proclaimed patron of Mexico City, followed by her acclamation as patron of all New Spain in 1750. Mexico was seen as a chosen nation, uniquely converted through the appearance of Mary, and there was speculation that the Indians were the ten lost tribes of Israel. Just as the United States would take over the myth of England as a chosen nation, adding its vision of itself as a paradisal promised land, so Mexico took over the myth of Spain as an elect people and interpreted Mexico as a promised land uniquely chosen by Mary.[69] The phrase from Psalm 147:20, *"non fecit taliter omni natione"* (it was not done so to any other nation), referring to Israel as a chosen people, was applied to Mexico, uniquely favored by Mary.[70]

The effort to provide biblical roots for the Mexican church was expressed in a controversial sermon preached on the feast of Guadalupe on December 12, 1794, by Fray José Servando Teresa de Mier. In this sermon, Mier speculated that St. Thomas had already evangelized Mexico in apostolic times and that the image of Guadalupe, identical to that seen by St. John in Revelation 12, had been revealed in Mexico at that time. He argued that the Nahuas had preserved in their religious traditions a distorted memory of this early evangelization—Quetzalcóatl was a dim remembrance of St. Thomas, and the image of Mary imprinted on St. Thomas's cloak was remembered in traditions about Teotenantzin (another name for the beloved Mother Goddess) and other goddesses. This sermon caused furious criticism, and its view was not generally accepted. But it represented early efforts to rehabilitate Nahuatl religion, to see it not simply as idolatry and demon worship, by arguing that its central religious figures contain memories of "true" religion, conveyed to the Mexicans in the apostolic age.[71]

In September of 1810, the parish priest of Delores, Miguel Hidalgo, raised the cry of rebellion against Spanish rule of Mexico. The Virgin of Guadalupe was imprinted on the banners of the revolution. The war cry of those who joined the rebellion was "Long live the Virgin of Guadalupe and death to the *gachupines*" (Spaniards born in Spain, who had continued to be the ruling elite of church and state in New Spain). The Virgin of Guadalupe, as the symbol of an elect Mexican national identity, had become the patron of revolution. But the top church leaders, still largely royalist, were by no means willing to let this national symbol be carried off by the rebels. More conservative Creole leaders saw Hildago and other revolutionaries as fomenting a class rebellion that would also undo the hierarchy of Creoles over mestizos and Indians. The priest revolutionaries, Hildago and José Maria Morelos, as well as many other rebels, were captured and executed.

Mexico would establish its independence from Spain, but under a Creole leadership that would curb deeper class and race transformation of society. By the mid-nineteenth century, however, Mexico had become deeply divided between liberals, who wanted a radical secularization of public life and separation of church and state, and conservatives, who wanted to retain the alliance of the Mexican state and the Catholic Church. Under the reform laws of Benito Juárez, much church land was confiscated, and the Catholic Church's control was removed from many areas of public life, such as education.

At the same time, a critical history of Mexico began to be developed by a new generation of historians, such as Joaquín García Icazbalceta (1824–1894). The long-delayed publication of the documents from the 1556 investigation of the Virgin of Guadalupe apparitions raised the question of the historicity of this tradition. Icaz-balceta clearly believed that the apparitions could not be defended as historical fact, although, as a faithful Catholic, he was reluctant to say so openly and accepted devotion to the Virgin as piety.[72]

The Catholic Church saw itself as deeply embattled by both the legal and the intellectual attacks of liberalism. It sought to position itself as the guardian of the true Catholic faith against both of these attacks. Its spokesmen reviled and sought to refute the historians. It sponsored a number of public displays of Guadalupan piety, such as the 1895 "coronation" of the Virgin of Guadalupe, to reclaim public space for the church in Mexico. At the same time, the Mexican Catholic Church began to realize that separation of church and state also freed the church itself from subordination to the state inherited from Spanish rule. By positioning itself in a new relation to the Vatican, as the head of an independent world church, the Mexican church began to reorganize itself and rebuild its educational and other institutions independently of the Mexican state.[73]

This use of Marian piety to defend the church against secular liberalism also reflected the struggles going on in Europe, with Pius IX's repudiation of liberalism in the Syllabus of Errors and the declaration of papal infallibility (1870). In France, the apparitions of Mary at Lourdes in 1858, followed by the promotion of mass pilgrimages to Lourdes, had become displays of the power of the French church against secular liberalism. This French Marian Catholicism influenced a similar politics of anti-liberalism through promotion of Guadalupan mass public piety in Mexico.[74] Despite the effort of the rebels of 1810 to claim Guadalupe for revolutionary change, Guadalupan piety appeared firmly in bed with rightist politics and hostility to critical historical thought at the end of the nineteenth century.

During the Mexican Revolution of 1910–1935, similar conflicts arose over the ideological ownership of Guadalupe. The followers of the peasant revolutionary

Emiliano Zapata carried the banner of Guadalupe. But Zapata was assassinated, and the revolution was "institutionalized" in the rule of the PRI (Party of the Institutionalized Revolution). Under President Plutarco Elías Calles (1924–1928), militant anticlerical laws were passed that imposed heavy fines and imprisonment for violating the constitutional separation of church and state by engaging in religious education or maintaining religious orders or Catholic trade unions. The church was prohibited any public display of religion, even the wearing of clerical garb in public.

These laws pushed Mexico into a new civil war, with rural priests risking execution for defying the laws. In this "Cristero" rebellion, parts of the rural peasantry arose against the urban elite of Mexico City. The Cristeros' slogan was "*Viva Cristo Rey y Santa Maria de Guadalupe.*" On their banners, the image of the Virgin of Guadalupe appeared in the white center between the green bars of the Mexican flag. Below the image of Mary were the words *Reina y Madre Nuestra, Salvanos* (our queen and mother, save us).[75] During this upheaval, the politics of Guadalupan piety were partly shifted. No longer only on the side of a landed conservative class, the church now stood with a rebellious poor peasantry, mestizo and Indian, who saw themselves as both Catholic and oppressed by the secular elites of the ruling party.

Not accidentally, it was precisely in the context of the Cristero rebellion that the movement to beatify Juan Diego arose. The figure of Juan Diego had been largely neglected in earlier Creole Guadalupan devotion, but now he became the perfect symbol for a pious Catholic who was at the same time a poor Indian. That Mary chose to reveal herself to such an Indian meant not only that Mexico itself was at root Indian but also that Mary's revelation had enshrined the union of Indian and Spaniard. In Juan Diego, the Catholic Church found a "Catholic" way of taking over the revolutionary claim that Mexico was a mestizo nation, a new people born of the merger of the two peoples. Mexico was both uniquely mestizo and Catholic—which cast militant secularism as a deviation from true Mexican identity.

This effort to canonize Juan Diego moved slowly, as had the earlier effort to prove the historicity of the apparitions. Canonization made it necessary to prove that Juan Diego had actually existed as a historical person. He was unknown in sixteenth-century records, appearing first in the apparition traditions of the mid-seventeenth century. Thus, the effort to canonize him flew in the face of historical criticism of these apparition traditions. Despite these questions, Pope John Paul II moved to beatify Juan Diego in 1990.[76] Juan Diego was proposed for canonization as a saint by this same pope in December of 2001 and canonized in July of 2002.[77] But the attempt to claim Juan Diego as a symbol of Mary's favor to the Mexican Indians goes back earlier, receiving a marked emphasis as far back as the 1930s. It has borne rich ideological fruit in new efforts to "indianize" Catholicism in recent decades.

The second half of the twentieth century saw a gradual reconciliation of the Catholic Church and the Mexican state. The laws against public displays of religion were allowed to remain unenforced and then were gradually rescinded. The Mexican church more and more reappeared in public space, to the alarm of a Mexican secularism concerned with maintaining a high wall of separation between church and state. But the political stances of the Catholic Church were no longer only on the right. Liberation theology and notions of a "preferential option for the poor" as the true Christian gospel had pushed the faith and politics of many priests and bishops to the left. The bishop of Cuernavaca, Sergio Mendez Arceo, was Marxist and pro-Cuban; the bishop of Chiapas, Samuel Ruíz, was pro-Indian and suspected by the Mexican government of standing behind the Zapatista rebellion of 1994.[78] Other Mexican prelates were suspected of conspiring to undermine these bishops of the left, siding with the Vatican's suspicions of liberation theology and with mon-eyed corporate elites. Thus, conflict among right, left, and center came to mark the politics of Catholic commitment. When the PRI was defeated in the election of 2000 and the new president, Vicente Fox, took office, he made a point of going first to Mass at the shrine of the Virgin of Guadalupe. A Mexican president in 2000 could now publicly present himself as a Guadalupano.

During the 1980s and 1990s, liberation theology, feminist theology, and "Indian" theology interacted to both reinterpret Guadalupe and reclaim indigenous religious traditions as positive. Liberation theology developed a reinterpretation of the tra-ditional Jewish and Christian dualism between the true God and idolatry. For lib-eration theologians, such as Pablo Richard, idolatry, or the worship of false gods, was seen as a false use of the name of God to justify violence, injustice, and death.[79] Such idolatry took place among nominal Christians whose "god" was money, power, or war. The true God was the God of life, the God of love and justice for all. This new understanding of the true God and idols allowed a new approach to the confrontation of Spanish Catholicism and the Nahua people.

In her article "Quetzalcóatl y el Dios Cristiano," Elza Tamez, professor of bib-lical studies at the Universidad Bíblico de América Latina in Costa Rica, applied this understanding of God and the idols to the Mexican conquest.[80] Tamez argues that the Nahuas had an authentic tradition of the God of life in Quetzalcóatl, but that the Aztecs distorted this native vision of a beneficent God whose representa-tive served the community and forbade human sacrifice. The Aztecs, she writes, co-opted Quetzalcóatl into their religion of war and human sacrifice, led by the war God Huitzilopochtli.

In effect, there was within Nahuatl religion both a true understanding of God as the God of life and a distorted view of God as an idol of death. But the Spanish also brought with them an idolatrous god of death that justified their violent conquest and the destruction of the Indians. This Spanish idol of death was far from the true God of life of Jesus Christ. The Indian leaders deplored the violence of this Spanish god but were also able to glimpse behind the Spanish teaching something of a true God of life who resembled Quetzalcóatl. Whether or not Tamez correctly interprets the Aztec tradition, her essay represents a new way for Christians to find positive religious meaning in indigenous religion and at the same time critique their own traditions, without imagining an apostolic evangelization of Mexico by St. Thomas. Tamez assumes a universal revelation of the true God accessible to peoples of all religions as well as a general tendency to will to power that distorts religion into a system of domination. As a Protestant, Tamez does not discuss the Tonantzin-Guadalupe relationship.

Brazilian Catholic feminist theologians Ivone Gebara and Maria Clara Bingemer attempted a feminist reinterpretation of Mary in their book *Mary, Mother of God, Mother of the Poor*.[81] Mary, in opting for the poor, also opts for women as the oppressed of the oppressed. Gebara and Bingemer sought to free "Marianismo" from the taint of being a tool of the conservative church to pacify and subordinate women. In Mary, women are empowered to struggle for justice, emulating Mary in the Magnificat, who lauds herself as the one through whom "the mighty are put down from their thrones and the poor lifted up" (Luke 1:52). Bingemer and Gebara see the Virgin of Guadalupe, in particular, as representing God's choice of the conquered, oppressed Indian people of the Americas and the vindication of their despised culture, uniting Mary with the Mother Goddess Tonantzin.[82]

The reinterpretation of the Virgin of Guadalupe as supporting the struggles for justice of the poor mestizos, the Indians, and women took on new creativity in the United States, where Chicanos as a whole see themselves as oppressed by the dominant Anglos. In the farmworkers' strikes, led by César Chávez, banners imprinted with the picture of the Virgin of Guadalupe led the movement of insurgent Mexican agricultural laborers.

In *Goddess of the Americas*, a group of essays written originally in English and authored mostly by Chicanos and Mexicans living in the United States, writers and artists skeptical of the historicity and piety of the traditional devotion nonetheless reclaim the meaning of Guadalupe.[83] Some authors celebrate Guadalupe as a covert continuation of Mexican goddess traditions. They see this presumed continuation of goddess traditions under the cover of Guadalupe as empowering their struggles as feminists. One such writer, Clarissa Pinkola Estés, author of *Women Who Run with the Wolves*,[84] imagines a Guadalupe who can lift up the women whom society despises and connect them with elemental earth energies:

> My Guadalupe is a young woman gang leader in the sky
> She does not appear as a woman in light blue
> She is serene, yes, with the serenity of a great ocean.
> She obeys, yes, as the dawn obeys the line of the horizon.
> She is sweet, yes, like an immense forest filled with sweet maple trees.
> She has a great heart, an enormous sanctity
> And like any young woman gang leader, a solid pair of hips.
> Her embrace sustains us all . . . [85]

The history outlined in this chapter indicates the remarkable ideological amplitude of the figure of the Virgin of Guadalupe. She can be adapted to Creole, mestizo, or Indian celebration of identity as well as the merger of these identities in "la Raza" (the new race). She can be used by the left and the right, revolutionaries and reactionaries, feminists and defenders of traditional femininity. In all this diversity, she is always a way of claiming "Mexicanidad" (Mexicanness), a Mexicanness that remains convinced, in the midst of victories and defeats, that, if all else fails, there is a divine mother who loves us. Or, in the words of Octavio Paz, "The Mexican people, after more than two centuries of experiments and defeats, have faith only in the Virgin of Guadalupe and the National Lottery."[86]

EIGHT

Mary and Wisdom
in Protestant Mystical
Millennialism

MARY AND FEMALE SYMBOLS IN THE REFORMATION

Paul Tillich, a leading twentieth-century Protestant theologian, declared, in the first volume of his *Systematic Theology:* "Just as Apollo has no revelatory significance for Christians, the Virgin Mary reveals nothing to Protestants."[1] This statement epitomizes the view that Mariology is simply a closed book for the Protestant tradition, a heretical growth to be excised by responsible New Testament exegesis. Yet this is not quite the last word for Reformation theology's response to Catholic Mariology. The Reformers themselves reveal a more nuanced view: not a total rejection but a refocusing of Mariology on its Christological core.

Martin Luther himself admitted to a warm affection for Mary that was strong in his Catholic youth and never entirely left him. In his *Table Talk*, Luther recounted an incident from his student days when he suffered a life-threatening wound, which evoked his spontaneous prayers to Mary: "The blood gushed from the wound and could not be stopped.... There [Luther] was in danger of death and cried out, 'Mary help!' 'I would have died,' he now added, 'with my trust in Mary.' Afterwards during the night, while he was in bed, the wound broke open. He almost bled to death and again prayed to Mary."[2] Luther told this tale ruefully, wishing that he had put his primary trust in Christ rather than Mary.

Nevertheless, Luther retained in his theology the main developments of patristic Mariology, rejecting disputed medieval additions. He had no question that Christ was born of the Virgin Mary, and he assumed Mary's virginity in Christ's birth.[3]

As did John Calvin, Luther supported the concept of Mary's perpetual virginity, and hence Jerome's argument that the "brothers and sisters of Jesus" in the New Testament were cousins, although Luther opined that her virginity was not important. Both Luther and Calvin argued for the doctrine of the Theotokos, on the Christological grounds that in Christ the two natures, human and divine, commingle, and hence Mary can be called Mother of God, although Calvin specifically refused to use this title lest it cause misunderstanding among Christians who did not understand its doctrinal basis.[4]

Luther eventually rejected the doctrine of the Assumption as lacking any scriptural basis.[5] He also saw the Immaculate Conception as violating the concept of universality of sin and the dependence of all humans on Christ's forgiveness, the same reason given by the theologians of the High Middle Ages. While Luther insisted that Mary, like all humans, was conceived in sin, he was open in his early writings to the possibility of purification in preparation for the virgin birth, an idea he later abandoned.[6] But most important for Luther and Calvin was that these divine gifts to Mary had nothing to do with any special merit on her part. Mary must never become a mediator, advocate, or means of grace in her own right. Rather, she must remain only an elect instrument of God for the birth of his son.

In their view, any development that made Mary a co-redemptrix, a focus of reverence in herself, rather than a sign pointing to the one means of redemption, Christ, had to be totally rejected. This also meant that the medieval split between Mary as the merciful, forgiving one, who intervenes to soften Christ's "severity" as judge, must be healed. Christ is both judgment and mercy, and Mary only a pointer to this oneness. There should be no trace of elevating her to divinity. Mary is solely human, not in the sense of "pure nature" but in the sense of sinful humanity, utterly dependent on divine grace. She can be seen as the "type" of the church, not as sinless Mother Church but simply as the type of the community of the faithful, redeemed by Christ's grace despite their unworthiness. Protestant images of Mary, such as Lucas van Leyden's *The Virgin with Two Angels* (1523), show her as a peasant woman with a fat baby. The two angels, despite their wings, look like peasant children peeking at the baby. There is nothing glorious or regal about this earthy figure (fig. 45).[7]

Key to any evangelical view of Mary is her "fiat" to God, by which she accepts her own role as elect instrument of God: "Be it done to me according to thy word." Here, Mary can be seen as the type or image of the true Christian relation to God, as *sola fide, sola gratia*. As one chosen by God to be a passive instrument in his redemptive work in Christ, Mary responds to grace through faith. This faithful

FIGURE 45
The Virgin with Two Angels, by Lucas van Leyden, 1523. (Yale University Art Gallery)

response does not itself rebound to some merit on her part but is the work of grace in her. In this sense, and only in this sense, can Mary be seen as the model of the church, of the life of faith through grace.[8]

The Reformers also discarded the role of saints as mediators or advocates who stand between individuals and Christ and who can be sources of help in themselves. Saints, like Mary, were simply examples of faithful Christians, not intermediaries. The effect of this rejection of a pluralistic world of saintly persons who mediate between ordinary Christians and Christ was the virtual elimination of any female images of the holy in Protestant spirituality, which consequently became more exclusively masculine.

This masculinization was augmented by the loss of any remnant of sophiology (Wisdom theology) in the works of the Reformers. The Wisdom of Solomon, a book that had been such a rich source of female personification of God's mediating Wisdom for the medieval tradition, was relegated to apocryphal status, no longer a revealed text for preaching or commentary. The female personification of Wisdom in Proverbs also was ignored. Luther and other Reformers continued to comment on the Song of Songs, but its bridal imagery lost its mystical meaning. For Luther, the Song of Songs signified the relation of the church to Christ, or the people of God to God. These people could be spoken of as a bride married to the bridegroom Christ—but simply in the sense of the church's election through grace received in faith, not in the sense of an ecstatic mutual communion: "[Solomon] makes God the bridegroom and this people the bride, and in this mode he sings how much God loves that people, how many and how rich the gifts He lavishes and heaps upon it, and finally how He embraces and cherishes the same people with such goodness and mercy which no bridegroom has ever embraced or cherished his bride."[9]

Although female symbols for the holy were virtually eliminated in magisterial Protestant spirituality, there remained a vivid female symbolism for evil. Witchcraft persecutions were renewed among Protestants of the sixteenth and seventeenth centuries, and images of witches figured prominently in popular iconography (fig. 46). The evil Church of Rome was represented as the Whore of Babylon from the book of Revelation. Protestant artists created vivid images of her pompous display surrounded by Catholic kings and prelates and crowned with the three-tiered papal tiara (fig. 47).

Any female leadership was to be strictly rejected, and women who assumed such leadership were themselves considered sources of evil in society. Commenting on Ecclesiastes 7:26—"And I have found more bitter than death the woman whose heart is snares and nets and whose hands are fetters; he who pleases God escapes

FIGURE 46

Witches concocting an ointment to be used for flying to the Sabbath. Etching by Hans Baldung Grien, 1514. (From Ernst and Johanna Lehner, *Devils, Demons, Death and Damnation* [New York: Dover Publications, 1971])

FIGURE 47

Illustration to Apocalypse 17, the Whore of Babylon, 1534. In *Biblia*, Martin Luther's translation of the Bible, published in Wittenberg in 1534. (Courtesy Bibliothèque nationale de France)

her, but the sinner is taken by her"—Luther wrote: "He is speaking about a woman who administers things and arrogates wisdom and ruling power to herself. He is not speaking about the wrath of women, although it is true that a woman has a more tempestuous nature than a man." Arguing that women therefore were not to be despised and that their weakness must be distinguished from their being as God's creation, Luther went on to insist that women's sphere was limited to the household by divine decree:

> For she was created to be around the man, to care for children and to bring them up in an honest and godly way and to be subject to the man. Men, on the other hand, are commanded to govern and have the rule over women and the rest of the household. But if a woman forsakes her office and assumes authority over her husband, she is no longer doing her own work, for which she was created, but a work that comes from her own fault and from evil. For God did not create this sex for ruling and therefore they never rule successfully.[10]

Luther himself was not without his mystical side, drawn from the traditions of the late medieval German mysticism of *gelassenheit*, or resignation to the will of God, even to the point of accepting one's own damnation. But by the end of the sixteenth century, the victory of Lutheran scholasticism virtually eliminated any focus on an inward transformative spirituality in favor of a strict acceptance of orthodox Lutheran doctrine. This dry acceptance of externalized doctrine "announced" to sinners soon created a revolt, however. This reaction was expressed in pietist "conventicles," which signaled a quest for a warmer spirituality that believers could experience inwardly as personal transformation and communion with God, not merely an acquiescence to "objective" doctrine.[11] The mystical side of Luther, as well as its roots in the medieval mystical tradition and its older sources in church fathers such as Origen and Gregory Nyssa, was reclaimed. In the process, the figure of Wisdom was rediscovered and redeveloped for some forms of Protestant mysticism, particularly those linked to renewed millennial hope.

WISDOM IN THE MYSTICISM OF JACOB BOEHME

A key figure in this development was the self-taught German mystic Jacob Boehme (1575–1624). Boehme was the son of a prosperous farmer who lived near the town of Gorlitz in Silesia. Jacob was apprenticed as a shoemaker and married in 1599 to a butcher's daughter, who bore him four sons. Throughout his life, he was an active businessman. But he also experienced mystical revelations, beginning about 1594. His Lutheran pastor, Martin Moller, had read medieval mysticism and created a prayer group, "the conventicle of God's real servants," which Boehme joined, to cultivate a more personal religious experience. The Gorlitz region was also influenced by a religious ferment of ideas, which included those of the Protestant spiritual thinker Caspar Schwenckfeld (1489–1551), who defended the idea of Christ's "celestial flesh"; the work of the alchemist Theophrastus Bombastus von Hohemheim, known as Paracelsus (1493–1541); the nature mystic Valentine Weigel (1533–1588); Renaissance Neoplatonism; and Jewish Kabbalism. All these traditions would find their echoes in the work of Boehme.[12]

In 1612, Boehme finished his first treatise, *Aurora*, or *Day-Dawning*, drawn from his revelatory experiences. By this time, Gregory Richter, a strict defender of Lutheran orthodoxy, had replaced Moller as pastor. Richter denounced Boehme's work and forbade him to write. Although Boehme kept silent for seven years, he continued to cultivate his mystical interests. In 1619, he began a series of treatises on his visionary understanding of creation, the fall, and redemption. He started to gather a community of enthusiastic supporters, but his new writings aroused the anger of Richter, who again denounced him. In March of 1524, Boehme was forced into exile by the municipal council and went for a short while to Dresden. Returning ill at the end of 1624, he died on November 17.

Boehme's followers Abraham von Franckenberg (1593–1652) and Johann Theodor von Tschech (1595–1649) carried his writings zealously throughout Europe, and his works were translated into many European languages. In 1661, his complete works appeared in English in a translation by John Sparrow (1615–1665). Boehme's influence on German poetry and philosophy was to be considerable, especially through the romantics Novalis, Fichte, Schelling, and Schlegel. Through Boehme, the vision of Wisdom as a female aspect of the divine flowed through mystical and millennialist thought and movements, both Protestant and Catholic, from the seventeenth into the nineteenth centuries.[13]

For Boehme, Wisdom arises out of the self-reflection of God as primal Abyss. From an original unmanifest state, God becomes manifest through self-reflection. Wisdom is the mirror through which God becomes self-conscious, both expressing the potentiality of God's being and disclosing the manifold beings of creation. Boehme speaks of Wisdom both as God's self-reflecting mirror and as the corporeality of the divine spirit through which all things are produced. She is not one member of the Trinity among the three of the divine self-disclosure, but she is the substance, or being, of the whole Trinity in which Son and Spirit subsist. As Father and Mother, God/Sophia is the source of our true life and being and that of the whole creation. As Boehme puts it in a prayer:

> You are our Father in whom we have received our life, and Your word is our mother that bore us out of Your creation and formed us after the image of Your revelation. Our soul and mind is, O God, Father, Your image, and our body is an image of Your outflowing Word. This Word is our eternal mother in whose body we are begotten and nourished.[14]

This self-manifestation of God in the mirror of divine Wisdom creates duality, or differentiation, in God, which is manifest in the plurality of created things, of which Wisdom is the collective expression and the material (maternal) ground of being. This differentiation is integrated in the Spirit as a harmonious synthesis. But it also becomes the basis for a contrariety of love and wrath in God when creatures seek to take possession of their own being and thus split the original harmony in which God's self-differentiated being and its extension in the manyness of creation originally existed.

For Boehme, as for the medieval mystical tradition generally, Lucifer, rather than Adam and Eve, is the first culprit of this primal fall, which transformed the original harmony of creation into hostile duality. Lucifer's sins were the refusal to subsist as a manifestation of the being of God and the attempt to seize dominion over the world as his own kingdom. He wished to seize the "mother," the maternal corporeality of being, as his own possession. This broke the original harmony and projected the split-off negativity of the original contrariety as a demonic, delusory universe, cut off from its source of being.

Both Lucifer and Adam were captured in their false desires, in the mother, and broke themselves off from resignation out of God and were captured by the will's spirit with the desire in the mother and gained immediately dominion over the creature. As a result Lucifer stayed in the angry, dark, inert fire sources, and the same fire was revealed in his will's spirit by which the creature in desire became an enemy to the love and meekness of God.[15]

This fall is recapitulated in Adam, but in a secondary and redeemable way. Adam, the collective human being, is God's second step (after the angels) to create an expression of God's self that reflects the fullness of God's self-manifestation in its spiritual and corporal (inner and outer) nature. Adam originally was the microcosm of the creation, imaging both God's self-manifestation and the external created world as the epitome of the whole. Adam was originally androgynous, containing both male and female, and being able to bring forth creations from him/herself. Adam's corporeality was "crystalline," or heavenly, manifesting the spiritual corporeality of Wisdom, the divine mother. Boehme writes: "This was the holy Paradise. Thus man stood in heaven and also in the world and was lord of all creatures of this world. . . . so man also was created in such an image and likeness according to time and eternity, but in an eternal immortal life that was without antagonism and opposition."[16]

But Adam, tempted by Lucifer, desires to take possession of his own kingdom rather than simply being an outflow of the being of God/Wisdom. Boehme sees this primal apostasy as expressed in Adam's "falling asleep," losing original unitary consciousness, and in this sleep falling into a duality of good and evil in which male and female are separated:

Then through the *fiat* God made from him woman, out of the *venus matrix*, that is, out of that characteristic which Adam had the begetter in himself; out of one body two, and he divided the characteristics of the *tinctures* [transformative elements] as into the element of watery and fiery constellations. . . . The self love-desire was taken from Adam and formed in the woman after his likeness. Therefore man now greatly desires the woman's *matrix*, and the woman desires the man's *limbus*, as the fiery element, the cause of the true soul in which the fire's *tinctur* is understood. These two were one in Adam and in this the magical birth consisted.[17]

This splitting of the primal androgynous Adam into the fiery and watery elements also awakens the desire for self-possession, the fall into an "I," or egoism, that loses its original unity with the divine ground of being. For Boehme, as for the Origenist tradition on which this idea depends, this causes a coarsening or hardening of the original spiritual corporeality of humanity. The human body becomes mortal and bestial, filled with lustful desires. Humans grow ashamed of their own bodies and must hide them with clothing.

Now was the vanity of the flesh awakened and the dark fire-world received governance and dominion in the vanity of earthiness. Immediately the beautiful heavenly image, of the heavenly, divine world's being faded. Here Adam and Eve died to the kingdom of heaven and awoke in the external world; the beautiful soul was corrupted to the love of God as to the holy power and characteristic and angry wrath awoke in its place in her, the dark fire-world, and she became in one part of her soul, in the inner nature, a half-devil, and in another part, the external world, a beast. This is the goal of death and the gates of hell.[18]

But God is unwilling to let his beautiful image, the human, fall into evil and alienation. God chooses to bring about what Boehme calls God's "counter-stroke" by becoming human and dying on the cross, covering divine wrath with divine love, and opening again the gates to paradise: "God became man that He might break death, and change hell into the great love again, and destroy the vanity of the devil."[19] The soul, sunk in its alienation and self-delusion, is "met by our Lord Jesus Christ, with God's love and wrath, who came into this world to bring to nothing the works of the Devil, to bring judgment over all godless acts. He spoke into it as with great power out of his suffering, passion and death, and smashed the devil's work in it and opened the way for it to His grace and He looked on it with His compassion and called it back again to be converted and repentant, because He wished to redeem it from such a spectre-like image and to lead it back again to Paradise."[20]

In Boehme's view, this work of Christ in becoming human, suffering, and dying for humanity is essentially an expression of God's love for human beings. But this act of love does not so much open new grounds for our return to paradise as it reveals to us the existing grounds, established as the true basis of our being in God from creation. Thus, Boehme can be said to have a "creation-based" spirituality. Our being in God is our true nature that still subsists, even though we are out of touch with it in our state of alienation. But the immediate effect of this revelation of God's love in Christ is to awaken the soul's terror and fear as it realizes the extent of its false and evil state of being and alienation from God. Thus, the first work of conversion is the experience of divine wrath and judgment:

> When it happened that the spark of divine light was revealed to it, it saw itself both in its work and will and was aware that it stood in the hell of God's wrath and knew it was a spectre and *monstrum* before God and the kingdom of heaven. It was so terrified at this that greatest anguish awoke in it, because the Judgment of God was revealed in it.[21]

This experience of divine wrath awakens a tug of war in the soul, in which the devil tries to convince the soul that its condition is hopeless and that the ways of the world are too comfortable to leave behind. Moreover, to leave worldly ways behind is to awaken the world's scorn and to risk loss of "worldly honour and majesty." Boehme describes with great power the confusion and distress of the soul, as it struggles with its inclination to repent and return to God, the tugs of worldly pleasure and comfort, and its fears of facing the full reality of its fallenness.[22]

For Boehme, conversion is fundamentally a transformation in the soul, from self-will to the "resigned will"—that is, giving up all self-will to will only what God wills in us. This conversion to the resigned will undoes the original act of apostasy of the fall and reunites the being of the creature with God as an outflowing of the being of the creator, rather than as separated self-possession and dominion in itself. Here, we see the continuity of Boehme's spirituality with the medieval mystical tradition of *gelassenheit*, expressed in radical form by mystics such as Marguerite Porete. Boehme, however, does not explore with the same psychological complexity as Porete all the ways the soul creates gestures in itself of resigning its own will and dying to the "I," or independent self, which are ever more subtle expressions of self-will (see chapter 6). Rather, Boehme seems to think that this act of resigning the "I" is possible for the soul as its true nature. But one must grow into this process, against the pulls of worldly comforts and the fears of divine wrath and judgment that reveal the extent of fallenness.

Sophia mysticism plays a key role for Boehme in this restoration of the soul to its union with God. Christ opens up the gates of paradise through his acts of unconditional love in his incarnation and death, but it is Sophia who reunites the soul with God. In a reverse bridal mysticism, Boehme images the soul as a male bridegroom, but a dependent and needy lover. Sophia is the queenly lady whose love restores the soul. In language reminiscent of Hadewijch and medieval *mystique courtoise*, Boehme portrays the soul as a knight errant, willing to risk all trials for the love of the heavenly lady. "For if a man wishes to obtain the noble Virgin Sophia, Her honour and love, he must make such a vow to Her in his resolution and mind." This means being willing to give up and lose all worldly honors and comforts rather than "lose the noble love of Sophia."[23]

In his 1622 treatise *True Repentance*, Boehme creates an extended dialogue between the soul and Sophia. The soul professes its undying love for Sophia, promises not to stray again from her love, and begs her for final transformation: "Now I discover your promised truth, O sweet Love. Let me not bend from You again. Give unto me Your crown of pearls and stay with me. Be my possession that I may eternally rejoice in You." Sophia, in turn, reproaches the soul for its unfaithfulness to her and recounts her many efforts to call it back to her when it had "taken the devil as a lover," "broken my marriage," . . . "and lost me, your God-given bride." Without the love of the soul, Sophia refers to herself as having become "a crushed being, without the strength of your fire's might."[24]

In these passages of "love play" between the soul and Sophia, it appears that not only does the soul need Sophia in order to transform itself into its original nature as image of God, but also Sophia needs the soul to give power to her spiritual purity. In the divine alchemy, the soul and Wisdom represent two principles, light and fire. Only when "married" together is the harmony of the spiritual world reestablished. Thus, Sophia says to the soul:

Without your fire's might I have not been able to be happy, for you are my husband; by you my own brightness is revealed. You are able to reveal my hidden miracles in your fire-life and lead them to majesty. Apart from me you are a dark house in which is only anguish and pain and an enemy's torment. O noble bridegroom, keep your face before me and give me your fire-beams. Lead your desire into me, and ignite me. By my meekness, I shall then change your fire-beams into white-light and direct my love through your fire-beams into your fire's essence and I shall kiss you eternally.[25]

Although the soul entreats its divine lady to give it the "pearl" of final transformation, she insists that this must be postponed. The soul is still marred by its long apostasy and must undergo a process of change through its love for her until it comes to full transformation. Ultimately, for Boehme, this can happen only at the final separation of "contraries" and the laying down of the gross external body in the future *eschaton* (the heavenly consummation of creation).

Boehme's belief in an original and future spiritual body that represents the unfallen and redeemed state is reflected in his Mariology. Mary represents original uncorrupted humanity before Adam's fall, which subsists in a hidden way within corrupted humanity, and which she transmits as her "woman's seed." Through this transmitted seed, she bears Christ, the representative of the renewed uncorrupted humanity, as the counter to Adam's transmission of the seed of the fall:

> . . . the promise of the covenant in the root of David in Mary the Virgin who was the internal kingdom of hidden humanity . . . in this Virgin Mary in the promised goal of the covenant, of which all the prophets had foretold, the eternally speaking Word, which has created all things according to its highest and deepest love and humility, moved in the name of JESUS, and brought the living, divine heavenly being into the heavenly part of Adam's corrupted humanity to which he had died in Paradise, into Mary's seed.[26]

Although human and a "daughter of Eve" in her external body, the Virgin Mary preserves in her internal being the original paradisal humanity that would reproduce itself "in a magical, heavenly manner, as in the true woman's seed of the heavenly being that was corrupted in Paradise."[27]

Although Boehme does not explicitly identify the Virgin Mary with Sophia, she appears to represent the original spiritual corporeality of Wisdom, lost in paradise but transmitted through her to Christ. Christ reopens the gates of paradise, but it is love for Sophia that leads the soul to that transformative union in which the paradise of uncorrupted soul and spiritual body is restored.

Boehme argues, however, that the threats to this transformed state remain as long as we are in the gross fallen body and surrounded by the fallen world ruled over by the devil. We are tempted to continue in our fallen state not only by the temptations of the world, the flesh, and the devil but also by the corruption of the church. For Boehme, the greatest trick of the devil is to distort the message of Christ's call to repentance into external doctrines and rational arguments. Redemption is not ideas, but transformation of the soul from self-will to the divine will. Those who are truly transformed love one another and transcend all sectarian division.

But the devil distorts the call to repentance into teachings about repentance, thus creating what Boehme calls the "mouth church" and the "stone church," where people argue about correct definitions and repudiate and persecute one another for errors of external rationality.[28] Clearly reflecting his own experiences of being denounced and persecuted by church orthodoxy, Boehme sees this "mouth and stone church" as hostile to the true children of God. Those who are truly transformed in God leave behind all worldly honors and spontaneously recognize and love one another. Such true Christians are threatening to those of the "mouth church," who want to talk and argue about repentance but not really live it. True Christians are ever the object of its wrath and scorn. Thus, one of the trials of those who would follow the way of Christ-Wisdom is that this path of life will draw persecution from those who pretend to represent Christ's church but are actually the devil's final snare to keep them tied to the world.

With truly resigned will, which surrenders the "I" to God's willing and working in them, Christians walk the path of transformed life. They are sustained by the inner community of like-minded souls who love and serve one another, but they can expect only hatred and scorn from those of the world and its "stone church." Their external selves still dwell in the world, although increasingly freed from its temptations. They await the final eschatological transformation in which the gross mortal body will be laid down and its manifestations in the world will disappear. Spiritual, or "crystalline," corporeality will be restored, and God and God's creation will return to their original harmony.

In this harmony, the separation of male and female will also be overcome and the spiritual androgyny of the original Adam restored.

This good power of the mortal body is to come again, to live or remain eternally in a beautiful, transparent crystalline, material characteristic in spiritual flesh and blood. Just as the good powers of earth, so the earth itself will be crystalline and the divine light will shine in all being. . . . There shall be neither man nor woman but all shall be like God's angels, androgynous virgins, neither daughter, son, brother nor sister but all one sex in Christ, all in one like a tree with its branches and yet separate creatures; but God all in all.[29]

WISDOM MYSTICISM IN JANE LEADE

Although Boehme's teachings may have aroused anger and opposition in his local church and among town leaders, small but enthusiastic bands of followers soon arose across Europe. One such group was organized in London by a marginalized clergyman, John Portage (1607–1681), together with the visionary Jane Leade (1623–1704), who formed what they called the Philadelphian Society. Leade was the daughter of a prosperous Norfolk family. Even as a teenager, she experienced deep religious sensitivity and once fled from a family Christmas party on hearing a voice whisper to her, "Cease from this. I have another Dance to lead thee in, for this is vanity."[30] At twenty, she married a distant relative, William Leade, and bore four daughters, two of whom died in infancy. Her husband died in 1670, when she was forty-seven, leaving her impoverished but also free to pursue her religious inclinations. She joined the Portage circle at this time and became acquainted with Boehme's thought. She was accepted as the leading visionary of the group and published a number of treatises of her own revelatory experiences.

Beginning in 1670, Leade experienced personal appearances of Sophia in which this heavenly woman promised to be her personal guide: "Sophia appeared to me in the figure of a woman with a very friendly and dignified appearance. Her countenance radiated like the sun and She was dressed in a garment of translucent gold." Sophia says to Leade:

> Look at me! I am the eternal Virgin Wisdom of God who you always wished to see just once. I am come to unveil to you my profound treasures of God's Wisdom, and I will be to you what Rebecca was to Jacob, a true and natural mother, for you will be begotten in my bosom, conceived and born anew. You will recognize something active in you which will leave you no rest until Wisdom has been born in the depths of your soul. Think about my words until I come to you again.

In a further vision three days later, Wisdom tells Leade: "Behold your Mother and know that you must enter into a covenant with me in order to be in harmony with the laws of the new creation which will be revealed to you."[31]

Leade's mystical thought follows the outlines of Boehme's theology. Wisdom is seen as emerging from the Abyss of God as God's divine self-reflection. Lucifer falls as a result of his effort to seize dominion in self-will. Adam, originally androgynous and with a spiritual, immortal body, falls into a gross mortal body with self-will. But Leade's visions concentrate on the restoration side of this worldview. She believes herself to be living at the end of the present fallen era and on the eve of the great restoration, in which the soul is being reborn through divine Wisdom and the fallen bodies are transformed into spiritual bodies. She is commissioned by Wisdom to spread this good news throughout the world in the short time that remains before the millennial transformation of creation.[32] The Philadelphians saw themselves not as a new church but as the community of spiritual renewal within all churches.

Leade sees visions of Wisdom's land as a spiritual kingdom presided over by Wisdom as princess. Wisdom is followed by a company of the redeemed, described as an "illustrious troop of [Heroines] divine, celestial Amazons, untaught to yield."[33] Led by their mother and bride, Wisdom, they create the heavenly metropolis, or mother city, constructed with brilliant architecture as the heavenly Jerusalem.[34] Leade, guided into the edges of this brilliant community, finds herself discomfited because she does not yet have a "clarified body" and is a "stranger in their region"— that is, she has not yet been totally transformed and attained a spiritual body.[35]

But Sophia, the "Majestical Princess" who rules this realm, speaks to her, saying that "this is the only thing that is worthy to be known." Leade is told that the time is coming when the beast (gross body and passions) will be tamed and the heavenly world renewed. The age of this world is spent, and Solomon's day is expected, in which Wisdom shall flow from the "life-magical tree." The "seed pearl" (the soul) presently smothered in the low valley will mount to its heavenly realm, "where Wisdom has her school." Sophia will once again move souls to know this high mystery. "Wisdom's theatre may be known by her own that are born anew. . . . Every prepared heart shall become Wisdom's spring of Holy Understanding and Theatre. . . . Now is beginning of a new creation."[36]

In Leade's 1683 treatise *Revelation of Revelations*, on the interpretation of the book of Revelation, she sees Wisdom as the "woman clothed with the sun" who is described in chapter 12 of this New Testament book. This woman, who flees into the wilderness to give birth to the messianic child, restores the capacity to give birth from oneself that was lost to Adam when he fell from paradise. God created Adam male and female as one, but in the fall the female was taken out of him. Virginal androgynous humanity is restored in the woman, who brings forth the messianic child to possess again what Adam and Eve lost. She is "greater than Mary." Leade speaks of her as a "female" androgyne. Her virginal acts are "not limited to male or female, for she may assume either according to her good pleasure. She is both male and female for angelical generation." She is rooted in the foundations of being, for she was born "from eternity before the creation of heaven and earth." She was before all as the "co-efficient creating partner of the Deity which formed all things out of nothing." She is "God's spouse and mate" and the "virgin matter out of which the soul was made." Now we are to "be born again out of her Virgin womb, as the mother of the true Virgin Church."[37]

Leade's originality lies in her translation of Boehme's bridal mysticism of male soul married to heavenly Wisdom into a female-centered vision in which she as a woman is reborn through Wisdom. In Wisdom, woman is restored to her original capacity to give birth from herself and bring forth a new humanity, no longer split into male and female, soul and body, but united in renewed harmony as God's image and self-expression. Wisdom is Leade's "mother-element," through which she herself is reborn. She is her heavenly counterpart, teacher, ruler, and leader of the heavenly kingdom of the redeemed. Through Wisdom, Leade claimed her own voice as visionary writer, teacher, and church leader of the messianic humanity of the Philadelphians.

WISDOM AND LOVE IN EMANUEL SWEDENBORG

Whereas Leade gave us a female-centered Wisdom mysticism, the Swedish scientist-mystic Emanuel Swedenborg (1688–1772) translated divine androgyny into an androcentric, socially male-dominant form. Swedenborg was the son of a Lutheran bishop, Jesper Swedberg, a pietist reformer and politically ambitious cleric.[38] (The name was changed to reflect the ennoblement of the family.) Emanuel Swedenborg's feelings of alienation from his father and from the conservative theological teachers of Uppsala University were translated into the pursuit of science, reflecting the new Enlightenment faith that all truth could be known by empirical investigation. He traveled and lived at various times in England, France, and the Netherlands, studying Newton and the new physics as well as chemistry, geology, and engineering. In Sweden, he was able to win appointments to the Royal Board of Mines, a royal franchise, and pioneer a series of inventions to facilitate mine work.[39]

Swedenborg then turned his interest to anatomy and traveled to Germany and France to study the physiology of the body, hoping to understand the mind-body relationship. Approaching the nature of the soul through minute study of the physical organs of the body, he became convinced that there exists a subtle life energy or substance of which the body itself is the manifestation and conduit. This spiritual energy is expressed in the organic material world, but it also exists in a higher form in the spiritual world that our souls enter after death.

In his later years, Swedenborg turned increasingly to this higher spiritual world and shocked his scientific colleagues in Stockholm with his conviction that he himself could converse with these ascended souls in the higher world. He also began to work out his theological views in treatises such as *Angelic Wisdom Concerning the Divine Love and Wisdom* (1763), the twelve-volume *Arcana Celestia* (1749–1756), *Heaven and Hell* (1758), and *The True Christian Religion* (1771). In his 1768 volume *Conjugial Love,* he explored particularly the sexual, gendered nature of bodies and souls and the continuation or realignment of conjugal relations in the next life.

In Swedenborg's view, God or the divine nature consists of the dynamic interaction of love and wisdom; all created things have their life from the interconnection of these two dynamic forces. Although Swedenborg sees the two genders as reflections of this divine duality and interconnection of love and wisdom, he does not discuss explicitly the female aspect of God. Rather, it seems that in God the two are united in an androcentric whole, although separated into two in humans.

> . . . Love together with Wisdom in its very essence is in God. For He loves everyone from Love in Itself and leads everyone from Wisdom in Itself. . . .
> It is from the fact that the Divine Essence is Love and Wisdom that all things in the universe have a relation to Good and Truth. For everything that proceeds from Love is called Love and what proceeds from Wisdom is called truth.[40]

Swedenborg goes on to relate these two principles to the energies of heat and light, "for heat corresponds to love and light to wisdom." He also connects love and wisdom to the *esse* and *existere* of God: "Because Divine Esse is Divine Love and Divine existere is Divine Wisdom. So these similarly are one distinctly. They are said to be one distinctly because love and wisdom are two distinct things, yet so united that love is of wisdom and wisdom is of love; for in wisdom love *is* and in love wisdom *exists*."[41]

For Swedenborg, the fullness of being in anything always comes from dynamic interaction of these two forces, love and wisdom or good and truth, rooted in the nature of God. This finds its ideal expression in marriage—or, rather, what he calls "conjugial love," which often does not coincide with actual legal marriage and can exist outside marriage. Swedenborg deplores the splitting of goodness and truth in much of culture, which allows people to speak of what is true apart from any question of what is good, and about what is good apart from any question of what is true. Fullness of life must always seek the marriage, or commingling, of these two principles. The inclination of men and women to seek each other in "conjugial" love is itself the expression of the quest on the physical level that finds its highest expression in spiritual, or "chaste," love between a man and a woman: "The male and the female were created to be the essential form of the marriage of good and truth. They are that form in their inmost principles and thence in what is derived from those principles in proportion as the interiors of their minds are opened."[42]

This view might suggest that each person is androgynous, that men and women have both goodness and truth. Modern Swedenborgians will draw out this possibility from his writings.[43] But Swedenborg himself insists on a strict, mutually exclusive complementarity of the two genders. He also asserts that humans remain either male or female in the next life and engage in "conjugial" relations in which they experience ideal complementarity, in contrast to the less than ideal relations of legal marriage in this life. "Since a man lives [as] a man after death and man is male and female and there is such a distinction between the male principle and the female principle, that one cannot be changed into the other, it follows that after death the male lives [as] a male and the female [as] a female."[44]

Swedenborg goes on to define the essential distinction between the two:

> In the masculine principle love is inmost and its covering is wisdom . . . whereas in the feminine principle the wisdom of the male is inmost and its covering is love thence derived. . . . the male is the wisdom of love and the female is the love of that wisdom. . . . That the female principle is derived from the male or that the woman was taken out of the man is evident (Genesis 2:21–2) . . . the character of the male is intellectual and that of the female character partakes more of the will principle . . . the male is born into the affection of knowing, understanding and growing wise and the female into the love of conjoining herself with that affection in the male.[45]

Swedenborg insists that these two principles exist in males and females distinctly, essentially, and totally. "They are not exactly similar in a single respect." "The male principle in the male is male in every part of his body, even the most minute, and also in every idea of his thought, and every spark of his affection; and the same is true of the female principle in the female."[46] From this, it follows that these two separate gender principles must continue as male and female in the next life and there seek their fullest "conjunction" in more ideally complementary relations. Swedenborg claimed to be in touch with a number of departed spirits and to have information about their new partners in the next life, which caused some consternation when the still living partner of such a departed person was told that the deceased had taken a different partner in heaven.[47]

Swedenborg's religious writings were widely circulated after his death and translated into many languages. Swedenborgian Societies were founded in a number of countries and continue to exist today. Since Swedenborgians tend to be educated professionals who pride themselves on a rational and scientifically provable spirituality, they have generally had the means to continue to promulgate his teachings. The Swedenborgian Church of North America, founded in 1817, split in 1870 over the issue of the infallibility of Swedenborg's writings. The conservative branch of the church, the General Church of the New Jerusalem of Bryn Athyn, Pennsylvania, believes that millennial redemption has already dawned spiritually through Swedenborg's revelatory writings and those who follow his teachings.[48]

But even conservative Swedenborgians today are being challenged by the contemporary feminist and gay movements, which question the teaching of strict gender complementarity. The Church of the New Jerusalem has historically rejected women's ordination and membership on governing boards, based on Swedenborg's views of gender complementarity, although this is beginning to change. The church argues that leadership demands male intellectual qualities, supposedly lacking in women. Because this lack is seen as essential and ontological and not a result of social biases, according to a strict reading of Swedenborgian anthropology, conservatives claim that the bar to women's ordination cannot be changed. It also follows that homosexual relations can never be acceptable as "conjugial" unions, since such relationships join two male or two female "principles" and fail to connect the male and female principles that are the basis of true union. Again, for traditional Swedenborgians, this is a matter of ontology and not social construction.

In the 1980s, protest began to find its way into the life of this conservative branch of the Swedenborgian church. Women began to demand leadership on governing boards and ordination,[49] and some gay thinkers sought to bend Swedenborgian anthropology in a way that allows greater diversity of partners.[50] But these efforts have been resisted by those who cling to the tradition of mutually exclusive complementarity, rejecting even the Jungian adaptation that males have a recessive femininity (*anima*) and females a recessive masculinity (*animus*).[51]

The more liberal wing of the Swedenborgian church, the General Convention of Swedenborgian Churches, has moved far ahead on these issues, however. It ordained its first woman in 1975 and its first openly gay person in 1997. Today, women make up almost half of its clergy and its leadership structure, as well as 75 percent of its seminarians. These followers see Swedenborg as a visionary yet also recognize that he was culture-bound. Thus, the liberal Swedenborgians feel free to reinterpret the anthropological reflection of divine androgyny as an interrelation of male and female qualities that are found in both men and women.[52]

WISDOM IN THE HARMONY SOCIETY

Another example of a theology of divine androgyny is found in the German millennialist sect known as the Harmony Society, founded by Johann Georg Rapp (1757–1847). The son of a farmer from Württenberg, Germany, Rapp adopted weaving as his trade, married in 1783, and settled in the town of Iptingen, near Stuttgart. After experiencing a religious conversion in which he became convinced that the established Lutheran church was corrupt, he began to gather a group of seekers around him. They broke with the church, refusing to have their children baptized or attend its services. The local civil and religious authorities investigated Rapp's separatists and threatened to expel them from the area.

In 1798, members of the group drew up their articles of faith, in which they declared themselves to believe only in the church as originally established by the apostles, which they regarded themselves as reestablishing. They opposed infant baptism, confirmation, governmental oaths, and military service. By this time, the group had also begun to practice communal living, community of goods, and celibacy. They believed that they were living in the last times of world history, awaiting the millennium. Rapp was deeply influenced by the teaching of Jacob Boehme and also by the writings of Emanuel Swedenborg and the German mystic Johannes Tauler.

Rapp's following grew rapidly; by 1802, some ten to twelve thousand believed in his teachings. The Württenberg government saw his movement as increasingly threatening and began new investigations. At this point, Rapp decided to migrate and take his followers to America. He began to see his community as the embodiment of the "woman clothed with the sun" of Revelation 12 and to believe that they must flee into the wilderness (America), there to await Christ's millennial advent. Rapp and an advance party selected a site, to be called Harmony, in Butler County, Pennsylvania. In 1805, some five hundred Harmonists signed a contract to live together communally, giving over their property to Rapp, who now called himself Father Rapp.

The hardworking Harmonists prospered, building an attractive village supported by orchards, grain fields, vineyards, and the sale of woolen cloth made from the wool of the sheep they raised. In 1814, the society moved west, buying thirty thousand acres in Indiana along the Wabash River. There, they built a second town of fine

brick houses, which included four community houses, granaries, mills, and a cruci-
form church building. In 1824, this entire town was sold to English socialist com-
munitarian Robert Owen. The Harmonists moved back to Pennsylvania, where they
founded their third and last communal town, called Economy. Rapp died in 1847 at
the age of eighty-nine, still expecting the imminent arrival of the millennium. Remnants of the society continued into the twentieth century, although it officially dis-
solved in 1906.[53]

In their religious system, the Harmonists adopted from Boehme a belief in divine androgyny and an original androgynous Adam. God is male and female, with
the divine Wisdom or Sophia manifesting the female aspect of God. Adam created
in God's image was also male and female until the fall, when the female was taken
out of "him" to become a separate being. Celibacy was seen as overcoming sexual
dualism and reestablishing the original biune Adam. Communal living reflected the
Harmonists' belief that they were reestablishing the original church of the apostles,
which held all goods in common. In their retreat to America, they sought to live a
way of perfection in preparation for Christ's second coming, in which the saints
would be transformed and live in androgynous spiritual bodies like that of the original Adam: "This is that first resurrection in which they expect the risen and trans-
figured saints to be fully restored to the image of God by being clothed in bodies
like unto Christ's glorious body and like the dual organization of Adam, when he
first left the creator's hand."[54]

The Harmonists cultivated a lively bridal mysticism focused on the figure of the
divine Sophia as their "goddess," whom they celebrated with many hymns of praise.
Their Sophia hymns are love songs that cast Wisdom as a spiritual spouse through
whose love the (male) Harmonist soul is transformed, frees itself from all carnal
love for human women, and becomes spiritually united with God.

One such hymn appeals to Sophia as guide:

O, Sophia, when thy loving hands carefully have guided my path
Through the thorny rose-bush, let my shadow soar;
You, the Harmonists' goddess, play now your golden strings;
Bind with loving golden chains those who follow you to the designated goal.

Another hymn celebrates the raptures of love with Sophia:

Sophia, from your glances rapture flows into my heart
When a friendly love delights my soul;

O the pure instincts your charm arouses in me,
This flame feeds the blessed heavenly love.

These lines acknowledge the lover's sinful suffering apart from Sophia's love and promises repentant faithfulness:

Sophia, you know my suffering for I have entrusted myself to you,
My praises of love shall resound from my lips for you,
What every prodigal avoids confessing I shall confess today. . . .
Separate I myself from you my limbs anxiously quiver;
My cheeks become pale and wane and from my eyes death shivers;
I sway weak and dying, resembling a moribund figure.

This hymn appeals to Sophia to free the lover from all carnal lust so that he may be spiritually transformed:

O, stay with me, Sophia, let me flee what is distasteful to you,
No matter what it be.
My heart will withdraw, O pure bride,
O make me free from all chains.

Let no Delilah sneak into my heart and rob me of my strength,
Let me be constant and true,
Let nothing ever weaken me through its false brilliance. . . .

O, heal what was wounded, cut what is unclean
Give me, noble Virgin, a virgin-heart;
Give me a hero's spirit for my sufferings;
Let brightly burn in me the light of truth.

I am aware that I cannot be spotless in my spirit, soul and body;
It will be given to me by you, You pure God's brilliance!
So, immaculate Spirit, mirror yourself in me.[55]

Although the Harmony Society consisted of both men and women, its government was highly authoritarian and patriarchal under the control of Father Rapp. Its Sophia mysticism centered on the relation of the male soul seeking its perfection through idealized love for its divine virgin bride, who would transform it into spiritual perfection and free itself from the carnal pleasures represented by phys-

ical women. How women Harmonists saw themselves in the light of this spirituality is unknown.

WISDOM IN SHAKER THEOLOGY

By contrast, the United Society of Christ's Second Appearing—the Shakers—a millennialist sect of English background, developed its belief in divine androgyny in
a much more egalitarian direction, with parallel roles for women alongside men at
every point in its theological and organizational system. The Shakers also were
influenced by Boehme through the English Philadelphians, although their primary
roots lay in a group of "shaking Quakers," or spiritual seekers, established by James
and Jane Wardley in London in the mid-eighteenth century. The Wardley Society
was joined by an unlettered, working-class English mystic, Ann Lee (1736–1784),
who was periodically imprisoned along with other society members for participating in ecstatic religious services.

During one such incarceration, Lee had a series of visions in which she saw that
the original sin of Adam and Eve lay in lustful sexual intercourse. Abstinence from
sex, she came to believe, was necessary to establish the redeemed humanity. Lee
also saw herself as chosen to be Christ's bride and messianic representative for
the establishment of this perfected millennial humanity.[56] A group of followers
gathered around Lee, accepting her divinely elected role. In 1772, Lee had another
vision, which directed the community to migrate to America, where they would
find a place prepared for them to await the messianic advent.[57] Landing in New
York in 1774, Lee and her followers found land in Niskeyuna, near Albany, New
York.

The Shakers were able to gather many converts in the environment of religious
enthusiasm of northern New York and New England in the 1770s and 1780s, but
they also aroused hostility from Americans who were suspicious of their celibacy
and female leadership. Lee and her brother, William Lee, were beaten in a raid by
one such hostile group, and Lee died of her injuries a few months later. The Shakers did not disappear with Lee's death, however. Rather, one of her American converts, Joseph Meacham, took up the leadership of the society and developed its
theological and organizational system. He chose Lucy Wright to be a co-leader.

The Shaker movement continued to expand into the first decades of the nineteenth
century, founding a number of new communal villages from New England to Ken-
tucky. Each local society was divided into families, with the collegiate leadership of
two elders and two elderesses, who acted as spiritual leaders, and two deacons and

two deaconesses, who managed the temporal affairs of the community. Central to the organizational plan worked out by Meacham was a dual male-female leadership, which was seen as reflecting the dual male-female nature of God and the dual male-female redemptive work of Christ and Mother Ann Lee. Celibacy, sexual equality, and community of goods were the keys to the perfected life to which the Shakers aspired.

Meacham's work as theological and organizational interpreter of Shakerism was followed by that of John Dunlavy, Calvin Green, and Benjamin Seth Young, who set down their foundational understanding of revelation in the *Testimony of Christ's Second Appearing*, first published in 1808. This Shaker Bible recasts the Christian Bible and church history in terms of the Shaker vision of divine, human, and Christological androgyny and the parallelism of male and female roles in creation and redemption.

Fundamental to Shaker theology is the belief that God is dual, both male and female. In Genesis 1:27, God is said to have created humanity in "their" image, male and female. It follows, then, for Shakers, that God is male and female, the divine prototype of the maleness and femaleness of God's image, humanity:

> All who profess the Christian name, mutually believe in *one* God, the eternal Father, the creator of heaven and earth; . . . they also believe in the first begotten *son* of God in man, the Saviour of the world, the redeemer of men. . . . the existence of the Son, while it proved the existence of the *Eternal* father proved also the existence of the *Eternal* mother.

According to the Shaker text, the very existence of a son argues for the existence of both a divine father and a divine mother, since there can be no son in either the natural or the spiritual world without both a mother and a father. It also argues that God's consultation with God's self in saying, "Let *us* make man in *our* image," makes it clear that God is more than one: "But it was not the Son with whom the Father spoke or counselled, or with any other being, angel or spirit, save only with the Eternal *Mother*, even *Divine Wisdom*, the Mother of all celestial beings. It was the *Eternal Two* that thus counselled together." The Shaker writers quote the Wisdom passages of Proverbs to show that the Bible recognizes the existence of divine Wisdom as the female partner of God in the creation of the cosmos. They then comment:

> Thus we may see the true order and origin of our existence descending through proper mediations, not only in the state of innocent nature, but

in the state of grace, proceeding from eternal *parentage*, the Eternal Two, as distinctly Two, as *Power* and *Wisdom* are two, and as the *Father* and *Mother* are two, yet immutably, unchangeably, *One Spirit*, One in *Essence* and in *substance*, one in *love* and in *design*, and so of the whole spiritual creation and household of God, *Father* and *Mother*, *Son* and *Daughter*, *Brother* and *Sister*, *Parents* and *children*, in which the order of the natural creation is a similitude.[58]

In the Shaker Bible, Adam was created as a duality both of living soul and animal body and of male and female, imaging the duality of God. But the creation of humanity is incomplete until woman is taken out of Adam and stands alongside him as his companion. This is not seen as a fall but as a completion of the human as male and female. Nevertheless, Eve is described as subordinate to Adam as mind must be subordinated to body. The fall is interpreted as a subverting of right order of male over female, soul over body. This subversion was expressed in lust, which is the root of all sin, wars, violence, and physical passions. The possibility of lust-free reproductive sex was thus lost by the original parents, and sex became an expression of sinful concupiscence.

Redemption takes the form of an increasing control over the lower passions, culminating in a new humanity that transcends sexual relations in a spiritual community of men and women. Jesus is the founder of this new humanity, himself the product of a virgin birth. But, for the Shakers, this redemptive foundation in Jesus is incomplete because it lacks the dispensation of spiritual power that enabled Jesus's followers truly to live the sinless, celibate life. Although they aspired to such a life, Christians of the last nineteen centuries have fallen below this ideal into fornication or else have sought to curb such fornication in marriage.

Only with the second appearing of Christ in a woman, Mother Ann Lee, does the empowerment of millennial humanity begin. She represents the Wisdom, or female, side of God. Without the revelation of this divine Wisdom, redemption in the "male line" remains incomplete and lacking in true transformative power. Just as Adam, the male human, was incomplete without Eve, so the new Adam, Christ, is incomplete without the new Eve, which the Shakers understand not as Mary but as a female counterpart to the male Christ, Ann Lee.

As then the first Adam was not complete, in the order of natural generation, without Eve, the first mother of the human race and children of this world, so neither could the second Adam be complete in the order of spiritual regeneration, without the second Eve, who of course would be manifested in the "first begotten of the dead," in the line of the female, and become the first mother of the redeemed, the children of the Kingdom of promise.[59]

God promised that, in the *restitution of all things*, a woman should stand in her proper lot and order, as the first Mother in the new creation, as Bride of the Redeemer, and co-worker with him in the work of man's redemption and thus according to the promises of God, she now really stands.[60]

The Shakers understood the Genesis 3:15 promise of God to Eve that "she and her seed would crush the serpent's head" (which the earlier Christian tradition understood as referring to Mary) as the promise of a messianic female counterpart to the male Christ. Although this promise took thousands of years to be kept, it was fulfilled in Ann Lee: " . . . thousands of years had passed away since the promise was made in the garden of Eden, concerning the *woman* . . . unto whom the promise was made."[61] This promise was renewed in the revelation of John concerning the "woman clothed in the sun" (Revelation 12). For the Shakers, this messianic mother of Revelation refers to Wisdom, as the mother of the male Christ, and also to the promise of a future manifestation of Wisdom in Ann Lee:

This vision represented Holy Wisdom, the Eternal Mother, who brought forth the "man-child," the Christ, who first appeared in the male order, and which the Dragon sought to devour. . . . Then the Eternal Mother brought forth her own likeness and representative, the Mother Spirit of Christ, in the woman, to whom "was given the two wings of a great eagle, that she might fly to her place from the face of the serpent." This is the woman, the *Daughter*, in the likeness of the Eternal Mother, even as the Son was in the likeness of the Eternal Father. And when this *Daughter*, who has now become the Mother of the new creation had escaped from the serpent's power, she was *nourished* in her place in the wilderness until the time of her manifestation.[62]

This messianic woman is now manifested in her American wilderness refuge as Mother Ann Lee:

These are the words of the Divine Spirit of prophecy, in relation to that peculiar personage whom we call "Mother." And in her and in her spiritual offspring of the present day, they were and are fulfilled, and are still being fulfilled. In obedience to the revelation and will of God and in love to the Lord her Redeemer, whom she worshipped and served, she did forsake her own people and her father's house. She left also the land of oppression and fled into this wilderness, the land of freedom, as the Lord directed her.

By her faithfulness and her toils, by her crossbearing, and self-denying life, by persecutions and deprivations and imprisonments she endured for the testimony of Christ against the hidden works and abominations of fallen man; and by her sorrows and sufferings of soul, her incessant tears and cries to God, she became a sanctified and "chosen vessel unto the Lord" that in her the word of God by the Prophet Jeremiah might be fulfilled, which says, "*The Lord hath created a new thing in the earth, A woman shall compass a man.*"

Through the valley of humiliation and sufferings she was brought; in the furnace of affliction she was tried, until her soul became cleansed and purified, and being thus prepared, she became a fit tabernacle and abode of the "*only begotten*" Daughter of the Most High, the *faithful witness*; and the true *representative of the Eternal Mother.*[63]

The Shaker theologians thus gather up all the female-oriented imagery of Hebrew scripture and the New Testament, much of which had been previously employed to speak of Mary and Mother Church, reinterpreting these symbols in a new coherent system of parallel maleness and femaleness. As God is male and female, Power and Wisdom, which only together make up the fullness of divinity, so the messianic humanity must be manifested in both the "male and the female line" for the full millennial church to come about. This church in turn must testify to its roots in the dual God and Christ by a parallel leadership of men and women, elders and elderesses, deacons and deaconesses. The consistency of the Shaker vision and practice is stunning.

True, the Shaker vision is not without its remnants of female subordination. It believed that Eve was closer to bodily nature, and Adam equally sinful because he overturned the "right order" (of male leadership). But, for the Shakers, this original inferiority of women is overcome in celibacy. Yet even in celibacy, the duality of male and female natures manifested itself in Shaker societies in the conventional dualism of "inner and outer" roles. Men did the outside work of the society (agriculture), and women did the indoor work (cooking, cleaning). Each performed different kinds of artisanry. Men predominated in the financial representation of the society to the outside world, a situation that changed only in the later nineteenth century, when women had become such an overwhelming majority of the society that they took over financial management.

Later Shaker women leaders, such as Anna White, elderess of the Society of New Lebanon, would confidently align Shakerism with both pacifism and feminism. Ann Lee is hymned as liberator of woman. Through celibacy, woman is freed from the rule of the husband and can claim the "absolute right to her own person":

> To Ann Lee may all reformers among women look as the one who taught and through her followers still teaches perfect freedom, equality and opportunity to woman. The daughters of Ann Lee, alone among women, rejoice in true freedom, not alone from the bondage of man's domination, but freedom also from the curse of that desire, "for her husband," by which through the ages he has ruled over her.[64]

In the examples of Protestant mysticism and millennialism presented in this chapter, we see that female symbolism, at first much diminished by the Reformers, enjoyed a remarkable renewal through Boehme, with the redevelopment of Wisdom theology and spirituality. This Wisdom mysticism lent itself to powerful explorations of both spousal and maternal imagery of Wisdom in relation to the soul seeking transformation. Wisdom mysticism can be developed in relatively or highly androcentric ways in which men privilege their love relation to Wisdom to the exclusion or marginalization of women. But, in the hands of a woman mystic, Jane Leade, or a community that looked to a woman, Ann Lee, as its founding mother, it can lead to significant efforts to reinterpret the tradition in a female-centered way or a more egalitarian way that grants equal roles to female and male in God, Christ, and the redemptive community.

NINE

Contested Gender Status and
Imagining Ancient Matriarchy

GENDER IN NINETEENTH-CENTURY THOUGHT

As industrialization developed, nineteenth-century western Europe and North
America saw a gradual loss of family-based economic production. Although poor
women were drawn into factory work, especially in textiles, and domestic service
continued as a sphere of low-paid female labor, it became increasingly difficult for
middle-class women to make a "respectable" living. The overwhelming view of the
male intellectual elite was that a woman's only acceptable role was that of wife and
mother, as determined by her biological nature, which also fixed her mental and psychological capacities. Male and female roles were governed by the notion of a rigid
complementarity of gender "natures." Women were seen as passive, intuitive, and
emotional; men as active, aggressive, and rational. These fixed gender natures assigned women to the dependent domestic sphere and men to the governance of both
society and the family.[1]

The American and French Revolutions signaled a shift from class-based, aristocratic societies to a new view of civil society based on equal rights of citizens. By
general agreement of most political theorists, however, the citizen class was limited
to propertied males; dependent persons, slaves, servants, and women were excluded.
Although men might rise from the servant class to become independent property
owners and hence citizens, women by their very nature were seen as permanent dependents, without the possibility of independent citizen status. The philosopher Immanuel Kant distinguished between active and passive citizenship and assigned

women to the latter category, whereas Georg Wilhelm Friedrich Hegel believed that women's gender nature excluded them from political life. For Hegel, women represented the particularity of family interests and as such were the enemies of the universal interests of the state and public life.[2]

This insistence on women's fundamental difference from men and their necessary confinement to the domestic sphere lent itself to both idealization and denigration of the feminine sex. The split between home and public life reflected an increasing split between two cultures and two moralities. Piety, self-sacrifice, and concern for others were considered part of women's nature, belonging to private life, whereas men by nature and role pursued rational self-interest in the secular, public sphere. Women were idealized and sentimentalized for their loving, self-giving spirit, even as many believed that these characteristics made them unfit for public political and economic life.

But not all women of nineteenth-century Europe and the United States passively accepted this assignment to dependency in the home. In the course of the century, groups of women contested these limited roles and argued that the apparently fixed "nature" of women was in fact socially constructed, not biological. Feminist writers such as Mary Wollstonecraft contended that women were made to appear less rational and capable only because they had been denied education and opportunities in larger spheres of activity.[3] Women began to organize to win access to higher education and better-paid professions, property rights, and legal status as voting citizens.

As women struggled for emancipation, the arguments against their capacities for education, more demanding work, and participation in public political life became more virulent. Educators such as Dr. Edward Clarke of Harvard College, author of the 1873 volume *Sex in Education*, insisted that women by their very nature had limited energy and declared that what energy they had was needed for their maternal functions. Any diversion of this limited energy into "brainwork" would deplete their capacity for maternity, rendering them sterile and infirm.[4] Medical experts echoed these views, insisting on women's weak and sickly nature and the dangers to their health posed by work, education, or even physical exercise outside what was strictly necessary for performing their domestic chores.[5] Producers of both "high" and "low" culture—philosophers, novelists, journalists, artists, and writers of popular musicals—attacked the "new woman" as threatening the social order and ultimately debasing the "true" nature of women, who were to be revered only when they limited themselves to domestic roles.[6]

In the context of this tense struggle over women's gender status, a small sector of anthropologists, classicists, socialists, and feminists began to discuss the idea that an ancient prepatriarchal, or matriarchal, society had once existed. This idea lent it-self to a variety of uses, both to argue for the normative nature of patriarchy as the highest and best form of society and to imagine matriarchy as a better world that had been lost and needed to be restored at some "higher" level. This chapter fo-cuses on the emergence and variable use of this concept of ancient matriarchy in nineteenth- and early twentieth-century thought. The purpose of this chapter is not to examine the historicity or nonhistoricity of this concept (a discussion that can be found in chapter 1) but rather to explore the various ways men and women of this period imagined the organization of gender and religion in ancient times and how they used these ideas as a mirror to picture how gender and religion could be or-ganized in their own societies.

To introduce this topic, I briefly examine a nineteenth-century French sociolo-gist, an American theologian, and a German philosopher as examples of how lead-ing theorists employed both the idealization and the denigration of women's nature to enforce the reigning views of women's necessarily limited sphere.

The first of these thinkers is French social philosopher August Comte (1798–1857). Comte both promoted and epitomized this period's confident faith in cultural progress. He believed that society had evolved through three stages from ancient times until the nineteenth century. In the first, or theological, stage, humanity attrib-uted the causes of things to deities or supernatural entities. This was the era of super-stition among ancient barbarian societies. In the second stage, that of the classical world and medieval Christianity, these religious entities were translated into meta-physical terms, as philosophical abstractions. These earlier social stages were being superseded in more modern times by scientific observation and experimentation, which permitted accurate knowledge of the physical nature of the universe. Comte called this scientific view of nature "positivism." He believed that it would bring a turn from a religion that worshipped alien gods and metaphysical forces to one that worshipped the ideal of humanity and humanism itself, leading to continual social progress.

In his 1848 volume *A General View of Positivism*, Comte discusses the salutary effects of positivism on society, including the working classes, women, and art. Women, he asserts, are naturally more moral than men and represent the ideals of humanity. But this moral superiority can be maintained only if women live a seg-regated life in the home. The worship of women as the epitome of human rational ideals was anticipated in medieval chivalry and Mariology, but this veneration had been vitiated by Catholicism's hostility to independent reason. Positivism, by con-trast, would harmonize reason and feeling.[7] Women, for Comte, are less capable of abstract thought than men and are the specialists in loving emotion. Social evolution has increasingly removed women from any arena of political authority and paid labor, in order to concentrate their influence within the family. It is from this realm as wife and mother that women can epitomize the ideals of love, which can then inspire all of society. By being segregated in the home and thus protected from the rough and tumble of society, women can play their highest role as "priestesses of Humanity," personifying "the purest principles of love."[8] The home, in effect, becomes the new sanctuary and temple for modern humanity, and woman its ideal embodiment.

In Comte's view, positivism will promote to the greatest degree possible both this segregation of women in the home and the worship of women as the epitome of human ideals. In an astounding picture of woman's "pedestalization," Comte gushes:

Positivism . . . encourages, on intellectual as well as on moral ground, full and systematic expression of the feeling of veneration for Woman, in public as well as in private life, collectively as well as individually. Born to love and to be loved, relieved from the burdens of practical life, free in the sacred retirement of their homes, the women of the West will receive from Positivists the tribute of deep and sincere admiration which their life inspires. They will feel no scruple in accepting their position as spontaneous priestesses of Humanity; they will fear no longer the rivalry of a vindictive Deity. . . . The enervating influence of chimerical beliefs will have passed away, and men in all the vigour of their energies, feeling themselves the masters of the known world, will feel it their highest happiness to submit with gratitude to the beneficent power of womanly sympathy. In a word, Man in those days will kneel to Woman and to Woman alone.[9]

The second example of the idealization of women comes from American Protestant theologian Horace Bushnell (1802–1876). Bushnell agreed that woman's nature represented the highest human ideals, although he cast this in Christian rather than secular terms. But he also wielded this argument to oppose the campaign for women's suffrage, which he characterized as "the reform against nature."[10] For Bushnell, women's enfranchisement represented only a corruption of their true womanly nature—and, with it, the corruption of the whole society. "Woman having once gotten the polls will have them to the end, and if we precipitate our American society down this abyss and make a final wreck of our public virtue in it, that is the end of our new-born, more beneficent civilization."[11]

Bushnell rises to theological heights to differentiate women from men by making the distinction between them analogous to the distinction between law and gospel:

The law, which is the man, goes before, rough-hewing the work of government. It is Sinai-like, and speaks in thunder. It commands, and, by sanctions of force, where force is wanted, vindicates its own supreme authority. . . . The gospel, meantime, coming after in order is the woman. It is subject as gospel to the husband, that is, to the law; it is made under the law, and the whole historic operation, by which it is organized, is itself obedience, submission, love and sacrifice. . . . If it can but write the law on the heart of transgressors, all its wifely ends or ambitions are answered. And this it is supposed to do by what is called grace; that is, by a way of approach so gentle, so winsome and lovely, and close to the manner of true womanly grace, as to be another, more effective, side of the divine power.[12]

In a startlingly gendered version of the doctrine of the "two Kingdoms," Bushnell argues that the law, as the realm of force and coercion of sinners, is necessarily suited only to males, as those capable of rule and force. Women, as the tender and loving sex, are incapable of such force and would only be corrupted by exercising it. They represent the higher kingdom of the gospel of divine love, through which human hearts are converted and persuaded to obey rather than being coerced by external rule. Only by being separated from the external realm of rule can women truly represent this higher realm of loving persuasion, which epitomizes divine grace. Thus, according to Bushnell, women are more Christlike than men—but by that very superiority are excluded from the lower realm of government.

The German philosopher Arthur Schopenhauer (1788–1860) saw human nature as torn by conflicting desires that express the foundational imperative of the will to live. The desire to maximize the will to live causes endless strife between and within persons and can never be fully satisfied. The only escape is a renunciation of desire, an idea that Schopenhauer took from Buddhism. Renunciation of will can also bring with it an element of compassion for others, as one's consciousness of one's own pain impels the effort to relieve the pain of others.

Although this ethic of renunciation of will and sympathy for the pain of others might suggest that women represent such self-sacrificing compassion for another's suffering, Schopenhauer rejects any idealization of women. Rather, he declares that women represent inferior beings, weak, passive, and trivial by nature, who use cunning and deception to control men. Women have no sense of justice and "are defective in reasoning and deliberation."[13] They are suited only for procreation; by nature, they bloom and fade early, lacking real strength. They are incapable of any intellectual or artistic achievement and should be excluded from education. They should be told to keep silent in theaters and other places of cultural life, as St. Paul once told them to keep silent in church. They are even ugly in physical appearance, undersized, with narrow shoulders, broad hips, and short legs—the opposite of masculine beauty.

Idealizing women, Schopenhauer believes, would subvert the manliness of men. Instead, women should be dealt with by contemptuous force, which keeps them firmly in their proper place as house servants of men. The West has erred, he argues, in its foolish veneration of women and its ideals of the "lady." It is the "Orientals" who know how to treat women as they should be treated. They reject monogamy and understand that men have a right to the use of many women. Polygamy provides for all women, while monogamy leaves many women without husbands and creates the hypocritical proliferation of prostitutes. Treat women with stern force, confine them to service to men, and they will be happy and accept their true role, which is to obey—this is Schopenhauer's prescription for gender relations.

Such a diatribe on women's inferiority would seem to be the opposite of Comte's sentimental idealization of women as "priestesses of Humanity" or Bushnell's warning that women, as the personification of higher divine grace, will be corrupted by embracing civil rights. In fact, however, it is the implied underside of the same argument. For all three thinkers, women are incapable of intellectual development and independent economic life and are suited only for motherhood and domestic service. When women fail to be persuaded that their true and highest destiny is to remain confined to this realm, when they persist in seeking education, suffrage, and professions, "right-thinking" men must employ force, coupled by forthright restatements of women's inferiority and their lack of capacity for reason and rule (activities reserved for males). Schopenhauer's frustrated misogyny represents the resort to violence that emerges when Comte's and Bushnell's idealization of women fails to convince.

BACHOFEN AND THE THEORY OF EARLIER MATRIARCHY

The personality of Johann Jakob Bachofen (1815–1887) was quite different from that of the pessimistic Schopenhauer. Also unlike Schopenhauer, who deeply resented his competent mother, Bachofen adored his young mother, who was not even twenty when he was born; he did not marry until after she died. At fifty, he married a beautiful twenty-year-old, who was much like his mother had been when he was a child.[14] But his assumptions about gender complementarity were not very different from those of Schopenhauer and from nineteenth-century norms generally. A Swiss jurist and historian of Roman law, Bachofen was fascinated by ancient Greek and Roman mythology, which he believed accurately reflected the social evolution of ancient society, from the pre-Greek cultures of the Mediterranean to Greek classical society, culminating in the Roman empire.

Based entirely on the "testimony" provided by ancient myth, Bachofen divides the evolution of ancient society into three phases. The oldest and most primitive, which he calls the hetaeric stage (from the Greek word *hetaera*, or courtesan), was characterized by male promiscuity; all men had sexual access to all women. This stage of society was related to a preagricultural economy, when wild plants were gathered for food, without cultivation.

Although women submitted to such sexual abuse for a long time, Bachofen assumes that the situation violated women's naturally chaste and monogamous preferences. At some point, he writes, women revolted against male sexual promiscuity and forced men to accept monogamous unions, which were dominated by women as mothers and in which descent of children was traced through the mother. This was the matriarchal phase of society. It was also related to agriculture and the planting of grain, which Bachofen sees as an innovation introduced by women, represented by the Greek Goddess Demeter.

In some cases, women's revolt against sexual promiscuity even took the form of Amazonianism, an effort of women to separate from men altogether. But Bachofen assumes that such female independence did not last long because women by nature are incapable of real independence. Thus, temporary moments of Amazonian life were quickly defeated by heroic men and erotic gods, such as Dionysus, that represented phallic sensuality:

One of the main causes of the rapid triumph of the new god was the extreme Amazonian form of the old matriarchy and the universal barbarism inseparable from it. The stricter the law of maternity, the less woman was able to sustain the unnatural grandeur of her Amazonian life. Joyfully she welcomed this god whose combination of sensuous beauty and transcendent radiance made him doubly seductive. The enthusiasm of women for his cult was irresistible. In a short time the Amazonian matriarchy's determined resistance to the new god shifted to an equally resolute devotion . . . one extreme followed another, showing how hard it is, at all time, for women to observe moderation.[15]

Matriarchal society, including its extreme form of Amazonianism, lacked a capacity for true order and discipline, which must be grounded in transcendent rationality and the idea of eternal life located in the heavenly realm—the highest stage of society and culture. This third stage could come about only through the overthrow of matriarchy and the suppression of its earth-bound cultural patterns, in favor of patriarchy, the rule of the father, the tracing of descent through the father, and male inheritance of property. In Greek mythology, this patriarchal revolution was represented by Apollo and by Athena, the male-identified Goddess who repudiated female birth for male generation. (She herself had no mother and was born from the head of her father, Zeus.) The patriarchal revolution reached its highest state of development in Roman law, as the expression of universal imperial rule. Unlike motherhood, which is based on the natural experience of the birth of a child from its mother, fatherhood is necessarily abstract and "fictive." One cannot confirm the identity of a child's father by natural experience; rather, fatherhood must be established juridically. Thus, father right, unlike mother right, is established by universal legal principles and therefore is the basis of abstract thought, in contrast to maternal thinking, which is rooted in bodily realities.

According to Bachofen, the ancient Greeks and Romans had passed through all three of these societal stages. He notes that one can discern the earlier hetaeric and matriarchal stages by hints in the mythology that reveal stern efforts to impose father rule over former mother rule. Bachofen argues, however, that some Mediterranean peoples of the Near East and Egypt failed to evolve to the more advanced stage reached by the patriarchal West. He theorizes that the inferiority of Asians and Africans relative to the superior Occidental (Western) people lies in their failure to emerge out of the promiscuous and matriarchal stages and to attain the higher reason of patriarchal society.

Bachofen employs a symbolic thinking that assumes both a gender hierarchy of masculine over feminine and a hierarchy of the Occident over Asian and African peoples. The hierarchies are conflated, and both are symbolized by the superiority of rational over irrational, mind over body, transcendence over immanence, sun over moon and earth, light over dark, active over passive, dynamic over static, ordered rule over sensual excess. Although the two earlier stages of society existed in the West, Bachofen assumes that they originated from the East and were foreign to the true Occidental spirit. Thus, he suggests an essentialism that differentiates Western men from Asian and African men and from all women in general. He writes, with typical rhetoric:

... the maternal mystery is the old element and the classic age represents a late stage of religious development . . . Hellenism is hostile to such a world. The primacy of motherhood vanishes and its consequences with it. The patriarchal development stresses a completely different aspect of human nature, which is reflected in entirely different social forces and ideals. In Egypt Herodotus finds the direct antithesis to Greek and especially Attic civilization. Compared to his Hellenic surroundings, Egypt struck him as a world upside down. . . . For Egypt is the land of stereotyped matriarchy, its whole culture is built essentially on the mother cult, on the primacy of Isis over Osiris; . . . [The] origins [of Pythagoreanism] lie, not in the wisdom of the Greeks, but the more ancient lore of the Orient, of the static African and Asian world.[16]

The most ancient stage of life is locked in what Bachofen calls "tellurism," the realm of spontaneous growth from the soil, which he continually relates to "muck," or wet swampy ground, and to unbridled sensuality. Matriarchy, with its monogamous conjugal life and human control over the earth through agriculture, represented a step up from this subordination to the purely physical world. But the spirit was still held in check by the bodily realm. The completion of the triumph of mind over body took place only with the assertion of patriarchy over matriarchy. Here, the principles of the transcendent intellect and the immortal soul asserted themselves over and beyond a world that knew only the coming to be and passing away of the material life process.

But the sensual, maternal world was not easily defeated. It returned again and again—with incursions from the inferior Orient; with the cult of the God of wine and intoxication, Dionysus; with Cleopatra's efforts to subvert Roman imperial rule; and finally with Oriental cults that sought to undermine Roman domination. These incursions from an inferior world had to be continually combated and sternly repressed by patriarchal rule, which was embodied in Roman law and superior rational morality. This rule is imaged as the transcendence of the solar over the lunar. For Bachofen, the moon lies between the mortal and the immortal worlds, while the sun ideally represents a transcendence over mortality altogether, establishing a realm freed from material process:

Wholly different and far purer is the third stage of solar development, the Apollonian stage. The phallic sun, forever fluctuating between rising and setting, coming to be and passing away, is transformed into the immutable source of light. It enters the realm of solar being, leaving behind it all idea of fecundation, all yearning for mixture with feminine matter. Dionysus merely raised paternity over the mother; Apollo frees himself entirely from any bond with woman. His paternity is motherless and spiritual, as in adoption, hence immortal, immune to the night of death which forever confronts Dionysus because he is phallic.[17]

Bachofen asserts that Roman law represents the final secure triumph of patriarchal transcendence over maternal and Oriental immanence:

Mankind owes the enduring victory of paternity to the Roman political idea, which gave it a strict juridical form and consequently enabled it to develop in all spheres of existence; it made this principle the foundation of all life and safeguarded it against the decadence of religion, the corruption of manners and a popular return to matriarchal views. Roman law maintained its traditional principle against all the assaults and threats of the Orient, against the spreading cult of Isis and Cybele and even against the Dionysian mystery.[18]

Although Roman law dealt the decisive blow that subjugated inferior matriarchy to superior patriarchy, establishing the victory of immortal mind over death-prone body, there is more than a hint that Bachofen sees Christianity as the final embodiment of this patriarchal principle of mind over body. Thus, he writes:

Roman is the idea through which European mankind prepared to set its own imprint on the entire globe, namely, the idea that no material law but only the free activity of the spirit determines the destinies of peoples. . . . the Asiatic passively bows to the most trifling natural phenomenon and wastes his mental energies in timidly hearkening to the slightest message of nature, but the Roman feels free to reject the augury and thus upholds the superiority of the human mind. Everywhere he regards himself as the first factor in historical life. Cutting the chains imposed on him by the naturalness of the Orient, he makes religion with all its fictions subservient to the purposes of the state . . . the restless striving that is the hallmark of European mankind came to the fore with Rome; that is why the world-wide victory of Rome prefaced the great struggle for freedom from natural necessity that marks the historical trend of Christianity.[19]

With these words, we see clearly that the triumph of patriarchy not only represents the triumph of superior Roman men over inferior women and Orientals in ancient times but also lays the basis for the right of European men in Bachofen's own time to colonize and rule over the rest of humanity, justifying the subjugation of Asians and Africans, then being conquered by European empires, as the right of higher over lower cultures.

CLASSICISTS AND ANTHROPOLOGY

Ideas of familial evolution from promiscuity to matriarchy to patriarchy were debated among anthropologists of the late nineteenth and early twentieth centuries. Given that a European education meant being immersed in the classics, this debate necessarily influenced how classicists interpreted the ancient Greek world. Anthropologist John Ferguson McLennan, in his 1885 volume *Patriarchal Theory*, connects matrilineal descent to the most primitive system of kinship based on the observable relation of the mother to her children and her daughters' children.[20] As long as female sexuality is not secured in an exclusive relation to one male, he writes, only the kinship of mother and child is certain; a child's paternity is uncertain and difficult to confirm. Matrilineal systems of kinship center the family on female descent and import males from other tribes, who father children but remain members of their own matriliny.

McLennan believed that early societies killed most of their women in infancy, with many men then monopolizing one woman. Capturing brides from other tribes and the ritualizing of this capture as a contract between men of exogamous tribes came to be the major ways of securing wives. Only when males transferred wives to their domiciles and secured exclusive control over the women's sexuality could the paternity of children be established. Patriliny, then, is possible only through rigid control that prevents a woman from having sexual encounters with anyone other than her husband, who then fathers "legitimate" children.

Edward Tylor's summary of then-current anthropological thought in the July–December 1896 issue of the influential journal *The Nineteenth Century* rejects Bachofen's concept of a stage of original promiscuity. Tylor claims that humans have always ordered kinship relations and that matriliny is simply one variant of such ordered systems of exogamous kinship, in which women stay in their own clan and their husbands are imported into the matrilocal context as laborers and begetters of children. These men may come and go, but the mother-child relation remains the secure basis of descent and inheritance. Tylor sees this as a prevalent form of social organization in early times, although not necessarily universal. It was still the social order of half of the peoples of "lower culture" in his day, although it was dying out with the influence of patrilineal forms preferred by the dominant "civilizations."[21]

As to the status of women in matriliny, Tylor describes women as "enjoying greater consideration" in such a system, although rule is in the hands of the male blood relatives of women, their brothers and uncles. By contrast, the brief article on "the matriarchate" in the eleventh edition of the *Encyclopaedia Britannica*, published in 1910–1911, tersely denies that women enjoy any "personal power" in matrilineal kinship systems, where they are considered "mere chattel."[22]

Among classicists, these anthropological debates became crucial to the interpretation of ancient Greek culture. Turning from literary to archaeological data, classicists uncovered far older worlds that lay behind the cultures of the Homeric era and fifth-century Athens. Beneath the apparently "rational" and anthropomorphic world of Greek art and literature was a shadowy realm of preclassical Greece, typified in Minoan Crete. This world was seen as chthonic rather than Olympian, rooted in the powers of the earth and the underworld, not the shining heavens. Most of all, it seemed to privilege women and goddesses in ways unthinkable to patriarchal Athens, with its male-controlled public space and secluded women. What was the relation between the two eras?

Sir Arthur Evans, archaeologist of the palace of Knossos in Minoan Crete, understood this early civilization as matriarchal, observing that it gave women preeminence and worshipped a goddess as the primary deity. Without hesitation, he interpreted the prominent role of women in Minoan art as a testimony to their high status. Commenting on representations of women in paintings of the bull-leaping games, he notes that women take the front seats at these shows and that male spectators are not admitted among them, "a sign of female predominance characteristic of the matriarchal stage."[23] Gilbert Murray, summarizing his work in *Five Stages of Greek Religion*, writes that powerful goddesses are related to a stage of human religion focused on the fertility of the earth, animals, and land. Women's fertility is related magically to the fertility of the land, both in the hunter-gatherer stage of human survival and in early agriculture.[24]

Jane Ellen Harrison (1850–1928), one of the first women scholars at Cambridge University, who continued to teach classics at Newnham College, devoted her life to trying to interpret the meaning of this evolution of Greek culture. Her central theme was the emergence of religion from pre-Hellenic chthonic patterns to Olympian forms and then to postclassical asceticism of the Orphic and gnostic type. Hovering behind her struggle was the question of women. Were women better off under the prepatriarchal chthonic religions? Was the rise of patriarchal Olympian religions a regression for women? What about women today? Her answer is allusive and ambiguous.

In her discussion of the "Making of a Goddess" in her 1903 volume *Prolegomena to the Study of Greek Religion*, Harrison sees this veneration of female power as related to a magical connection between female fecundity and that of the earth. Men looked with awe at the female capacity to bring forth children and connected it with the spontaneous growth of animals and plants gathered in the wild, and then with the fertility of the planted land. The goddess was first the "lady of the Wild Things" and then the "Corn Mother." Harrison rejects an original stage of promiscuity prior to matriarchy, citing Tylor's 1896 article as the best account "known to me" of the matriarchal human family system that she presumes was prevalent in the early Mediterranean world in pre-Hellenic times.[25]

Harrison describes the relation of women and men as freer in this matrilineal culture. At that time, women chose their male partners and promoted their heroic activities rather than being possessed by men and reduced to being servile household workers and sexual instruments. Thus, Harrison comments on the representations of Demeter and Kore:

> The relation of these early matriarchal, husbandless goddesses, whether Mother or Maid, to the male figures that accompany them is one altogether noble and womanly, through perhaps not what the modern mind holds to be feminine. It seems to halt somewhere half-way between Mother and Lover, with a touch of the patron saint. Aloof from achievement themselves, they choose a local hero for their own to inspire and protect. They ask of him, not that he should love and adore, but that he should do great deeds.[26]

Harrison interprets the misogynist Greek images of women, such as Juno, the grumbling wife of Zeus, and Hesiod's portrayal of Pandora as the troublesome wife who causes evil to come into the world, as the distortions of patriarchy, which must deny the earlier independence and power of women. Powerful goddesses who remain in Hellenic culture, such as Athena, herself once a local Kore, must be made motherless, her partnership with the male hero turned against women's capacity for motherhood. But when Harrison turns to evaluate the effect that the advent of Olympian patriarchy had on women's status, she becomes oddly ambivalent. While admitting that this was a temporary setback for women, she sees it as necessary for a larger evolution of religion and culture.

For Harrison, the earlier veneration of women as the magical source of earth's fecundity was based on a falsehood. Once men recognized this falsehood and realized their own superior power, they were bound to subjugate women and despise their weakness. This was an unfortunate but necessary step to a more advanced stage of religion and culture, glimpsed in Pythagorean and Orphic culture, in which women could be released from biological necessity and set free to share in the higher human capacities of mind and spirit denied to them by patriarchy. Commenting on Hesiod's depiction of the beautiful but evil Pandora, Harrison opines:

> Through all the magic of a poet . . . there gleams the ugly malice of theological animus. Zeus the Father will have no great Earth-goddess, Mother and Maid in one, in his man-fashioned Olympus, but her figure *is* from the beginning, so he re-makes it; woman, who was the inspirer, becomes the temptress; she who made all things, gods and mortals alike, is become their plaything, their slave, dowered only with physical beauty, and with a slave's tricks and blandishment. To Zeus, the archpatriarchal *bourgeois*, the birth of the first woman is but a huge Olympian jest.
>
> Such myths are a necessary outcome of the shift from matriarchy to patriarchy, and the shift itself, [in] spite of a seeming retrogression, is a necessary stage in a real advance. Matriarchy gave to women a false because a magical prestige. With patriarchy came inevitably the facing of real fact, the fact of the greater natural weakness of woman. Man the stronger, when he outgrew his belief in the magical potency of woman, proceeded by a pardonable practical logic to despise and enslave her as the weaker. The future held indeed a time when the non-natural, mystical truth came to be apprehended, that the stronger had a need, real and imperative, of the weaker. Physical nature had from the outset compelled a certain recognition of this truth, but that the physical was a sacrament of the spiritual was a hard saying, and its understanding was not granted to the Greek, save here and there where a flicker of the truth gleamed and went through the vision of philosopher or poet.[27]

What does this mean? What is this better stage that awaited women in a future in which the physical was perceived to be a sacrament of the spiritual? In her *Epilegomena to the Study of Greek Religion*, a brief fifty-page text written in 1921 to sum up her reflection on the evolution of religion, Harrison attempts an answer but, unfortunately, without returning to the question of female status.[28] Here, she details what she sees as the pre-Olympian stage of religion. In this stage of "primitive ritual," there are neither gods nor priests. Rather, the community devises rituals to embody its two primary concerns for life, the expulsion of evil (barrenness and famine) and the encouragement of the good (fertility and good harvests). As these ritual patterns become developed and institutionalized, a literary and theological superstructure is erected upon them, imagining our projected desires for good against evil embodied in immortal deities, like ourselves but without impermanence. Humans then fall down and worship their own projections and construct systems of self-blame and repentance for their own mortality. Harrison sees this Olympian stage of religion as fading today, as the temporal means of life is secured by science. But this frees the human spirit to move on to a higher stage of religion, which she speaks of all too briefly as the "Religion of Today."

Harrison sees this highest stage of religion as ascetic, anticipated by the ascetic religions of late antiquity. Asceticism frees us from the biological imperative and thus allows the human spirit to soar into higher, eternal cultural creations, such as poetry and the scholarly search for truth. Although Harrison doesn't explicitly say so, one can infer from her earlier comments that at last women could be freed by this ascetic stage of religion to join men as equal companions in a new way in the tasks of the spirit's heavenly quests for truth, goodness, and beauty, presumably no longer "aloof from achievements themselves." Is Harrison thinking of herself in this context, as a female celibate scholar at Cambridge University? Is a secularized form of monasticism Harrison's vision of the highest stage of religion?

SOCIALISM: MATRIARCHY AS PRIMITIVE COMMUNISM

A very different evaluation of the meaning of early matriarchy for the human future was developed by socialists. Both Karl Marx and his colleague Frederick Engels were deeply interested in the anthropological debates on the development of the family, and they read Bachofen, McLennan, and others with great interest. They eventually adopted the American anthropologist Lewis Morgan, with his studies on American Indian family systems, as their authority on these issues. Morgan, in his 1877 study *Ancient Society: Researches in the Lines of Human Progress from Savagery Through Barbarism to Civilization*, argued that the earliest humans were promiscuous.[29] From original promiscuity, there developed a group family pattern in which all men of each generation of a tribe were seen as married to all women. This pattern gradually grew more restricted, with the sister group of one gens seen as married to the brother group of another, while excluding sex with their own blood brothers. Eventually, a pairing relation of a man and a woman developed, but with easy separation and still within a communal household. In all these stages of the early family, found in savagery and barbarism, descent through the mother was the rule for tracing kinship and inheritance.

Engels adopted this scheme in his major work on this subject, *The Origin of the Family, Private Property, and the State* (1884).[30] For Engels, the shift from the matrilineal and matrilocal communal family to patriarchy took place with the accumulation of property, beginning with the domestication of animals and the development of herds of cattle, which were defined as private property in the hands of a chief, belonging to him personally rather than to the clan. This chief, wishing his property to be handed down to his own male children—rather than to his sister's children, as in the matrilineal system—overthrew the old pattern of "mother right" and began a system of patrilineal descent and inheritance of property. The development of slavery soon followed, with slaves becoming a second type of private property to be inherited by a man's children. A class hierarchy of lords over slaves thus arose within the patriarchal family itself, and women were redefined as subjects to their lords within this property relationship.

Engels dramatically describes the development of the patriarchal family not as an advance but as the "fall" of women and the advent within the family itself of the nucleus of the class antagonisms between ruling owners and oppressed workers, *qua* women and slaves. This class antagonism will define the rest of social history from the rise of early "civilizations" to modern capitalism. In ringing tones, Engels declares:

> The overthrow of mother right was the *world-historic defeat of the female sex*. The man seized the reins in the house also, the woman was degraded, enthralled, the slave of the man's lust, a mere instrument for breeding children. This lowered position of women, especially manifest among the Greeks of the Heroic and still more of the Classical Age, has become gradually embellished and dissembled and, in part, clothed in milder form, but by no means abolished.[31]

For Engels, early patriarchy was the rule of a chief over a clan of dependents, including several wives, their children, and slaves. The increasing restriction of legal marriage to one wife, or monogamy, in no way abolished the hierarchy of the male head of family over wife, children, and slaves. Chastity was expected only of the wife, in order to procure legitimate descendants. Male sexuality was never so limited; men were allowed to range over a variety of other sex objects who did not become legal wives. Women were restricted to unpaid household labor and thus dependent on their husbands for economic survival.

Late antiquity and the medieval love lyric began the ideal of romantic love between a woman and a man, but such love was conceivable only as adultery, not within marriage. In Engels's view, no genuinely equal and mutual love could develop between husband and wife within marriage, since the relationship was essentially one of property, between owner and owned. He predicts that truly egalitarian love partnerships could begin to develop among the proletariat, where women are forced out of their homes into factory labor by economic necessity. Although labor conditions are oppressive, the women's status as workers makes them economically independent and thus able to enter into a love relation with a man as a free and equal partner.

This beginning of truly equal monogamous love would be fulfilled under socialism, when collective ownership of the means of production by the workers would abolish the property relation between owners and workers. Without the oppressive conditions of capitalist production, women would take their place as economic equals in productive labor and hence as personal equals with men. Engels was confident that socialism not only would liberate women as workers through economic equality but also would allow the realization of the bourgeois ideal of monogamous love, which had been unrealizable under capitalist conditions.[32] (Engels himself lived out this idea by being paired in a faithful relationship with a working-class woman without benefit of legal marriage.)[33]

Engels's view became the official doctrine of Marxist thought, which looked back to this writing as its foundational text. This analysis was spelled out in a major work by the German socialist August Bebel, *Die frau und der socialismus* (1883), translated into English in 1904 as *Women Under Socialism*.[34] Bebel repeats the arguments made by Morgan and Engels that original promiscuity developed gradually into more restrictive forms of communal marriage that nonetheless continued to be based on female descent. This gave women of the family not only persuasive influence but also political power:

The mother is the head of the family; and thus arises the "mother-right," which for a long time constitutes the basis of the family and inheritance. In keeping therewith—so long as descent was recognized in the female line— woman has a seat and a voice in the councils of the gens; they voted in the election of the sachems and of the military chiefs and deposed them. . . . The woman is the real guide and leader of this family community; hence she enjoys a high degree of respect, in the house as well as in the affairs of the family community concerning the tribe. She is judge and adjuster of disputes and frequently performs the ceremonies of religion as priestess. The frequent appearance of Queens and priestesses in antiquity, their controlling influence, even there where their sons reigned, for instance, in the history of old Egypt, are results of mother-right. Mythology in that epoch assumes predominantly female characters: Astarte, Ceres, Demeter, Latona, Isis, Frigga, Freia, Gerdha, etc. Woman is considered inviolable, matricide is the blackest of all crimes. . . . In defense of women men are spurred to highest valor. Thus did the effects of the mother-right, gyneocracy, manifest themselves in all the relations of life among the peoples of antiquity—among the Babylonians, the Assyrians, the Egyptians, the Greeks, before the time of the Heroes, among the people of Italy, before the founding of Rome, among the Scythians, the Gauls, the Iberians and Cantabrians, the Germans of Tacitus, etc. Woman, at that time, takes in the family and in public life a position such as she has never since taken.[35]

Like Engels, Bebel assumes that all this was overthrown by the rise of private property. With the dissolution of the old female-centered gens, the male took over the rule of the family and developed the state to protect these property relations. Woman was subjugated to man and lost her old prerogatives based on mother right. A double standard was imposed, demanding strict chastity from women, while men remained promiscuous. All had been equally provided for in the mother-ruled communal gens, but patriarchy, based on private property, created the oppression of women: "The reign of the mother-right implied communism, equality for all; the rise of father-right implied the reign of private property and with it the oppression and enslavement of women."[36]

For Bebel, this subjugation of women can be ended only under socialism, in which private property is superseded by collective ownership. Socialism is a restoration of the equality of all, of original matriarchal communism on a more advanced level: "Socialism creates in this nothing new; it merely restores, at a higher level of civilization and under new social forms, that which prevailed at a more primitive stage and before private property began to rule society."[37] Woman under socialism will be socially and economically independent: "She is peer of the man, the mistress of her lot." All vestiges of domination and exploitation will be overcome. She will have an equal education and will be able to develop her mental powers. She can choose her occupation and will work "under conditions identical with the man." She will also be free in her choice of love; she "woos or is wooed, and closes the bond from no consideration other than her own inclinations." The revolutionary goals of "liberty, equality, and fraternity," unrealizable under capitalist conditions, will flourish fully under socialism: "Democracy in government, brotherhood in society, equality in rights and privileges and universal education foreshadow the next higher plane of society to which experience, intelligence and knowledge are tending."[38]

Bebel's work was widely disseminated among feminist socialist groups at the turn of the century. In their publications, these groups frequently referred to an original communist and matriarchal stage of history, followed by the advent of patriarchy and the exploitation of the working class. They believed that socialism would be the agent for the emancipation of women as workers. Among U.S. socialist women, the Women's National Committee of the Socialist Party of America made Bebel's book a required study text for their groups in the first decades of the twentieth century.[39] In the pages of *The Progressive Woman*, the publication of the Women's National Committee, socialists frequently discussed these views.[40] They argued that the industrial revolution was freeing women from the confinement and unpaid labor of the household, allowing them to relate to men more as equals and leading working women to demand ever more equal conditions for their labor and the development of their skills, although these goals would be fully attainable only under socialism.

MATRIARCHY AMONG WOMEN'S SUFFRAGE LEADERS

One of the first feminists to make use of the theory of early matriarchy was Matilda Joslyn Gage, one of the three major leaders of the National Woman Suffrage Association, along with Elizabeth Cady Stanton and Susan B. Anthony, from the 1860s to 1900. Gage was a member of the editorial board for Stanton's *Woman's Bible*, which critically reviewed the biblical basis of women's oppression.[41] With Stanton, Gage was the major writer of the multivolume *History of Woman Suffrage* and tirelessly researched evidence of women's oppression and historical resistance to patriarchy.[42] She was one of the first to investigate the persecution of witches as evidence of an attempt to destroy women's culture.[43]

Gage's parents adopted the Swedenborgian faith.[44] She herself was a free thinker who was deeply suspicious of Christianity, which she saw as the mainstay of women's oppression. She vehemently opposed Susan B. Anthony's efforts to effect a merger of the American and National Woman Suffrage Associations. (The two organizations had split after the Civil War over the issue of delaying women's suffrage in favor of the enfranchisement of freed slaves.)[45] This merger brought conservative Christian women, such as Frances Willard and the members of the Women's Christian Temperance Union, into the mainstream of the suffrage movement. Gage saw the presence of such Christian women as undermining the more radical visions of social transformation held by many in the suffrage movement, using the movement instead for conservative goals such as temperance.[46]

In her 1893 volume *Woman, Church, and State,* Gage seeks to demonstrate woman's original ascendancy in matriarchal times and the key role of Judaism and Christianity in her subjugation by patriarchy. In contrast to the tradition of male patriarchalists, including socialists, Gage does not identify the matriarchal stage of history as "primitive"; rather, she sees it as a time of high culture. She describes how women held exclusive power in economic, political, and religious affairs during that period:

> A form of society existed at an early age known as the Matriarchate or Mother-rule. Under the Matriarchate, except as son and inferior, man was not recognized in either of these great institutions, family, state or church. A father and husband as such had no place in the social, political or religious scheme; woman was ruler in each. The primal priest on earth, she was also supreme as goddess in heaven.[47]

Gage does not believe that patriarchy attained a sudden victory. Instead, she sees a gradual inclusion of males in cultures that retained substantial female leadership and venerated the maternal principle in goddess worship. Thus, she attributes the achievements of all the classical cultures of Egypt, Greece, and Rome to their retention of matriarchal elements. As long as the feminine was recognized as "a component and superior part of divinity," civilizations remained just, peaceful, and highly cultured. Far from being a society based on promiscuity, "under the matriarchate, monogamy was the rule, neither polyandry nor promiscuity existed."[48]

According to Gage, such mother-ruled societies continued in the non-Christian East into recent centuries. At a time when Christian cities in Europe were rude and unsanitary, such matriarchal societies enjoyed high culture. Thus, she describes the culture of Malabar, India, at the time of its discovery and conquest by the Portuguese in the fifteenth century: " . . . they were not so much surprised by the opulence of their cities, the splendor of all their habits of living, the great perfection of their navy, the high state of the arts, as they were to find all this under the control and government of women." Gage emphasizes that this high culture existed at a time when Christian Europe was struggling against the church for freedom of the press, when the Inquisition was persecuting free thought, when education was crude, and when women were forbidden all participation in public life. For Gage, this cultural superiority was closely related to the worship of feminine rather than masculine deities. In Europe, the feminine principle had been "entirely eliminated from divinity," and a "purely masculine God [had become] the universal object of worship." By contrast, in Malabar, "cleanliness, peace, the arts, a just form of government, the recognition of the feminine both in humanity and in the divinity were found."[49]

Gage relates the feminine principle and its worship to spirituality and intelligent wisdom, whereas masculinity is related to force, violence, sexual promiscuity, and materialism. In her view, the key to the fall from high feminine to low masculine societies came about through Judaism and the continuation of its religious viewpoint in Christianity.[50] This rule of masculine principles not only subjugated women socially but also introduced prostitution and polygamy: "The Patriarchate under which Biblical history and Judaism commenced, was the rule of men whose lives and religion were based on passions of the grossest kind, showing but few indications of softness or refinement." To produce many children, "polygamy was instituted, becoming as marked a feature of the patriarchate as monogamy was of the Matriarchate."

Not until the patriarchate were wives regarded as property, the sale of daughters as a legitimate means of family income, or their destruction at birth looked upon as a justifiable act. Under the Patriarchate society became morally revolutionized, the family, the state, the form of religion entirely changed. The theory of a male supreme God in the interests of force and authority, wars, family discord, the sacrifice of children to appease the wrath of an offended deity are all due to the patriarchate.[51]

Gage finds remnants of the feminine even in the Jewish and Christian views of God, however. She cites the Jewish Shaddai ("the Breasted God") and the Christian Holy Spirit as representing continued elements of goddess worship, although these were denied and repressed by the church. (Although it is usually translated in English as "the Lord Almighty" [Gen. 17:1], the root of the word "Shaddai" is "breast." In the plural, it could be translated as "many-breasted one.")[52]

Patterns of violence, wars, the subjugation of the female sex, and the sexual and physical violation of women have continued in Christianity, Gage observes. She declares that Christianity has been "of little value to civilization."[53] She describes people who are freeing themselves from the Christian church and aspiring to a higher level of spirituality and critical thought:

We have now reached a period in history when investigation is taking the place of blind belief, and the truth, capable of making man free, is once again offered. It is through a recognition of the divine element in motherhood as not alone inhering in the primal source of life but extending throughout creation, that it will become possible for the world, so buried in darkness, folly and superstition, to practice justice toward women.[54]

The full flowering of this new religious consciousness will bring about a millennial transformation of society: "A brighter day is to come for the world, a day when the intuitions of woman's soul shall be accepted as a part of humanity's spiritual wealth, when force shall step backward, and love, in reality, rule the teachings of religion; and may women be strong in the ability and courage necessary to bring about this millennial time."[55]

The great revolution manifest in the women's suffrage movement is not limited to winning the vote, Gage argues. Its deepest meaning is the rebellion of women against those teachings of the Christian church that have hitherto sanctified their oppression: "During the ages, no rebellion has been of like importance with that of Woman against the tyranny of Church and State; none has had its far reaching effects. We note its beginnings; its progress will overthrow every existing form of these institutions; its end will be a regenerated world."[56]

Although Gage was the most radical and outspoken, she was not the only suffrage leader to harbor a belief in an original matriarchal age linked to a higher, more just, and peaceful civilization and to see the goal of women's emancipation as ultimately tied to religious change. In her commentary on Genesis 3 in *The Woman's Bible*, Elizabeth Cady Stanton expresses her belief that a long period of female rule had preceded patriarchy. For eighty-five thousand years of human development, she asserts, women reigned supreme in a matriarchal form of society. Only in the barbarian era did males "seize the reins of government," imposing a patriarchal system of rule.

Stanton sees God as androgynous, containing both male and female elements, and describes the suppression of the feminine aspect of God as a cultural and moral disaster. She predicts that humanity will emerge from patriarchal government and religion to what she terms the "Amphiarchate," a shared rule of women and men as equals. In that new age, men and women will worship an androgynous God, recognizing the true laws of the universe, which strive for a dynamic harmony of male and female elements.[57]

Carrie Chapman Catt, head of the merged National American Woman Suffrage

Association when Susan B. Anthony retired in 1900 and a leader in the women's peace movement, also believed in a peaceful and progressive era of human society under matriarchal rule. She used her travels to investigate evidence of the survival of matriarchal societies into the twentieth century. In a 1914 article in *Harper's Magazine*, "A Survival of Matriarchy," she reported on the matriarchal Menangkabau peoples of Malaysia.[58] She argues that they have resisted efforts by patriarchal Hindu and Muslim peoples to impose patriarchal patterns upon them. She describes their society as peaceful and prosperous, free from rape or prostitution, thus refuting the assumption that matriarchy belongs to a primitive and sexually promiscuous stage of society. With its egalitarian patterns, this society is able to enter directly into the more advanced, democratic culture that is emerging in the world as patriarchy fades, skipping entirely the distorted patriarchal period of development.

ROBERT BRIFFAULT: THE DEFENSE OF MATRIARCHAL ORIGINS

In the 1920s, the anthropological tradition that had supported a belief in original matriarchy was being discredited. The new school of anthropology under Franz Boas promoted investigation of each culture as distinct and rejected the belief in a universal history in which every culture passes through the same stages. The 1920s also saw the collapse of the Victorian women's culture that believed in a superior "feminine" principle linked to women's maternal nature. This culture had nurtured the women's movement of the late nineteenth century. The suffragists in their long white dresses and big hats, with their firm faith in women's moral superiority and their abhorrence of "gross male sexuality," now seemed quaintly old-fashioned to a new "flapper" culture that sought to reclaim women's sexuality and to be "pals" rather than mothers to men.[59]

The last major anthropologist to defend the belief in a matriarchal stage of society was Robert Briffault, who published a three-volume work, *The Mothers*, in 1927, written to refute Edward Alexander Westermarck's reaffirmation that the family had always been patriarchal.[60] Briffault assembles a vast amount of information cross-culturally to argue for a universal stage of matriarchal organization of the family, preceding patriarchy. He traces the matriarchal family back to the animal family, in which the mother establishes the core family and cares for and feeds her young. Men, Briffault asserts, lack the nurturing instinct and must be socialized by the female to care for children.[61]

Although he praises females as more naturally loving and caring than males, he also sees women as inherently less intelligent, lacking an interest in and capacity for abstract thought. Thus, all higher culture that demands abstract thought comes from men and presupposes the dominance of male rule.[62] Briffault is ambivalent about women's emancipation. He sees women's difference, grounded in instinct, as complementing the male tendency to abstraction and loss of contact with bodily and earthy realities. Consequently, he deplores the notion of a female emancipation in which women would lose their distinctiveness and simply imitate male patterns of culture.[63] His praise of the maternal values that underlie matriarchy are thus rooted in a complementarian anthropology that wishes to keep women "different" and hence tied to particular "instinctual" roles in relation to male "intelligence."

Theories of early matriarchy, as this chapter demonstrates, were always theories about male and female nature, and they carried imaginations of ideal society. Male matriarchalists generally cultivated some version of a complementarian anthropology in which women embody instinct and earthy elements, while males represent mind and spirit. Victorian feminist matriarchalists reversed this pattern, although they also assumed dual-gender principles: femininity is spiritual, peaceful, and asexual; masculinity is "grossly" sexual, materialist, and violent. Socialists, however, usually ignored innate gender natures, striving for an economically based equality of the sexes that would then allow personal sexual parity.

Male matriarchalists generally saw matriarchy as a culturally inferior stage, tied to bodiliness that would be transcended by masculine spirit. The feminine is valuable as a "difference" to be preserved against the threat of a modern "egalitarianism." Their model of history is one of progress from "lower" to "higher," although with some ambivalence about what has been lost in this process. Socialists and feminists, by contrast, saw matriarchy as a germ of an original Eden, a better state that is to be recovered on a higher level—that is, a secular version of a fall and redemption pattern. Both socialist and feminist matriarchalists were millenarian, imagining a more advanced society emerging in the near future through women's emancipation and recovery of a lost past.

Racial hierarchy lurks around the edges of much of this thought about ancient matriarchy and the rise of patriarchy, linked to gender hierarchy. Inferior racial and religious groups were seen as less rational and masculine, more emotional, somatic, and feminine. This view is obvious in Bachofen, as pointed out earlier, but it is also found in others. Morgan declared that only two peoples, the Semitic and the Aryan, had attained civilization by unassisted self-development; all other peoples, he argued, moved from barbarism to civilization through the influence of these two. Engels followed Morgan in this opinion.[64] The Aryans were seen as the most important of the two: "The Aryan family represents the central stream of human progress, because it produced the highest type of mankind and because it has proved its intrinsic superiority by gradually assuming the control of the earth."[65] Morgan saw this evolution as guided by divine providence, as "part of the plan of the Supreme Intelligence to develop a barbarian out of a savage and a civilized man out of this barbarian."[66]

Harrison also used ethnic stereotypes, speaking of the "cold purity" of the northern European peoples as having a natural affinity for male gods and patriarchal social patterns, as distinct from the "passions" of the south, which were linked to goddesses and matriarchy.[67] Gage reversed the gender-ethnic hierarchy but nevertheless linked it to spirit-matter dualism. In her view, all pagan peoples possessed a superior morality and spirituality based on the veneration of the maternal. Jews are uniquely "gross," violent, and materialist, she claimed, and Christianity inherits this from the Jews.

Although the theory of original matriarchy was eclipsed among anthropologists in the period from the 1920s to the 1960s, it never entirely disappeared. Briffault kept the argument alive, not only with his massive work in 1927 but also in debates with fellow anthropologists, such as Bronislaw Malinowski, into the 1950s.[68] Through the 1960s, both classicists and socialists continued to draw on literatures from the pre–World War I era that enshrined a belief in a matriarchal stage of history, although they used the theory for quite different agendas.[69] Thus, when feminism as a movement for women's emancipation was reborn in the late 1960s, the literature of early matriarchy was available for rediscovery and embrace as a vision of an alternative world of women that had once existed and hence might exist again.

The connection of matriarchy with religion, specifically with goddesses and goddess worship, had been implied in various ways in the nineteenth-century literatures, even among socialists such as Bebel. In the twentieth century, this assumed correlation of goddesses and matriarchy, or the high status of women, would give birth to new religious movements that sought to revive goddess worship as part of a new valuing of women and the feminine in society and nature. It is to these developments that we turn in the next chapter.

TEN · The Return of the Goddess

In the early 1970s, sectors of the new women's movement, seeking a feminist spirituality, began to reclaim the ideas of original matriarchy and the primacy of a female deity. Nineteenth- and early twentieth-century anthropologists such as Bachofen and Briffault, who had written about an original matriarchy, were rediscovered. Their work was received with surprise and joy and was seen as proof of the "truth" of human history that had been kept from women by a patriarchal conspiracy. For these new feminists, however, such ideas were not simply theories about original female power that might buttress a new equality; they were also the foundations for a new, or renewed, religion. Circles of women and some men gathered around worship of the "Goddess," presumed to be the original deity of human history.

Goddess worship was linked to "female" values that promoted peace, harmony with nature, equality, and love for all. In opposition, "masculine" values, enshrined in the male supreme deity of Judaism, Christianity, and Islam, promoted male domination, aggressive violence, subjugation of women, and exploitation of the earth. The reclaiming of Goddess worship took on the vision of a redemption of humanity and the earth from the nadir of violence and destruction that had been unleashed by patriarchal religion and rule.

THE BEGINNINGS OF FEMINIST WICCA

Two books published in the 1970s were important in popularizing the feminist reclamation of matriarchy and Goddess worship: Elizabeth Gould Davis's *The First Sex*

(1971) and Merlin Stone's *When God Was a Woman* (1976).[1] Davis argues that women literally were the original human beings, reproducing parthenogenetically. Males were the result of a mutation, she theorizes, arising when one of the X chromosomes of the female was broken into a Y. Davis notes that males with double YY chromosomes are criminals, suggesting that all males by nature are half criminals, with a violent, aggressive nature different from that of women. Davis speculates that an early lost civilization, composed only of women, was the original source of culture. This civilization, vegetarian and pacific, worshipped the female solely and invented all the arts and agriculture. But with a shift in the earth's poles, Antarctica, once tropical, was lost into the ice, and this culture was destroyed. Descendants of its people traveled across the earth, planting matriarchal civilizations.

The mutant males were originally smaller than women, who kept them under control. Davis speaks of males as only "glorified gonads" and the "frightened victims" of women. But women's habit of selecting large males as mates gradually produced men who were larger and stronger than women. At a certain point, men revolted against female domination and took revenge, harboring a vast hatred of women because of their lingering memory of women's original primacy and superiority. Davis sees this patriarchal revolution as originating from pastoral nomads, exemplified by the Hebrews. She refers to these Semites as cultureless barbarians who had "never achieved a civilization of their own."[2] They overthrew the goddess civilizations, enthroning in place of the goddess a male deity of strife, vengeance, and male domination.

Although the Semites were the prime source of patriarchy, it is the Christian church that spread this malignancy, Davis declares. She describes Christianity as imbued with a "psychopathic determination to degrade the female and annihilate her soul." It spread "like a bloody stain," bringing rapine wherever it touched. But goddess-worshipping Celtic cultures of Europe continued to resist and covertly enthroned a substitute goddess, in the figure of Mary. Davis credits the Puritans of the seventeenth century with the final triumph of patriarchal domination, eliminating any female divinity.[3] The nineteenth century virtually prohibited the economic independence of women. But women's resistance is again arising, Davis predicts, and will soon bring a matriarchal counterrevolution to save humanity from destruction.

She describes this matriarchal counterrevolution of the coming "Aquarian Age" in apocalyptic tones:

The ages of masculism are now drawing to a close. Their dying days are lit up by a final flare of universal violence and despair such as the world has seldom before seen. Men of goodwill turn in every direction seeking cures for their perishing society, but to no avail. Any and all social reforms superimposed on our sick civilization can be no more effective than a bandage on a gaping and putrefying wound. Only the complete and total demolition of the social body will cure the fatal illness. Only the overthrow of the three-thousand-year-old beast of masculist materialism will save the race.

In the new science of the twenty-first century, not physical force but spiritual force will lead the way. Mental and spiritual gifts will be more in demand than gifts of a physical nature. Extrasensory perception will take precedence over sensory perception. And in this sphere women will again predominate. She who was revered and worshiped by early man because of her power to see the unseen will once again be the pivot—not as sex but as divine woman— about whom the next civilization will, as of old, revolve.[4]

Merlin Stone is less apocalyptic in her vision of the future and describes a somewhat less dramatic shift from goddess worship and female power to patriarchy and worship of a male god. She speculates that originally the male role in procreation was unknown, with the woman seen as the sole parent. Matrilineal societies, which venerated the female as the Divine Ancestress, were then the rule. She does not construe this earlier society as one of female domination, although she is vague about this. Rather, men played their role alongside women, although it was a role structured by their lineage from their mothers, not their fathers.

According to Stone, the Indo-Europeans, who invaded from the north sometime around the middle of the third millennium (with some earlier waves going back to 4000 BCE), were responsible for the overthrow of these matrilineal, goddess-worshipping societies. The Indo-Europeans already had an aggressive, militaristic society, worshipping a supreme male war god and driving horse-drawn war chariots. Stone argues that the Jews were the primary carriers of this patriarchal overthrow of goddess worship. But since this contradicts her thesis that the Indo-Europeans are to blame, she speculates that Abraham was influenced by a "conclave of Indo-Europeans" who had migrated to his native city of Ur. She also believes that the Levites were Indo-Europeans, imposing patriarchy and male monotheism on the goddess-worshipping Hebrew tribes of Canaanite culture.[5]

Like Davis, Stone sees the Christian church as the vehicle for spreading patriarchy and male monotheism to the West, although she also mentions the "Mohammedans" as carrying this revolution forward in the East. These two religions "finish the job of killing the Goddess." But with the advent of the Enlightenment and feminism in the nineteenth and twentieth centuries, women began to revolt against male domination. Stone ends with the modest hope that men and women will find a new way of living together in mutual respect, seeing "the world and its riches as a place that belongs to every living being on it." Only then can we "begin to say we have become a truly civilized species."[6] Stone in this book does not call for a new goddess-worshipping religion or imagine an apocalyptic return to female predominance, although she would later become very interested in the rise of new religious movements centered on the Goddess.

THE LEADERSHIP OF Z. BUDAPEST AND STARHAWK

The 1970s also saw the growth of feminist "witchcraft," in which Z. (Zsuzsanna) Budapest played a key role. Modern witchcraft as a goddess-worshipping religion was developed in England in the 1940s by Gerald Gardener, who blended the speculative theories of British anthropologist Margaret Murray with ceremonial magic. (Murray had argued that medieval witchcraft was the survival of ancient goddess-worshipping paganism, which Christianity sought to repress.)[7] Gardener believed that worship of the Goddess and the Horned God (a male consort, with horns and goat legs, like the Greek God Pan) survived in secret covens that had handed down their teachings and practices into the twentieth century. He claimed to have been initiated into the "craft" in 1939 by one of the last surviving covens in England. Gardener's version of witchcraft, however, was male-dominated; the feminine deity was an enhancement of a male-centered complementarity. It fell to Z. Budapest to synthesize the ceremonial practices of witchcraft, or Wicca, with the feminist liberation movement of the 1970s.[8]

Budapest explained that she derived her knowledge of witchcraft from her mother, who in turn had been taught by a woman from a hereditary line of witches. Budapest's mother, Masika Szilagyi, was born in rural Hungary of a suffragist mother, Llona. Budapest claimed that Masika had no father, having been conceived "immaculately" in her mother's womb, without male fertilization. As a tiny infant, Masika was nurtured by Victoria, an old servant who worked in the house and was a witch. Victoria taught Masika the arts of witchcraft, "how to bless and how to curse; how diseases are cured with natural herbs; how to understand the language of animals; how to read tarot cards and omens; how to speak with spirits."[9] Budapest situated these practices in the context of the emerging women's movement, dubbing her group the "Susan B. Anthony Coven Number One." She opened a shop of witch-craft books and material in Venice, California, and began to train groups of women in the "craft."[10]

Budapest assumes the "sacred history" of an original matriarchal society and a later "fall into patriarchy." She holds that goddess worship was once the universal religion, expressing the feminine life principle of the universe. She describes the matriarchal era as a golden age that prioritized love as the ruling power of society and cultivated the arts of health and beauty. Jewelry, painting, bathing and care of the body, superior sewage systems, refined feelings, and sexual pleasure charac-terized matriarchal civilizations, she argues. Men in such societies were content to remain identified with their mothers, growing from sons into lovers, but not seek-ing domination.[11]

The ancient matriarchies exiled aggressive males who rejected this mother-centered relationship with women. These exiled males, Budapest theorizes, were the root of the patriarchal revolt against original matriarchy. They formed gangs that lurked on the edge of matriarchal civilizations, gathering strength to attack them, to seize, rape, and enslave the women. Such male hordes swarmed into Greece and the Near East from the north. Some were partly integrated into matriarchal civi-lizations, but gradually the males rose to dominance and overthrew female rule. With the overthrow of mother rule came a religious war that subordinated and then even-tually eliminated the worship of the goddess, substituting an aggressive god of pa-triarchal male dominance. The ancient male god as son and lover of the mother was transformed into a warrior father god of male rule over women.[12]

Budapest believes that the essence of Judaism can be characterized by this back-lash of patriarchal war against goddess spirituality. Christianity, she observes, has certain muted echoes of goddess religion, especially in the worship of Mary. But its dominant ethos expresses the Jewish war against the goddess, and it has become the primary vehicle for spreading this war as a global faith. The Asian religions also preserve some feminine elements but are basically patriarchal.[13] Feminist Wicca represents a rediscovery and redevelopment of the original matricentric religion of life. It is emerging as the spiritual expression of the revolt against patriarchy in mod-ern times. Patriarchal religions and societies represent the principles of death and are inherently destructive. They are digging their own graves and threatening to destroy the ecological balance of the earth. Thus, feminist Wicca embodies a strug-gle of life against death, for the very survival of humanity and the earth.

In Budapest's thealogy, the Goddess symbolizes the immanent life process of the universe. This life principle is one of plurality in dynamic interconnection, symbolized as trinity, or threeness.[14] Maleness has its place within this female-centered plurality, as the expression of the dying and rising of life within the sustaining female life principle. Patriarchal maleness, however, splits off this male function of dying and rising from its maternal matrix, distorting it into death in a purely destructive sense. Patriarchal gods thus are typically war gods, gods of death and destruction. In patriarchal religion and culture, dynamic plurality in interconnection is distorted into mutually exclusive dualities of "good" and "evil." The body, the woman, and the earth are both subordinated and identified with the negative pole in male-dominant dualisms.

The ultimate goal of feminist Wicca is not only to restore the worship of the feminine life principle but also to integrate the male principle of dying and rising back into it. Thus, men who accept their position as mother-identified, nondominant males have their place in Wicca. But Budapest herself practices what she calls "Dianic" witchcraft exclusively for women.[15] She sees this female-separatist form of witchcraft as necessary in order to form the basis for resistance to patriarchal destructive power and to wean women away from their interiorization of subordination to patriarchy.

Dianic witch covens do not admit male members or teach men the secrets of the craft, since there is too much danger that men will use the power of spells, blessings, and curses to injure women. Men who show the proper feminist spirit are allowed to learn herbology, the healing arts, and the general philosophy of Wicca, but not its core rituals.[16] The Dianic covens consider this strategy of exclusion as part of a necessary transition to a new society. Once women's full equality is won, which implies the conversion of men to the female-identified life principle and acceptance of their own place within it, then men can enter more fully into the mysteries of Wicca.

Budapest's two key books, self-published in 1979 and 1980, *The Holy Book of Women's Mysteries, Part I,* and *The Holy Book of Women's Mysteries, Part II,* partly belie this secrecy by making these mysteries available to the general public. Presumably, such description attracts interested practitioners but does not give them the actual tools to practice the craft without initiation. These books express the general worldview and thealogy of Wicca, although they are largely liturgical handbooks on how to practice the craft. The first book expounds the calendar of the eight "sabbaths" of the Sacred Wheel of the year: the Winter Solstice (December 21), Candlemas (February 3), the Spring Equinox (March 21), May Eve (April 30), the Midsummer Solstice (June 21), Lammas (August 1), Samhain (September 21), and Hallowmas (October 31), detailing rites for the observance of each sabbath.

In the second book, Budapest describes the necessary tools: the setup of the altar, the knife, the wand, the cord, the chalice, the pentagon, the cauldron, candles, oils, and incenses. She explains the meaning of various oils, perfumes, and colors as well as the functions of healing herbs. The volume contains instructions for gathering a coven, casting a sacred circle, and raising a "cone of power" in the group. (A "cone of power" is a practice of chanting that creates focused group energy.) Details concerning the interpretation of dreams, changing the weather, and divination are also included. Various kinds of spells are delineated, such as spells for sustaining health, winning the love of another, influencing the mind of another, achieving success in school or work, getting a job, changing one's luck, and attracting money. Negative spells also have their place: spells to stop harassment, to hex a rapist, to protect against danger, to punish someone who has brought harm, even to free political prisoners. But spells may not be used frivolously. One must be sure that the persons hexed are truly guilty. The basic ethic of the craft is summed up in the phrase "Harm none and do what thou wilt."[17]

A witch may practice the craft both in a tightly bonded coven, led by a high priestess, and alone, in her own home before a personal altar. In community, the rites of the year and ritual circles are performed; alone, a witch may engage in rituals of daily life, such as self-blessing or blessing of the day and night, as well as casting spells for bringing good fortune and hexing evildoers. In addition, mass celebrations, or "groves," bring together many women at major festivals or gatherings. Celebrations are typically carried out "sky clad"—naked, save for flowers and jewelry—and thus demand care in selecting protected venues.

Budapest's view of the role of the high priestess is somewhat hierarchical. This priestess is given the dominant role in teaching others, orchestrating rituals, and managing the flow of energy in the group. Budapest cautions against extreme egalitarianism that refuses to recognize and venerate the high priestess, warning that it can lead to resentment, anger, and ultimately chaos. She also points out the necessity of having an assistant who is attuned to the energy of the high priestess and helps orient the group toward her leadership.[18]

Z. Budapest's most important disciple as thealogian-theorist and organizer-teacher of feminist Wicca is undoubtedly Starhawk (Miriam Simos), although Starhawk also credits other teachers and claims to have been initiated and trained in the "faery" tradition going back to the Old Religion of the British Isles.[19] Starhawk, as a trained psychotherapist, brings a sophisticated sense of the processes of personal healing and group dynamics to her practice and theory of Wicca.

Starhawk grew up in the Jewish tradition and began college at the University of California at Los Angeles in 1968. Her interest in witchcraft was sparked by discussion of the subject in an anthropology class. She and a friend then offered their own class in witchcraft as a way of learning about it themselves. Only in the early 1970s did she meet real Wiccans, particularly Z. Budapest, and begin to attend women's rituals, under Budapest's leadership. After an unsuccessful move to New York City, with the hope of becoming a published novelist, she returned to California and moved to San Francisco, where she started to meet other members of the growing pagan community and to teach classes in ritual (from which her covens, such as the Compost Coven, were formed).[20]

From her teaching and practice in forming communities, Starhawk wrote her first major book on feminist Wicca, *The Spiral Dance: A Rebirth of the Ancient Religion of the Great Goddess,* published first in 1979. In the 1980s, she became increasingly involved in antiwar and ecological activism. From this political experience, she began to shape a perspective on feminist Wiccan spirituality and ritual that was integrally linked to and expressed through political action. These further developments of her thought are reflected in her 1982 and 1987 books, *Dreaming the Dark: Magic, Sex, and Politics* and *Truth or Dare: Encounters with Power, Authority, and Mystery.*[21]

Starhawk also taught for more than ten years in Dominican priest Matthew Fox's Institute of Culture and Creation Spirituality, based at the Catholic Holy Names College in Oakland.[22] This association brought her into contact with new forms of Christian feminist and ecological spirituality remarkably similar to the worldview that she was developing in feminist Wicca. This experience, among others, broadened Starhawk's worldview ecumenically, leading her to recognize patterns of spirituality in other religions similar to her own perspective. She no longer assumed a simple dichotomy that cast Christianity and other "patriarchal religions" as solely destructive and Wicca as the sole positive religion, a view that Z. Budapest tended to reflect in her 1970s work.[23]

In the 1989 revised edition of *The Spiral Dance,* Starhawk notes the ways her worldview changed over the decade since the book's initial publication, although most of its essentials remained the same. One area of change was her view of maleness and femaleness. Her earlier work reflected an essentialist view of distinct female and male "energies" found predominantly either in women or in men. By the late 1980s, she had rejected this Jungian-influenced dichotomy, in favor of seeing both women and men as complex wholes, each with a full range of energies.[24] Patriarchal cultures, she asserts, have split men and women into dualities, assigning a certain profile of powers to men and complementary or negative opposites to women, but this distorts the true capacities of both sexes. Likewise, goddess and god are neither role models for women and men nor manifestations of dual energies in the cosmos; rather, they reflect complex interconnections within and between both men and women.

Starhawk does not accept the Dianic form of separatist witchcraft practiced by Z. Budapest, seeking instead to include both women and men in her covens. Increasingly, she has moved away from a dualistic scheme of female and male roles as Goddess and Horned God in these covens in favor of a view that sees these capacities in both genders. Starhawk's political work also sensitized her to class and ethnic diversity and the necessity of recognizing a plurality of cultural perspectives. She sees her brand of Wicca as a revival of traditional forms of shamanism from the British Isles. In her view, many cultures throughout the world, particularly the nonwhite world, have never completely lost their shaman traditions. Witches such as herself need to respect the shamanism of other ethnic groups rather than seeing their own perspective as universal or trying to appropriate the traditions of other groups.[25]

This embrace of cultural diversity makes Starhawk ecumenical toward the many kinds of shamanistic traditions throughout the world. She also sees remnants of immanent spirituality in traditional patriarchal religions, such as Christianity, that are reemerging and being renewed through the challenges of feminism and ecological crisis. She believes that Wiccans should not demonize other groups as the "enemy"— a pattern of patriarchal religion from which they themselves have suffered—but should instead be prepared to embrace life-giving spirituality wherever it is found.[26]

This ecumenism and the embrace of diversity do not obviate a basic distinction in Starhawk's thought between a life-giving spirituality of immanence of life in and through all things, promoting complex interconnection and community, in contrast to patterns of estrangement that divide the world between heaven and earth, good and evil, men and women, and set up systems of domination of some over others. But she has come to see the tension between immanent interconnection and community versus estrangement and domination as complexly situated in various religions and cultures. As a person raised in the Jewish tradition, Starhawk avoids the anti-Semitic Jew-blaming found in many earlier goddess traditions, even in the work of Z. Budapest. Rather, she celebrates elements of goddess worship found in Jewish esoteric traditions such as Kabbalah, while recognizing the patterns of patriarchy found in normative Judaism.[27]

Starhawk also critiques the tendency toward hierarchy and the dominant role of the high priestess found in Budapest's work.[28] She seeks to overcome all elements of "power over" in her communities and to develop patterns of relationship that are more genuinely circular and egalitarian, while recognizing that some persons in a group have particular talents and skills. Any community needs recognized leadership, she argues, but this might take the form of recognizing a great diversity of gifts and roles and circulating these roles over time rather than setting up one person as a permanent high priestess.

This work of community building leads Starhawk to differentiate three kinds of power: "power over," "power within," and "power with."[29] "Power over," or domination, is the form of power foundational to patriarchal cultures. It expresses a view of power as the control and use of some by others and has so shaped our consciousness that it has come to be identified with the very nature of consciousness itself. The work of feminist spirituality and ritual is a long process, not only of resisting systems and cultures of domination outside Wiccan groups but also of exorcising the many ways those within this movement continue to interiorize patterns of power that assume either control over others or passivity toward such control. In Starhawk's practice, magic, ritual, trance, and visualization increasingly coincide with processes of inward growth by which persons free themselves from their inner demons of self-hate and are able to enter into a community of equals.[30]

Wiccan spirituality is about freeing individuals and communities from these patterns of domination, or "power over," by linking each person in themselves and in community with their own inner power. By coming in contact with their own inner worth, beauty, talents, and life force, women and men can overthrow the internalized patterns of domination and subjugation within and among them. But Wiccan spirituality is more than simply coming in contact with one's own inner power. There is also a need to find new ways of respecting and interacting with each other's power in a way that is not based on new forms of control. This kind of relation to one another's power Starhawk calls "power with."[31]

Becoming tuned to one another's power allows a member of the community to offer inspired suggestions for action and the others to intuitively develop a consensus about supporting such actions, recognizing that they feel "right" rather than being threatened by the creativity of others. The community thus avoids both the negative side of egalitarianism, as a flattening of all to a common dullness, and the tendency to stab natural leaders in the back. This concept of "power with" is key to Starhawk's effort to recognize special talents and capacities for leadership without setting up new hierarchies.

Starhawk's political activism in the antiwar and ecological movements, including brief incarcerations, brought her into intimate contact with the violence of the military and the police. This contact deepened her analysis of the subtle and complex combinations of direct violence and the internalization of passivity, self-hatred, and horizontal violence among the oppressed. In her later books, descriptions of the jail experiences of women who had been arrested for participating in protests provide graphic illustrations of the psychosocial processes of control and resistance to control.[32] In recent years, she has developed perceptive methods of channeling group energy into nonviolent demonstrations against oppressive world power, such as the World Trade Organization, helping to avoid chaotic outbreaks of violence that justify police retaliation.[33]

"Magic" as the transformation of consciousness in relation to outward circumstances takes on a more overt political aspect in her thought and work. Protest rituals conducted at a nuclear test site or a weapons factory merge symbolic and political action. It has become evident to Starhawk that feminist spirituality must be more than individual or small-group solutions to personal problems, although that remains an important aspect. There must also be systemic change of the economic, political, and social systems of domination and oppression.[34]

Starhawk preserves the basic Wiccan view of history, but it becomes more inclusive of diverse histories in her developing thought. She believes that there was once a time of matricentric culture, where deity was seen as the immanent life force of the whole universe, linking all peoples, men and women, with one another in complex interconnection and community. Every people originally had forms of religion that expressed this matricentric society and values. This culture and its forms of social relationships were gradually subverted at different times in the transition from Paleolithic to Neolithic and Bronze Age cultures, but remnants of it survived in the many forms of shamanism found in every culture, better preserved in some than in others.[35]

Key to the patriarchal revolution was the development of systems of domination by a few and oppression of others, ratified by a worldview of dualistic hierarchies. The inner core of patriarchal culture is estrangement, the estrangement of mind from body, men from women, thought from feeling, humans from the earth. These patterns of domination and estrangement are now bringing humans to a stage of such global violence, militarism, and ecological pollution that life on earth itself is threatened. A new consciousness—found in feminist Wicca, but also in many renewed forms of earth-centered spirituality in religions throughout the world—represents the rising of the human and earth spirit to resist this destructive onslaught and reverse the patterns of domination and estrangement.[36]

Although Starhawk sees the roots of the patriarchal revolution in ancient societies of five or six thousand years ago, she argues that these patterns of estrangement and destructive domination significantly intensified much more recently, in the transition to modernity in Europe in the sixteenth and seventeenth centuries. Drawing on the work of historian of science Carolyn Merchant,[37] Starhawk sees this as the decisive period of the shift from an organic to a mechanistic view of the natural world and the human place in it.

Christianity, although patriarchal, preserved covertly many elements of earlier goddess-worshipping cultures and continued to see the divine as an immanent organic power of life in all things. The sixteenth and seventeenth centuries saw not only the culmination of attempts to destroy the last remnants of European shamanism, by labeling witchcraft as "devil worship," but also a series of other economic and cultural shifts that made the patterns of domination and estrangement much more rigid.

In the epilogue of *Dreaming the Dark*, expanded in the 1997 edition, Starhawk seeks to epitomize the many aspects of the pervasive estrangement and domination now spreading as a global culture, from Western roots, threatening the destruction of the whole earth.[38] In England, the center of the initial shift to modernity, these new patterns were expressed in developments such as the enclosure movement, which uprooted peasants from the land, turning them into a landless proletariat for the new industrial economy or foot soldiers for colonialist expansion. The rise of the market economy; expanding Western colonialist control over Asia, Africa, and Latin America and warring against the earlier cultures of those areas; subjugation of peoples and lands; the professionalization of knowledge and institutionalized education; the removal of women particularly from forms of knowledge passed down in the family and from participation in the work of a family-based economy—all these are aspects of a shift to a more total system of estrangement and domination.

Desacralization of the universe is key to shaping the world into resources for appropriation into an industrial and market economy. This shift to a new stage of the culture of domination and estrangement did not take place without struggle: the persecution of witches; the war on many popular protest groups, such as the Diggers and Ranters in seventeenth-century England;[39] crusades against the cultures of indigenous peoples of the non-Western world. In this compact conclusion of her book, Starhawk joins the Wiccan "sacred story" of the persecution and survival of European witchcraft with many other stories of oppressed people both within the Western world and in postcolonial struggles in the non-Western world.

THE THEALOGY OF CAROL CHRIST

Perhaps the leading thealogian seeking to create a comprehensive account of the religious and ethical worldview implied by Goddess thought and practice is Carol

Christ. Christ grew up in California in a family of mixed religious traditions: Catholic, Protestant, Christian Scientist. She attended a Presbyterian church as a child and adolescent. As an undergraduate at Stanford University, she was attracted to the study of Hebrew scripture and Jewish thought, especially to the work of Martin Buber. She went on to do graduate work in religion at Yale. While completing a degree in theology, she was drawn to literature as a source for the spiritual quest, both women's literature, such as that of Doris Lessing, Margaret Atwood, Kate Chopin, Adrienne Rich, and Ntozake Shange, and also the Jewish Holocaust novels of Elie Weisel. She wrote her doctoral dissertation on Weisel's stories, and her first book, *Diving Deep and Surfacing*, grew from her studies of women's literature.[40]

Christ's early work in religion and literature was an attempt to connect theology to the experiences of people's lives, her own and those of others. Christ was also inspired by the feminist insights that "the personal is political" and that "theology begins with experience." In her work, she consistently combines reflection on her personal journey with theological reflection, using a model that she has come to call "embodied embedded thinking."[41]

The study of Weisel and Jewish history shocked Christ into a realization of the deep evils that had been perpetrated by Christian anti-Judaism, culminating in the Holocaust. Feminist writings and the feminist movement made her increasingly aware of how Christianity was permeated with patterns of thought that legitimated the subordination of and contempt for women and modeled divine power after the male warrior. For these reasons, she became increasingly alienated from Christianity and found it impossible to go to church.

In 1974, while writing about Elie Wiesel's anger at God for not intervening to stop the Holocaust, she expressed her own anger at God for not preventing the oppression and violation of women. In the silence that followed, she heard a still, small voice saying, "In God is a woman like yourself. She shares your suffering."[42] In 1975, through Naomi Goldenberg, her fellow student at Yale, Christ became aware of the Wiccan movement and the work of Z. Budapest. Back home in California, Christ was introduced to the women's spirituality movement. Later that year, she and Goldenberg took an alternative university class on witchcraft from Starhawk.[43]

As Christ was drawn into the Goddess movement, she began to participate in rituals with Starhawk and also to create her own rituals and group. She experienced the Wiccan movement as "coming home" to a worldview that had always been her deepest intuition, but one that she had been discouraged from validating by her androcentric upbringing and education. She began to articulate her rejection of Christianity in favor of the Goddess in academic meetings, such as the Women and Religion section of the American Academy of Religion, and in major articles such as the much reprinted "Why Women Need the Goddess."[44]

Most of the leading feminist theologians, however, declined to follow her in this new option or to validate her new path. She felt betrayed by this response from feminists in religious studies but took heart at the growing number of ordinary women who were being drawn into the Goddess movement.[45] She was also increasingly aware that her new "journey to the Goddess" was imperiling her chances of finding employment in religious studies, where jobs were open mainly to Christians.

Leaving religious studies for women's studies allowed Christ to refocus her career goals. She married, found a promising job at San José State University in California, and seemed to settle into the trajectory of the typical American academic dream, with a large house and mortgage. In a few years, however, she began to experience deep burnout from the academic rat race, driving the polluted freeways between home and work, teaching students who were often uninterested and were taking her courses merely to fulfill requirements. Her marriage was falling apart. She had begun to journey to Greece during the summers to study and teach Goddess traditions in their ancient settings, and she finally decided to give up her academic career and move permanently to Greece, settling at first on the island of Lesbos, where the poet Sappho had lived in ancient times.[46]

Although Christ says that she "never for one moment looked back" from this decision,[47] she went through a period of deep depression in the early 1990s. An intense love relationship had ended. She felt unable to write, experiencing writer's block. Feelings of isolation and failure and the fear that she was unlovable resurfaced and brought suicidal thoughts. She even felt abandoned by the Goddess and was angry at her. The refrain "no one loves you, no one will ever love you, you might as well die" echoed in her mind.[48] She spent most of her time renovating a newly purchased apartment in Athens, hoping to welcome her parents to Greece for their first visit. Instead, she received word that her mother had been diagnosed with cancer.

Christ's trip back to her parents' home to be with her mother in her dying days became a revelatory turning point. As her mother died, Christ felt bathed in an ambiance of love and experienced the deepest nature of the universe as embodied love.[49] This experience decisively resolved her uncertainty as to whether the Goddess was simply a metaphor for oneself or the sum total of an indifferent "nature" (the views of two of her closest friends, Naomi Goldenberg and Judith Plaskow) or whether the Goddess represented an embodied personal power within and beyond us who cares for us. Christ now felt that she had the experiential basis for clearly choosing the latter view.[50]

At the same time, she examined her relation to her father and found that it explained the roots of her tendencies to feel abandoned, betrayed, and despairing. She realized that her father, the son of an alcoholic father, had compensated by establishing a rigid pattern of control, acted out in demands for perfection and judgmental criticism toward her. Her tendency to believe that she could never be good enough and was always going to prove unlovable had its roots in how her father had related to her.[51]

These experiences and insights enabled Christ to return to her adopted home in Greece, pull out of her feeling of despair, and regain her creative energy. The process of bringing a group of women on a "goddess" pilgrimage to the island of Crete, where she led them in retracing and performing rituals at the sites of ancient goddess worship in Minoan culture, reconnected her with her experience of the Goddess. This reassured her that the Goddess had not abandoned her but indeed continued to love her and would always love her. "My muse returned. Words were flowing out of me, the more poetic words I came to Greece to write. I would return again and again to the mountains and caves of Crete, by myself, with friends and with other pilgrims. My life would be filled with amazing grace, love abounding and overflowing."[52]

Building on her new energy and insights, Christ was able to complete a manuscript she had started some years before, which explained the thealogy of the Goddess in a more systematic way. It was published in 1997 as *Rebirth of the Goddess: Finding Meaning in Feminist Spirituality*. Further work in this direction appears in her book *She Who Changes: Re-Imagining the Divine in the World*, in which she integrates process theology into Goddess thealogy. Her more recent work brings together both her new stage of psychological development and her experiences of living in Greece and experiencing the Greek goddesses in their ancient home, allowing her to modify and nuance the understanding of the Goddess that she had drawn from the tutelage of the Wiccan movement in the United States.

One aspect of Wiccan religion that Christ has come to reject through her experiences in Greece is the concept and practice of magic. She identifies the idea of magic as part of a very American and patriarchal quest for control, based on the belief that individuals can bend reality to their will. She also sees this quest for control duplicated in New Age spirituality in the United States, which can imply that individuals can get whatever they want and that if they have bad experiences, it is because they have "chosen" them.[53] Christ, by contrast, insists that we are only partially in control of our lives and that many things happen to us, good and bad, which we do not choose. She herself seeks to let go of control and "go with the flow," becoming able to interact with events outside her control rather than becoming upset when everything does not go as planned.[54]

Her life in Greece has given her a critical perspective on the Goddess movement in the United States. She sees American Goddess spirituality as heavily based on ideas that seek to "create" the Goddess through focusing their will and energy to "raise a cone of power." This practice reflects a lack of groundedness in a land whose history bespeaks a long tradition of the presence of the Goddess. Euro-Americans are uprooted people who left lands in Europe that had such histories. They despoiled the indigenous peoples of the Americas without ever integrating with their culture. Instead, their myths have centered on conquest of the land and a historical destiny and selection by a God unconnected with the land in which they live.[55]

By contrast, the Greeks live in a land dotted with sites of prepatriarchal goddess worship. Even though their culture and religion are patriarchal, under the surface the people of Greece still live in continuity with these earlier roots. Many little churches signal a cave or other holy site of earlier goddess worship, often linked in Crete with sacred trees. Their icons celebrate Mary as the "all holy" (Panagia), also linked with sacred trees. Christ herself has warmed to these aspects of Greek folk Christianity and has shared in the veneration of icons and sacred myrtle trees with communities of Orthodox nuns in areas such as Crete, which she believes are continuing elements of the ancient religion. Her goddess tours include visits to such communities of nuns, as well as trips to caves and ruins of ancient palaces, as part of a living history still inscribed in the Cretan land and its people.[56] Christ describes the Greek people, men as well as women, as being much more in touch with their bodies and feelings than Americans are, and she writes that they have taught her to "let go" and be in touch with the natural flow of life.[57]

Although Christ still affirms the "sacred history" of original matrifocal societies in which humans were in harmony with one another and the land, societies that were then overthrown by patriarchy, her reading and her response to critics have nuanced her account. She firmly rejects the description of this "prepatriarchal" time as "matriarchy."[58] Rather, she sees it more as an egalitarian complementarity, in which women as well as men had their spheres of power and expertise. Women's areas of life were equally venerated and not subordinated to those of men. In preindustrial subsistence societies, such as parts of rural Greece, much of that pattern of complementary power and skill continues, although the female sphere has been devalued in official rhetoric and women disempowered.[59]

The "fall into patriarchy" in her account has also become more complex—it is less a dramatic overthrow of a female-dominated utopian society by horse-riding outsiders and more a complex process in which both internal evolution and outside invasion played roles. As early gardening societies in which women played a predominant role changed to plow agriculture, men took control of the land and its produce. The invention of bronze and iron created more powerful weapons. Warfare spread and with it the enslavement of the conquered. Those who had developed these militaristic and hierarchical patterns conquered those who remained more pacific and imposed their patterns on these peaceable peoples. Christ considers warfare as the key development that created patriarchal patterns of society and its supporting ideologies.[60]

Myths of the defeat and slaying of a goddess supported the transition to the new society. In other cases, goddesses were co-opted to become auxiliary supporters of the patriarchal order. Goddess religion is partly an attempt to resurrect, through imaginative reading of early artifacts, the patterns of egalitarian harmony among men, women, and nature that existed in prepatriarchal times. It is also partly a modern development that seeks to deconstruct the patterns of patriarchal religion and envision how its alienated hierarchical dualisms could be reintegrated into a life-giving communion. The victory of a new society is not guaranteed by some all-powerful deity. Rather, one can only try in many small ways to create more life-giving patterns of relationship and to hope that it is not too late to prevent some massive destruction of life on earth by global warfare and ecological devastation.[61]

In her efforts to give a more comprehensive account of thealogy, parallel to the traditional topics of systematic theology, Christ seeks to avoid any simple reversal of patriarchal dualisms. It is not enough simply to value the female, the body, the earth, the emotions, and the unconscious, although this may be a necessary starting point. Rather, one must overcome the dualistic hierarchy of male and female, mind and body, heaven and earth, feeling and thinking, dark and light, the one and the many, transcendence and immanence, transforming them into a new interactive unity.[62]

Her definition of the Goddess as "intelligent embodied love as the ground of all being" seeks to glimpse this kind of vision. Polytheism and monotheism are integrated in a vision of a Goddess with many names, experienced in many ways in different cultures and lands, but manifesting an underlying unity of the earth and all its beings. Christ also allows that we need to widen this definition to include the universe, though she wishes to focus primarily on our planet, the earth.[63] The Goddess (who can also be called by male metaphors, although Christ finds the female metaphor preferable in order to jolt our minds out of their traditional patterns) is the immanent life energy in all things. But the Goddess is more than simply the sum of what is. In some ways, she is also transcendent—not in the sense of being split off into a disconnected heaven, but in the sense of an interactive, loving relation with existing beings. She is both mind and body, spirit and matter, not as a dualism of one against the other, but as one embodied energy and spirit. Here, Christ draws on process theology for a description of the Goddess as the power of loving persuasion that calls beings into transformative response, but who also suffers when beings refuse to respond and instead relate to one another with hostility.[64]

For Christ, life is inherently finite. There is no heaven of immortal life beyond this earth. Although she believes that love outweighs tragedy, we all encounter irreparable losses that cannot be remedied or justified; such losses are part of natural life, and we have to accept them.[65] There is also massive unjust violence and loss of life, which we should resist and try to prevent by undoing the systems that cause such injustice. We live on in the many new beings that arise from the disintegrating bodies of dead animals and plants and in the spirits and memories of those who come after us—in other words, we live on in the ongoing body of Gaia (Earth)-Goddess. We need to accept our own finitude and integrate ourselves into the cycles of life rather than trying to resist death.[66] Life goes on precisely through the rhythms of birth, growth, disintegration, death, and rebirth. The Goddess lives in this cyclical rhythm of life.

In response to the essentialist/anti-essentialist debate, Christ insists that biology matters. Men and women have different bodies, which give them different experiences and capacities. Unlike men, women menstruate; they give birth and suckle babies. Goddess religion celebrates and valorizes the female body and its functions and thus restores beauty and dignity to that which has been devalued in patriarchal religions. But beyond these particular differences, Christ sees men and women as much the same. They have similar intellectual and moral capacities. Men are as capable of loving tenderness as women, and women are as capable of hatred and evil as men. Patriarchy has constructed men and women into false opposites. Women need to learn to love their particularities as females, and men need to both value these female particularities in women and get back in touch with their own bodies and feelings.[67] To do this, it is particularly important for men to participate in childbirth and child raising. All humans need to reintegrate ourselves into the rhythms of Gaia, into the earth life process, in order to reconstruct a harmonious way of life with one another on earth.

For Christ, the root of evil in human life is the denial of love.[68] To deny love is not only to distort one's own life but also to set off a chain reaction that distorts loving relationships for generations to come. She sees this pattern in the relation of her father to the alcoholism of his father, and, in turn, in her father's controlling inability to love her wholeheartedly. Denial of love causes endless suffering, making us blame ourselves for our unhappiness rather than recognizing the source of our suffering.

Christ argues that patriarchal cultures enshrine relationships of control, domination, and violence. The distortion of relations caused by the denial of love is transmitted not only between parents and children but also in schools, religion, the military, the arts—in all the institutions of society. She thus sees in her own family experience a key element that helps to explain human failure to love and to relate to one another in life-giving ways.

Christ believes that the symbol of the Goddess has the metaphorical power to unsettle deeply rooted cultural symbolisms that enshrine and perpetuate these patterns of violence, hierarchy, and domination. This belief gives urgency to her decision to focus the energies of her life on the rebirth of the Goddess in contemporary Western culture. For her, the Goddess is a symbol who radiates a transforming power that calls us to change all the institutions of dominating societies and cultures.[69]

THE DEVELOPING NEOPAGAN MOVEMENT

In the mid-1970s, the neopagan movement began to organize on national and regional levels and to seek legal status as a recognized American religion. On March 1, 1975, some forty witches from fifteen California covens came together in Oakland to explore their differences and commonalities. On that day, they founded an organization called the Covenant of the Goddess and designated a committee to draft a charter and by-laws. On the summer solstice of that year, 150 witches and pagans gathered at a retreat in California's Mendocino County for midsummer festival, where they unanimously ratified the charter and by-laws of the Covenant of the Goddess.

The organization seeks to carefully balance centralizing functions and local control. A national board handles issues of legal standing and questions about the craft as a whole. The governing body is the grand council, made up of representatives of all member covens. Board members cannot vote at council meetings. Covens geographically close enough to meet on a regular basis have local councils, which sponsor festivals, set up training programs, and establish the credentials of member covens. The Covenant of the Goddess does not ordain, but it does issue ministerial credentials to members designated by particular covens. The Covenant does not make pronouncements about the legitimacy of any group that does not join the organization, but it has "determined that we who are members of the Covenant are of the same religion and respect some essentially identical Craft Laws."[70]

Representatives of the Covenant of the Goddess participated in meetings of the Parliament of the World's Religions in Chicago (August 28 to September 5, 1993), Capetown, South Africa (December 1–8, 1999), and Barcelona, Spain (July 7–13, 2004). The participation of the Covenant and other neopagan groups aroused criticism from conservative and orthodox Christians, but their presence was affirmed by the organizers of the parliament. The parliament, first held in Chicago in 1893, has typically been a forum for smaller religious groups seeking recognition in American culture vis-à-vis dominant forms of Christianity.[71] In more recent meetings of the parliament, groups such as Sikhs, Jains, and Baha'i have also been well represented.

The Covenant of the Goddess held workshops and prepared papers and pamphlets for distribution at the 1993, 1999, and 2004 parliaments, explaining who they were to the other participants and the general public. One of these papers, written by Selene Fox, leader of the Circle Sanctuary of Mt. Horeb, Wisconsin, is titled "I Am Pagan."[72] It is an appealing, two-page description of her faith as a pagan:

I am Pagan. I am part of the whole of Nature. The Rocks, the Animals, the Plants, the Elements, and Stars are my relatives. Other humans are my sisters and brothers, whatever their races, colors, genders, sexual orientation, nationalities, religions, lifestyles. Planet Earth in my home. I am part of this large family of Nature, not the master of it. I have my own special part to play and I seek to discover and play that part to the best of my ability. I seek to live in harmony with others in the family of Nature, treating others with respect.

The paper talks about the eight seasonal festivals held by the Covenant and the celebrations that mark the seasons of life: "I celebrate the changing seasons, the turning of the Wheel of the Year. . . . I also honor the seasons of life within my life's journey, beginnings, growth, fruition, harvest, endings, rest and beginnings again. Life is a Circle with many cycles. With every Ending comes a new Beginning, within Death there is the promise of Rebirth." Fox then describes magic as "intentional consciousness change." Citing the Wiccan Rede (credo), "And it harm none, do what you will," she discusses magic as healing rituals, "to help and to heal others, myself and the Planet."

Theologically, Fox defines herself as a pantheist, "acknowledging the Divine is everywhere and in everything." All that has a physical body also has a spiritual body. The physical and the spiritual are intertwined. Creator and Creation are interconnected. Although she honors many manifestations of the divine in gods and goddesses, Fox also finds a oneness underlying all things: "I honor Divine Oneness, the

Unity of All." She describes paganism as a tolerant, nonproselytizing religion, although it is open to anyone truly interested. There is no one "right way for everyone. There are many paths up the mountain of spiritual understanding."

According to Fox, paganism is a religion concerned about ecology, militarism, and social justice:

> I hear the cries of Mother Earth who is upset with the harm being done to the environment by humankind. I am dismayed by the pollution of the air, the soil and the waters, and by the domination games being played by nations with the fire of nuclear missiles and other weapons of mass destruction. I am also concerned about the spiritual pollution on the Planet, selfishness, hatred, greed for money and addiction, violence and despair. Yet as I perceive these problems, I also perceive cleansing and healing happening on Planet Earth at this time. I know that I can help in at least a small way to bring Planet Earth into greater balance by seeking balance in my own life, by being a catalyst for restoring balance in the lives of others, and by working for a better environment.

Fox concludes with these words: "I am pagan. Nature spirituality is my religion and my life's foundation. Nature is my spiritual teacher and holy book. I am part of Nature and Nature is part of me. My understanding of Nature's inner mysteries grows as I journey on this spiritual path."

In their ecumenical outreach, the Covenant of the Goddess and other groups, such as EarthSpirit in Massachusetts, define themselves as seeking solidarity with any spiritual path that embraces similar concerns about the sacredness of all life.[73] One does not find in this literature diatribes against Christians or Jews as inherently patriarchal or opposed to nature. There is a special affinity with the indigenous shamanist religions found throughout the world, such as those of American Indians or Africans. Wicca itself is defined as a revival of the "ancient, pre-Christian indigenous religion of Europe."[74]

As Wiccan and neopagan groups became more public, they also faced virulent attacks led by fundamentalist Christians. The most serious threat to Wiccan religious freedom came from the 1985 attempt by Senator Jesse Helms and Representative Robert Walker to deny tax-exempt status to any group defined as "promoting satanism or witchcraft." Their amendment to HR 3036 defined "Satanism" as "the worship of Satan or the powers of evil" and "witchcraft" as "the use of powers derived from evil spirits, the use of sorcery or the use of supernatural powers with malicious intent."[75] Although Wiccans reject Satanism, or the worship of evil powers, completely, viewing Satan as a Christian idea they do not accept, they realized that this amendment would very likely be applied to them. Concerted nationwide organizing eventually defeated the amendment. Additionally, Wiccans have sought to rescind local laws against fortunetellers, which are often used to discriminate against Wiccan tarot readers, astrologers, and "metaphysical advisors." They also organize protests when Wiccans are discriminated against in any field of employment, such as teaching, simply because of their religion.

The Lady Liberty League was organized in 1985 under the Circle Sanctuary to defend Wiccans against all forms of legal and privately organized discrimination and to promote their acceptance in various public sites, such as schools, prisons, and even the U.S. Army.[76] Groups such as the American Civil Liberties Union have aided Wiccans in these struggles. Through its attorneys and communications network, the Lady Liberty League has taken on an array of cases, including those involving the rights of students to wear symbols of their faith in schools, the rights of pagan students in high schools and colleges to form recognized student groups for worship or study, the acceptance of Wiccan ministers as chaplains in the military and in prisons, state recognition of Wiccans as clergy for weddings, and the right to gather in privately owned camp grounds for festivals or worship without harassment.

Considerable progress has been made in the last fifteen years in the acceptance of Wiccans as chaplains. The U.S. Army's *Military Chaplain's Handbook* contains an accurate portrayal of Wiccans in chapter 7, under "other groups," a category that includes the Native American Church, the Baha'i Faith, and the Church of Scientology.[77] Wiccans have also served as chaplains in some prisons; priestess Rev. Jamyi Witch at the Waupun Correctional Institute in Wisconsin is one example.

The Wiccan religious liberty network also keeps its eye on the media, protesting the equation of Wiccans with Satanism or Nazism. In the spring 2001 *Intelligence Report* published by the Southern Poverty Law Center in Montgomery, Alabama, an article entitled "The New Romantics" discussed Asatru, or Odinist, pagans as dangerous racists, in a way that could easily be construed as including all Wiccans or pagans. Although some Odinists, who seek to revive what they regard as "Norse paganism," do espouse elements of white supremacy, this type of racist paganism is repudiated by other pagans.[78] The Liberty League won a clarification of this distinction from Mark Potok, editor of the SPLC *Intelligence Report*.

The Covenant of the Goddess supports tolerance of differences between member covens on how to interpret paganism. Some pagans, such as Starhawk, are pacifist and reject participation in any violence, while others see the warrior life as part of historical paganism. The Covenant does not take a stand on pacifism, accepting both conscientious objectors and those who embrace a warrior ethic.[79] But tolerance clearly has its limits. For example, the Covenant has drawn boundaries and rejected racist forms of paganism. In making such a distinction, the Covenant follows lines similar to those of liberal religion in the United States generally.

Despite constant efforts to define themselves as peaceful, life-affirming nature worshippers, who do not even believe in—much less worship—the devil, Wiccans and pagans continue to be attacked as "devil worshippers," by Christian conservatives. Seizing on the terms "witch" and "witchcraft" for this movement, Christian conservatives attempt to define Wiccans and pagans in language drawn from the witch persecutions of the late medieval and Reformation periods. The access to media commanded by Christian fundamentalism greatly outweighs that of pagans and Wiccans, putting them at great disadvantage in their ability to define themselves in American public culture. Nevertheless, their successes in the army, prisons, and schools suggest that neopagans are on their way to being accepted within the rubric of American constitutional religious liberty.

Another important indication of the normalization of Goddess-centered paganism in American religion was the acceptance, in 1987, of the Covenant of Unitarian Universalist Pagans (CUUPs) within the Unitarian Universalist denomination. CUUPs is an affiliate network of pagan-identified Unitarian Universalists who develop chapters for ritual and education within local churches and seek to educate the denomination on the national level about paganism. CUUPS also networks with the larger pagan community in the United States. Unitarian Universalists have accepted "earth-centered traditions which celebrate the sacred circle of life and instruct us to live in harmony with the rhythms of nature" as the sixth source of Unitarian Universalist tradition, alongside others, such as Judaism and Christianity. This source is understood to include contemporary neopaganism as well as Native American and other indigenous religious traditions. Unitarian Universalist pagans also promote interreligious dialogue between pagans and other religious traditions.[80]

In my view, it is the duty of liberal and progressive Christians to defend the religious liberties of Wiccans and pagans. This is the case for several reasons. First, Wicca is a positive movement that affirms the life values that Christians should also affirm, even if Christians might not agree with Wiccans on some aspects of their theologies or on some historical details, such as the existence of an original matricentric civilization overthrown by patriarchal warriors or the view that the witch-hunts in Christian history targeted a goddess-worshipping religion.[81] (Wiccans are becoming much more nuanced in these historical claims, in any case.)

Second, although the witchhunts in the thirteenth to seventeenth centuries may not have actually targeted goddess worshippers, these attacks were an egregious crime against innocent and largely poor and powerless women, men, and children. Christians have never repented of this crime or publicly repudiated it. It is high time to do so and to make clear that the people targeted in these persecutions were not Satanists, but harmless people. In the process, Christians must also reject use of the language of that era's witch persecutions against a contemporary religious movement that seeks to be life-affirming and to promote peaceful, harmonious relations among all peoples and the earth.

Beyond the question of religious liberty for Wiccans, many common values are shared by Wiccans and ecofeminists merging from Christianity and other mainstream historic religions. Is ecumenical dialogue possible between Christian ecofeminists and Wiccans? Is a new frontier of religious vision, largely shared across these religious communities today, emerging in response to the challenges of ecological crisis and militarism in modern societies and the questioning of traditional patriarchal religions? It is to these questions that I turn in the concluding reflections of this book.

CONCLUSION

In light of the long history traced in this volume, the question I wish to address here is this: what conclusions can we draw from this complex story of how gender has functioned symbolically in ancient Near Eastern, Mediterranean, and western European religious systems? I do not have any final answer to this question. I find this history puzzling in many ways and will continue to mull over its implications long after this book is published.

In the dominant story line that comes from thealogians such as those discussed in chapter 10, the implications are clear. There was once a culture, they assert— possibly worldwide, for most of human history, until the last few thousand years— in which a matricentric, if not matriarchal, society flourished. Humans were in harmony with one another and nature, and a female-personified deity expressed the immanent life energy that cycled through the earth as one community. This happy culture was overthrown by patriarchy and its female deity repressed, replaced by a male monotheism that enshrined estrangement, hierarchy, domination, and violence. Any continuing ways in which deity is symbolized as female/feminine can only be survivals of that earlier, matricentric religion, continuing covertly within patriarchy. The suppression of all female symbolism, not only for deity but even for the collective human, is the dominant agenda of patriarchal religion, which reached its climax in Puritan Protestantism. The truth about the original matricentric society and culture began to be discovered in nineteenth-century anthropology and archaeology. Now there is a full-fledged rediscovery of this earlier culture, together with its redevelopment, which must serve as a redemptive alternative to these long dark ages of violence and domination from which we currently suffer.

Although I am very sympathetic to the need for a redemptive alternative to the systems of violence that threaten humanity and the earth, I find myself skeptical of a great deal of this explanatory story line. We cannot know with much certainty what the cultures were like before written history in the ancient Near East or elsewhere. I find it likely that preagricultural gatherer societies were more egalitarian, in the sense of having little class hierarchy, but gender arrangements may have varied. At best, perhaps some had parallel spheres for men and women, where both were more or less equally valued.

I doubt the existence of female-dominated societies in which the relations between men and women, humans and nature, were totally harmonious. I suspect that some of the tensions from which later hierarchy developed were present earlier in nascent form. The growing ability to accumulate and concentrate wealth allowed these nascent tensions to become explicit. These are, of course, guesses based on complex sets of fragmentary evidence pulled together from many sources.

The powerful goddesses we find during the second and first millennia BCE in societies in Mesopotamia, Palestine, Egypt, and Greece—such as Inanna/Ishtar, Anat, Isis, and Demeter—do not strike me as survivals of some original, pro-woman, great goddess who goes back to Paleolithic times. Kingly and queenly gods and goddesses, I believe, were inventions reflecting the same process by which urban society, social hierarchy, and literacy were developing sometime in the fourth to third millennia BCE. Such immortal, aristocratic gods and goddesses themselves reflected a split between ordinary humans and physical nature and celestial beings who came to be located in the mountains, the underworld, and especially the heavens, identified with the stars and planets.

In earlier times, humans surely experienced energies that circulated in themselves, male and female, and in the animals, plants, and earth around them. But why visualize these energies as gods and goddesses, personified as ruling-class humans yet separated by their immortality? The process of social separation and projection that generates such an image of deities is itself complex and needs to be explained rather than assumed to be aboriginal.

By the time for which we have literary texts, this process was already well developed. Gods and goddesses were presumed to exist in some space in the heavens, separated from humans, mostly personified as humans, although sometimes with animal attributes (especially in Egypt). These deities were immortal, in contrast to humans as mortals, although some also died and rose. They were much more powerful than humans, imaged as an aristocracy writ large. The idea of gods and goddesses, therefore, enshrined a concept of cosmological hierarchy that itself was built on and reflected the development of class hierarchy.

There were surely earlier ways of imaging spheres of the natural world, and human male and female interaction with it, that were not yet constructed as "aristocrat-morphic" gods and goddesses. But we cannot readily imagine how such images were "thought about" without some ability to "hear" the voice of those earlier people. What became imaged as goddesses likely had roots in the imaginations of human females in relation to human and nonhuman life processes. But goddesses such as Inanna, depicted in epics, hymns, and poetry in the most ancient writing, do not seem to me to be a survival of some earlier way of symbolizing the female, within and beyond humans, that valued and promoted women as a gender group. Rather, these goddesses seem to be a new construction that developed in the context of the first urban, hierarchical societies.

Such concepts of goddesses bear the clear marks of classist and, indeed, royal ideology. Creating these goddesses was the work of men and women of the royal and priestly classes, reflecting their interests and validating their roles. One cannot ascertain a decisive difference between the imaginings of men and women in these classes. The writing of the high priestess Enheduanna makes it clear that a priestess of this class created hymns that reflected the royal ideology of her father, Sargon. True, the Goddess Inanna empowered her as well, but Enheduanna was empowered as a representative of a royal family, as a royal princess and high priestess, not as a representative of special gender characteristics or because of her role as "woman."

Of the ancient goddesses described in this volume, I consider Demeter a major exception to this theme of royal ideology. It is true that her priests were the established male leaders of the Eleusinian city-state, and her cult was understood as servicing the whole society. Yet her story suggests something of the anger felt by women against abuse by males. In the Thesmophoria, described in chapter 2, we get at least a hint of a community of women who gathered yearly to speak of their own needs as women—and perhaps also about their anger at male abuse of them and their daughters.

When we turn to the early Hebrew religious world, we see something closer to the pattern of developing patriarchal monotheism, with the survival of goddesses from the Canaanite world. But the concept of Yahweh and "his Asherah" was also embraced by Israelite men; we can only guess whether Israelite women especially valued Asherah as a way to address their particular interests as females. Although the consolidation of patriarchal monotheism led to the gradual repression of this female consort of Yahweh, the story took an unexpected turn after the exile in Babylonia. No sooner was the Goddess apparently finally excluded from the rebuilt temple than we find a new Goddess being invented.

This was Wisdom. She was not on the edges but in the center of the imagination of a new male teaching class and was used to image the foundations of the universe and the embodiment of Jewish revelation and learning. But was this Hebrew Goddess feminist? Was she the creation of women? Was she the reflection of women's roles? Did she empower women? The answer to all these questions is mostly no, although her image might have been modeled on idealized mothers and wives.

Goddesses did not disappear from the Mediterranean world during the Hellenistic and Roman eras, even though patriarchal social structures by then were long established. On the contrary, religious rites focusing on goddesses such as Cybele and Isis flourished across the empires. Most of what we know of these rites reflects the views of male leaders and initiates, but women participated as priestesses and devotees. Unfortunately, we hear about these women from male friends or in artistic representations rather than in their own voices. What did devotion to the Goddess mean to these women?

Likewise, the diverse movements called gnosticism feature floridly androgynous visions of deity as well as startling reversals in the roles of female figures, such as Eve. A new female figure, Norea, Eve's daughter, plays the role of the heroine against the cosmic powers and as mother of the redeemed humanity. In the gnostic Christian gospels, Mary Magdalene and other women disciples play leading roles, and their presence is defended against misogynist disciples, such as Peter. Yet the theology and anthropology of these writings feature femaleness as mostly derivative of a dominant maleness, linked with error and material existence to be given up in order to return to the higher spiritual world. Women are included in the redeemed community. A demonic maleness that rules the fallen cosmos is subverted, but in ways that are ambivalent for women's ordinary sexual and bodily existence.

Early Christianity appropriated the Jewish Wisdom tradition, while mostly masculinizing it in ways that veiled its female personification. Yet Christianity unleashed new role models for women as virgins and ascetics, who renounced marriage for a new independence and female bonding in women's religious circles and communities. As bridal soul and Mother Church, a new female symbolism for the individual and collective human in relation to God was elaborated. Late patristic and medieval Christianity shaped an increasingly exalted female mediatrix and object of devotion in Mary, Our Lady. Never touched by sin, incorruptible, ascending to the celestial realm immediately after death to be crowned as queen of heaven, appearing in endless visions, and celebrated in tens of thousands of pieces of art, she is functionally the Christian Goddess, although officially she is simply the representative of our original nature, our best human potential.

The existence of women's religious communities in medieval Christianity also allowed female mystical theologians to flourish, to teach, to write, to have their work circulated and preserved for future generations. Thus, for the first time in Western history, we have a large body of women's religious writings, not just an occasional fragment of the work of a female religious writer. Here, we find an extraordinary elaboration of a theology of female-personified Wisdom shaped by and for women's empowerment.

Mainstream Protestantism eliminated most of this devotion to Mary, female saints, and personified Wisdom. But a whole new stream of mystical millennialist Protestantism arose on the edges of official Protestantism and redeveloped a theology of Wisdom that restored a female personification to God as mediator of creation and redemption.

Yet much of this elaboration of Mariology and bridal mysticism throughout Christian history was the work of men, not women. Rather than totally repressing female symbols for deity and for the individual and collective human, Jewish and Christian men, within patriarchal societies and religious systems, continually reinvented the "religious feminine." What does this mean? Inverting Carol Christ's feminist query, "Why do women need the Goddess?" I ask, in light of this history, "Why do men need the Goddess?" Why do they periodically reinvent female personifications of the divine and of the individual and collective human, even imagining themselves as brides and as mothers, impregnated, giving birth, and nursing children with full breasts?

A full answer to this question would require psychoanalytic directions that go well beyond my expertise. Writers such as Michael Carroll have explored the psychic role played by Marian devotion in the lives of celibate Catholic males and mostly pronounced it sick-making.[1] I do not automatically rush to this judgment. I simply wish to make the obvious point that most of the goddesses that we know about from art and literary texts in the ancient Near East and Western religion were invented by men to serve male interests. What are these male interests that the Goddess serves?

In the ancient Near East, goddesses such as Inanna/Ishtar, Anat, and Isis were figures who protected men in power. Politically, goddesses seem to have played a key role in installing upstart men in power, elevating them, through marriage, into the older systems of divine and royal legitimacy. Ecologically, in a natural environment in which yearly drought threatened survival, the Goddess was the sustaining power behind the renewal of life, the figure who called the dying lover, husband, or daughter back to life, restoring the fertility of the earth. In a world threatened by war, the Goddess rode in front of the war chariot of the king with lightning bolts in her hands and brought defeated captives to crouch under his foot. In Egypt, the young pharaoh depended on his mother, Isis, to birth him, to protect and nurture him, and to secure his ascendancy to the throne, seated on her lap.

As ancient empires expanded and men felt ever more vulnerable to "fickle Fortune," the Goddess Isis played new and more individualized roles of protection. Through her transforming power, Lucius was rescued from a disastrous fall into asinine bondage, restored to his humanity, and assured of ongoing protection of his good fortune under her mantle. Did men, nurtured by mothers in patriarchal families, assume that divine females were more caring, more accessible, more reliable intermediaries in the volatile world of shifting forces of life and death than male deities?

When we move to the world of early Judaism and then of Christianity, in which a male monotheistic God and heterosexist culture reigned officially, we find a new problem for male spirituality and its relation to the divine. In this setting, for males to love God meant that a human male must love a divine male. The structure of spirituality in male monotheism was homoerotic. As Christianity in particular gave priority to the celibate male as spiritual leader, males whose psychosexual orientation was homoerotic may have been particularly attracted to such leadership. Yet the official heterosexist ethic forbade an explicit elaboration of male-male eros, such as that in classical Greece. Thus, male lovers of a male God or Christ were forced to veil the homoerotic structure of their spirituality by imagining themselves as females, as blushing brides led to the marriage bed with Christ, longing to be kissed "by the kisses of his mouth."[2]

One way that heterosexual males, perhaps seeking an alternative to this homoerotic spirituality, could open up other vistas of spirituality was by reinventing female spiritual love objects. Mary, as God's bride and mother, could also become the bride and love object of the male devotee. By imaging her as virginal mother, the male devotee could also become the beloved child, nurtured by a mother who belonged to him alone, rescued from the phallic father who would defile her through the sexual act by which the child was conceived. Another option for Christian males was to rediscover the female, or Wisdom, side of God and envision the soul as bridegroom and lover, ever seeking the gracious response of his celestial lady love.

Male bridal mysticism, whether imaging the soul as the bride of a male Christ, a child-lover nurtured by Mary, or a bridegroom of Wisdom, was, however, hardly positive toward women. On the contrary, it was primarily a spirituality by which the male devotee turned away from and despised relationships with actual women, imagining such relationships as debasing to his soul, to devote himself to these more elevating celestial loves. Misogyny was the covert and often overt subtext of male spirituality that seeks the love of God, as father, mother, bridegroom, or lady love.

What, then, of women in this construction of gendered spirituality? Can a Jewish Goddess—Wisdom or Shekinah—or a Christian Goddess—Holy Spirit, Wisdom, or Mary—be converted to feminism? Again, we have to admit that our evidence for answering this question is scanty. Most of the record of women's devotion to female religious symbols has been silenced, by excluding women from teaching and writing and by failing to preserve their work as part of the teaching tradition. A contemporary Mexican feminist, seeking to understand how women relate to the Virgin of Guadalupe, might approach this question with sociological research, by interviewing Mexican women and asking them to express their relationship to La Morena (the Dark Virgin).[3] But such a method of inquiry is not available to us for women of past generations.

Those women of medieval and early modern religious communities who did gain access to teaching, writing, and transmission of their thoughts were themselves marginal to the dominant church teaching institutions. What they knew of Mary or Wisdom they learned from male teachers and male-constructed texts. Yet even with all these handicaps, what has come down to us from medieval women mystics such as Hildegard of Bingen, Mechthild of Magdeburg, Hadewijch, Marguerite Porete, Julian of Norwich, and others, as well as more recent figures such as Jane Leade, makes it evident that women can make tentative and sometimes very bold reconstructions of these female symbols to express their own relation to them and redemptive transformation in and through them.

For Hildegard of Bingen, female-personified spiritual beings encompassed the entire cosmos and salvation history from start to finish. Mechthild imaged a male Christ who not only was her lover but also kneeled to her as his beloved. Hadewijch engaged in a gender-bending fluidity of identity, as bride of Christ and as bridegroom seeking a fickle celestial lady love. Marguerite Porete trumped one-eyed Lady Reason and Holy Church the Little with a triumphant Lady Love, who liberated her into Holy Church the Great, beyond the spiritual reach of institutional male clerical power. Even in her fiery death at their hands, Marguerite Porete rose, superior to their hostile power, which could not control or dominate her soaring spirit.

Julian of Norwich, in her anchorite cell, created a more homey vision of God as kindly father and kindly mother, both reassuring the troubled soul that no one is finally rejected by God, that in the end "all will be well." Jane Leade imagined Wisdom as a celestial sister leading her to a liberating kingdom of transformed life, in which all that is corruptible has been left behind.

One might well say that all these spiritual visions, built mainly on flight from finitude, physical sexuality, and the body, are hardly the liberating messages that feminist women seek today. But these women were operating with cosmologies and views of the self that differ from ours. They reshaped the gender symbolism of these spiritualities in a way that clearly made them agents of their own lives and visionaries in their own right, as well as prophetic and pastoral teachers for their communities, who valued them and carefully preserved their teachings for us to read today. This is surely some part of feminism.

Today we are in quite a different situation. Thanks to two centuries of feminist teaching and organizing, women, particularly in the West, have legal access to all levels of education. We can teach in most venues of scholarship. We have property rights and access to income in our own names. We can study these inherited religious traditions and seek to reshape them in ways that will overcome sexist hierarchy in all its social and symbolic ramifications. Yet these and similar goals have hardly been fully accomplished. Public communication media still seek to make the very word "feminism" an object of derision. Fundamentalist backlash in all the patriarchal religious traditions seeks to reestablish female subjugation and its ideological justifications and resocialize women to accept this. We still have a long way to go.

But the battle has been joined in a more decisive way than in any previous centuries since the shaping of patriarchal, hierarchical societies in antiquity. Precisely because women and men have caught a new vision of gender mutuality no longer built on domination and subordination and have begun to reorganize their relations to embody this, those who seek to maintain traditional patterns have grown more hostile and aggressive. With the U.S. administration headed by George W. Bush, the war against women has become increasingly explicit in every area, but particularly in the arena of reproductive rights. Renewed apocalyptic language of a male warrior God crusading against evil buttresses the many efforts to establish a new level of neocolonial hegemony of the Western elite male. Silencing feminist critique— or trivializing it as simply the token inclusion among the seats of power of an African American female who is totally subservient to the Bush agenda—is a key weapon in the arsenal of the renewed power of domination.[4]

Feminists interested in the religious aspects of overcoming patriarchy have pursued several strategies. Some have seen the most meaningful road as the reclaiming of prophetic, liberative themes in Judaism and Christianity and seeking to reinterpret them for feminism within their historical communities. Others have sought religions such as Buddhism or Hinduism, with no male god, no god at all, or a great plurality of goddesses, which can be claimed for a feminist spirituality.[5] Yet another group has despaired of any effort to reinterpret established religious systems shaped by millennia of patriarchy, instead seeking to reach back to an earlier time before the rise of patriarchy for some original feminist alternative, to be repristinated today for a new revolutionary transformation of self and society.

Although I regard this notion of a prepatriarchal feminist alternative as mythical rather than literal history, it clearly speaks to deep psychocultural structures in our culture that lie in many religious traditions, including Christianity. One might say that the lost feminist alternative is not so much a literal historical era of the past as it is a symbol of faith in the possibility of a better self and society despite their distortion by systems of domination. This faith is rooted in a deep sense that we do indeed have a better self and capacity for good social relations that can be resurrected from beneath the patterns of alienation. Its validity, like that of the myth of the Garden of Eden on which it is built, is theological rather than historical. For this reason, this symbol of a utopian prepatriarchal past to be recovered today speaks powerfully and convincingly to many people's intuitive feelings, even as it arouses skepticism from others when it is defended as literal history.

I regard all these paths as equally legitimate. There are difficulties but also rich creativity to be found in each of these paths of the feminist religious quest. I personally am more inspired by the first path. That we are not likely to clearly identify feminist goddesses and cultures from prepatriarchal histories means that reclaiming goddesses from the ancient Near East, such as Inanna, Isis, or Demeter, or Kali and Durga from India, is also a work of feminist reinterpretation for today, not a ready-made feminist spirituality that we can lay hold of literally and reproclaim in its ancient historical form. This means taking responsibility for our own work of reinterpretation and new myth-making today, not engaging in a kind of "feminist fundamentalism," which insists that it is reclaiming the "old-time religion."

I also see a great deal of convergence among the different roads of interpretation of an ecofeminist spirituality, whether it be Vandana Shiva speaking from an Indian context and reclaiming Shati as the female power of the universe, or Ivone Gebara of Brazil reimagining the Christian Trinity as a dialectic of immanent relationships of life energy, or Selene Fox of the Circle Sanctuary honoring the cycle of life that continually renews nature as the context in which she stands.[6] These many visions converge on a considerable degree of common ground.

There is no one source for this emerging commonality.[7] Rather, its roots lie in the processes by which we are all responding to similar challenges and coming up with similar solutions in the context of a twenty-first-century world threatened by military violence, economic exploitation, and ecological collapse. It is based on a shared recognition that a male hierarchical concept of the divine is a major ideological reinforcement of these patterns of social domination. This recognition is creating views of the divine and of humanity and the earth in relation to the divine that, if not exactly the same, have a great deal of similarity. One can perhaps begin to speak of an ecumenical and interreligious common ground of ecofeminist theology and spirituality.

Characteristics of a common ecofeminist theology include rejecting the idea of splitting the divine from the earth, whether as "god" or "goddess" or as personified immortal entities, located in some supercelestial realm outside the earth. The very concept of a god is deconstructed. Instead, the divine is seen as the matrix of life-giving energy that is in, through, and under all things, sustaining and renewing life. This is not simply pantheism, in the sense of a reduction of life-giving energy to what "is," for what "is" includes great superstructures of dominating power. Rather, this life-giving matrix is pan-en-theist, or immanently transcendent and transcendently immanent. That is to say, it not only sustains the cycling seasons but also empowers us to struggle against the hierarchies of dominance and to seek to re-create relationships of mutuality.

This divine energy for life and renewal of life in and through all things can be imaged as female or male in ways that celebrate our diverse bodies and energies, rather than in ways that reinforce traditional gender stereotypes. But it is neither male, female, nor anthropomorphic in any essential or exclusive sense. It is the font of life that wells up to create and re-create all living things in ecozoic community. It calls us to repent of power over others and to reclaim power within and power with one another, to use Starhawk's critical categories.

This is a vision of life energy that calls us all into life-giving community from many strands of tradition, culture, and history. This common theology, I believe, must also call us to stand shoulder to shoulder and arm in arm to oppose the systems of economic, military, and ecological violence that are threatening to undo the very fabric of planetary life. This, as Thomas Berry has said, is the "great work" of our generation.

NOTES

INTRODUCTION

1. A note here on capitalization: Christians have established the tradition of capitalizing the word "god" when it refers to the god of the Bible and Christian faith and lowercasing it in reference to all other gods and goddesses. This practice reflects their view that only the biblical god is the true god and all others are false and nonexistent idols. This is not the view of this book. The policy I have followed here is to lowercase the words "god" and "goddess" when they are used in a more generic way, including references to the Hebrew or Christian god. I capitalize the word "god" or "goddess" when it refers to a particular god or goddess, such as the Goddess Isis, or to the biblical and Christian God as a statement of belief. I also capitalize "goddess" in statements about this deity as object or expression of faith in the contemporary goddess religions.

2. Walter Otto, *Dionysus: Myth and Cult*, trans. Robert B. Palmer (Bloomington: Indiana University Press, 1965); Jane Ellen Harrison, *Prolegomena to the Study of Greek Religion* (1903; New York: Meridian Books, 1955); Jane Ellen Harrison, *Themis: A Study of the Social Origins of Greek Religion* (1912; New York: University Books, 1962). For a discussion of Harrison's thought, see chapter 9 of this volume.

3. Philip Merlan, author of *From Platonism to Neoplatonism* (The Hague: M. N. Nijhoff, 1953), was one of my mentors at Scripps College.

4. I developed this thesis of three interactive spiritualities—pagan, prophetic, and mystical-contemplative—primarily in lectures to students. The thesis is presumed but not specifically explicated in my published writing, although my book *Women-Church: Theology and Practice of Feminist Liturgical Communities* (San Francisco: Harper and Row, 1986) refers to the nature-renewal roots of Jewish and Christian liturgy (pp. 99–104).

5. In a number of writings in the mid-1960s, I advanced a critique of the traditional Catholic view of sexuality and the reproductive roles of women. See, for example, "The Difficult Decision: Contraception," in *The Experience of Marriage: The Testimony of Catholic Laymen*, ed. Michael Novak (New York: Macmillan, 1964), pp. 69–81; "A Question of Dignity, a Question of Freedom," in *What Modern Catholics Think of Birth Control*, ed. William Birmingham (New York: New American Library, 1964), pp. 233–240; and "Birth Control and the Ideals of Marital Sexuality," in *Contraception and Holiness*, ed. Thomas Roberts, S.J. (New York: Herder and Herder, 1967), pp. 72–91.

6. Rosemary Radford Ruether, "Male Chauvinist Theology and the Anger of Women," *Cross Currents* 21, no. 2 (Spring 1971): 173–184.

7. Although I was invited to teach at Harvard through the funds of the Chauncey Stillman Chair of Roman Catholic Studies, the faculty there decided that I was not sufficiently senior to hold this title and gave me instead the title of Visiting Lecturer in Catholic Studies. I jokingly referred to myself during that year of teaching as sitting "under" the Stillman Chair rather than "on" it, a story I recounted at the November 2002 Harvard conference on recovering the history of feminism in religion.

8. E. O. James, *The Cult of the Mother Goddess* (New York: Praeger, 1959).

9. Anne L. Barstow, "The Prehistoric Goddess," in *The Book of the Goddess, Past and Present: An Introduction to Her Religion*, ed. Carl Olson (New York: Crossroads, 1983), pp. 7–15.

10. See, for example, Kay Martin and Barbara Voorhies, *The Female of the Species* (New York: Columbia University Press, 1975). For a fuller account of feminist anthropology and its view of the development of gender roles, see chapter 1 of this volume.

11. For her development of this typology, broadened into what she called "Type 1, Type 2, and Type 3" feminist thinkers, see Carol Christ, "Symbols of Goddess and God," in *The Laughter of Aphrodite: Reflections on a Journey to the Goddess* (San Francisco: Harper and Row, 1987), pp. 135–160.

12. This interchange was sparked particularly by Naomi Goldenberg's book *The Changing of the Gods: Feminism and the End of Traditional Religion* (Boston: Beacon Press, 1979). My article "A Religion for Women: Sources and Strategies" (*Christianity and Crisis*, December 10, 1979, pp. 307–311) sought to evaluate positive and negative aspects of Goldenberg's thesis that the Jewish and Christian symbols are to be rejected as totally pro-male and hostile to women. In the light of Goldenberg's and Christ's responses to my critique, I further elaborated my view in "Goddesses and Witches: Liberation and Counter-Cultural Feminism" (*Christianity and Crisis*, September 10–17, 1980, pp. 842–847).

13. This claim is found in a recent article by Naomi Goldenberg; see "Witches and Words," *Feminist Theology* 12, no. 2 (January 2004): 203–211.

14. Charlene Spretnak, ed., *The Politics of Women's Spirituality: Essays on the Rise of Spiritual Power Within the Feminist Movement* (Garden City, N.Y.: Anchor Books,

1982); Riane Eisler, *The Chalice and the Blade: Our History, Our Future* (San Francisco: Harper and Row, 1987).

To clarify, the term "matriarchal" refers to a society dominated by women as mothers; a "matricentric" society is centered on women as mothers but is not dominated by them.

15. Cynthia Eller, *The Myth of Matriarchal Prehistory: Why an Invented Past Won't Give Women a Future* (Boston: Beacon Press, 2000). This book evoked outraged responses from some adherents of the Gimbutas thesis. See also its hostile treatment in Naomi Goldenberg's article "Witches and Words." My review of the book appears in the *Anglican Theological Review* 83, no. 3 (Summer 2001): 894–895.

16. On ecological rethinking, see, for example, the volumes in the series Religions of the World and Ecology, edited by Mary Evelyn Tucker and John Grim for Harvard University Press, which focus on ten world religions and the recovery of their traditions in light of the ecological challenge. The series covers Judaism, Christianity, Islam, Buddhism, Hinduism, Jainism, Confucianism, indigenous religions, Sikhism, and Daoism.

Brazilian liberation theologian Leonardo Boff has been particularly notable in his efforts to include the new perspectives of ecology and feminism in his work; see, for example, his *Ecology and Liberation* (Maryknoll, N.Y.: Orbis Press, 1995); and *Cry of the Earth, Cry of the Poor* (Maryknoll, N.Y.: Orbis Press, 1997). His efforts have been criticized, however, by Brazilian ecofeminist theologian Ivone Gebara; see her *Out of the Depths: Women's Experience of Evil and Salvation* (Minneapolis: Fortress Press, 2002), pp. 163, 164.

The efforts of indigenous theologies are expressed in the movements to create a "teología india" in the Latin American context. See, for example, *Teología india: Sabiduria indigena, fuente de esperanza* (Peru: IDEA, 1997).

17. The major book that expresses this vision of an alternative society is a project of the International Forum on Globalization: see John Cavanagh et al., *Alternatives to Economic Globalization* (San Francisco: Berrett-Koehler, 2002).

18. In an infamous quotation, Pat Robertson defines feminists as compelling women to "leave their husbands, kill their children, practice witchcraft, destroy capitalism, and become lesbians." See Rosemary R. Ruether, *Christianity and the Making of the Modern Family: Ruling Ideologies, Diverse Realities* (Boston: Beacon Press, 2000), pp. 174, 275n58.

CHAPTER 1: GENDER AND THE PROBLEM OF PREHISTORY

1. See James Mellaart's account of this development in *The Neolithic of the Near East* (London: Thames and Hudson, 1975).

2. See Anne Baring and Jules Cashford, *The Myth of the Goddess: Evocation of an Image* (London: Penguin, 1991). See also Marija Gimbutas, *The Civilization of the Goddess* (San Francisco: HarperSanFrancisco, 1991), p. 222.

3. See Richard B. Lee and Irven DeVore, eds., *Man the Hunter* (Chicago: Aldine, 1968), a symposium collection; refer particularly to the article by Sherwood L. Washburn, C. S. Lancaster, William Laughlin, and Jules H. Steward, "Hunting and Evolution," pp. 293–346.

4. See Melanie G. Wiber, *Erect Men and Undulating Women: The Visual Imagery of Gender, "Race," and Progress in Reconstructive Images of Human Evolution* (Waterloo, Ont.: Wilfred-Laurier University Press, 1997).

5. See Joan M. Gero, "Genderlithics," and Russell G. Handsman, "Whose Art Was Found at Lepenski Vir?" in *Engendering Archaeology: Women and Prehistory*, ed. Joan M. Gero and Margaret W. Conkey (Cambridge, Mass.: Blackwell, 1991), pp. 329–365.

6. Johann Jakob Bachofen, *Myth, Religion, and Mother Right: Selected Writings of J. J. Bachofen*, trans. Ralph Manheim (Princeton, N.J.: Princeton University Press, 1967); Sir Arthur Evans, *The Palace of Minos at Knossos*, 4 vols. (London: Macmillan, 1921–1936).

7. Lewis H. Morgan, *Ancient Society: Researches in the Lines of Human Progress from Savagery Through Barbarism to Civilization* (New York: Henry Holt, 1877); Frederick Engels, *The Origin of the Family, Private Property, and the State*, ed. Eleanor B. Leacock (1884; New York: International Publishers, 1972).

8. Engels, *Origin of the Family*, p. 218.

9. Matilda Joslyn Gage, *Woman, Church, and State: A Historical Account of the Status of Woman Through the Christian Ages, with Reminiscences of the Matriarchate* (1893; Watertown, Mass.: Persephone Press, 1980).

10. For an overview of the work of Franz Boas, see Regna Darnell, *And Along Came Boas: Continuity and Revolution in Americanist Anthropology* (Philadelphia: John Benjamin, 1998).

11. Robert Lowie, *Primitive Society* (New York: Boni and Liveright, 1920), pp. 184–185.

12. For a critique of "origins" research as legitimation of dominant social forms, see Margaret W. Conkey, "Original Narratives: The Political Economy of Gender in Archaeology," in *Gender at the Crossroads of Knowledge: Feminist Anthropology in the Postmodern Era*, ed. Micaela di Leonardo (Berkeley: University of California Press, 1991), pp. 102–139.

13. Elman R. Service, *Primitive Social Organization: An Evolutionary Perspective* (New York: Random House, 1962).

14. Elman R. Service, *The Hunters* (Englewood Cliffs, N.J.: Prentice-Hall, 1966), p. 11.

15. Lionel Tiger, *Men in Groups* (New York: Random House, 1969).

16. Service, *Primitive Social Organization*, p. 43.

17. See M. Kay Martin and Barbara Voorhies, *The Female of the Species* (New York: Columbia University Press, 1975), table 7-1, p. 181; also Frances Dahlberg, ed., *Woman the Gatherer* (New Haven, Conn.: Yale University Press, 1981).

18. Margaret Ehrenberg, *Women in Prehistory* (Norman: Oklahoma University Press, 1989), pp. 46–50.

19. Ibid., pp. 39, 42–43.

20. Martin and Voorhies, *Female of the Species*, pp. 184–187.

21. Lee and DeVore, *Man the Hunter*, pp. 3, 85–89.

22. Martin and Voorhies, *Female of the Species*, pp. 201–202; see also Jane C. Goodale, *Tiwi Wives* (Seattle: University of Washington Press, 1971).

23. Martin and Voorhies, *Female of the Species*, pp. 197–199.

24. See Cheryl P. Claassen, "Gender, Shellfishing, and the Shell Mound Archaic," in Gero and Conkey, *Engendering Archaeology*, pp. 276–300.

25. Martin and Voorhies, *Female of the Species*, pp. 229–241.

26. For a description of trade in Neolithic Anatolia, see James Mellaart, *Earliest Civilizations of the Near East* (New York: McGraw-Hill, 1965), pp. 124–125.

27. Martin and Voorhies, *Female of the Species*, pp. 241–246.

28. See Peggy Reeves Sanday, *Female Power and Male Dominance: On the Origins of Sexual Inequality* (Cambridge: Cambridge University Press, 1981). Sanday studied 150 preindustrial societies. She characterized 32 percent as egalitarian in the sense that economic power and political power were balanced, with no aggressive violence against women. She described 28 percent of the societies as markedly male-dominated. Although women performed much of the labor, they were excluded from economic and political decision making and subjected to a high level of male violence, beating, and rape. Finally, Sanday characterized 40 percent of the societies as conflictual, in which women had considerable economic power, based on their productive labor, but were excluded from political decisions. Although men in these societies lacked full dominance, they had developed patterns of cultural hostility to women, male bonding that excluded women, and myths and rituals of male overthrow of female power.

29. See, for example, William Barnett's review of Marija Gimbutas's *The Language of the Goddess* (*American Journal of Archaeology* 96, no. 1 [1992]: 170–171) and Ruth Tringham's review of Gimbutas's *The Civilization of the Goddess* (*American Anthropologist* 95, no. 1 [1993]: 196–197).

30. Marija Gimbutas, *Gods and Goddesses of Old Europe, 7000–3500 B.C.* (Berkeley: University of California Press, 1974; republished with a new introduction as *Goddesses and Gods of Old Europe, 6500–3500 B.C.* [Berkeley: University of California Press, 1982]); Marija Gimbutas, *The Language of the Goddess* (San Francisco: HarperSanFrancisco, 1989); Gimbutas, *Civilization of the Goddess*; Riane Eisler, *The Chalice and the Blade: Our History, Our Future* (San Francisco: Harper and Row, 1987); Charlene Spretnak, ed., *The Politics of Women's Spirituality: Essays on the Rise of Spiritual Power Within the Feminist Movement* (Garden City, N.Y.: Anchor Books, 1982).

31. See Valerie Abrahamsen, "Essays in Honor of Marija Gimbutas: A Response," *Journal of Feminist Studies in Religion* 13, no. 2 (Fall 1997): 69–74.

32. Gimbutas, *Civilization of the Goddess*, p. 324.

33. Cynthia Eller, *The Myth of Matriarchal Prehistory: Why an Invented Past Won't Give Women a Future* (Boston: Beacon Press, 2000).

34. See, for instance, the following works by Marija Gimbutas: "Achilleion, a Neolithic Mound in Thessaly: Preliminary Report on 1973 and 1974 Excavations," *Journal of Field Archaeology* 1 (1974): 277–302; *Figurines: Neolithic Macedonia as Reflected in Excavations at Anza, Southeast Yugoslavia*, Monumenta Archaeologica 1 (Los Angeles: Institute of Archaeology, University of California at Los Angeles, 1976), pp. 198–241; "Gold Treasures at Varna," *Archaeology* 30, no. 1 (1977): 44–51.

35. Compare the introduction to Gimbutas's 1974 *Gods and Goddesses of Old Europe*, pp. 13–15, with that of the 1982 *Goddesses and Gods of Old Europe*, pp. 9–15.

36. Gimbutas, *Civilization of the Goddess*, p. 263.

37. See Eller, *Myth of Matriarchal Prehistory*, pp. 119–133; and Lynn Meskell, "Goddesses, Gimbutas, and New Age Archaeology," *Antiquity* 69 (1995): 74–86.

38. See Meskell, "Goddesses, Gimbutas, and New Age Archaeology"; and Margaret W. Conkey and Ruth Tringham, "Archaeology and the Goddess: Exploring the Contours of Feminist Archaeology," in *Feminisms in the Academy*, ed. Domna C. Stanton and Abigail J. Stewart (Ann Arbor: University of Michigan Press, 1995), pp. 199–247. Also see Margaret Conkey and Ruth Tringham, "Rethinking Figurines: A Critical View from Archaeology to Gimbutas, the "Goddess," and Popular Culture," in *Ancient Goddesses: The Myths and the Evidence*, ed. Lucy Goodison and Christine Morris (London: British Museum Press, 1998), pp. 22–45.

39. Gimbutas, *Civilization of the Goddess*, p. 335.

40. See Martin and Voorhies, *Female of the Species*, pp. 225–228; see also Judith K. Brown, "Economic Organization and the Position of Women Among the Iroquois," *Ethnohistory* 17 (1970): 151–167.

41. See the discussion among J. D. Clark, Irven DeVore, F. C. Howell, Richard Sharp, and Colin Turnbull, "Use of Ethnography in Reconstructing the Past," in Lee and DeVore, *Man the Hunter*, pp. 287–289.

42. Compare Gimbutas, *Goddesses and Gods*, p. 237; and Gimbutas, *Language of the Goddess*, p. xxii.

43. See Gimbutas, *Language of the Goddess*, p. 265; and Gimbutas, *Civilization of the Goddess*, p. 245. Gimbutas seems to have gotten this odd idea from D. O. Cameron, *Symbols of Birth and Death in the Neolithic Era* (London: Kengen Deane, 1981), figure 7-19. See the discussion in Eller, *Myth of Matriarchal Prehistory*, p. 146.

44. Gimbutas, *Civilization of the Goddess*, pp. 351–401.

45. Ibid., pp. 347–348. See also Marija Gimbutas, *The Living Goddesses*, ed. Miriam Robbins Dexter (Berkeley: University of California Press, 1999), pp. 165–171, as well as the discussion of matriarchy among the Celts and Basques, pp. 172–187.

46. Ruth Tringham and Dušan Krstić, ed., *Selevac: A Neolithic Village in Yugoslavia*,

Monumenta Archaeologica 15 (Los Angeles: Institute of Archaeology, University of California at Los Angeles, 1990); Silva Marinescu-Bâlcu, *Tîrpeşti: From Prehistory to History in Eastern Romania*, trans. Georgeta Bolomey, Oxford British Archaeological Reports, International Series 107 (Oxford: BAR, 1981); David W. Anthony, "Nazi and Ecofeminist Prehistories: Ideology and Empiricism in Indo-European Archaeology," in *Nationalism, Politics, and the Practice of Archaeology*, ed. Philip Kohl and Clare Fawcett (Cambridge: Cambridge University Press, 1996), pp. 1–32.

47. Gimbutas, *Civilization of the Goddess*, p. 252.

48. James Mellaart, *Çatal Hüyük: A Neolithic Town in Anatolia* (London: Thames and Hudson, 1967).

49. See James Mellaart, Udo Hirsh, and Belkis Balpinar, *The Goddess from Anatolia*, 4 vols. (Milan: Eskenazi, 1989).

50. Anne L. Barstow, "The Uses of Archaeology for Women's History: James Mellaart's Work on the Neolithic Goddess at Çatal Hüyük," *Feminist Studies* 4, no. 3 (October 1978): 7–18.

51. Mellaart, *Çatal Hüyük*, pp. 68–69.

52. See Mellaart, *Neolithic of the Near East*, p. 101.

53. Mellaart, *Çatal Hüyük*, pp. 208, 209.

54. Barstow, "Uses of Archaeology for Women's History."

55. Mellaart, *Çatal Hüyük*, p. 60. See also Ian Hodder, ed., *On the Surface: Çatalhöyük, 1993–1995*, Çatalhöyük Project, vol. 1, British Institute of Archaeology at Ankara monograph 22 (Cambridge: McDonald Institute for Archaeological Research and Çatalhöyük Research Trust, 1996); Ian Hodder, "The Past as Passion and Play: Çatalhöyük as a Site of Conflict in the Construction of Multiple Pasts," in *Archaeology Under Fire: Politics, Nationalism, and Heritage in the Eastern Mediterranean and Middle East*, ed. Lynn Meskell (London: Routledge, 1998), pp. 124–139.

56. Mellaart, *Çatal Hüyük*, plates 52, 54, 55, 56, 57, 61, 62, 63, 64, and pp. 170–176; Mellaart, Hirsh, and Balpinar, *Goddess from Anatolia*, vol. 1, plates 2, 5–12, pp. 8–9.

57. See Mellaart, *Çatal Hüyük*, pp. 101, 110, 111, 113, 114, 115, 116, 117, 121–122, 124, 125. Lotte Motz has disputed the exaggerated focus on fertility and motherhood as the meaning of Paleolithic and Neolithic figurines generally; she suggests that the spread-legged figure in Çatal Hüyük may be engaged in ritual genital display, not birth. See Motz, *Faces of the Goddess* (Oxford: Oxford University Press, 1997), p. 125.

58. See Mellaart, *Çatal Hüyük*, fig. 27, p. 115; fig. 38, p. 125; fig. 40, p. 127. One such figure has a slightly raised belly with red concentric circles, which causes Mellaart to pronounce this figure "clearly pregnant" (pp. 113–114).

59. Ibid., fig. 29, p. 116. The paired figures are shown in fig. 23, p. 109; and fig. 26, p. 113.

60. Ibid., pp. 166–168; Mellaart, Hirsh, and Balpinar, *Goddess from Anatolia*, plate 13, 1-2, p. 58.

61. Mellaart, *Çatal Hüyük*, pp. 101, 106, 107, 111, 126, 128; fig. 21, p. 107; figs. 41 and 42, p. 128.

62. See Eller, *Myth of Matriarchal Prehistory*, p. 147.

63. Mellaart, *Çatal Hüyük*, plate 67 and fig. 52, p. 184.

64. Ibid., figs. 49, 50, 51, pp. 182–183; plate 83, p. 184.

65. Peter Ucko, *Anthropomorphic Figurines of Predynastic Egypt, and Neolithic Crete, with Comparative Material from the Prehistoric Near East and Mainland Greece* (London: A. Szmidla, 1968), pp. 356, 361, 369. I have made my own survey of the hundreds of female figurines in Gimbutas's three volumes and have found only three of a woman with child: see *Goddesses and Gods*, p. 144; *Language of the Goddess*, fig. 58, p. 37; and *Civilization of the Goddess*, fig. 8-3, p. 311.

66. See David Horrobin, *The Madness of Adam and Eve: How Schizophrenia Shaped Humanity* (London: Bantam, 2001), pp. 76–77, for the suggestion that fat Neolithic figures may refer to this survival value.

67. Conkey and Tringham suggest that some archaeologists have too readily lent themselves to promoting the fertility goddess idea: "In one form or another some archaeologists have provided the authentication, intentionally or unintentionally," citing Mellaart as an example ("Archaeology and the Goddess," p. 108).

68. See the two major collections of articles: Rita Wright, ed., *Gender and Archaeology* (Philadelphia: University of Pennsylvania Press, 1996); and Gero and Conkey, *Engendering Archaeology*. For a useful bibliography through 1992, see Elisabeth A. Bacus, *A Gendered Past: A Critical Bibliography of Gender in Archaeology*, Technical Reports no. 25 (Ann Arbor: University of Michigan Museum of Anthropology, 1993).

69. Tringham, Review, *Civilization of the Goddess*, p. 197.

70. Meskell, "Goddesses, Gimbutas, and New Age Archaeology," p. 76.

71. For a critique that presents the concept of the nuclear family with working husband and dependent children as a middle-class, twentieth-century ideology, see Rosemary R. Ruether, *Christianity and the Making of the Modern Family: Ruling Ideologies, Diverse Realities* (Boston: Beacon Press, 2000).

72. See Ehrenberg, *Women in Prehistory*, pp. 99–107; also Martin and Voorhies, *Female of the Species*, pp. 276–332.

CHAPTER 2: GODDESSES AND WORLD RENEWAL
IN THE ANCIENT MEDITERRANEAN

1. See Susan Pollock, *Ancient Mesopotamia: The Eden That Never Was* (Cambridge: Cambridge University Press, 1999), pp. 150–171. Also see Denise Schmandt-Besserat, *Before Writing: From Counting to Cuneiform*, 2 vols. (Austin: University of Texas Press, 1992).

2. Nisaba is the Goddess of grain storage and the arts of writing and accounting; see Tikva Frymer-Kensky, *In the Wake of the Goddesses: Women, Culture, and the Biblical Transformation of Pagan Myth* (New York: Free Press, 1992), pp. 34, 39–40.

3. See Joan Goodnick Westenholz, "Enheduanna, En-priestess, Hen of Nanna, Spouse of Nanna," in *Dumu-e2-Dub-ba-a: Studies in Honor of Ake W. Sjoberg*, ed. Hermann Behrens, Darlene Loding, and Martha Roth (Philadelphia: University Museum, 1989), pp. 539–556. On *naditu* and other women trained as scribes, see Rivkah Harris, *Gender and Old Age in Mesopotamia: The Gilgamesh Epic and Other Ancient Literature* (Norman: University of Oklahoma Press, 2000), pp. 149–150.

4. See Pollock, *Ancient Mesopotamia*, pp. 45–116. Also see Hans Nissen, *The Early History of the Ancient Near East, 9000–2000 BC* (Chicago: University of Chicago Press, 1988), pp. 129–164; and Guillermo Algaze, *The Uruk World System: The Dynamics of Expansion of Early Mesopotamian Civilization* (Chicago: University of Chicago Press, 1993).

5. Pollock, *Ancient Mesopotamia*, pp. 94–96.

6. See "Enki and Nimmah: The Creation of Humankind," in *Myths of Enki: The Crafty God*, ed. Samuel Noah Kramer and John Maier (Oxford: Oxford University Press, 1989), pp. 31–33.

7. Pollock, *Ancient Mesopotamia*, pp. 117–148; J. Nicholas Postgate, *Early Mesopotamia: Society and Economy at the Dawn of History* (London: Routledge, 1992), pp. 126–128, 230–240.

8. For a major study of the various forms of servitude in the neo-Babylonian period, see M. A. Dandamaev, *Slavery in Babylonia* (De Kalb: Northern Illinois University Press, 1984). See also Igor Diakonoff, "Slaves, Helots, and Serfs in Early Antiquity," *Acta Antiqua Academiae Scientiarum Hungaricae* 22 (1974): 45–78; and I. J. Gelb, "Prisoners of War in Early Mesopotamia," *Journal of Near Eastern Studies* 32 (1973): 70–98.

9. See Susan Pollock, "Women in a Man's World: Images of Sumerian Women," in *Engendering Archaeology: Women and Prehistory*, ed. Joan Gero and Margaret Conkey (Cambridge, Mass.: Blackwell, 1991), pp. 366–387.

10. Rivkah Harris, "Independent Women in Ancient Mesopotamia," in *Women's Earliest Records: From Egypt and Western Asia*, ed. Barbara S. Lesko (Atlanta: Scholars Press, 1989), pp. 150–156.

11. See Rita P. Wright, "Technology, Gender, and Class: Worlds of Difference in Ur III Mesopotamia," in *Gender and Archaeology* (Philadelphia: University of Pennsylvania Press, 1996), pp. 79–110. Also see Samuel Noah Kramer, "The Women of Ancient Sumer," in *La femme dans la Proche-Orient antique*, ed. J. M. Durand (Paris: Éditions Recherche sur les Civilisations, 1989), pp. 107–155; Kazuya Maekawa, "Female Weavers and Their Children," *Acta Sumerologica* 2 (1980): 81–125; and Kazuya Maekawa, "Collective Labor Service in Girsu-Lagash: The Pre-Sargonic and Ur III Periods," in *Labor in the Ancient Near East*, ed. M. A. Powell (New Haven, Conn.: American Oriental Society, 1987), pp. 49–72.

12. Thorkild Jacobsen, *Treasures of Darkness: A History of Mesopotamian Religion* (New Haven, Conn.: Yale University Press, 1976), pp. 73, 79–91.

13. See the chart of the Sumerian pantheon in Samuel Noah Kramer and Diane Wolk-

stein, *Inanna, Queen of Heaven and Earth: Her Stories and Hymns from Sumer* (New York: Harper and Row, 1981), pp. ix–xi.

14. Jacobsen, *Treasures of Darkness*, pp. 81–84.

15. Kramer and Maier, *Myths of Enki*, pp. 38–56.

16. Ibid., pp. 57–68.

17. Jacobsen, *Treasures of Darkness*, pp. 86–92.

18. Goddesses as patrons of cities were included in divine assemblies, however; see ibid., pp. 86–91.

19. Kramer and Maier, *Myths of Enki*, pp. 22–30, 33–37; also Jacobsen, *Treasures of Darkness*, pp. 104–110.

20. Jacobsen, *Treasures of Darkness*, pp. 229–230. See also Neal Walls, "Desire in Death's Realm: Sex, Power, and Violence in 'Nergal and Ereshkigal,'" in his *Desire, Discord, and Death: Approaches to Near Eastern Myth* (Boston: American Schools of Oriental Research, 2001), pp. 127–182.

21. For the full text, see "The Creation Epic," in *Ancient Near Eastern Texts Relating to the Old Testament*, ed. James P. Pritchard (Princeton, N.J.: Princeton University Press, 1950), pp. 60–72. This text has been extensively studied; see Jacobsen, *Treasures of Darkness*, pp. 165–192.

22. The Code of Hammurabi, promulgated in 1726 BCE, reflects a strictly patriarchal and hierarchical society that had less acknowledgment of women's independent property rights than earlier legal documents would seem to indicate; see "Code of Hammurabi," in Pritchard, *Ancient Near Eastern Texts*, pp. 163–180.

23. Ibid., p. 119.

24. William W. Hallo and J. J. A. Van Dijk, *The Exaltation of Inanna* (New Haven, Conn.: Yale University Press, 1968), pp. 15–19. For another translation of this hymn and also two other others by Enheduanna, see Betty de Shong Meador, *Inanna, Lady of the Largest Heart: Poems of the Sumerian High Priestess, Enheduanna* (Austin: University of Texas Press, 2000).

25. Meador, *Inanna*, pp. 31–35.

26. Kramer and Wolkstein, *Inanna*, pp. 30–34.

27. Ibid., p. 37.

28. Ibid., pp. 37–47.

29. Ibid., p. 52.

30. Ibid., p. 71.

31. *Epic of Gilgamesh* 3.4.6–7; Pritchard, *Ancient Near Eastern Texts*, p. 79. Gilgamesh was the semidivine king of Erech, hero of a collection of stories making up this epic.

32. "Prayer of Lamentation to Ishtar," Pritchard, *Ancient Near Eastern Texts*, p. 384.

33. Ibid., p. 385.

34. See Rivkah Harris's interpretation of the persona of Inanna as one of liminal-

ity and contradictions expressed in carnival (*Gender and Old Age*, pp. 158–171). Enhe-duanna's hymns to Inanna also depict her gender-bending; see Meador, *Inanna*, pp. 124, 127, 162–167.

35. For a critique of the modern scholarly ideas concerning sacred prostitution, a concept derived from Herodotus's unreliable comments, see Phyllis Bird's essay " 'To Play the Harlot': An Inquiry into an Old Testament Metaphor," in Bird, *Missing Persons and Mistaken Identities: Women and Gender in Ancient Israel* (Minneapolis: Fortress Press, 1997), pp. 219–236. Also see Jerrold S. Cooper, "Sacred Marriage and Popular Cult in Early Mesopotamia," in *Official Cult and Popular Religion in the Ancient Near East*, ed. E. Matsushima (Heidelberg: Universitatsverlag C. Winter, 1993), pp. 81–96. Samuel Noah Kramer assumes that the rite was sexually enacted (*The Sacred Marriage Rite: Aspects of Faith, Myth, and Ritual in Ancient Sumer* [Bloomington: Indiana University Press, 1969], pp. 49–66), but this assumption has been questioned by others. Mesopotamian cults believed that the god's statue embodied the god, and they used it to carry out many rites: being put to bed, awakening, feeding, and bathing. Thus, a rite of sexual union could also have been carried out using the statue rather than having humans engage in intercourse. Undoubtedly, an abundance of prostitutes of various classes existed, including sophisticated courtesans who, it was believed, taught the refinements of sexual pleasure as a "civilizing art." Inanna was seen as their patron, but that does not imply that they were respected. For a discussion, see Jean Bottero, *Mesopotamia: Writing, Reasoning, and the Gods* (Chicago: University of Chicago Press, 1992), pp. 165–198.

36. N. Wyatt, *Religious Texts from Ugarit: The Words of Ilimilku and His Colleagues* (Sheffield, U.K.: Sheffield Academic Press, 1998), p. 14; D. Pardee, "Ugaritic Inscriptions," in *The Oxford Encyclopedia of Archaeology in the Near East*, ed. E. M. Meyers (Oxford: Oxford University Press, 1997), vol. 5, p. 264.

37. For an account of these ritual texts, see Gregorio del Olmo Lete, *Canaanite Religion, According to the Liturgical Texts of Ugarit* (Bethesda, Md.: CDL Press, 1999).

38. See Wyatt, *Religious Texts*, p. 21.

39 For a discussion of Baal's parentage, see Neal H. Walls, *The Goddess Anat in Ugaritic Myth* (Atlanta: Scholars Press, 1992), pp. 929–933.

40. Wyatt, *Religious Texts*, pp. 39, 41. Standard translation of these texts is found in Pritchard, *Ancient Near Eastern Texts*, pp. 129–155. I use the translations from Wyatt's *Religious Texts*, which represents fifty years of careful work on these texts.

41. KTU 1.3, ii, 5–35; Wyatt, *Religious Texts*, pp. 72–75. (KTU is the abbreviation used for *Die Kelalphabetischen Texte aus Ugarit*, the texts of the Ugaritic tablets.)

42. See J. B. Lloyd, "Anat and the 'Double' Massacre in KTU 1.3 ii," in *Ugarit, Religion, and Culture: Proceedings of the International Colloquium on Ugarit, Religion, and Culture, Edinburgh, July 1994*, ed. N. Wyatt, W. G. E. Watson, and J. B. Lloyd (Munster: Ugarit-Verlag, 1996), pp. 151–165.

43. KTU 1.3, iii, 15–20, and 1.3, iii, 37–42; Wyatt, *Religious Texts*, pp. 78, 79.

44. KTU 1.3, iv, 40–45; Wyatt, *Religious Texts*, p. 82.

45. KTU 1.10, iii, 5–10, and 1.11; Wyatt, *Religious Texts*, pp. 158–159, 161.

46. Neal H. Walls (*The Goddess Anat*) argues that Anat is sexually inactive and that Baal's sexual relations are with his harem of wives, not with Anat. This view is also found in P. L. Day, "Anat," in *Dictionary of Deities and Demons in the Bible*, ed. K. Van der Toorn, B. Becking, and P. W. van der Horst (Leiden: Brill, 1995), col. 62–77. These texts seem to clearly dispute this version.

47. KTU 1.3, v, 1–6; Wyatt, *Religious Texts*, p. 84.

48. KTU 1.4, iv, 41–44, and 1.4, v, 5; Wyatt, *Religious Texts*, pp. 100–101.

49. KTU 1.4, v, 20–27, and 1.4, vii, 59; Wyatt, *Religious Texts*, pp. 102, 111.

50. KTU 1.5, vi, 10–22; Wyatt, *Religious Texts*, pp. 126–127.

51. KTU 1.6, i, 1–25; Wyatt, *Religious Texts*, pp. 128–130.

52. KTU 1.6, ii, 30, and 1.6, ii, 31–35; Wyatt, *Religious Texts*, p. 135. (I follow Pritchard, *Ancient Near Eastern Texts*, p. 140, ii, 36, for the translation "in the field she sowed him," rather than using Wyatt's language, "on the steppe she abandoned him.")

53. KTU 1.6, iii, 5–9; Wyatt, *Religious Texts*, p. 137.

54. KTU 1.6, v, 5, and 1.6, vi, 35; Wyatt, *Religious Texts*, pp. 140, 143.

55. KTU 1.17–1.19; Wyatt, *Religious Texts*, pp. 248–312.

56. See Pritchard, *Ancient Near Eastern Texts*, p. 155.

57. The term *compañera*, for a woman, has been used in the context of Latin American revolutionary relationships between men and women. It suggests a partnership that is at once sexual, loving, and loyal, at times childbearing, yet unmarried, with each partner remaining independent. The partnership is one of equality and joint effort, including militant struggle, for a common historical purpose.

58. R. E. Witt, *Isis in the Greco-Roman World* (London: Thames and Hudson, 1971), pp. 46–58.

59. See J. Gwyn Griffiths, *Plutarch's de Iside et Osiride* (Cambridge: University of Wales Press, 1970), esp. intro., pp. 5–110.

60. "Creation by Atum," in Pritchard, *Ancient Near Eastern Texts*, p. 3. On brother-sister marriages in Egypt, see J. Gwyn Griffiths, *The Origins of Osiris* (Berlin: Verlag Bruno Hessing, 1966), pp. 132–143.

61. See fig. 2, "Osiris in the erica tree with Isis and Nephthys," first century BCE, Denderah; figs. 7 and 8, "Isis and Nephthys guarding the sarcophagus of Ramses III," twentieth dynasty, c. 1194–1163 BCE; fig. 12: "Nephthys and Isis guarding the inner doors of the third shrine of Tutankhamun," c. 1325 BCE; all found in Anne Baring and Jules Cashford, *The Myth of the Goddess: Evocation of an Image* (London: Penguin, 1991), pp. 229, 236–237, 244.

62. Ibid., pp. 235, 250–251.

63. Fig. 18, "Isis with King Seti I on her lap"; and fig. 19, "Isis suckling Seti I"; ibid., p. 251.

64. See E. A. Wallis Budge, *Osiris: The Egyptian Religion of Resurrection* (New York: University Books, 1961), pp. 305–347 and frontispiece plate.

65. Baring and Cashford, *Myth of the Goddess*, p. 238; also see fig. 9, "Osiris with wheat growing from his body, watered by priest," the Ptolemaic temple of Isis at Philae, in ibid., p. 238.

66. "Theology of Memphis," Pritchard, *Ancient Near Eastern Texts*, pp. 5–6.

67. Compare Plutarch's story of Isis as a nurse in the palace of Byblos (chap. 15), in Griffiths, *Plutarch's de Iside et Osiride*, p. 141, with Demeter as a nurse in the palace of Celeus in Eleusis, in *Homeric Hymns*, trans. Hugh G. Evelyn White (New York: Putnam, 1920), pp. 301–309. On the Isis cult at Byblos, see Griffiths, *Plutarch's de Iside et Osiride*, pp. 319–321.

68. See fig. 10, "Isis helping Seti I to raise the *Djed* pillar of Osiris," nineteenth dynasty, c. 1300 BCE, Temple of Seti I, Abylos; fig. 3, "Isis as a Kite conceiving Horus"; both in Baring and Cashford, *Myth of the Goddess*, pp. 242, 230. On the phallic character of the Osiris story, see Tom Hare, *ReMembering Osiris: Number, Gender, and the Word in Ancient Egyptian Representational Systems* (Stanford: Stanford University Press, 1999), pp. 22–23; figs. 3.6 and 3.7, pp. 120–121.

69. See Budge, *Osiris*, p. 94.

70. Text and translation in E. A. Wallis Budge, *The Gods of the Egyptians* (London: Methuen, 1904), pp. 222–240.

71. Griffiths, *Plutarch's de Iside et Osiride*, pp. 145, 151.

72. Ibid., pp. 145–146.

73. "The Contest of Horus and Seth for the Rule," in Pritchard, *Ancient Near Eastern Texts*, pp. 14–17. For a Freudian interpretation of this contest between Horus and Seth as well as Horus's relation to Isis, see Neal Walls, "On the Couch with Horus and Seth," in his *Desire, Discord, and Death*, pp. 93–125.

74. "The God and His Unknown Name," in Walls, *Desire, Discord, and Death*, p. 12.

75. Ibid., p. 14.

76. Contemporary Goddess thought sees the theme of mother-son lovers as central to Goddess worship; see Baring and Cashford, *Myth of the Goddess*, esp. pp. 1–45. But this theme is not confirmed in these ancient Near Eastern goddess traditions. This view seems to have been derived from James Frazer's interpretation of the relation of Cybele and Attis as mother and son; see his *The Golden Bough: A Study of Magic and Religion* (New York: Macmillan, 1942), pp. 347–348, 356.

77. See "To Demeter," in White, *Homeric Hymns*, pp. 289–313. Also see George E. Mylonas, *Eleusis and the Eleusinian Mysteries* (Princeton, N.J.: Princeton University Press, 1961), p. 3.

78. "To Demeter," lines 480–484.

79. On the history of the site, see Mylonas, *Eleusis*, pp. 23–186.

80. Ibid., pp. 20–22, 229–237. Only at the very end of the existence of the sanctuary was this tradition broken, when a Mithraic shrine was added to the Eleusinian area; the last Hierophant was also a priest of Mithras (ibid., pp. 8, 183, 313).

81. Ibid., pp. 243–280.

82. On this cult, see Lewis Richard Farnell, *The Cults of the Greek States* (Oxford: Clarendon Press, 1907), vol. 3, pp. 89–92.

83. See Lotte Motz, *The Faces of the Goddess* (Oxford: Oxford University Press, 1997), p. 129.

84. These stories of Demeter's rape by Zeus and Poseidon come from Pausanias (8:42) and Clement of Alexandria, *Protrepticus* 2.22; see Motz, *Faces of the Goddess,* p. 126.

85. See Aristophanes, *Lysistrata,* in *Complete Greek Drama,* ed. Whitney J. Oates and Eugene O'Neill (New York: Random House, 1938), vol. 2, pp. 805–859.

CHAPTER 3: THE HEBREW GOD AND GENDER

1. Norman K. Gottwald, *The Politics of Ancient Israel* (Louisville, Ky.: Westminster John Knox Press, 2001), pp. 166–167. For a discussion of the idea that the exodus story was appropriated by Saul as a national charter myth of the new royal power, see Karel van der Toorn, *Family Religion in Babylonia, Syria, and Israel: Continuity and Change in the Forms of Religious Life* (Leiden: Brill, 1996), pp. 291–302, 349–351, 375–376.

2. See Mark S. Smith, *The Early History of God: Yahweh and Other Deities* (San Francisco: Harper and Row, 1989); Robert Karl Gnuse, *No Other Gods: Emergent Monotheism in Israel* (Sheffield, U.K.: Sheffield Academic Press, 1997); and Bob Becking, Meindert Dijkstra, Karel Vriezen, and Marjo C. A. Korpel, *Only One God? Monotheism in Ancient Israel and the Veneration of the Goddess Asherah* (Sheffield, U.K.: Sheffield Academic Press, 2001). For a contrary view, see Jeffrey H. Tigay, *You Shall Have No Other Gods: Israelite Religion in the Light of Hebrew Inscriptions,* Harvard Semitic Studies 31 (Atlanta: Scholars Press, 1986).

3. See Saul M. Olyan, *Asherah and the Cult of Yahweh in Israel* (Atlanta: Scholars Press, 1988); Tilde Binger, *Asherah: Goddesses in Ugarit, Israel, and the Old Testament* (Sheffield, U.K.: Sheffield Academic Press, 1997); J. A. Emerton, "Yahweh and His Asherah: The Goddess or Her Symbol?" *Vetus Testamentum* 49, no. 3 (1999): 315–337; Judith M. Hadley, *The Cult of Asherah in Ancient Israel and Judah: Evidence for a Hebrew Goddess* (New York: Cambridge University Press, 2000).

4. Binger, *Asherah,* pp. 94–109.

5. Judith Hadley, "Yahweh and 'His Asherah': Archaeological and Textual Evidence for the Cult of the Goddess," in *Ein Gott allein? JHWH-Verehrung und biblischer monotheismus im kontext der israelitischen und altorientalischen religionsgeschichte,* ed. Walter Dietrich and Martin A. Klopfenstein (Freiburg: Universitätsverlag Freiburg, 1994), pp. 235–268.

6. See Tikva Frymer-Kensky, *In the Wake of the Goddesses: Women, Culture, and Biblical Transformation of Pagan Myth* (New York: Free Press, 1992), pp. 159–160; and John B. Burns, "Female Pillar Figurines of the Iron Age: A Study in Text and Artifact," *Andrews University Seminary Studies* 36, no. 1 (1998): 23–50.

7. See Gale Yee, "'She Is Not My Wife and I Am Not Her Husband': A Materialist Reading of Hosea 1–2," *Biblical Interpretation* 9, no. 4 (2001): 345–383 (reprinted in Gale A. Yee, *Poor Banished Children of Eve: Woman as Evil in the Hebrew Bible* [Minneapolis: Fortress Press, 2003], pp. 81–109); and N. K. Gottwald, "From Tribal Existence to Empire: The Socio-Historic Context for the Rise of the Hebrew Prophets," in *God and Capitalism: A Prophetic Critique of the Market Economy*, ed. J. Mark Thomas and Vern Visick (Madison, Wisc.: WIAR Editions, 1991), pp. 11–29.

8. Olyan, *Asherah*, pp. 3–22.

9. Ibid. See also Susan Ackerman, *Under Every Green Tree: Popular Religion in Sixth-Century Judah* (Atlanta: Scholars Press, 1992).

10. Smith, *Early History of God*, pp. 152–153.

11. Frymer-Kensky, *In the Wake of the Goddesses*, pp. 83–99.

12. See Howard Eilberg-Schwartz, *God's Phallus: And Other Problems for Men and Monotheism* (Boston: Beacon Press, 1994), p. 86.

13. Frymer-Kensky, *In the Wake of the Goddesses*, pp. 187–198.

14. Smith, *Early History of God*, pp. 7–11.

15. Ibid., p. 51; A. Mazar, "The 'Bull Site': An Iron Age I Open Cult Place," *Bulletin of the American Schools of Oriental Research* 247 (1982): 27–42; A. Mazar, "On Cult Places and Early Israelites: A Response to Michael Coogan," *Biblical Archaeologist Review* 15, no. 4 (1988): 45.

16. Smith, *Early History of God*, pp. 41–61. See also van der Toorn, *Family Religion*, pp. 240–241, 316–338.

17. Smith, *Early History of God*, pp. 52–53. See also John Day, *God's Conflict with the Dragon and the Sea: Echoes of a Canaanite Myth in the Old Testament* (Cambridge: Cambridge University Press, 1985).

18. Smith, *Early History of God*, pp. 61–64.

19. Ibid., pp. 63–64.

20. John Gardner and John Maier, eds., *Gilgamesh* (New York: Knopf, 1984), tablet 1, col. iv, p. 77.

21. Eilberg-Schwartz, *God's Phallus*, pp. 139–141.

22. Frymer-Kensky, *In the Wake of the Goddesses*, pp. 97–98.

23. Phyllis Trible has argued that this language makes God androgynous; see these two works by Trible: "Depatriarchalizing in Biblical Interpretation," *Journal of the American Academy of Religion* 12 (1973): 39–42; and *God and the Rhetoric of Sexuality* (Philadelphia: Fortress Press, 1978). For critiques of this view, see J. W. Miller, "Depatriarchalizing God in Biblical Interpretation," *Catholic Biblical Quarterly* 48 (1986): 609–616;

M. Gruber, "The Motherhood of God in Second Isaiah," *Revue Biblique* 90 (1983): 351–359; and J. J. Schmitt, "The Motherhood of God and Zion as Mother," *Revue Biblique* 92 (1985): 557–569.

24. Gardner and Maier, *Gilgamesh*, tablet 6, col. 1, p. 149. Neal Walls interprets the spurning of Inanna by Gilgamesh as a homoerotic preference for his relation with Enkidu; see Walls, "The Allure of Gilgamesh," in *Desire, Discord, and Death: Approaches to Near Eastern Myth* (Boston: American Schools of Oriental Research, 2001), pp. 34–68.

25. Eilberg-Schwartz, *God's Phallus*, p. 3.

26. Smith, *Early History of God*, pp. 41–45; Else K. Holt, "' . . . Urged on by his wife Jezebel': A Literary Reading of I Kgs 18 in Context," *Journal for the Study of the Old Testament* 9, no. 1 (1995): 83–96; Yigael Yadin, "The 'House of Ba'al' of Ahab and Jezebel in Samaria and That of Athalia in Judah," in *Archaeology in the Levant*, ed. Roger Moorey and Peter Parr (Warminster, U.K.: Aris and Phillips, 1978), pp. 127–135.

27. Yee, "'She Is Not My Wife,'" pp. 348–350.

28. For discussion of Herodotus's description, see L. M. Epstein, "Sacred Prostitution," in *Sex Laws and Customs in Judaism* (New York: Bloch, 1948), pp. 152–157.

29. See Phyllis Bird, "'To Play the Harlot': An Inquiry into an Old Testament Metaphor," in *Missing Persons and Mistaken Identities: Women and Gender in Ancient Israel* (Minneapolis: Fortress Press, 1997), pp. 219–236; C. J. Fisher, "Cultic Prostitution in the Ancient Near East? A Reappraisal," *Biblical Theology Bulletin* 6 (1976): 225–236; R. A. Oden, "Religious Identity and the Sacred Prostitution Accusation," in *The Bible Without Theology: The Theological Tradition and the Alternatives to It* (San Francisco: Harper and Row, 1987), pp. 137–153; Richard A. Henshaw, *Female and Male: The Cultic Personnel, the Bible, and the Rest of the Ancient Near East* (Allison, Pa.: Pickwick, 1994), pp. 218–256.

30. Christopher R. Seitz, *Theology in Conflict: Reactions to the Exile in the Book of Jeremiah* (Berlin: de Gruyter, 1989); Angela Bauer, *Gender in the Book of Jeremiah: A Feminist Literary Reading* (New York: Lang, 1998); Joseph Blenkinsopp, *Ezekiel* (Louisville, Ky.: John Knox Press, 1990).

31. Peggy L. Day, "Adulterous Jerusalem's Imagined Demise: Death of a Metaphor in Ezekiel XVI," *Vetus Testamentum* 50 (2000): 285–309; Peggy L. Day, "The Bitch Had It Coming to Her: Rhetoric and Interpretation in Ezekiel 16," *Biblical Interpretation* 8 (2000): 231–254; Julie Galambush, *Jerusalem in the Book of Ezekiel: The City as Yahweh's Wife*, Society of Biblical Literature Dissertation Series 130 (Atlanta: Scholars Press, 1992).

32. Sororal polygyny (marriage to two sisters) was common in Israel at this time; see Naomi Steinberg, *Kinship and Marriage in Genesis: A Household Economic Perspective* (Minneapolis: Fortress Press, 1993), pp. 45–46, 115–134, 152.

33. Mary E. Shields, "Gender and Violence in Ezekiel 23," *Society of Biblical Literature Seminar Papers* (Atlanta: Scholars Press, 1998), vol. 1, pp. 86–105; Fokkelien van Dijk-Hemmes, "The Metaphorization of Woman in Prophetic Speech: An Analysis of

Ezekiel 23," in *On Gendering Texts: Female and Male Voices in the Hebrew Bible*, ed. Athalya Brenner and Fokkelien van Dijk-Hemmes (Leiden: Brill, 1993), pp. 167–176.

34. For an analysis of the rhetoric of sexual abuse and its implications for psychology, see Renita J. Reems, *Battered Love: Marriage, Sex, and Violence in the Hebrew Prophets* (Minneapolis: Fortress Press, 1995). See also T. Drorah Setel, "Prophets and Pornography: Female Imagery in Hosea," in *Feminist Interpretations of the Bible*, ed. Letty Russell (Philadelphia: Westminster, 1985), pp. 86–95.

35. For a discussion of when the poems were first assembled, see Michael V. Fox, *The Song of Songs and the Ancient Egyptian Love Songs* (Madison: University of Wisconsin Press, 1985), pp. 186–190; and Athalya Brenner, *The Song of Songs* (Sheffield, U.K.: JSOT Press, 1989), pp. 57–61. A fragment of the Song at Qumran shows that the poem had attained a degree of sanctity before the first century CE; see Fox, *Song of Songs*, p. 189.

36. Rabbi Akiva declared: "Whoever warbles the Song of Songs at banqueting houses, treating it like an ordinary song, has no portion in the World to Come" (Tosefta Sanhedrin 12:10); see Fox, *Song of Songs*, pp. 249–250.

37. Phyllis Trible positions the Song of Songs in this eschatological relation to the "love relation of God and humanity gone awry"; see Trible, *God and the Rhetoric of Sexuality*, pp. 72–143.

38. Brenner, *Song of Songs*, pp. 65, 89–90.

39. See Shelomo Dov Goitein, "Women as Creators of Biblical Genres," trans. M. Carasik, *Prooftexts* 8 (1988): 1–33.

40. I follow Fox's interpretation here, understanding the girl's darkness to refer to sunburned skin from outdoor work, not to ethnicity (Fox, *Song of Songs*, p. 101).

41. See Fox's interpretation of the seal and the brothers' comments about their little sister in ibid., pp. 169, 171–173.

42. In Rabbi Akiva's words: "For all the writings are holy, but the Song of Songs is the holy of the holies" (Mishna Yadayim. 3:5).

43. Fox, *Song of Songs*, pp. 181–183.

44. Ibid., pp. 52, 55.

45. Samuel Noah Kramer, *The Sacred Marriage Rite* (Bloomington: Indiana University Press, 1969), pp. 85–106.

46. See, for example, Bernard of Clairvaux, *On the Song of Songs*, trans. Kilian Walsh (Spencer, Mass.: Cistercian Publications, 1971). Also see chapter 6 of this volume.

47. See Eilberg-Schwartz, *God's Phallus*, pp. 164–168, 183–186; and Fiona C. Black, "Unlikely Bedfellows: Allegorical and Feminist Readings of the Song of Songs 7:1–8," in *A Feminist Companion to the Song of Songs*, ed. Athalya Brenner (Sheffield, U.K.: Sheffield Academic Press, 1993), pp. 104–129.

48. H. Ringgren, *Word and Wisdom: Studies in the Hypostatization of Divine Qualities and Functions in the Ancient Near East* (Lund, Sweden: Hakan Ohlssons Boktryckeri, 1947), pp. 34–36; Claudia V. Camp, *Wisdom and the Feminine in the Book of Proverbs*

(Decatur, Ga.: Almond Press, 1985), pp. 72–77; Roland E. Murphy, "The Personification of Wisdom," in *Wisdom in Ancient Israel: Essays in Honor of J. A. Emerton*, ed. John Day et al. (Cambridge: Cambridge University Press, 1995), pp. 222–233; Judith E. McKinley, *Gendering Wisdom the Host: Biblical Invitations to Eat and Drink* (Sheffield, U.K.: Sheffield Academic Press, 1996), pp. 38–44.

49. C. Bauer-Kayatz, *Studien zu Proverbien 1–9*, Wissenschaftliche Monographien zum Alten und Neuen Testament, vol. 22 (Neukirchen-Vluyn: Neukirchener Verlag, 1966); Hans Conselmann, "The Mother of Wisdom," in *The Future of Our Religious Past*, ed. John Robinson (New York: Harper and Row, 1971), pp. 230–243.

50. Bernhard Lang, *Wisdom and the Book of Proverbs: A Hebrew Goddess Redefined* (New York: Pilgrim Press, 1986), pp. 126–131.

51. John Day, "Foreign Semitic Influences on the Wisdom of Israel and Its Appropriation in the Book of Proverbs," in Day, *Wisdom in Ancient Israel*, pp. 55–70.

52. Judith M. Hadley, "Wisdom and the Goddess," in Day, *Wisdom in Ancient Israel*, pp. 234–243.

53. Leo G. Perdue, "Wisdom and Social History in Proverbs 1–9," in *Wisdom, You Are My Sister: Studies in Honor of Roland E. Murphy*, ed. Michael L. Barre (Washington, D.C.: Catholic Biblical Association of America, 1997), pp. 78–101.

54. Comments on the meaning of personified Folly abound: see, for example, these three essays in *A Feminist Companion to the Wisdom Literature*, ed. Athalya Brenner (Sheffield, U.K.: Sheffield Academic Press, 1995): Gale A. Yee, "'I Have Perfumed My Bed with Myrrh': The Foreign Woman in Proverbs 1–9," pp. 110–126; Gale A. Yee, "A Socio-Literary Production of the Foreign Woman in Proverbs," pp. 127–130; and Meike Heijerman, "Who Would Blame Her? The 'Strange Woman' in Proverbs 7," pp. 100–109. See also Joseph Blenkinsopp, "The Social Context of the 'Outsider Woman' in Proverbs 1–9," *Biblica* 72 (1991): 457–473; McKinley, *Gendering Wisdom the Host*, pp. 81–99; and Claudia V. Camp, *Wise, Strange, and Holy: The Strange Woman and the Making of the Bible* (Sheffield, U.K.: Sheffield Academic Press, 2000), pp. 40–71.

55. Camp, *Wisdom and the Feminine*, pp. 99–103.

56. See Yee, "'I Have Perfumed My Bed with Myrrh,'" p. 121.

57. See McKinley, *Gendering Wisdom the Host*, pp. 44–56.

58. Ibid., pp. 56–58.

59. The term *'amon* has been translated as either "master worker" or "little child"; see Prov. 8:30 and note, *Holy Bible, Revised Standard Version* (New York: Thomas Nelson, 1952), p. 669.

60. See Leo G. Perdue, *Wisdom and Creation: The Theology of the Wisdom Literature* (Nashville: Abingdon Press, 1994), pp. 77–92.

61. Ibid., pp. 248–250.

62. Ibid., pp. 184–186.

63. For the history and interpretation of the Wisdom of Solomon, see Silvia Schroer,

"The Wisdom of Solomon," in *Searching the Scriptures*, ed. Elizabeth Schussler Fiorenza (New York: Crossroads, 1993–1995), vol. 2, pp. 17–38.

64. Ibid., pp. 291–322; William Horbury, "The Christian Use and the Jewish Origins of the Wisdom of Solomon," in Day, *Wisdom in Ancient Israel*, pp. 182–196.

65. For possible reflections of women's counseling roles as prophetesses, mothers, and wives, see Silva Schroer, "Wise and Counseling Women in Ancient Israel: Literary and Historical Ideals of the Personified *Hokma*," in Brenner, *Feminist Companion to the Wisdom Literature*, pp. 67–84. See also Schroer's commentary on the Wisdom of Solomon in Fiorenza, *Searching the Scriptures*, vol. 2, pp. 17–38, for a possible reference to the Therapeutae.

66. Carol A. Newsom, "Women and the Discourse of Patriarchal Wisdom: A Study of Proverbs 1–9," in *Gender and Difference in Ancient Israel*, ed. Peggy L. Day (Minneapolis: Fortress Press, 1989), pp. 142–146.

CHAPTER 4: SAVIOR GODDESSES
IN THE MYSTERY RELIGIONS AND GNOSTICISM

1. Examples of such studies from the History of Religions School include Franz Cumont, *Oriental Religions in Roman Paganism* (New York: Dover, 1911); and Richard Reitzenstein, *Hellenistic Mystery-Religions: Their Basic Ideas and Significance*, trans. John E. Steely (1910; Pittsburgh: Pickwick Press, 1978). See Gilbert Murray, *Four Stages of Greek Religion* (New York: Columbia University Press, 1912), p. 103; later, *Five Stages of Greek Religion* (New York: Columbia University Press, 1930).

2. Murray, *Four Stages of Greek Religion*, p. 103.

3. See, for example, John Herman Randall, *Hellenistic Ways of Deliverance and the Making of the Christian Synthesis* (New York: Columbia University Press, 1970).

4. This is the argument made in Giulia Sfameni Gasparro, *Soteriology and Mystic Aspects in the Cult of Cybele and Attis* (Leiden: Brill, 1985).

5. Lynn E. Roller, *In Search of God the Mother: The Cult of the Anatolian Cybele* (Berkeley: University of California Press, 1999), pp. 63–115.

6. Roller (ibid., pp. 9–24, 168–169) argues that the idea of irrational, ecstatic rites as "oriental" is itself a Greek stereotype of the "oriental," which has been picked up and repeated in the more recent stereotypes of "oriental" religion in modern European scholarship, as in Cumont's *Oriental Religions in Roman Paganism*.

7. Ibid., pp. 177–182, 237–259; compare with Gasparro, *Soteriology and Mystic Aspects*, p. 26.

8. Roller, *In Search of God the Mother*, pp. 263–325; also Maarten J. Vermaseren, *Cybele and Attis: The Myth and Cult* (London: Thames and Hudson, 1977), pp. 38–63.

9. Vermaseren, *Cybele and Attis*, pp. 113–124. See also Gasparro, *Soteriology and Mystic Aspects*, pp. 84–106, on the lack of eschatology as central to these rites. Compare Robert Turcan, *The Cults of the Roman Empire* (Oxford: Blackwell, 1996), pp. 44–47.

10. Gasparro, *Soteriology and Mystic Aspects*, pp. 107–118; Turcan, *Cults of the Roman Empire*, pp. 49–65. See also Robert Duthoy, *The Taurobolium: Its Evolution and Terminology* (Leiden: Brill, 1969).

11. See Reginald E. Witt, *Isis in the Greco-Roman World* (Ithaca, N.Y.: Cornell University Press, 1971), pp. 46–58; Frederick Solmsen, *Isis Among the Greeks and Romans* (Cambridge, Mass.: Harvard University Press, 1979), pp. 1–26; and Sharon Kelly Heyob, *The Cult of Isis Among Women in the Greco-Roman World* (Leiden: Brill, 1975), pp. 2–10. See also Turcan, *Cults of the Roman Empire*, pp. 76–78.

12. An earlier form of the story has been attributed to Lucian of Samosata, but this is doubtful. See an excerpt from this novel in Apuleius, *The Golden Ass*, trans. Robert Graves (New York: Pocket Library, 1955), pp. 261–264. The original story probably goes back to the *Metamorphoses*, by Lucian of Patras; see Harold E. Butler, "Apuleius," in *Oxford Classical Dictionary*, ed. Max Cary et al. (Oxford: Clarendon Press, 1957), pp. 73–74.

13. Apuleius, *The Golden Ass*, pp. 238–239.

14. Ibid., p. 252. See also Turcan, *Cults of the Roman Empire*, pp. 119–121.

15. Robert Graves, introduction to Apuleius, *The Golden Ass*, pp. x–xi.

16. See Homer *Odyssey* 4.561–569; Hesiod *Work and Days* 167–173.

17. Franz Cumont, *Astrology and Religion Among the Greeks and Romans* (New York: Putnam, 1912), pp. 1–35.

18. Plato *Timaeus* 41–42.

19. See Herbert J. Rose, "Transmigration," in Cary et al., *Oxford Classical Dictionary*, p. 921.

20. "Poimandres," in Hans Jonas, *The Gnostic Religion: The Message of the Alien God and the Beginnings of Christianity* (Boston: Beacon Press, 1958), p. 153.

21. Margherita Guarducci, ed. and trans., *Epigraphii Graeca* 4.263; quoted in Jocelyn Godwin, *Mystery Religions in the Ancient World* (San Francisco: Harper and Row, 1981), p. 36.

22. Burke R. Lawton, "Shoel in Ancient Hebrew and Jewish Literature" (PhD diss., Northwestern University, 1918).

23. Rachel Z. Dulin, "Old Age in Hebrew Scripture: A Phenomenological Study" (PhD diss., Northwestern University, 1962).

24. See Lawrence Mills, *Avesta Eschatology Compared with the Book of Daniel and Revelation* (Chicago: Open Court Press, 1908).

25. The apocalypses of the second century BCE think of the risen ones as joining those alive at that time in temporal life. Only in later apocalypses of the first centuries BCE and CE do we find the idea of an eternal kingdom separated from a temporal one. This development was traced in Rosemary R. Ruether, "A Historical and Textual Analysis of the Relationship Between Futurism and Eschatology in the Apocalyptic Texts of the Inter-Testamental Period" (BA diss., Scripps College, 1958), chap. 4.

26. See Catherine Keller's book *The Face of the Deep: A Theology of Becoming* (New York: Routledge, 2002); see also her essay "No More Sea: The Lost Chaos of the Eschaton," in *Christianity and Ecology*, ed. Rosemary R. Ruether and Dieter I. Hessel (Cambridge, Mass.: Harvard University Press, 2000), pp. 183–198.

27. See, for example, Philo *On the Creation of the World*, secs. 7–10.

28. Philo *On Drunkenness* 30–32, in *Philo*, ed. F. H. Colson and G. H. Whitaker (New York: Putnam, 1930), pp. 333, 335.

29. Philo *On the Creation of the World*, secs. 47, 53.

30. Philo *On the Therapeutae;* for a translation, see Natum N. Glazer, ed., *The Essential Philo* (New York: Schocken Books, 1971), pp. 311–330.

31. Jorunn Buckley describes this diversity of views in her study of six gnostic systems; see *Female Fault and Fulfillment in Gnosticism* (Chapel Hill: University of North Carolina Press, 1986).

32. See Michael A. Williams, "Variety in Gnostic Perspectives on Gender," in *Images of the Feminine in Gnosticism*, ed. Karen L. King (Philadelphia: Fortress Press, 1988), pp. 2–22.

33. Karen L. King, "Sophia and Christ in the *Apocryphon of John*," in King, *Images of the Feminine in Gnosticism*, pp. 158–176.

34. See George W. MacRae, "The Jewish Background on the Gnostic Sophia Myth," *Novum Testamentum* 12 (1970): 86–101.

35. *Apocryphon of John* II, 2, 13; in *The Nag Hammadi Library in English*, ed. James M. Robinson (San Francisco: Harper and Row, 1977), p. 99.

36. The many names for this figure are all variations on the word "thought": Pronoia means "forethought," Epinoia means "thought as purpose," and Ennoia means "the act of thinking."

37. Robinson, *Nag Hammadi Library*, pp. 100–102.

38. The term "wisdom of the thought" indicates that she is a version of the first female emanation that is the Thought of God (see note 36 above).

39. Robinson, *Nag Hammadi Library*, pp. 103–104.

40. The figure of a man with a lion face and a serpent wrapped around his body was a typical image of the lord of time and fate in Mithraism; the image seems to have been drawn from this tradition. See Franz Cumont, *Mysteries of Mithra* (Chicago: Open Court Publishers, 1910), pp. 105, 106; also Leroy A. Campbell, *Mithraic Iconography and Ideology* (Leiden: Brill, 1968), plate 11 (from Ostia), p. 312; and plate 16 (from Florence), p. 665.

41. Robinson, *Nag Hammadi Library*, pp. 105–106.

42. The *Apocryphon of John* text claims to interpret the Genesis passage but gives it a different meaning: "Do not think it is as Moses said, 'above the waters.' No, but when she had seen the wickedness which had happened, and the theft which her son had committed, she repented. And forgetfulness overcame her in the darkness of ignorance and

she began to become ashamed." (IV, 21, 13–14 adds "and she did not dare to return but she was moving about. And the moving was going to and fro.") See Robinson, *Nag Hammadi Library*, p. 106.

43. Ibid., pp. 110–112. The Berlin Codex makes the female powers speak as the eagle from the tree, while the Nag Hammadi II version Christianizes it as "I" (Christ); see King, "Sophia and Christ in the *Apocryphon of John*," pp. 158–176.

44. The *Hypostasis of the Archons* was composed in Greek, probably in Egypt; Bentley Layton places it in the third century CE (Robinson, *Nag Hammadi Library*, p. 152).

45. Ibid., p. 153.

46. Ibid., p. 154.

47. Ibid., p. 155.

48. Ibid., p. 156.

49. Ibid., pp. 156–157.

50. Ibid., pp. 157–160.

51. The *Trimorphic Protennoia* is contemporaneous with the *Apocryphon of John* and attained its final form about 200 CE, according to editor John D. Turner; see ibid., p. 461.

52. Ibid., pp. 461–462.

53. Ibid., p. 467.

54. Deirdre J. Good protests the scholarly interpretation of the gnostic Sophia as only a negative "cosmic Eve," arguing that this view neglects her celestial component in the pleroma as an expression of the female First Thought (*Reconstructing the Tradition of Sophia in Gnostic Literature* [Atlanta: Scholars Press, 1987]).

55. For the Greek medical background of this view of the female's "formlessness," see Richard Smith, "Sex Education in Gnostic Schools," in King, *Images of the Feminine in Gnosticism*, pp. 345–360.

56. As noted in this chapter, the *Apocryphon of John* and the *Hypostasis of the Archons* differ on whose image is reflected in the waters. The former describes it as the image of Perfect Man, which inspired the archons to try to imitate him in Adam; whereas the latter writes that it is the female spiritual power, inspiring the archons to make Adam in order to attract the female downward.

57. On Norea, see two essays in King, *Images of the Feminine in Gnosticism:* Anne McGuire, "Virginity and Subversion: Norea Against the Powers," pp. 239–258; and Birger A. Pearson, "Revisiting Norea," pp. 265–275.

58. Although the authors represented in *Images of the Feminine in Gnosticism* insist that "symbolism is not sociology" and that we know little about the actual roles played by women in gnostic groups, we do know that one gnostic group, that of Simon Magnus, appointed a woman, Helen, to represent the female deity; see Madeleine Scopello, "Jewish and Christian Heroines in the Nag Hammadi Library," in King, *Images of the Feminine in Gnosticism*, pp. 71–95.

59. The image of Mary Magdalene as a prostitute comes from confusing the unnamed

woman in Luke 7:37–48 with the Mary Magdalene who is cured of "seven devils" by Jesus in Luke 8:2. This confusion belongs to the exegetical work of Pope Gregory the Great in the sixth century, particularly in his Homily 33. See also Susan Haskin, *Mary Magdalene: Myth and Metaphor* (London: HarperCollins, 1993), pp. 95–97.

60. The leading woman disciple in these gnostic writings is variously called Maria, Mariam, or Mariamme. This woman is Mary Magdalene. She is not to be confused with Mary, the mother of Jesus, who is identified as such when she appears in some of the writings.

61. The Sophia of Jesus Christ is a Christianization of a pre-Christian religious tract, called Eugnostos the Blessed, that converted this writing into a revelation discourse of the risen Christ with his disciples. The aim of both tracts was to establish a superceles-tial world beyond the visible world. Christ is seen as coming from this supercelestial world and revealing knowledge of it to his followers. The Sophia of Jesus Christ exists in a Coptic translation, found in the Nag Hammadi library, and also in a Coptic version in the Berlin Codex, found in 1896 and sold to the Berlin Museum. There is also a Greek fragment in the Oxyrhynchus papyri. The Eugnostos may go back to the first century CE; its Christianization, in the Sophia of Jesus Christ, probably occurred in the early second century CE. For an English translation, by Douglas M. Parrott, see Robinson, *Nag Hammadi Library,* pp. 206–228.

62. The Dialogue of the Savior is a fragmentary and composite text with parallels to the Gospel of Thomas. Originally written in Greek sometime in the second century CE, it exists only in a Coptic translation in the Nag Hammadi Codices. For an English translation, by Helmut Koester and Elaine Pagels, see ibid., pp. 229–238.

63. The First Apocalypse of James probably emerged from a Jewish-Christian gnos-tic group around the end of the second century CE. It exists in two Coptic codices. For an English translation, by William R. Schoedel, see ibid., pp. 242–248.

64. The Gospel of Thomas was composed as early as the second half of the first century CE and may have been written originally in Aramaic or Syriac. Several frag-ments in Greek survive, and a Coptic translation was found in the Nag Hammadi Codices. For an English translation, by Thomas O. Lambdin, see ibid., pp. 117–130.

Concerning the demand that women go through a double transformation "upward," see Jorunn Buckley, "An Interpretation of Logion 114 in the *Gospel of Thomas,*" in her *Female Fault and Fulfillment in Gnosticism,* pp. 84–104.

65. The Gospel of Philip is a collection of theological teachings about ethics and the sacraments. It comes from the late second to third centuries CE and is known only as a Coptic translation in the Nag Hammadi Codices. For an English translation, by Wesley W. Isenberg, see Robinson, *Nag Hammadi Library,* pp. 131–151.

Also see Jorunn Jacobsen Buckley, "'The Holy Spirit Is a Double Name': Holy Spirit, Mary, and Sophia in the *Gospel of Philip,*" in King, *Images of the Feminine in Gnosticism,* pp. 211–227.

66. The Pistis Sophia is a long composite document that takes the form of conversations between the risen Lord and his disciples. The document is known from 1773 when it was purchased by a British manuscript collector, Thomas Askew. It comes from Egypt and was written in the third century CE. For an English translation, see *Pistis Sophia*, trans. Carl Schmidt and Violet McDermot (Leiden: Brill, 1978); quotations from 1.17, 1.36, 2.72, 4.146.

67. The Gospel of Mary exists in the Berlin Codices. The Coptic manuscript dates to the early fifth century CE, while the Greek fragment goes back to the early third century CE. The translation by George MacRae and R. Mcl. Wilson in Robinson, *Nag Hammadi Library*, pp. 471–474, uses androcentric language. Karen King offers an inclusive-language translation, which she sees as closer to the original meaning, and gives preference to the Greek fragment over the Coptic translation; see King, "Gospel of Mary," in *The Complete Gospels*, ed. R. J. Miller (Sonoma, Calif.: Polebridge Press, 1992), pp. 357–366.

For further detailed commentary on the Gospel of Mary, see Karen King, "The Gospel of Mary," in *Searching the Scriptures: A Feminist Commentary*, ed. Elizabeth S. Fiorenza (New York: Crossroads, 1994), vol. 2, pp. 601–635.

68. The Greek fragment suggests that only Levi goes out to preach the gospel, whereas the Coptic version suggests that all the disciples, including Mary Magdalene, go out to preach; see King, "Gospel of Mary"; and Karen King, *The Gospel of Mary of Magdala: Jesus and the First Woman Apostle* (Santa Rosa, Calif.: Polebridge Press, 2003), p. 18.

CHAPTER 5: THE SPIRITUAL FEMININE IN NEW TESTAMENT AND PATRISTIC CHRISTIANITY

1. For a critique of the ideology which held that orthodoxy was the original Christianity of Jesus's teachings and that heresy (gnosticism) was a later deviation, see Walter Bauer, *Orthodoxy and Heresy in Earliest Christianity* (Philadelphia: Fortress Press, 1971).

2. On the mingling of apocalyptic and Wisdom traditions at the time of the rise of Christianity, see Silva Schroer, *Wisdom Has Built Her House: Studies on the Figure of Sophia in the Bible* (Collegeville, Minn.: Liturgical Press, 1996), p. 122. Schroer counters the view of Luise Schottroff that the Wisdom tradition is elitist, in contrast to the prophetic tradition, which is egalitarian and is the primary tradition for women concerned about a liberating gospel. This debate is discussed in Elizabeth S. Fiorenza, *Jesus: Miriam's Child, Sophia's Prophet: Critical Issues in Feminist Christology* (New York: Continuum, 1994), pp. 155–157.

3. See Ben Witherington, *Jesus the Sage: The Pilgrimage of Wisdom* (Minneapolis: Fortress Press, 1994), pp. 85–117.

4. The apocalyptic tradition is represented by the book of Daniel in the Hebrew Bible

and by Revelation in the New Testament, together with the inter-testamental apocalypses; see R. H. Charles, *The Apocrypha and Pseudepigrapha of the Old Testament* (Oxford: Clarendon Press, 1913), vol. 2.

5. On the early fusion of the creation narrative from Wisdom and the eschatological narrative of apocalypse in the Christological hymns, see Witherington, *Jesus the Sage*, pp. 252–253, 290. Stevan Davies sees the fusion of Wisdom and Kingdom language into an early realized eschatology in the Gospel of Thomas, which he views as a mid-first-century document, parallel to Q. Thomas's theology of baptismal-realized eschatology that existed among some of the Corinthians against whom Paul was reacting in Corinthians 1–4; see Davies, *The Gospel of Thomas and Christian Wisdom* (New York: Seabury Press, 1983), pp. 77–78, 138–147.

6. Witherington argues for the position that Jesus identified himself as Wisdom (*Jesus the Sage*, pp. 203–204). Davies sees the union of Kingdom and Wisdom language as possibly going back to Jesus but notes that this is different from Jesus actually identifying himself as Messiah or Wisdom (*Gospel of Thomas*, p. 98).

7. New Testament scholars have long disputed the idea that Jesus called himself Messiah. See Marcus J. Borg's discussion of a noneschatological Jesus in his *Jesus in Contemporary Scholarship* (Valley Forge, Pa.: Trinity Press International, 1994), pp. 47–96.

8. For a discussion of the Wisdom background of these Christological hymns, see Elizabeth S. Fiorenza, "Wisdom Mythology and the Christological Hymns of the New Testament," in *Aspects of Wisdom in Judaism and Early Christianity*, ed. Robert L. Wilken (Notre Dame: Notre Dame University Press, 1975), pp. 17–41.

9. For a discussion of the likelihood that the hymn was given a Christian editing to add references to the church and the blood of the cross, see Edward Lohse, *Colossians and Philemon* (Philadelphia: Fortress Press, 1971), pp. 53–54.

10. See Davies, *Gospel of Thomas*, pp. 100–104.

11. On Wisdom in the Q tradition, see Witherington, *Jesus the Sage*, pp. 219–235; and Fiorenza, *Jesus*, pp. 139–145.

12. See Witherington, *Jesus the Sage*, pp. 341–368. Also see Celia M. Deutsch, *Lady Wisdom, Jesus, and the Sages: Metaphor and Social Context in Matthew's Gospel* (Valley Forge, Pa.: Trinity Press International, 1996), pp. 49–54; and M. Jack Suggs, *Wisdom Christology and Law in Matthew's Gospel* (Cambridge, Mass.: Harvard University Press, 1970), pp. 57, 97.

13. See Fiorenza, *Jesus*, pp. 141–145.

14. See John Ashton, "The Transformation of Wisdom: A Study of the Prologue of John's Gospel," *New Testament Studies* 32 (1986): 161–186.

15. See particularly Sharon H. Ringe, *Wisdom's Friends: Community and Christology in the Fourth Gospel* (Louisville, Ky.: Westminster John Knox Press, 1999), pp. 46–63.

16. The term "friends" in John 15:12–15 echoes language from the Wisdom of

Solomon 8:28, where it is said that Wisdom "enters into holy souls and makes them God's friends and prophets." On the importance of friendship as a model of community in John, see Ringe, *Wisdom's Friends*, pp. 64–83.

17. On the role of Philo in the shift from Wisdom to Logos, see Schorer, *Wisdom Has Built Her House*, p. 39; Fiorenza, "Wisdom Mythology," p. 34; and Ringe, *Wisdom's Friends*, p. 43.

18. See Witherington, *Jesus the Sage*, pp. 386–387, for an insistence that Jesus's maleness necessitates the male grammatical gender in describing his divinity. Also see Raymond Brown, *The Gospel of John* (New York: Doubleday, 1966), vol. 1, p. 523.

19. Fiorenza, *Jesus*, pp. 152–154.

20. To contrast the books included in the Greek canon, still the basis for the Catholic Bible today, and the Hebrew canon followed by Protestants, see *The Jerusalem Bible* (Garden City, N.Y.: Doubleday, 1966), pp. xv–xvi.

21. The modern Orthodox writer Sergius Bulgakov has developed a Sophiology in which Wisdom is the *ousia*, or ground of being, that sustains the three persons of the Trinity; see Bulgakov, *Sophia, the Wisdom of God: An Outline of Sophiology* (Hudson, N.Y.: Lindesfarne Press, 1993).

22. "The Gospel of Philip," 17a, in *The New Testament Apocrypha*, ed. Wilhelm Schneemelcher (Louisville, Ky.: Westminster John Knox Press, 1991), vol. 1, p. 190.

23. "The Gospel of the Hebrews," frag. 3, is quoted in Jerome's commentary on Isaiah 40:9 (M. Adriaen and F. Glorie, eds., *Corpus Christianorum Series Latina* [Turnholti, Belgium: Brepols, 1963], vol. 73, p. 459). The translation of the Gospel of the Hebrews is found in Schneemelcher, *New Testament Apocrypha*, vol. 1; see p. 177.

24. James H. Charlesworth, ed. and trans., *The Odes of Solomon: The Syriac Texts* (Missoula, Mont.: Scholars Press, 1977).

25. See Susan Ashbrook Harvey, "Feminine Imagery for the Divine: The Holy Spirit, the Odes of Solomon, and Early Syriac Tradition," *St. Vladimir's Theological Quarterly* 37, no. 2 (1993): 115; and Susan Ashbrook Harvey, "The Odes of Solomon," in *Searching the Scriptures: A Feminist Commentary*, ed. Elizabeth S. Fiorenza (New York: Crossroads, 1994), vol. 2, pp. 86–96. See also Sebastian Brock, "The Holy Spirit as Feminine in Early Syriac Literature," in *After Eve: Women, Theology, and the Christian Tradition*, ed. Janet M. Soskice (London: Collins, 1990), pp. 71–85.

26. See Sebastian Brock, *The Holy Spirit in the Syrian Baptismal Tradition*, vol. 9, Syrian Church Series (Bronx, N.Y., 1979). The milk and honey baptismal Eucharist is found in the third-century *Apostolic Tradition*, attributed to Hippolytus; see Paul Bradshaw, Maxwell Johnson, and L. Edward Phillips, eds., *The Apostolic Tradition of Hippolytus: A Commentary* (Minneapolis: Fortress Press, 2002), chap. 21. Also see Andrew McGowan, *Ascetic Eucharists: Food and Drink in Early Christian Ritual Meals* (Oxford: Clarendon Press, 1999), pp. 107–117.

27. Charlesworth, *Odes of Solomon*, pp. 42 (Ode 8.14), 124 (Ode 35.5), 138 (Ode 40).

28. Ibid., pp. 82–83 (Ode 19).

29. Ibid., pp. 98 (Ode 24), 108 (Ode 28), 29 (Ode 6), 66 (Ode 14.8).

30. Ibid., pp. 120 (Ode 33), 126–127 (Ode 36).

31. Clement of Alexandria *The Instructor* 1.6, translated in *Ante-Nicene Fathers*, ed. A. Cleveland Coxe (Buffalo, N.Y.: Christian Literature Publishing, 1885), vol. 2, pp. 215–222.

32. See Harvey, "Feminine Imagery," p. 137; and Sebastian Brock, trans., *A Garland of Hymns from the Early Church* (McLean, Va.: St. Athanasius' Coptic Publishing Center, 1989), pp. 63–68. Concerning the feminine in Ephrem's language for the Spirit, see Sebastian Brock, *The Luminous Eye: The Spiritual World Vision of Saint Ephrem* (Kalamazoo, Mich.: Cistercian Publications, 1988), pp. 168–172.

33. Gregory Nyssa is quoted in Verna E. F. Harrison, "Male and Female in Cappadocian Theology," *Journal of Theological Studies* 41, no. 2 (October 1990): 441.

34. Ibid., p. 442.

35. Gregory Nazianzus, "Fifth Theological Oration: 'On the Holy Spirit,'" in *The Christology of the Later Fathers*, ed. E. R. Harvey and C. Richardson, Library of Christian Classics (Philadelphia, Md.: Westminster Press, 1954), vol. 3, p. 198.

36. Jerome's commentary on Isaiah 40:9–11 (Adriaen and Glorie, *Corpus Christianorum Series Latina*, vol. 73, pt. 1, p. 459).

37. See Harrison, "Male and Female in Cappadocian Theology," pp. 442–471.

38. Augustine, *On the Trinity*, 12.12.17, in *St. Augustine: The Trinity*, trans. Stephen McKenna (Washington, D.C.: Catholic University Press of America, 1963), p. 359; Kim Power, *Veiled Desire: Augustine on Women* (New York: Continuum, 1996), pp. 140–143.

39. See Harvey, "Feminine Imagery," pp. 120–121; and Harvey, "Odes of Solomon," p. 96. For a more extended discussion, see Brock, "The Holy Spirit as Feminine," pp. 75–85.

40. See Adele Yarbro Collins, "Feminine Symbolism in the Book of Revelation," *Biblical Interpretation* 1, no. 1 (1993): 27.

41. On Hippolytus's commentary on the Canticle, see Berthold Altaner, *Patrology* (New York: Herder and Herder, 1960), p. 186.

42. Origen *Prologue 1*, in *The Song of Songs, Commentary and Homilies*, trans. R. P. Lawson (Westminster, Md.: Newman Press, 1957), p. 21.

43. Ibid., pp. 22–24.

44. Ibid., 1.1 (pp. 59–61), 2.1 (pp. 91–93), 3.9 (pp. 199–200).

45. Origen *De Principiis* 2.1.4, in *Origen: On First Principles*, trans. G. W. Butterworth (New York: Harper and Row, 1966).

46. For an account of Origen's catechetical school, see Eusebius *Ecclesiastical History* 6.18.2. Gregory Thaumaurgus attended the school and wrote an account of the curriculum taught there in his panegyric on Origen. The Neoplatonic philosopher Porphyry also commented that the Greek philosophers were part of Origen's curriculum; see Eusebius *Ecclesiastical History* 6.19.7–8.

47. Origen *Prologue 1*, 1.1 (Lawson, pp. 61–62).

48. See Erwin R. Goodenough, *By Light, Light: The Mystic Gospel of Hellenistic Judaism* (Amsterdam: Philo Press, 1969).

49. See Mary Astell, *The Song of Songs in the Middle Ages* (Ithaca, N.Y.: Cornell University Press, 1990), pp. 1–24.

50. Some of this discussion reflects Rufinus's Latin translation of Origen's commentary on the Song of Songs; see Lawson, *Song of Songs*, pp. 200–201.

51. Gregory Nyssa, *Commentary on the Song of Songs*, trans. with introduction by Casimir McCambley (Brookline, Mass.: Hellenic College Press, 1987), Homily 1, p. 47.

52. Ibid., Homily 7, pp. 145–146.

53. Charles Christopher Mierow, trans., *The Letters of St. Jerome* (Westminster, Md.: Newman Press, 1963), epistle 22.25, p. 158.

54. Methodius, *The Symposium: A Treatise on Chastity*, trans. Herbert Musurillo (Westminster, Md.: Newman Press, 1958), Logos 2, Theophilia's speech, pp. 48–58.

55. Ibid., pp. 76, 87.

56. Ibid., pp. 42, 44–46.

57. Tertullian *De Anima* 43, in *The Writings of Tertullian*, ed. Alexander Roberts and James Donaldson, Ante-Nicene Christian Library (Edinburgh: T. & T. Clark, 1870), vol. 2, p. 509.

58. Methodius, *Symposium*, p. 66.

59. Carolyn Osiek, ed., *Shepherd of Hermas* (Minneapolis: Augsburg Press, 1999), 2.1–4 (pp. 46–48).

60. Ibid., 2.4 (p. 58).

61. Ibid., 3.1–2 (pp. 60–61), 3.8 (p. 76).

62. Ibid., 3.9 (p. 80).

63. Ibid., 3.10–13 (pp. 83–84).

64. See Joseph C. Plumpe, *Mater Ecclesia: An Inquiry into the Concept of the Church as Mother in Early Christianity* (Washington, D.C.: Catholic University of America Press, 1943), pp. 18–80.

65. Cyprian, *The Unity of the Church*, trans. Maurice Bevenot (Westminster, Md.: Newman Press, 1957), 5.6 (p. 48).

66. Power, *Veiled Desire*, pp. 236–237.

67. Ambrose *De Virg.* 1.31; Augustine *Serm.* 190.2; Augustine *de Virg.* 7. For discussion, see Power, *Veiled Desire*, pp. 187–189.

68. Raymond E. Brown, ed., *Mary in the New Testament* (Philadelphia: Fortress Press, 1978), pp. 53, 286–287.

69. Ibid., pp. 74–77, 107–111.

70. Walter J. Burghardt believes that this analogy goes back to the beginning of the second century in the writings of Papias, bishop of Hierapolis; see Burghardt's "Mary in Eastern Patristic Thought," in *Mariology*, ed. Juniper B. Carol (Milwaukee: Bruce Publishing, 1957), vol. 2, pp. 88–89.

71. Justin Martyr *Dialogue with Trypho* 100, in *The Ante-Nicene Fathers*, ed. Alexander Roberts and James Donaldson (Grand Rapids, Mich.: Eerdmans, 1950), vol. 1, p. 249.

72. Irenaeus *Against Heresies* 3.22.4, in ibid., vol. 1, p. 455.

73. Ibid., 5.19.1 (p. 547).

74. On the significance of Jesus being called "Mary's son," and a view of him as the illegitimate child of Mary, see Jane Schaberg, *The Illegitimacy of Jesus: A Feminist Theological Interpretation of the Infancy Narratives* (San Francisco: Harper and Row, 1987).

75. "The Proevangelium of James," in *Apocryphal Gospels, Acts, and Revelations*, trans. Alexander Walker (Edinburgh: T. & T. Clark, 1873), pp. 1–15.

76. Ibid., chaps. 19–20, pp. 11–12.

77. Tertullian *De Monogamia* 8; see also his *De Carne Christi* 4, in which he assumes that Jesus was born naturally, against the views of the heretic Marcion.

78. Origen *Homily VII on Luke* 1.39–45, in *Homilies on Luke*, trans. Joseph T. Lienhard (Washington, D.C.: Catholic University of America Press, 1996), p. 30.

79. Jerome, "On the Perpetual Virginity of the Blessed Virgin Against Helvidius," in *Dogmatic and Polemical Works*, trans. John N. Hritzu, vol. 53, the Fathers of the Church (Washington, D.C.: Catholic University of America Press, 1965), pp. 3–43.

80. Jerome *Adversus Jovinius*, in *Jerome: Letters and Select Work*, ed. Philip Schaff and Henry Wace, series 2, *Nicene and Post-Nicene Fathers* (Grand Rapids, Mich.: Eerdmans, 1954), pp. 346–416. See also David G. Hunter, "Resistance to the Virginal Ideal in Late Fourth Century Rome: The Case of Jovinian," *Theological Studies* 48 (1987): 45–64.

81. Jovinian was condemned by synods at Rome under Pope Siricius (392 CE) and at Milan under Ambrose (393 CE).

82. For a discussion of the history and theology of this controversy, see Giovanni Miegge, *The Virgin Mary: The Roman Catholic Marian Doctrine* (London: Lutterworth Press, 1955), pp. 53–67. Also see Burghardt, "Mary in Eastern Patristic Thought," pp. 119–125.

83. For the "Tome of Leo" that provided the Roman view of the two natures and one person in Christ, as well as the Chalcedonian decree, see Edward R. Hardy and Cyril C. Richardson, eds., *Christology of the Later Fathers* (Philadelphia: Westminster Press, 1954), pp. 359–374.

84. Miegge, *The Virgin Mary*, pp. 59–60, 67. Also see Stephen Benko, *The Virgin Goddess: Studies in the Pagan and Christian Roots of Mariology* (Leiden: Brill, 1993), pp. 250–262.

85. "The Gospel of Bartholomew" in Schneemelcher, *New Testament Apocrypha*, vol. 1, p. 543.

86. Ibid., pp. 544–545.

87. "The Book of John Concerning the Falling Asleep of Mary," in Walker, *Apocryphal Gospels*, pp. 504–514.

88. "On the Passing of Mary," in ibid., pp. 529–530.

89. See Mary Clayton, *The Apocryphal Gospels of Mary in Anglo-Saxon England* (Cambridge: Cambridge University Press, 1998), p. 15.

90. Augustine *De natura et gratia*, chap. 36; see Miegge, *The Virgin Mary*, p. 110.

91. See the discussion in Marina Warner, *Alone of All Her Sex: The Myth of the Cult of the Virgin Mary* (New York: Knopf, 1976), xxii.

CHAPTER 6: FEMININE SYMBOLS IN MEDIEVAL RELIGIOUS LITERATURE

1. For a readable overview of medieval Mariology, see Marina Warner, *Alone of All Her Sex: The Myth of the Cult of the Virgin Mary* (New York: Knopf, 1976), esp. pp. 81–331.

2. John Damascene *On the Falling Asleep of the Mother of God* 2.14, in Paul F. Palmer, ed., *Mary in the Documents of the Church* (Westminster, Md.: Newman Press, 1952), p. 60.

3. Nicephorus Callistus Xanthopoulous *Ecclesiastical History* 15.4.14, in F. C. Baur, *Die Epochen der Kirchlichen Geschichtsschreibung* (Hildesheim: Georg Olms, 1962).

4. Warner, *Alone of All Her Sex*, p. 88.

5. See Elizabeth of Schönau, "The Resurrection of the Blessed Virgin," in *Elizabeth of Schönau: The Complete Works*, ed. and trans. Anne L. Clark (New York: Paulist Press, 2000), pp. 209–212.

6. Bernard of Clairvaux, Letter 174; quoted in full in Giovanni Miegge, *The Virgin Mary: The Roman Catholic Marian Doctrine* (London: Lutterworth Press, 1955), p. 114.

7. Thomas Aquinas *Summa Theologica* 3.27.1–6; quoted in Miegge, *The Virgin Mary*, pp. 116–117.

8. Duns Scotus, commentary on Book 4 of Peter Lombard's *Sentences*, 1.3.3.1; quoted in Miegge, *The Virgin Mary*, p. 124.

9. Daniel A. Dombrowski and Robert Deltete, *A Brief, Liberal, Catholic Defense of Abortion* (Urbana: University of Illinois Press, 2000).

10. See Warner, *Alone of All Her Sex*, pp. 242–243; Heiko Oberman, *The Harvest of Medieval Theology: Gabriel Biel and Late Medieval Nominalism* (Durham, N.C.: Labyrinth Press, 1983), pp. 283–286.

11. Miegge, *The Virgin Mary*, p. 127.

12. Bernard of Clairvaux, "Sermon on the Octave of the Assumption of the Blessed Virgin Mary," quoted in ibid., pp. 138–139.

13. This tale is recounted in Alfonso de Liguori's *Glories of the Most Holy Mary* (1750); see Miegge, *The Virgin Mary*, p. 148.

14. Concerning this concept of "pure nature" and its application to Mary, see Oberman, *Harvest*, pp. 47–49, 300–302, 309.

15. Ibid., p. 294.

16. Ibid., pp. 298–303. Also see Miegge, *The Virgin Mary,* pp. 155–177; and Warner, *Alone of All Her Sex,* pp. 206–223.

17. See Tim Unsworth, "Mary as Co-Redemptrix," *National Catholic Reporter,* July 18, 1997.

18. See these works by Hildegard of Bingen: *Scivias,* ed. Adelgundis Fuehrkoetter, *Corpus Christianorum: Continuatio Mediaevalis,* vol. 43–43a (Turnholti, Belgium: Brepols, 1978) (English edition: *Hildegard of Bingen: Scivias,* trans. Mother Columba Hart and Jane Bishop [New York: Paulist Press, 1990]); *The Book of the Rewards of Life,* trans. Bruce W. Hozeski (New York: Garland Press, 1994); *Hildegard of Bingen's Book of Divine Works,* ed. Matthew Fox and trans. Robert Cunningham (Santa Fe, N. Mex.: Bear and Company, 1987).

19. Barbara Newman has produced an elegant edition and translation of the *Symphonia* (Ithaca, N.Y.: Cornell University Press, 1988).

The letters are available in *Letters of Hildegard of Bingen,* trans. Joseph L. Baird and Radd K. Ehrman, 2 vols. (New York: Oxford University Press, 1998). A modern Latin edition of Hildegard's letters is found in L. van Acker, ed., *Corpus Christianorum* (Turnholti, Belgium: Brepols, 1991).

20. The original illuminated manuscript done under Hildegard's supervision in her own scriptorium was taken to Dresden during World War II, where it disappeared. The nuns of Eibingen, however, had prepared a hand-painted facsimile in the 1920s that still exists; see Barbara Newman, *Sister of Wisdom: St. Hildegard's Theology of the Feminine* (Berkeley: University of California Press, 1987), pp. 17–18.

21. See Hildegard *Book of Divine Works* 1.7 (pp. 13–14); and Newman, *Sister of Wisdom,* p. 62.

22. Hildegard *Book of Divine Works* 8.2 (pp. 206–207), 9.14 (p. 219).

23. Ibid., 4.11 (p. 86).

24. This quotation uses Barbara Newman's more literal translation of *O Virtus Sapientie;* see Newman, *Symphonia,* Song 2, pp. 100–101.

25. Hildegard *Book of Divine Works* 2.2 (p. 26).

26. Ibid., image of the Second Vision (p. 23).

27. See Newman, *Sister of Wisdom,* pp. 51–52, 67–69, 163–164.

28. Ibid., p. 49.

29. See Hildegard *Book of the Rewards of Life* 1.46 (p. 25), 4.38 (p. 191); and Newman, *Sister of Wisdom,* p. 49.

30. Hildegard *Book of the Rewards of Life* 4.38 (p. 191).

31. Image in Hildegard *Scivias* 3.9 (Hart and Bishop, p. 449).

32. Hildegard *Book of Divine Works* 8.2 (p. 207).

33. Ibid., 1.7 (pp. 13–14); Hildegard *Scivias* 1.2.2–9 (Hart and Bishop, pp. 74–76).

34. Hildegard *Scivias* 1.1 (Hart and Bishop, p. 67); Hildegard, Letter 23 to the Prelates of Mainz, in Baird and Ehrman, *Letters,* vol. 1, pp. 76–79. See also Newman, *Sister of Wisdom,* pp. 111–112.

35. Hildegard *Book of Divine Works* 2.27 (pp. 62–63), 4.18 (p. 95).

36. Ibid., 3.14 (p. 73).

37. Ibid., 4.100 (p. 123).

38. Newman, *Sister of Wisdom,* pp. 159–160.

39. Ibid., p. 176.

40. In this quotation, I have used Newman's more literal English translation of *O Virga Mediatrix,* but with my translation of *clausi pudoris tui orto;* see Newman, *Symphonia,* Song 18, pp. 124–125.

41. Ibid., Song 10, pp. 114–115.

42. Newman, *Sister of Wisdom,* pp. 198–204.

43. Hildegard *Scivias* 3.3 (Hart and Bishop, pp. 343–354).

44. Ibid., 1.5 (Hart and Bishop, pp. 133–136); Newman, *Sister of Wisdom,* pp. 205–211.

45. Hildegard *Scivias* 1.3 (Hart and Bishop, pp. 93–105); Newman, *Sister of Wisdom,* pp. 211–218.

46. See the image in Hildegard *Scivias* (Hart and Bishop, p. 167).

47. Image in ibid. (Hart and Bishop, p. 235); Newman, *Sister of Wisdom,* pp. 188–195.

48. Image in Hildegard *Scivias* (Hart and Bishop, p. 491).

49. Hildegard *Book of Divine Works* 10.20 (p. 244); Newman, *Sister of Wisdom,* pp. 238–244.

50. Hildegard, Letter 23, in van Acker, *Corpus Christianorum,* pp. 65–66.

51. Hildegard *Scivias* 3.11 (Hart and Bishop, pp. 493–514); Hildegard *Book of Divine Works* 10.28–32 (pp. 252–258).

52. Hildegard *Book of Divine Works* 4.78 (p. 113).

53. Hildegard defended her practice of clothing her nuns in white robes and golden crowns as an anticipation of the music of paradise restored in the virginal community in song; see Letter 52R, in Baird and Ehrman, *Letters,* vol. 1, pp. 128–130.

54. Bernard of Clairvaux, *On the Song of Songs,* trans. Kilian Walsh (Spencer, Mass.: Cistercian Publications, 1971), vol. 1, Sermon 3.1, p. 16.

55. Ibid., Sermon 8.9 (Walsh, p. 52).

56. Bernard of Clairvaux, *On the Song of Songs,* trans. Irene Edmonds (Kalamazoo, Mich.: Cistercian Publications, 1980), vol. 4, Sermon 82.2, p. 172.

57. Ibid., Sermon 69.7 (Edmonds, p. 34).

58. Bernard, *On the Song of Songs,* vol. 1, Sermon 8.6 (Walsh, p. 49).

59. Bernard of Clairvaux, *Life and Works of Saint Bernard: Eighty-Six Sermons on the Song of Solomon,* trans. Samuel J. Eales (London: John Hodges, 1896), Sermon 57.10, p. 345.

60. Bernard, *On the Song of Songs,* vol. 1, Sermon 3.1 (Walsh, p. 20).

61. See Caroline W. Bynum, *Jesus as Mother: Studies in the Spirituality of the High Middle Ages* (Berkeley: University of California Press, 1982), p. 31.

62. Bernard, *On the Song of Songs*, vol. 1, Sermon 12.1 (Walsh, p. 77), Sermon 18 (Walsh, pp. 133–139).

63. Ibid., Sermon 9.7 (Walsh, pp. 58, 59).

64. Bernard, *Eighty-Six Sermons*, Sermon 38.4 (Eales, p. 245).

65. Bernard, *On the Song of Songs*, vol. 1, Sermon 12.9 (Walsh, p. 84).

66. Ibid. (Walsh, p. 85).

67. Ibid., Sermon 3.4 (Walsh, p. 23).

68. Ann W. Asell's *The Song of Songs in the Middle Ages* (Ithaca, N.Y.: Cornell University Press, 1990), while well done and insightful, goes too far, in my view, toward an identification of medieval views of the soul with Jungian theories of the *anima*.

69. Barbara Newman, *From Virile Woman to WomanChrist: Studies in Medieval Religion and Literature* (Philadelphia: University of Pennsylvania Press, 1998), pp. 137–167.

70. Newman notes that the literature of courtly love, such as Gottfried's *Tristan*, adopted language from Cistercian bridal mysticism. She also discusses Richard of St. Victor's treatise *The Four Degrees of Violent Charity* (c. 1170) in terms of the psychological relation of sexual and spiritual love; ibid., pp. 159–160, 164–165.

71. See Hadewijch, Letters 29 and 30, Poems in Stanzas 29, in *Hadewijch: The Complete Works*, ed. Mother Columba Hart (New York: Paulist Press, 1980), pp. 114, 119, 207–212. When Hadewijch does see herself as mother in relation to her young Beguines (Letter 29), she does not connect this with impregnation by Christ.

72. On Mary Magdalene in the thought of the three Beguine mystics, see Mechthild of Magdeburg, *The Flowing Light of the Godhead*, trans. Frank Tobin (New York: Paulist Press, 1998), 5.23, 6.9 (pp. 203, 235–236); Hadewijch, Poem 3 in Couplets, in *Hadewijch: The Complete Works*, p. 323; Marguerite Porete, *The Mirror of Simple Souls*, ed. Ellen L. Babinsky (New York: Paulist Press, 1993), chaps. 76, 93, 124 (pp. 150, 168, 202–206).

73. Mechthild, *Flowing Light*, 1.22 (p. 50). The word "jubilus" meant rapture or ecstasy; see p. 341n33, in Tobin's translation.

74. Ibid., 3.9 (p. 114).

75. Ibid., 1.22 (pp. 50, 51).

76. Ibid., 2.22 (p. 87), 1.44 (p. 62).

77. Ibid., 1.2 (p. 30), 1.4 (p. 44), 3.2 (p. 108).

78. Ibid., 4.11 (p. 155), 3.10 (pp. 118–119).

79. Hadewijch's identity and the exact dates of her birth and death are disputed. Mother Columba Hart concludes only that "she probably lived in the middle of the thirteenth century" (introduction to *Hadewijch: The Complete Works*, p. 3).

80. Ibid., Poems in Stanzas 8 (pp. 147–148), 6 (p. 141), 39 (pp. 240–241), 10 (p. 153).

81. Ibid., Poems in Stanzas 7 (p. 145), 15 (p. 165), 28 (p. 206), 11 (p. 155), 14 (p. 164), 28 (p. 207).

82. Ibid., Poems in Stanzas 4 (pp. 138–139).

83. Ibid., Vision 10 (p. 288).

84. Ibid., Vision 12 (p. 296).

85. Ibid., Vision 13 (p. 298).

86. Newman, *From Virile Woman to WomanChrist*, p. 156.

87. Hadewijch, Letter 10, in *Hadewijch: The Complete Works*, pp. 118–119.

88. See Robert E. Lerner, *The Heresy of the Free Spirit in the Later Middle Ages* (Berkeley: University of California Press, 1972).

89. Marguerite names these scholars as Brother John, a Franciscan; Dom Franco, a Cistercian of the abbey of St. Villiers; and Godfrey of Fontaines, a Master of Theology (Porete, *Mirror of Simple Souls*, chap. 41 [pp. 221–222]).

90. The text was identified as the work of Marguerite Porete by Romana Guarnieri ("Il movimento del Libero Spirita," *Archivo Italiano per la storia della pietà* 4 [1965]: 351–708), and a critical edition was published by Romana Guarnieri and Paul Verdeyen in *Corpus Christianorum: Continuatio Mediaevalis*, vol. 69 (Turnholti, Belgium: Brepols, 1986). See Porete, *Mirror of Simple Souls*, introduction by Ellen L. Babinsky, p. 43; and Elizabeth A. Petroff, *Medieval Women's Visionary Literature* (Oxford: Oxford University Press, 1986), pp. 281, 283n13.

91. Porete, *Mirror of Simple Souls*, chap. 118 (pp. 189–194).

92. Ibid., chap. 60 (pp. 137–138).

93. On the inferiority and "one-eyedness" of Reason, see, for example, ibid., chaps. 9 (p. 87), 13 (pp. 94–96), 36 (p. 117), 53 (pp. 130–131), 116–117 (pp. 186–188).

94. Ibid., chap. 6 (p. 84); see also chaps. 8 (pp. 85–86), 13 (p. 94).

95. Ibid., chaps. 19 (pp. 101–102), 41 (p. 121), 43 (pp. 122–123), 49 (p. 127), 121 (p. 196).

96. Ibid., chaps. 123 (p. 202), 133 (pp. 216–217).

97. For the patristic exploration of this idea that apart from God our reality is the Nihil of pre-creation, into which we fall in sin, see, for example, Athanasius, *On the Incarnation of the Word* (New York: Macmillan, 1946).

98. Porete, *Mirror of Simple Souls*, chap. 34 (p. 115).

99. Ibid., chaps. 58 (p. 135), 80 (p. 155), 134–135 (pp. 217–218).

100. Ibid., chap. 1 (p. 80).

101. Julian of Norwich, *Showings*, ed. Edmund Colledge and James Walsh (New York: Paulist Press, 1978), chaps. 1–2 (pp. 125–129). For the Middle English version of the short and long texts, see *The Book of Showings to the Anchoress Julian of Norwich*, ed. Edmund Colledge and James Walsh (Toronto: Pontifical Institute of Mediaeval Studies, 1978), pts. 1 and 2.

102. See Grace M. Jantzen, *Julian of Norwich: Mystic and Theologian* (London: SPCK Press, 1987), pp. 21–25.

103. This view on the nature of evil is developed particularly in Julian's Parable of the Servant (Julian, *Showings,* chap. 51 [pp. 267–278]). For a discussion, see Jantzen, *Julian of Norwich,* pp. 190–196.

104. See chapter 39 of *Showings,* where Julian speaks of sinful souls being healed by the medicines of contrition, compassion, and longing for God, so that the wounds of sin are seen by God as honors. In chapter 56 of the long text, she says that the pains of sin are themselves redemptive: "When our sensuality by the power of Christ's passion can be brought up into the substance, with all the profits of our tribulation which our Lord can make us obtain through mercy and grace" (Julian, *Showings,* p. 289).

105. See ibid., chap. 27 (pp. 224–226), long text. For an insightful discussion of the resistance by Julian and other women mystics to the doctrine of eternal damnation of souls who die unrepentant, see Barbara Newman, "On the Threshold of Death: Purgatory, Hell, and Religious Women," in *From Virile Woman to WomanChrist,* pp. 108–136.

106. Julian, *Revelations of Divine Love,* chap. 58 (p. 159), long text: trans. James Walsh (New York: Harper and Row, 1961).

107. Ibid., chaps. 58–59 (pp. 159–161).

CHAPTER 7: TONANTZIN-GUADALUPE

1. David Carrasco, *Daily Life of the Aztecs: People of the Sun and Earth* (Westport, Conn.: Greenwood Press, 1998), p. 226; see also Tzvetan Todorov, *The Conquest of Mexico: The Question of the Other,* trans. Richard Howard (New York: Harper and Row, 1984).

2. For a study of the work of Andres de Olmos and Bernadino de Sahagún, see particularly Munro S. Edmonson, ed., *Sixteenth Century Mexico: The Work of Sahagún* (Albuquerque: University of New Mexico Press, 1974).

3. On the question of sources for Mesoamerican history, see David Carrasco, *Quetzalcóatl and the Irony of Empire: Myths and Prophecies in the Aztec Tradition* (Chicago: University of Chicago Press, 1992). For information about the work of Miguel Léon-Portilla in the development of Nahua studies, see J. Jorge Klor de Alva, "Nahua Studies, the Allure of the 'Aztecs,' and Miguel Léon-Portilla," in Miguel Léon-Portilla, *The Aztec Image of Self and Society: An Introduction to Nahua Culture* (Salt Lake City: University of Utah Press, 1992), pp. vii–xxiii.

4. Roberta H. Markman and Peter T. Markman attempt a discussion of the female figurines of preclassical village culture, but their views are heavily dependent on theories posited by Joseph Campbell and Marija Gimbutas rather than on detailed archaeological work in the region; see *The Flayed God: The Mythology of Mesoamerica; Sacred Texts and Images from Pre-Columbian Mexico and Central America* (San Francisco: HarperSanFrancisco, 1992), pp. 29–55.

5. Miguel Léon-Portilla, *Aztec Thought and Culture: A Study in the Ancient Nahuatl Mind,* trans. Jack Emory Davis (Norman: University of Oklahoma Press, 1963), p. 90.

6. Markman and Markman, *The Flayed God*, p. 66.

7. Ibid.; also see p. 127, a translation of a text probably from Francisco Andrés de Olmos, *Historia de los Mexicanos por sus pinturas*, on "the Creation of the World."

8. Ibid., p. 127. On the personality of Tezcatlipoca, see Inga Clendinnen, *Aztecs: An Interpretation* (Cambridge: Cambridge University Press, 1991), pp. 79, 83.

9. From Bernadino de Sahagún, *Florentine Codex: General History of the Things of New Spain*, ed. and trans. Arthur J. O. Anderson and Charles E. Dibble (Santa Fe, N. Mex.: School of American Research; Salt Lake City: University of Utah, 1950–1978), bk. 6, 210; Carrasco, *Daily Life of the Aztecs*, p. 41.

10. See Rosemary A. Joyce, *Gender and Power in Prehispanic Mesoamerica* (Austin: University of Texas Press, 2000), pp. 133–175. Also see Elizabeth M. Brumfield, "Weaving and Cooking: Women's Production in Aztec Mexico," in *Engendering Archaeology: Women and Prehistory*, ed. Joan Gero and Margaret Conkey (Cambridge, Mass.: Blackwell, 1991), pp. 224–251.

11. Rosemary Joyce argues that the Aztecs saw the newborn baby as gender-neutral, to be gender differentiated by transformative rituals that assigned dress, hair styles, and work roles (*Gender and Power*, pp. 145–149, 177).

12. See Alfredo Lopez-Austin, "La parte femenina del cosmos: Los opuestos complementarios," *La mujer en el mundo prehispanico: Arqueología Mexicana* 5, no. 29 (January–February 1998): 6–13.

13. Sahagún, *Florentine Codex*, bk. 1, 8.

14. Ibid.; see also Markman and Markman, *The Flayed God*, pp. 188–189.

15. Sahagún, *Florentine Codex*, bk. 2, 102.

16. Carrasco, *Daily Life of the Aztecs*, pp. 115–116.

17. Sahagún, *Florentine Codex*, bk. 1, 11.

18. Léon-Portilla, *Aztec Image*, pp. 187–188.

19. See Cecilia F. Klein, "Teocuitlatl, 'Divine Excrement': The Significance of 'Holy Shit' in Ancient Mexico," *Art Journal* 52, no. 3 (1993): 20–27.

20. Sahagún, *Florentine Codex*, bk. 1, 12 (pp. 10, 11).

21. Joyce, *Gender and Power*, p. 173; Susan D. Gillespie, *The Aztec Kings: The Construction of Rulership in Mexican History* (Tucson: University of Arizona Press, 1989), pp. 62–63, 224–225.

22. Carrasco, *Daily Life of the Aztecs*, pp. 53–54. See also Alfredo Lopez-Austin, *Cuerpo humano e ideología: Las concepciones de los antiquos Nahuas* (Mexico: Universidad Nacional Autonoma de Mexico, 1980), vol. 1, pp. 223–262.

23. Sahagún, *Florentine Codex*, bk. 6, 93.

24. From the *Leyenda de los soles*, translated in Markman and Markman, *The Flayed God*, pp. 132–133.

25. From Sahagún, *Florentine Codex*, bk. 7 (pp. 3–9); quoted in Markman and Markman, *The Flayed God*, pp. 121–125.

26. Markman and Markman, *The Flayed God*, p. 77.

27. This story is contained in the sixteenth-century work *Histoyre de Mechique*, by French cartographer André Thevet; a translation by F. M. Swenson appears in Markman and Markman, *The Flayed God*, p. 213.

28. From the *Leyenda de los Soles*, translated in Markman and Markman, *The Flayed God*, pp. 134–135.

29. Ibid., pp. 135–136.

30. Clendinnen, *Aztecs*, pp. 95, 135, 209.

31. One version of the hero's story of Quetzalcóatl appears in Sahagún's *Florentine Codex*, bk. 3, on the origins of the gods. Another version comes from the *Annales de Cuauhtitlán*, written in Nahuatl about 1570. Both versions are translated in Markman and Markman, *The Flayed God*, pp. 353–377.

32. The major study of this understanding of Quetzalcóatl and the ideal city is Carrasco, *Quetzalcóatl and the Irony of Empire*.

33. Ibid.

34. The story of the birth of Huitzilopochtli and the killing of Coyolxauhqui has been translated from Nahuatl by Miguel León-Portilla and is reprinted in Miguel León-Portilla, ed., *Native Mesoamerican Spirituality* (New York: Paulist Press, 1980), pp. 220–225. It also appears in Markman and Markman, *The Flayed God*, pp. 381–386.

35. See Eduardo Matos Moctezuma, *The Aztecs* (New York: Rizzoli, 1989), color plate 3, pp. 36–37, for the picture of the Coyolxauhqui stone in situ at the base of the stairs of the Temple Major in Mexico City.

36. This story comes from the *Cronica Mexicayolt*, written in 1609 by Hernando Alvarado Tezozomoc, the grandson of the Aztec king Motecuhzoma and great-grandson of Azayacatl; translated by Thelma D. Sullivan, it appears in Markman and Markman, *The Flayed God*, pp. 395–396.

37. See Cecelia F. Klein, "Rethinking Cihuacóatl: Aztec Political Imagery of the Conquered Woman," in *Smoke and Mist: Mesoamerican Studies in Memory of Thelma D. Sullivan*, ed. J. Kathryn Josserand and Karen Dakin (Oxford: BAR International Series, 1988), pp. 237–277.

38. Mari Carmen Serra Puche and Karina R. Durand V., "Las mujeres de Xochitecatl," *Arqueología Mexicana* 5, no. 29 (January–February 1998): 20–27.

39. Markman and Markman, *The Flayed God*, p. 369.

40. James Lockhart, *The Nahuas After the Conquest: A Social and Cultural History of the Indians of Central Mexico, Sixteenth Through Eighteenth Centuries* (Stanford, Calif.: Stanford University Press, 1992), p. 205.

41. Ibid., pp. 1–58.

42. See J. Jorge Klor de Alva, "Aztec Spirituality and Nahuatized Christianity," in *South and Mesoamerican Native Spirituality: From the Cult of the Feathered Serpent to the Theology of Liberation*, ed. Gary H. Gossen (New York: Crossroads, 1993), pp. 179–180.

43. Ibid., pp. 203–260.

44. Gonzalo de Sandovar and his army camped on this hill by order of Cortés, according to the account of the siege found in Bernal Díaz del Castillo, *La verdadera historia de la conquista de la Nueva España;* see Stafford Poole, *Our Lady of Guadalupe: The Origins and Sources of a Mexican National Symbol, 1531–1797* (Tucson: University of Arizona Press, 1995), pp. 65, 253n72.

45. See Jacques LaFaye, *Quetzalcóatl and Guadalupe: The Formation of Mexican National Consciousness, 1531–1813* (Chicago: University of Chicago Press, 1976), pp. 217–224; D. A. Brading, *The Mexican Phoenix: Our Lady of Guadalupe: Image and Tradition Across Five Centuries* (Cambridge: Cambridge University Press, 2001), pp. 36–37.

46. Brading, *Mexican Phoenix*, pp. 74–75.

47. LaFaye, *Quetzalcóatl and Guadalupe*, pp. 238–242; Brading, *Mexican Phoenix*, pp. 268–271. For the text of Montúfar's investigation, see Ernesto de la Torre Villar and Ramiro Navarro de Anda, eds., *Testimonios historicos guadalupanos* (Mexico: Fondo de Cultura Económica, 1982), pp. 36–141. See also Poole, *Our Lady of Guadalupe*, pp. 58–60.

48. LaFaye, *Quetzalcóatl and Guadalupe*, pp. 239, 326nn14, 15, from Montúfar's *Investigación*.

49. Sahagún, *Florentine Codex*, bk. 3, 352; quoted in Brading, *Mexican Phoenix*, pp. 214–215; and Poole, *Our Lady of Guadalupe*, pp. 78–79.

50. See Louise M. Burkhart, "The Cult of the Virgin of Guadalupe," in Gossen, *South and Mesoamerican Native Spirituality*, pp. 198–227.

51. Brading quotes a letter from Viceroy Martin Enriquez on September 21, 1575, to Philip II on the church at Tepeyac (*Mexican Phoenix*, p. 214).

52. Lockhart, *Nahuas After the Conquest*, p. 246.

53. Poole, *Our Lady of Guadalupe*, pp. 51–52, 63, 70, 215–216.

54. Brading, *Mexican Phoenix*, pp. 52–53, 54–55; also Poole, *Our Lady of Guadalupe*, p. 67.

55. Miguel Sánchez, *Imagen de la Virgen Maria, Madre de Dios de Guadalupe. Milagrosamente aparecida en la Ciudad de Mexico. Celebrada en su historia, con la profecia del capitula doce des Apocalipsis* (Mexico City: Imprenta de la Viuda de Bernardo Calderon, 1648); translated in part in Donald Demarest and Coley Taylor, *The Dark Virgin: The Book of Our Lady of Guadalupe* (New York: Coley Taylor, 1956), pp. 63–96.

56. A new annotated translation of the entire de la Vega text is available in Lisa Sousa, Stafford Poole, and James Lockhart, *The Story of Guadalupe: Luis Laso de la Vega's Huei tlamahuicoltica of 1649* (Stanford, Calif.: Stanford University Press, 1998), pp. 48–125.

57. Poole, *Our Lady of Guadalupe*, pp. 102–103, 222–223.

58. See Carrasco, *Daily Life of the Aztecs*, pp. 14, 17.

59. On these earlier Nahuatl accounts, see Burkhart, "Cult of the Virgin of Guadalupe," p. 215.

60. On the identification of the author of de la Vega's account with Valeriano, see Poole, *Our Lady of Guadalupe*, pp. 83–84, 166–169.

61. Sousa, Poole, and Lockhart, *Story of Guadalupe*, pp. 1–47.

62. Luis Laso de la Vega, "Carta al autor," in Sánchez, *Imagen de la Virgen Maria*, p. 38; see Lafaye, *Quetzalcóatl and Guadalupe*, pp. 246, 327n33.

63. LaFaye, *Quetzalcóatl and Guadalupe*, pp. 246–247.

64. Poole, *Our Lady of Guadalupe*, p. 71. It is not clear whether such alms were ever sent back to the shrine at Extremadura and, if they were, when this practice ceased.

65. For an account of the testimonies and a critique of their credibility, see ibid., pp. 127–143.

66. See Brading, *Mexican Phoenix*, pp. 76–95. For an English translation of the Tanco text, see Demarest and Taylor, *Dark Virgin*, pp. 99–112.

67. Brading, *Mexican Phoenix*, pp. 96–97.

68. Ibid., pp. 108–110.

69. On sixteenth-century Spain's view of itself as an elect people, see ibid., pp. 33–36.

70. Ibid., p. 75. On Creole patriotism in sermons of the late seventeenth and eighteenth centuries, see Poole, *Our Lady of Guadalupe*, pp. 151–155, 179–187.

71. Brading, *Mexican Phoenix*, pp. 201–212. See also Poole, *Our Lady of Guadalupe*, pp. 207–212. For an account of the tradition that St. Thomas preached in Mexico in apostolic times and is remembered in the figure of Quetzalcóatl, see Jacques LaFaye, "St. Thomas-Quetzalcóatl, Apostle of Mexico," in *Quetzalcóatl and Guadalupe*, pp. 177–208.

72. Brading, *Mexican Phoenix*, pp. 258–287.

73. See particularly Brading's discussion of the "coronation" and the politics of ultramontanism in late nineteenth-century Mexico (ibid., pp. 288–310).

74. On the rightist politics of Marian public devotion in Europe, see Nicholas Perry and Loreto Echeverria, *Under the Heel of Mary* (London: Routledge, 1988), esp. pp. 119–122 on Lourdes.

75. Brading, *Mexican Phoenix*, pp. 311–322.

76. Ibid., pp. 331–341.

77. See John Allen, "He May Not Be Real, But He Is Almost a Saint," *National Catholic Reporter*, January 23, 2002, p. 3.

78. See Gabriela Videla, *Sergio Mendez Arceo: Un Señor Obispo* (Cuernavaca: Correo del Sur, 1982); and Gary MacEoin, *The People's Church: Bishop Samuel Ruíz and Why He Matters* (New York: Crossroads, 1996).

79. Pablo Richard, *The Idols of Death and the God of Life: A Theology* (Maryknoll, N.Y.: Orbis Press, 1983).

80. Elza Tamez, "Quetzalcóatl y el Dios Cristiano," in *Cuadernos de teología y cultura*, no. 6 (San José, Costa Rica, 1992), translated as "Reliving Our Histories: Racial and Cultural Revelations of God," in *New Visions for the Americas: Religious Engage-*

ment and Social Transformation, ed. David Batstone (Minneapolis: Fortress Press, 1993), pp. 33–56.

81. Ivone Gebara and Maria Clara Bingemer, *Mary, Mother of God, Mother of the Poor* (Maryknoll, N.Y.: Orbis Press, 1989).

82. Ibid., pp. 144–154.

83. Ana Castillo, ed., *Goddess of the Americas: Writings on the Virgin of Guadalupe* (New York: Riverhead Books, 1996).

84. Clarissa Pinkola Estés, *Women Who Run with the Wolves: Myths and Stories of the Wild Woman Archetype* (New York: Ballantine, 1992).

85. Clarissa Pinkola Estés, "La ruta de corizon roto," in *La Diosa de las Américas: Escritos sobre la Virgen de Guadalupe* (New York: Vintage Español, 2000), p. 87; my translation from the Spanish.

86. Octavio Paz, foreword to Lafaye, *Quetzalcóatl and Guadalupe*, p. xi.

CHAPTER 8: MARY AND WISDOM
IN PROTESTANT MYSTICAL MILLENNIALISM

1. Paul Tillich, *Systematic Theology* (Chicago: University of Chicago Press, 1951), vol. 1, p. 128.

2. Martin Luther, *Table Talk*, vol. 54 of *Luther's Works*, ed. Theodore G. Tappert (Philadelphia: Fortress Press, 1967), p. 15.

3. Martin Luther, *Sermons on the Gospel of St. John, 14–16*, vol. 24 of *Luther's Works*, ed. Jaroslav Pelikan (Philadelphia: Fortress Press, 1995), p. 320.

4. Thomas A. O'Meara, *Mary in Protestant and Catholic Theology* (New York: Sheed and Ward, 1966), pp. 109–137.

5. Martin Luther, *The Catholic Epistles*, vol. 30 of *Luther's Works*, ed. Jaroslav Pelikan (Philadelphia: Fortress Press, 1995), p. 351; Martin Luther, *Sermons 2*, vol. 52 of *Luther's Works*, ed. Hans J. Hillerbrand (Philadelphia: Fortress Press, 1974), p. 682; O'Meara, *Mary*, p. 118.

6. O'Meara, *Mary*, p. 119.

7. See Jaroslav Pelikan, *Mary Through the Centuries: Her Place in the History of Culture* (New Haven, Conn.: Yale University Press, 1996), p. 152.

8. Ibid., p. 159.

9. Martin Luther, *Ecclesiastes, Song of Solomon, Last Words of David, 2 Samuel 23:1–7*, vol. 15 of *Luther's Works*, ed. Jaroslav Pelikan and Hilton C. Oswald (Philadelphia: Fortress Press, 1995), p. 193.

10. Ibid., p. 130.

11. The classic of Lutheran pietism is the work by Johann Arndt, *True Christianity* (New York: Paulist Press, 1979).

12. Peter Erb, ed., *Jacob Boehme: The Way to Christ* (New York: Paulist Press, 1978), introduction, pp. 4–5.

13. See Rufus M. Jones, *Spiritual Reformers in the Sixteenth and Seventeenth Centuries* (London: Macmillan, 1914).

14. Boehme *On Holy Prayer* 55 (Erb, pp. 111–112).

15 Boehme *On True Resignation* 1.5 (Erb, p. 115).

16. Boehme *On the New Birth That Is* 2.10, 2.11 (Erb, pp. 144–145).

17. Ibid., 2.18 (Erb, p. 147).

18. Ibid., 2.23 (Erb, p. 148).

19. Ibid.

20. Boehme *Conversation Between an Enlightened and an Unenlightened Soul* 23 (Erb, p. 230).

21. Ibid., 24 (Erb, pp. 230–231).

22. Ibid., 27 (Erb, pp. 231–242).

23. Boehme *On True Repentance* 29 (Erb, p. 40).

24. Ibid., 47 (Erb, p. 58).

25. Ibid.

26. Boehme *The New Birth That Is* 3.6, 3.7 (Erb, p. 150).

27. Ibid.

28. Ibid., 5.3, 6.12, 6.13 (Erb, pp. 156, 162).

29. Boehme *The Supersensual Life* 46 (Erb, p. 187).

30. Preface, "The Wars of Solomon and the Peaceable Reign of Solomon" (London, 1700); reproduced in Nils Thune, *The Behemists and the Philadelphians: A Contribution to the Study of English Mysticism in the Seventeenth and Eighteenth Centuries* (Uppsala: Almquist and Winsells Boktryckeri, 1948), pp. 68–69.

31. See Thomas Schipflinger, *Sophia-Maria: A Holistic View of Creation* (York Beach, Maine: Samuel Weiser, 1998), pp. 221–222.

32. See especially Jane Leade, "Message to the Philadelphian Church," in *A Fountain of Gardens Watered by the Rivers of Divine Pleasure and Springing Up in All the Variety of Spiritual Plants* . . . (London: 1697–1701), p. 270. These visions are dated from January to December 1678. (Many of Jane Leade's original manuscripts are now available online at www.passtheword.org/Jane-Lead.)

33. Leade, *Fountain of Gardens*, pp. 311–312.

34. See Catherine F. Smith, "Jane Leade: The Feminist Mind and Art of a Seventeenth Century Protestant Mystic," in *Women of Spirit: Female Leadership in the Jewish and Christian Traditions*, ed. Rosemary R. Ruether and Eleanor McLaughlin (New York: Simon and Schuster, 1979), p. 194.

35. Leade, *Fountain of Gardens*, p. 325.

36. Ibid., pp. 326–336.

37. Jane Leade, *Revelation of Revelations, Particularly as an Essay Toward an Unsealing, Opening, and Discovering the Seven Seals, the Seven Thunders, and the New Jerusalem State* (London: A. Sowle, 1683), pp. 38–44.

38. See Signe Toksvig, *Emanuel Swedenborg: Scientist and Mystic* (New Haven, Conn.: Yale University Press, 1948), pp. 14–29. Toksvig sees Bishop Swedberg as a very negative figure, who caused his son to rebel against him. For an alternative view, see Ernst Benz, *Emmanuel Swedenborg: Visionary Savant in the Age of Reason* (West Chester, Pa.: Swedenborg Foundation, 2002), pp. 3–19.

39. Toksvig, *Emanuel Swedenborg*, pp. 30–70.

40. Emanuel Swedenborg, *Angelic Wisdom Concerning the Divine Love and Wisdom*, trans. Clifford Harley and Doris H. Harley (London: Swedenborg Society, 1969), secs. 29, 31. Swedenborg wrote in Latin. There are dozens of English translations, a situation that allows different interpretations of his ideas.

41. Ibid., secs. 32, 14.

42. Emanuel Swedenborg, *Conjugial Love* (New York: American Swedenborg Publishing Society, 1871), sec. 83.

43. See Dorothea Harvey, "Swedenborg and Women's Spirituality," in *Rooted in Spirit: A Harvest of Women's Wisdom*, ed. Alice B. Skinner (West Chester, Pa.: Chrysalis Books, 1999), pp. 6–11.

44. Swedenborg, *Conjugial Love*, sec. 32.

45. Ibid., secs. 32–33.

46. Ibid., sec. 33.

47. Toksvig, *Swedenborg*, pp. 314–324.

48. Mary Ann Meyers, *A New World Jerusalem: The Swedenborgian Experience in Community Construction* (Westwood, Conn.: Greenwood Press, 1983). See also Marguerite Beck Block, *The New Church in the New World: A Study of Swedenborgianism in America* (New York: Holt, Rinehart and Winston, 1932).

49. Myers, *New World Jerusalem*, pp. 144–147.

50. See Carl Ernst Yenetchi, "The Role of Gender in Marriage: A Swedenborgian View," *Studia Swedenborgiana* 10, no. 1 (October 1996): 63–73.

51. See John K. Billings, "The Spiritual Origins of Sexuality and Genders: The Difference That Makes the Difference," *Studia Swedenborgiana* 10, no. 1 (October 1996): 45–62.

52. James Lawrence, the Swedenborgian House of Studies of the Pacific School of Religion, personal communication to the author, April 8, 2003. See also Lawrence's article "Risking on the Side of Compassion," *The Messenger*, November 1996, pp. 139–142.

53. For a good sketch of the history of the Harmony Society, see Carl J. R. Arndt, "George Rapp's Harmony Society," in *America's Communal Utopias*, ed. Donald E. Pitzer (Chapel Hill: University of North Carolina Press, 1997), pp. 57–87.

54. See Hilda Adam Kring, *The Harmonists: A Folk-Cultural Approach* (Metuchen, N.J.: Scarecrow Press, 1973), p. 13; citing Aaron Williams, *The Harmony Society* (Pittsburgh: W. S. Haven, 1866), p. 99.

55. Kring, *The Harmonists*, pp. 113–120.

56. *Testimonies of the Life, Character, Revelations, and Doctrines of Mother Ann Lee,* 2nd ed. (Albany, N.Y.: Weed, Parson, 1888), pp. 2–6.

57. Ibid., pp. 6–7.

58. *Testimony of Christ's Second Appearing* (the Shaker Bible), 4th ed. (Albany, N.Y.: Van Benthuysen, 1856), secs. 5, 7 (p. 504).

59. Ibid., sec. 17 (p. 506).

60. Ibid., sec. 22 (p. 507).

61. Ibid., sec. 29 (p. 508).

62. Ibid., secs. 30, 32, 33 (pp. 508, 509).

63. Ibid., secs. 35, 37, 38 (pp. 517–518).

64. Anna White and Leila S. Taylor, *Shakerism: Its Meaning and Message* (Columbus, Ohio: Fredereick J. Heer Press, 1904), p. 256.

CHAPTER 9: CONTESTED GENDER STATUS
AND IMAGINING ANCIENT MATRIARCHY

1. For an overview, see Rosemary R. Ruether, *Christianity and the Making of the Modern Family: Ruling Ideologies, Diverse Realities* (Boston: Beacon Press, 2000), pp. 83–106.

2. For Kant's and Hegel's views of women, see Ellen Kennedy and Susan Mendus, *Women in Western Political Philosophy: Kant to Nietzsche* (New York: St. Martin's Press, 1987), pp. 21–43, 127–258.

3. Mary Wollstonecraft, *A Vindication of the Rights of Women* (1792; London: Dent, 1929).

4. Edward H. Clarke, *Sex in Education; or, A Fair Chance for the Girls* (1873; New York: Arno Press, 1972).

5. See, for example, G. J. Barker-Benfield, *Horrors of the Half-Known Life: Male Attitudes Toward Women and Sexuality in Nineteenth-Century America* (New York: Norton, 1976); and Cynthia E. Russell, *Sexual Science: The Victorian Construction of Womanhood* (Cambridge, Mass.: Harvard University Press, 1986).

6. Katherine Rogers vividly represents the attacks found in nineteenth-century British musicals and journalism; see "The Drooping Lily: The Nineteenth Century," in Katherine Rogers, *The Troublesome Helpmate: A History of Misogyny in Literature* (Seattle: University of Washington Press, 1966), pp. 189–225.

7. August Comte, *A General View of Positivism,* trans. J. H. Bridges (London: Trubner, 1865), p. 245; originally published in French in 1848.

8. Ibid., p. 253.

9. Ibid., p. 288.

10. Horace Bushnell, *Women's Suffrage: The Reform Against Nature* (New York: Scribner, 1869).

11. Ibid., p. 31.

12. Ibid., pp. 65–66.

13. Arthur Schopenhauer, "On Women," in *Essays: The Works of Schopenhauer,* ed. Will Durant (New York: Simon and Schuster, 1928), p. 449.

14. See Joseph Campbell, introduction to Johann Jakob Bachofen, *Myth, Religion, and Mother Right: Selected Writings of J. J. Bachofen,* trans. Ralph Manheim (Princeton, N.J.: Princeton University Press, 1967), pp. xxxiv.

15. Bachofen, *Myth, Religion, and Mother Right,* pp. 100–101.

16. Ibid., p. 89.

17. Ibid., p. 115.

18. Ibid., p. 118.

19. Bachofen, "Myth of Tanaquil," in ibid., pp. 237–238.

20. John Ferguson McLennan, *Patriarchal Theory* (London: Macmillan, 1885).

21. Edward B. Tylor, "The Matriarchal Family System," *The Nineteenth Century* 40 (July–December 1896): 81–96.

22. *Encyclopaedia Britannica,* 11th ed. (1910–1911), s.v. "The Matriarchate," vol. 17, p. 889.

23. Arthur Evans, *The Palace of Minos at Knossos* (London: Macmillan, 1921–1936), vol. 3, pp. 58, 227.

24. Gilbert Murray, *Five Stages of Greek Religion* (New York: Columbia University Press, 1925), pp. 15–55. Murray calls the first stage "Saturnia Regna."

25. Claiming that the ancient goddesses "reflect another condition of things, a relationship traced through the mother, a state of society known by the awkward term matriarchal," Harrison added a footnote referring to Tylor's article in the July–December 1896 issue of *The Nineteenth Century,* describing the article as the "clearest and most sensible statement of the facts as to this difficult subject known to me" (*Prolegomena to the Study of Greek Religion* [1903; New York: Meridian Books, 1955], p. 261, 261n2).

26. Ibid., p. 273.

27. Ibid., p. 285.

28. Jane Harrison, *Epilegomena to the Study of Greek Religion* (1921; New York: University Books, 1962), pp. xvii–lvi. This volume was printed along with her book *Themis: A Study of the Social Origins of Greek Religion.*

29. Lewis H. Morgan, *Ancient Society: Researches in the Lines of Human Progress from Savagery Through Barbarism to Civilization* (New York: Henry Holt, 1877), p. 50.

30. Frederick Engels, *The Origin of the Family, Private Property, and the State,* ed. Eleanor B. Leacock (1884; New York: International Publishers, 1972).

31. Ibid., pp. 120–121.

32. Ibid., pp. 144–146.

33. On Karl Marx's family life and relation to Engels and his female companion, see Yvonne Kapp, *Eleanor Marx,* 2 vols. (New York: Pantheon, 1976).

34. August Bebel, *Women Under Socialism,* 33rd ed., trans. Daniel de Leon (New York: New York Labor News Press, 1904).

35. Ibid., pp. 23, 24.

36. Ibid., p. 30.

37. Ibid., p. 343.

38. Ibid., p. 349.

39. See Rosemary R. Ruether, "Radical Victorians," in *Women and Religion in America*, ed. Rosemary R. Ruether and Rosemary Skinner Keller, vol. 3, *1900–1968* (San Francisco: Harper and Row, 1968), p. 22.

40. See Josephine Conger-Kaneko, "Women and Socialism," *The Progressive Woman* 5, no. 55 (December 11, 1912): 8; and Theresa Malkiel, "Women and Socialism," *The Progressive Woman* 6, no. 68 (February 6, 1913): 6, 15. Excerpts from these articles can be found in Ruether, "Radical Victorians," pp. 22–24.

41. Elizabeth Cady Stanton, *The Woman's Bible*, pts. 1 and 2 (1895, 1898; Seattle: Coalition Task Force on Women and Religion, 1974).

42. Elizabeth Cady Stanton, Susan B. Anthony, and Matilda Joslyn Gage, *History of Woman Suffrage*, 6 vols. (Rochester, N.Y.: National American Woman Suffrage Association, 1881–1922).

43. See Matilda Joslyn Gage, *Woman, Church, and State: A Historical Account of the Status of Woman Through the Christian Ages, with Reminiscences of the Matriarchate* (1893; Watertown, Mass.: Persephone Press, 1980), pp. 94–128, on the persecution of witches.

44. Sally Roesch Wagner, introduction to ibid., p. xxx.

45. See Eleanor Flexner, *Century of Struggle: The Women's Rights Movement in the United States*, rev. ed. (Cambridge, Mass.: Harvard University Press, 1996), pp. 143–148.

46. See Wagner, introduction to Gage, *Woman, Church, and State*, pp. xxxi–xxxix.

47. Gage, *Woman, Church, and State*, p. 8.

48. Ibid., p. 9.

49. Ibid., p. 11.

50. For a Jewish feminist critique of anti-Judaism in this matriarchal tradition, see Annette Duam, "Blaming the Jews for the Death of the Goddess"; and Judith Plaskow, "Blaming the Jews for the Birth of Patriarchy"; both in *Nice Jewish Girls*, ed. Evelyn Torton Beck (Trumansburg, N.Y.: Crossing Press, 1982), pp. 303–309, 298–302.

51. Gage, *Woman, Church, and State*, p. 21.

52. Ibid., p. 22. On the translation of El Shaddai as "many-breasted one," see www.goodnewsinc.net/v4gn/shaddai.html.

53. Gage, *Woman, Church, and State*, p. 243.

54. Ibid., p. 23.

55. Ibid., p. 245.

56. Ibid., p. 246.

57. Stanton, *Woman's Bible*, p. 25.

58. Carrie Chapman Catt, "A Survival of Matriarchy," *Harper's Magazine* 128, April 1914, pp. 738–748. Excerpts can be found in Ruether, "Radical Victorians," pp. 19–22.

59. See Ruether, *Christianity and the Making of the Modern Family*, pp. 118–121.

60. Robert Briffault, *The Mothers: A Study of the Origins of Sentiments and Institutions*, 3 vols. (New York: Macmillan, 1927).

61. Robert Briffault, "The Origin of Love," in ibid., vol. 1, pp. 117–160.

62. See, for example, Briffault, *Mothers*, vol. 3, p. 45.

63. Ibid., pp. 507–521.

64. Engels, *Origin of the Family*, p. 27.

65. Morgan, *Ancient Society*, p. 553.

66. Ibid., p. 554.

67. Harrison, *Prolegomena*, p. 299.

68. Ashley Montagu, ed., *Marriage, Past and Present: A Debate Between Robert Briffault and Bronislaw Malinowski* (Boston: Sargeant, 1956).

69. See, for example, Evelyn Reed, *Problems of Women's Liberation: A Marxist Approach* (New York: Pathfinder Press, 1971), which recapitulates Engels's views for an audience of New Left feminists of the late 1960s.

CHAPTER 10: THE RETURN OF THE GODDESS

1. Elizabeth Gould Davis, *The First Sex* (Baltimore: Penguin, 1971); Merlin Stone, *When God Was a Woman* (London: Harcourt Brace Jovanovich, 1976). Stone's book was originally titled *The Paradise Papers*.

2. Davis, *First Sex*, pp. 34–36, 140–141.

3. Ibid., pp. 202, 203, 241, 286–293.

4. Ibid., p. 339.

5. Stone, *When God Was a Woman*, pp. 103–104, 179.

6. Ibid., pp. 160, 241.

7. See Gerald B. Gardener, *Witchcraft Today* (1954; New York: Citadel Press, 1970). Margaret Murray's major books are *The God of the Witches* (1931; London: Oxford University Press, 1970); and *The Witch-Cult in Western Europe* (1921; Oxford: Oxford University Press, 1971).

8. For a critical history of modern witchcraft, see James W. Baker, "White Witches: Historic Fact and Romantic Fantasy," in *Magical Religion and Modern Witchcraft*, ed. James R. Lewis (Albany, N.Y.: SUNY Press, 1996), pp. 171–192.

9. Z. Budapest, *The Holy Book of Women's Mysteries, Part II* (Los Angeles: Susan B. Anthony Coven Number One, 1980), p. 168.

10. See Starhawk's account of her first meeting with Z. Budapest in Starhawk, *The Spiral Dance: A Rebirth of the Ancient Religion of the Great Goddess*, 2nd rev. ed. (San Francisco: HarperSanFrancisco, 1989), p. 3.

11. See Z. Budapest, *Holy Book of Women's Mysteries, Part I* (Los Angeles: Susan B. Anthony Coven Number One, 1979), pp. 86–87; and Budapest, *Holy Book of Women's Mysteries, Part II*, pp. 129–134.

12. Budapest, *Holy Book of Women's Mysteries, Part II*, p. 212.

13. Ibid., p. 215.

14. Ibid., p. 16.

15. Ibid., pp. 23–25.

16. Ibid., p. 135.

17. Ibid., pp. 75–76, 55.

18. Ibid., pp. 19–20.

19. Starhawk, *Spiral Dance*, pp. 5, 18–19.

20. Ibid., pp. 2–5.

21. Starhawk, *Dreaming the Dark: Magic, Sex, and Politics* (Boston: Beacon Press, 1982); Starhawk, *Truth or Dare: Encounters with Power, Authority, and Mystery* (San Francisco: Harper and Row, 1987).

22. In the early 1980s, Father Matthew Fox moved his program on Creation-Centered Spirituality from Mundelein College in Chicago to Holy Names in Oakland. I had been providing the program's lectures on feminist theology, but I was unable to continue lecturing at Holy Names. Fox asked me to recommend another feminist in the Bay Area, and I recommended Starhawk. At that time, Fox was unfamiliar with Starhawk, but he took my suggestion and invited her to teach. Her work was well received, although in the 1990s Fox would be criticized by the Vatican and conservative Catholics for having invited a "witch" to teach at Holy Names.

23. See Starhawk, *Spiral Dance*, pp. 249, 202–203n. Compare with Budapest, *Holy Book of Women's Mysteries, Part II*, p. 46.

24. Starhawk, *Spiral Dance*, pp. 8–9.

25. Ibid., pp. 16–17, 32, 214. Also see Starhawk, *Truth or Dare*, pp. 18–19.

26. Starhawk, *Truth or Dare*, pp. 317–318.

27. Ibid., p. 65; Starhawk, *Spiral Dance*, p. 36.

28. Starhawk, *Spiral Dance*, p. 10.

29. Starhawk, *Dreaming the Dark*, pp. 1–15; Starhawk, *Truth or Dare*, pp. 8–19.

30. For Starhawk's definition of magic and her comments on using trance to face the "self-hater," see Starhawk, *Truth or Dare*, pp. 24–26, 176–178.

31. Ibid., p. 10.

32. See, for example, the description of the confrontation between the women jailed for blockading the Livermore nuclear weapons lab and the guards at Camp Parks, the nearby facility where they were held, which had been a World War II relocation camp for Japanese Americans, in ibid., pp. 4–5.

33. Starhawk, *Webs of Power: Notes from the Global Uprising* (Gabriola Island, B.C.: New Society Publishers, 2002).

34. Starhawk, *Dreaming the Dark*, pp. 154–182; Starhawk, *Truth or Dare*, p. 256.

35. See Starhawk, *Spiral Dance*, pp. 16–19; Starhawk, *Truth or Dare*, pp. 32–67.

36. See the chapter on resistance and renewal in Starhawk, *Truth or Dare*, pp. 312–340.

37. Carolyn Merchant, *The Death of Nature: Women, Ecology, and the Scientific Revolution* (San Francisco: Harper and Row, 1980).

38. Starhawk, *Dreaming the Dark: Magic, Sex, and Politics,* 15th anniv. ed. (Boston: Beacon Press, 1997), pp. 183–219.

39. Ibid., pp. 208–210.

40. Carol Christ, *Diving Deep and Surfacing: Women Writers on Spiritual Quest* (Boston: Beacon Press, 1980). Christ has not written a systematic account of her life but does refer to it in comments scattered throughout her writings. See her *Laughter of Aphrodite: Reflections on a Journey to the Goddess* (San Francisco: Harper and Row, 1987), pp. 3–8, 106.

41. Carol Christ, *She Who Changes: Re-Imagining the Divine in the World* (New York: Palgrave Macmillan, 2003), p. 143.

42. Carol Christ, personal communication to the author, August 15, 2003.

43. Christ, *She Who Changes,* p. 106.

44. Carol Christ, "Why Women Need the Goddess," reprinted in Christ, *Laughter of Aphrodite,* pp. 117–132. On the process of writing this paper and presenting it to a panel of the American Academy of Religion, see ibid., pp. 107–108.

45. Ibid., pp. 14–16, 107.

46. For reference to this decision, see Carol Christ, *Rebirth of the Goddess: Finding Meaning in Feminist Spirituality* (New York: Routledge, 1997), pp. 3, 147.

47. See Christ's *Odyssey with the Goddess: A Spiritual Quest in Crete* (New York: Continuum, 1995), p. 13.

48. Ibid., p. 16.

49. Ibid., pp. 18–23.

50. See Christ, *Rebirth of the Goddess,* p. 39.

51. See Christ, *Odyssey with the Goddess,* pp. 55–58.

52. Ibid., p. 164.

53. Christ, *Rebirth of the Goddess,* pp. 41–42, 124–125.

54. See Christ, *Odyssey with the Goddess,* pp. 80–82, 159–160.

55. Christ, *Rebirth of the Goddess,* pp. 41, 45.

56. Christ, *Odyssey with the Goddess,* pp. 33–35, 92–94.

57. See, for example, Christ's story "Reluctant Guests at Dionysian Rites," in ibid., pp. 39–42.

58. Christ, *Rebirth of the Goddess,* pp. 50, 58–59.

59. Ibid., pp. 50–60.

60. Ibid., pp. 60–62.

61. Ibid., pp. 62–67, 158–159, 170–176.

62. Ibid., pp. 98–104.

63. Ibid., pp. 107–109, 109–112, 90, 91.

64. Ibid., pp. 102, 104–106. See also Christ's essay "Feminist Theology in Post-Traditional Thealogy," in *The Cambridge Companion to Feminist Theology*, ed. Susan Frank Parsons (Cambridge: Cambridge University Press, 2002), p. 88.

65. Christ, *Rebirth of the Goddess*, pp. 130–132.

66. Ibid., pp. 132–134.

67. Ibid., pp. 148–150.

68. Ibid., pp. 138–139.

69. Christ, personal communication to the author, August 15, 2003.

70. Flyer, "Who We Are," prepared for the Parliament of the World's Religions, 1993, 1999, Covenant of the Goddess, p. 2. See the home page of the Covenant of the Goddess, www.cog.org.

71. In the 1893 parliament, Hinduism was represented by Swami Vivekananda, among others. There were five Buddhists, among them Reverend Dharmapala, Soyen Shaku, and Takayoahi Matsuyama. Confucianism was represented by Fung Kwang Yu and Kung Hsein Ho, and Jainism by Muni Amaramji. There were no Sikhs or Baha'i.

72. Circle Sanctuary, Box 219, Mt. Horeb, Wisc. 53572. See the sanctuary's Web site, located at www.circlesanctuary.org.

73. EarthSpirit can be reached at PO Box 723-N, Williamsburg, Mass. 01096. The group's Web site is located at www.earthspirit.com.

74. High Priestess Phyllis W. Curott, "A Portrait of Wicca," available online at www.silcom.com/~origin.

75. Appropriations Bill for 1986, HR 3036, Amend. 705, 99th Cong., 1st sess., *Congressional Record* 131 (1985): 25074; see Catherine Cookson, "Report from the Trenches: A Case Study of Religious Freedom Issues Faced by Wiccans Practicing in the United States," *Journal of Church and State* 39 (Autumn 1997): 738.

76. For reports, see www.circlesanctuary.org/liberty.

77. Cookson, "Report from the Trenches," p. 728n11.

78. See www.circlesanctuary.org/liberty/report/summer2002.htm, p. 2. For a general account of Odinism or Asatru, see Lewis, *Magical Religion and Modern Witchcraft*, p. 208.

79. See Starhawk, "Why Pagans May Be Conscientious Objectors to War"; and Tony Dominello, "A Wiccan and the Warrior Ethic"; both part of the Covenant of the Goddess information packet, pp. 28, 29. See www.cog.org.

80. For more information on CUUPs, see the Web site www.cuups.org.

81. For a critique of Margaret Murray's view of witchcraft as a survival of goddess-worshipping paganism and a historical account of the witch persecutions in Europe, see my chapter "Witches and Jews: The Demonic Alien in Christian Culture," in Rosemary Ruether, *New Woman, New Earth: Sexist Ideologies and Human Liberation*, 2nd ed. (Boston: Beacon Press, 1995), pp. 89–114.

CONCLUSION

1. See these two works by Michael P. Carroll: *The Cult of the Virgin Mary: Psychological Origins* (Princeton, N.J.: Princeton University Press, 1989); and *Madonnas That Maim: Popular Catholicism in Italy Since the Fifteenth Century* (Princeton, N.J.: Princeton University Press, 1992).

2. On the homoerotic character of male monotheistic spirituality, see Jeffrey M. Kripel, "A Garland of Talking Heads for the Goddess: Some Autobiographical and Psychoanalytical Reflections on the Western Kali," in *Is the Goddess a Feminist? The Politics of South Asian Goddesses*, ed. Alf Hiltebeitel and Kathleen M. Erndl (New York: New York University Press, 2000), pp. 239–268; and Howard Eilberg-Schwartz, *God's Phallus: And Other Problems for Men and Monotheism* (Boston: Beacon Press, 1994).

3. Jeanette Rodriguez, *Our Lady of Guadalupe: Faith and Empowerment of Mexican American Women* (Austin: University of Texas Press, 1994).

4. George W. Bush's administration proved to be very astute in managing to reject affirmative action in principle and yet select men and women of color who completely support its agenda as token race and gender "cards."

5. Rita Gross has argued that Buddhism is liberating for women precisely because it not only lacks a male god but has no god at all; see her *Buddhism After Patriarchy: A Feminist History, Analysis, and Reconstruction of Buddhism* (Albany, N.Y.: SUNY Press, 1993).

6. Vandana Shiva, *Staying Alive: Women, Ecology, and Development* (London: Zed, 1989); Ivone Gebara, *A Longing for Running Water: Ecofeminism and Liberation* (Minneapolis: Fortress Press, 1999), pp. 137–171; flyer, "Who We Are," prepared for the Parliament of the World's Religions, Capetown, South Africa, December 1999, Covenant of the Goddess.

7. Carol Christ suggests that ecofeminist Christians are "stealing" from Goddess thealogy; see her "Feminist Theology in Post-Traditional Thealogy," in *The Cambridge Companion to Feminist Theology*, ed. Susan Frank Parsons (Cambridge: Cambridge University Press, 2002), p. 8.

INDEX

Note: *Italicized page numbers indicate figures.*

Aztec religion: assumptions about, 203; dynamic plurality in, 195–96; origin stories of, 199–201; paired male and female deities in, 9, 190–91, 192–94; priesthood of, 194–95; sacrifices in, 196–99
Aztec state: dual authority in, 196; rebellion against, 203–4

Baal (god): Anat's relationship with, 57–60; worship of, 76, 81–82; Yahweh's appropriation of, 76–78
Babylonia: astrology of, 107; creation myth of, 48; exile in, 74, 76; hymns of, 50, 52, 55
Bachofen, Johann Jakob: background of, 254–55; hierarchies of, 272; as influence, 20; on original matriarchy, 15–16, 255–59; on "original" promiscuity, 259–60
Baha'i faith, 293, 295
Balkans, Neolithic: cultural achievements of, 23, 37
baptism: Cyprian on, 146; function of, 143, 145, 174, 333n5; milk and honey in, 133; in rites of Cybele, 102–3
Barbelo, 112, 113, 118–19
Barstow, Anne, 3, 29–30
Bartholomew (disciple), 123, 153
Bebel, August, 265–66, 267, 273
Beguine love mysticism, 176–77, 180–87
beloved: nature renewal linked to, 41; in Song of Songs, 86–90. See also love; love mysticism
Berlin Codex, 112, 330n43
Bernard of Clairvaux, 160, 162, 176–79
Berry, Thomas, 308
Bible: divine council of gods in, 74; eschatological writings in, 110; on Mary, 148; on monotheism, 76; Sánchez's narrative in context of, 210–11; Wisdom literature of, 90–97; women's oppression and, 267; Yahweh as

mother goddess in, 79–80; Yahweh as war god in, 78–79. See also New Testament; Song of Songs (Song of Solomon)
Biel, Gabriel, 165
bilineal descent, 19
Bingemer, Maria Clara, 218
blood, 101–2, 134
Boas, Franz, 16, 271
body: corn as consubstantial with, 198; duality of, 196; gender differences of, 291; as mortal and bestial, 229; patriarchal embodiment of mind over, 258–59; soul joined to, 162; Swedenborg's study of, 236. See also figurines, female; figurines, male
Boehme, Jacob: background of, 226–27; followers of, 234, 240, 243; Leade's translation of, 236; on Wisdom, 227–33
Boff, Leonard, 311n16
Bonaventure, 160
bows: gender assigned to, 60, 81
"bridal chamber" sacrament, 123–24
bridal mysticism. See love mysticism
Briffault, Robert, 271–73
Buber, Martin, 286
Budapest, Z. (Zsuzsanna): role of, 277–78, 281, 282, 286; theaology of, 278–80
Buddhism, 253, 307, 357n71, 358n5
Bulgakov, Sergius, 334n21
bull symbolism and cult: Baal and, 58; in Çatal Hüyük, 26–27, 30–32; in taurobolium, 102–3; Yahweh and, 77
Burghardt, Walter J., 336n70
burial rites, 29, 31–34, 109
Bush, George W., 6, 306, 358n4
Bushnell, Horace, 252–53
Bustamante, Francisco de, 207–8
Byblos: Osiris cult in, 65

Cain, 116
Calcolithic era, 13
Calvin, John, 221

Coatlicue (goddess), 199–200, *200*
Code of Hammurabi, 318n22
Colón, Cristobal, 190
colonialism, 190, 203, 259
communism, 263–67
compañera, 61, 320n57
complementary spiritualities concept, 2
Comte, Auguste, 251–52
Confucianism, 357n71
Conkey, Margaret, 35–36, 316n67
contemplative spirituality, 2, 309–10n4
Cortés, Hernán, 199, 206, 346n44
corvée labor, 42–43
cosmos and cosmology: Aztec conception of, 193–94, 200–201; as circle/
wheel, 168, *169;* eschatology rooted
in, 110; as estates of deities, 46, 300–
301; female-identified power in, 112,
120–22; hierarchy of, 301; Hildegard's
visions of, 167, 168, *169;* levels of
alienation in, 140–41; Mary as containing, 155; as series of concentric circles,
107–8; soul's origin as beyond, 108–9
Council of Basel, 162
Council of Chalcedon, 153
Council of Ephesus, 153
Covenant of the Goddess, 292–96
Covenant of Unitarian Universalist
Pagans (CUUPs), 296
Coyolxauhqui (goddess), 199–200, *201*
creation: beginning of new, 235–36; God
in relation to, 167–68, 186; harmony
of duality in, 228; as preordained, 170;
of Wisdom, 94–95; Wisdom as God's
partner in, 244–45
creation myths: in *Apocryphon of John,*
113–15; Aztec, 196–201; Babylonian,
48; biblical, 79–80; in Heliopolis, 61;
Philo on, 111; Sumerian, 43
Crete: goddess pilgrimage to, 288; patriarchal society in, 27; sacred trees in, 289
Cristero revolution, 216
cult of fertility, 31–32

cuneiform, 42
Cybele, 99, 100–103, *101, 102,* 321n76
Cyprian of Carthage, 145–46, 166

Dagan (god), 57
Daniel (king), 60
Davies, Stevan, 333nn5–6
Davis, Elizabeth Gould, 274–76
Day, John, 90
Day of Blood, 101–2
Day of Rejoicing (Hilaria), 102
death: Folly linked to, 92–94; of mystery
deities, 100; Osiris as symbol of, 63,
64; Yahweh as separate from, 76–
77. *See also* afterlife; burial rites;
underworld
deities: as androgynous, 194, 195; as
distant, immortal, powerful, 46, 300–
301; paired male and female, 9, 190–
91, 192–94; process of generating,
300; relations among, 45–47; as "role
models," 54–56; universalism of,
104–5. *See also* goddesses; gods
de la Cruz, Mateo, 212, 213
de la Vega, Luis Laso, 211–12
Demeter (goddess): agriculture linked
to, 255; depiction of, *70;* as exception
to royal ideology, 301; interpreting
representations of, 261; Isis conflated
with, 64; Persephone's rape and, 65,
69–71; rites for, 71–72
Dialogue of the Savior, 123, 331n62
Diego, Juan, 206, 207, 208, 210–11, 216
Dionysus (god): cult of, 99, 109; Osiris
conflated with, 64; as return of maternal, 257–58; as symbol of phallic
sensuality, 255
divine: androgyny of, 10; as life-giving
energy, 308; masculine identified with,
164; plurality of, 137. *See also* female
divine
domestication of plants and animals, 28,
264

domestic sphere: women relegated to, 249–54

Dominicans, 162

dove metaphor, 133–34

Dumuzi (god), 51, 51–53, 54, 89

Dunlavy, John, 244

Earth (Ki, goddess), 45

EarthSpirit, 294

Ecclesia. *See* Christian church (Ecclesia)

ecofeminist spirituality, 24, 281, 293–94, 307, 308

ecological movements, 2

ecumenism concept, 6

egalitarian complementarity concept, 289

egalitarianism, 20, 265, 282–83

egalitarian mutualism, 86–87, 90, 306

Egypt: exodus from, 73–74; hellenized culture of, 98; Isis in cosmology of, 61–69; love poetry of, 88–89; matriarchal elements in, 268; as matriarchy, 257

Eilberg-Schwartz, Howard, 80, 81

Eisler, Riane, 6, 21

El (god), 57, 58–59, 74, 76, 77. *See also* Yahweh (god)

Eleleth (Great Angel), 117–18

Eleusinian mysteries: Demeter-Persephone myth in, 69–72; historical location of, 98–99; hopes for afterlife in, 100; secret information imparted in, 109

Elijah, 75–76

Elisha, 75–76

Elizabeth of Schönau, 160

Eller, Cynthia, 6, 22

embodied embedded thinking (model), 286

Enbilulu (god), 46

endogamy, 91–94

Engels, Frederick: on mother right, 15–16, 263–65, 266; racial hierarchy of, 272–73

Enheduanna (goddess), 42, 50, 301

Enhil (god), 45, 53–54

Enki (god): complaints to, 49; in relations among deities, 45; rivalries of, 47–48; in Sumerian creation myth, 43; underworld realm and, 53–54

Ennoia, 112, 113, 329n36

ensoulment concept, 162

Ephrem, 134–35

Epinoia, 112, 114, 115, 329n36

Ereshkigal (goddess), 45, 48, 53–54

eschatology: baptismal-realized, 333n5; celestial view of, 107–8; in hellenistic Judaism, 109–12; in Isis cult, 103–6; protology fused with, 129–30; turn toward, 99–100, 106

essentialist views, 4, 291

Estés, Clarissa Pinkola, 219

eternal age concept, 110

Etruscans, 27

Eugnostos of the Blessed (text), 122–23, 331n61

Eumolpids, 71

Eustochium, 142

Evans, Arthur, 15, 260

Eve: Ann Lee as new, 245–47; Christian church as, 143; as female spiritual power, 116; Hildegard on, 170–71, 172; lustful sexual intercourse of, 243, 245; Mary as new, 150; maternal spiritual power and, 120–21; origin of, 115; role reversal of, 302; as Wisdom figure, 112

evil: denial of love as root of, 291–92; depictions of, *176*, *224;* female symbols of, 223; as human and animal, 174; presence of, 188; ritual for expulsion of, 262–63

Ezekiel, 82–83, 84–85

fall: effects of, 156, 229; gender acquired in, 111, 141–42; right order subverted in, 245

Gage, Matilda Joslyn: background of, 267–68; hierarchies of, 273; as influence, 20; on original matriarchy, 16, 268–70

Gaia (goddess), 291

Galli (castrated priests of Attis), 101

gardener: use of term, 50

Gardener, Gerald, 277

gardening, 19–20, 38, 39

gathering (of food), 14–15, 17, 18. *See also* foraging societies

gay movement, 239–40

Geb (god), 61

Gebara, Ivone, 218, 307

gender: absence of, 135, 141–42; assigned to bows, 60, 81; complementarity of, 238–39, 249, 255, 272, 289; contrasting interpretations of, 14–20; of God, 134–37, 141–42; nineteenth-century construction of, 249–54; reversal of, 121–22, 126; segregation by (classical Greece), 72; separation by, after fall, 111, 141–42; in socialist thought, 272; symbolism of, 122–26; of Trinity, 132–37

gender hierarchy: acceptance/subversion of, 174; assumptions of, 256; racial hierarchy linked to, 272–73

gender relations: in Çatal Hüyük, 29–30; conflict and collaboration in, 39; in Mesoamerican worldviews, 9; nineteenth-century construction of prehistoric, 3–4

German poetry and philosophy, 227

Germanus, 159

Gero, Joan, 35–36

gestation, 162

Gilgamesh, 54–55, 81, 318n31, 324n24

Gimbutas, Marija: basic argument of, 21–28, 30, 35–37, 104–5; collection of, 34; debate on scholarship of, 6, 35, 36–37; as influence, 343n4

gnosticism: celestial system as male in,

120; complementarity of male and female in, 121–22; complexity of, 8; diversity of, 112; female disciples in, 122–26; female spiritual powers in, 112–22, 302; opposition to, 127; plurality of male and female divine in, 137

God: Adam as imaging, 170–71; as androgynous, 240, 241, 244–48, 270; deconstructing concept of, 308; divine wrath of, 227, 230–31; duality of, 227–28, 230–31, 244, 245; familial language for, 188–89; "Farnearness" of, 187; as father/son/spirit and as lady love, 180; feminine aspects of, 127; gender of, 134–37, 141–42; humans' unification with, 110, 112; Jesus as mediator with, 164; levels of alienation from, 140–41; Mary as mother of, 152–58; in relation to creation, 167–68, 186; "Thought" of, 118–20. *See also* Jesus; Spirit; Trinity; Word of God; Yahweh (god)

Goddess: definitions of, 290–91; devotion to, 302; as embodied personal power, 287; as immanent life process of universe, 278–79; men's need for, 303–5; as monotheistic focus of religion, 35; quest for, 21–22. *See also* Goddess worship; Mother Goddess

goddesses: androcentric, 9; capitalization and, 309n1; defeat and slaying of, 290; as deities or females, 81; fertility linked to, 59, 60, 61, 70, 71, 72, 316n67; as inventions vs. survivals, 300, 301; Love as, 183–84; marginalization of, 47–49; as men's inventions and protection, 303–4; reclaiming ideas of, 8, 274–77; of war, 57–58, 59, 78, 79, 304. *See also specific goddesses*

Goddess worship: Christianity's assimilation of, 191; Carol Christ's experience with, 286–87; egalitarian harmony as hope in, 290; emergence of, 3, 4;

Herodotus, 82, 257
Hesiod, 261, 262
Hidalgo, Miguel, 214
hierarchy: class, 42–44, 174, 264, 301; cosmological, 108, 301; gender, 174, 256, 272–73; racial, 256, 272–73; rejection of tendency toward, 282–83
Hildegard of Bingen: on Adam and Eve, 170–72; drawings by, *169*, *171*, *173*, *175*, *176;* on Ecclesia (the church), 172–74; visions of, 166–67, 168, *171;* white garb and, 174, 176, 340n53; on Wisdom, 167–68, 305
Hinduism, 307, 357n71
Hippolytus of Rome, 138
Hodder, Ian, 30
Holocaust, 286
Holy Spirit. *See* Spirit
Holy Trinity. *See* Trinity
Homer, 106–7
Horned God, 277, 282
horses, 27–28
Horus (god): conception and birth of, 65–66; death of Osiris and, 64–65; depictions of, *62*, *67;* kingship of, 68–69; Seth's challenge of, 67–68
Hosea: on Israel as sexually promiscuous wife, 82–83, 85; on Israel's apostasy, 77–78; reform movement linked to, 75–76
houses: of Çatal Hüyük, 28–30; different sizes of, 26; miniature, 23; sculptures in niches of, 33–*34*
Huehuetéotl (god), 194
Huitzilopochtli (god), 199–200, 218
humanity: deities as "role models" for, 54–56; fallen condition of, 188; feminine symbols for, 137–46; gender as ephemeral in, 135; God's control of conception of, 80; God's final unification with, 110, 112; gods'/goddesses' relations with, 43–44, 54–55; Jesus Christ as expression of God's love for,

229–30; Mary as representative of, 164–65, 171–72, 232; repentance and remorse of, 170–71; separated into male and female after fall, 111, 141–42; will of, 166. *See also* family; social organization
hunting: in Çatal Hüyük, 28; gender roles in, 14–15, 17, 38; scavenging as preceding, 18
Hurrian people, 57
hymns: cosmologic Christology in, 129–31; to Inanna/Ishtar, 50, 52, 55; to Osiris, 65; to Wisdom/Sophia, 241–43
Hypostasis of the Archons: Apocryphon of John compared with, 330n56; description of, 115–18; origin of, 330n44

Icazbalceta, Joaquín García, 215
identity: countercultural, 22; national, 214–15
idolatry: concerns about, 205–6, 207, 211; reinterpretations and, 217
Ilimilku (scribe), 57
Immaculate Conception: debates on, 148, 150–52, 160, 162–63; depiction of, *149*, *163;* doctrine of, 158; rejection of, 221
immortality: of deities, 300–301; of soul, 110–11. *See also* afterlife
Inanna/Ishtar (goddess): ambition of, 46; Anat compared with, 56–57; complaints of, 49; depictions of, *49*, *51*, *52*, *53;* as goddess of royals, 55–56; as invention vs. survival, 301; Isis compared with, 62; liminality of, 56, 318–19n34; men protected by, 303; in relations among deities, 45; as "role model," 54–55; sacred marriage of, 50–53, 81, 89; victory attributed to, 79; Wisdom figure and, 90, 92
individualism, 100. *See also* eschatology
Indo-Europeans, 276–77
industrialization, 18–19, 249, 267

infanticide, female, 259
Inquisition, 184, 187, 269
Institute of Culture and Creation
　Spirituality, 281
intermarriage, 91–94
internationalism, 98–99
Iraq: attack on, 6
Irenaeus, 134, 150
Iroquois society, 25
irrigation, 42–43
Isaiah, 78, 79
Ishtar. *See* Inanna/Ishtar (goddess)
Isis (goddess): death of Osiris and, 64–
　65; depictions of, *62, 63, 67;* magic
　powers of, 68–69; men protected by,
　303–4; as mother of Horus, 62, 65–
　66, 67–68; Osiris's relationship with,
　61–62; Wisdom figure and, 90
Isis cult: cosmologic Christology com-
　pared with, 130; depictions of, *104,
　105;* eschatology in, 103–6; rites of,
　99, 103–6
Islam, 6, 159
Israel: God as warrior and mother god-
　dess in, 78–80; God's calling of, 140;
　as God's wife, 81–86, 90; Mary as part
　of, 148; Mexico compared with, 214;
　name of, 77; origin of, 73–74. *See also*
　Hebrew people; Judaism

Jacobsen, Thorkild, 44–45
Jainism, 293, 357n71
James, E.{ths}O., 2–3
James (disciple): Proevangelium of, 151–
　52, 156, 158, 160; role of, 123, 148
Jeremiah, 78, 82–84
Jeroboam (king), 77
Jerome, 135, 142, 152, 221
Jerusalem: as God's bride, 110; Islamic
　conquest of, 159; as sexually promis-
　cuous wife, 82–85
Jesuits: apostolic Christianity of, 205–
　6, 207; on Immaculate Conception,

162–63; on Virgin of Guadalupe
　as unique revelation, 213
Jesus: as bridegroom, 137–40, 142–43,
　145–46, 172–73, 176–87, 223; cruci-
　fixion of, 166, *175;* dual female-male
　redemptive work of, 244–48; Eve as
　humanity of, 170–71; female disciples
　of, 122–26; form of Protennoia in,
　119; God-manhood of, 146, 152–58,
　164–65, 221; as God's counter-stroke,
　229–30; Mary as mediatrix with, 164;
　Mary as mother of, 152–58; Mary's
　conception of, 132; Mary's death and,
　156; as messianic expression, 121; as
　new Adam, 150, 245–47; resurrection
　of, 127–28, 148; theological meaning
　of, 128–31; Wisdom and, 131, 134,
　333n6
Jezebel, 81
Job, 78, 95
John (disciple): Gospel of, 130–31, 138,
　148, 333–34n16; vision of, 112–13.
　See also Apocryphon of John
John Damascene, 159–60
John Paul II (pope), 166, 216
Jovinian, 337n81
Joyce, Rosemary, 344n11
Júarez, Benito, 215
Judaism: assumptions about, 73–74; as
　backlash against goddess spirituality,
　278; developing patriarchal monothe-
　ism in, 301–2; eschatology of (hel-
　lenistic), 109–12; Messiah as male in,
　131; patriarchal fundamentalism surge
　in, 6; reclaiming prophetic, liberative
　themes in, 307; as reinterpreted syn-
　thesis, 1–2; role in women's oppres-
　sion, 268–70; thealogy's exclusion
　of, 5. *See also* Hebrew people; Israel
Judas (disciple), 123
Julian of Norwich, 187–89, 305–6,
　343n104
Jungianism, 179, 281

Juno (goddess), 261
justice and mercy, 164
Justin Martyr, 150

Kabbalism, 226, 282
Kant, Immanuel, 249–50
Khirbet el-Qom inscriptions, 74
kingship: Baal's struggle for, 57–61;
    fertilizing power linked to, 51–53;
    goddess as power behind, 61, 68–69;
    Inanna's power and femaleness linked
    to, 56; Isis as representative of, 62;
    military defense linked to, 43, 44;
    mythic cycles central to, 50–54
knowledge, 177–78. See also Wisdom
Kore (goddess), 261
Kramer, Samuel Noah, 89
Kuntillet Ajrud inscriptions, 74
Kurgans, 27–28

Lady Liberty League, 295
land ownership, 39, 43–44, 264–66
late Paleolithic era, 13
law: as male, 253; neopagan movement
    and, 294–95; patriarchal society linked
    to, 256, 257–58
Lazarus, 178
Leade, Jane, 234–36, 306, 349n32
Leade, William, 234
leadership: in Goddess worship move-
    ment, 277–85; Reformation's rejection
    of female, 223, 225; of Shakers, 243,
    247–48; Swedenborgians on, 239–40
Lee, Mother Ann, 243–47
Lee, William, 243
Leo (pope), 153
León-Portilla, Miguel, 192
Levi (disciple), 124–25
Leviathan, 78
Leyden, Lucas van, 222
liberation theology, 217
life principle concept, 278–79
Lockhart, James, 212

Logos (Word). See Word of God
"lost souls" concept, 185–86
Lourdes, apparitions of Mary at, 215
love: denial of, as root of evil, 291–92;
    Engels on, 265; as female, 185; gospel
    of, 253; knowledge linked to, 177–78;
    Swedenborg on, 237–39; two kinds
    of, joined, 180–87; Wisdom as, 167
love mysticism: Beguines on, 176–77,
    180–87; bridal soul as merging with
    church in, 182–83; Cistercians on,
    176–79; Jesus Christ as bride in, 137–
    40, 142–43, 145–46, 172–73, 176–87,
    223; men's need for, 303–5
love poetry, 86–90
Lowie, Robert, 16
Lucifer, 170, 228, 234
Luke (disciple): Gospel of, 130, 147, 148,
    150; statue carved by, 206–7
Luther, Martin, 220–21, 223, 225, 226

Ma'at (goddess), 90
Madonna of Misericordia, 146, 147
magic: as intentional consciousness
    change, 293; of Isis, 68–69; protest
    rituals as, 284; as quest for control,
    288–89
Magna Mater (Great Mother): as all
    deities in one, 104–5; depictions of,
    101, 102; in gnosticism, 120–22; Mary
    as, 153–58; rites of, 99
Malabar (India): as matriarchal society,
    268–69
male and maleness: bull symbols of, 32;
    essentialist view of, 4; as rational part,
    142; Starhawk on, 281–82
male elites: as female in relation to God,
    81–86, 90; as preparing for soul's
    ascent, 108–9; Wisdom figure created
    by, 91–92. See also Therapeutae
male power, 25, 47–49
Malinalxoch (goddess), 200
Malinowski, Bronislaw, 273

mother-son lovers, 321n76

Motz, Lotte, 315n57

"mouth and stone church" concept, 233

Mummu-Tiamat (goddess), 48–49

Murray, Gilbert, 99, 106, 260

Murray, Margaret, 277

mystery religions: assumptions about, 99–100; cult of Isis and Osiris as, 61; rites of, 100–106; secret information imparted in, 109; sources on, 8. *See also* Eleusinian mysteries

mysticism: of Boehme, 227–33; dangers of, 186; of Leade, 234–36; resignation to will of God in *(gelassenheit)*, 226, 230–31. *See also* love mysticism

mystique courteoise (concept), 180

myths: of defeated goddess, 290; of exodus, 73–74; Gimbutas's narrative as, 22; patterns of thought in, 41; socialists on, 266; of U.S. vs. Greece, 289. *See also* creation myths

naditu (cloistered priestesses), 42, 44

Nag Hammadi Codex, 112, 330n43

Nahar (god), 58

Nahua peoples: Christianity adapted by, 204–5; decimation of, 203; female figurines of, 200–201, *202;* gender beliefs among, 193, 344n11; reinterpreting religion of, 217–18; sources on, 191; worldview of, 197. *See also* Aztec religion

Nahuatl language: documents in, 203, 211–12; word for Mary in, 205

Nammu (goddess), 43, 45

Nanahuatzin (god), 197

Nanna (god), 53–54

National American Woman Suffrage Association, 270–71

National Woman Suffrage Association, 267

Native American Church, 295

Native Americans, 15, 25, 263

nature: cyclical rhythm of, 291; death to, 184; desacralization of, 285; gods as power in, 45; imaging spheres of, 301; Isis as goddess of, 103–4; renewal of, 41, 102, 304; in Song of Songs, 87, 88, 89; woman as, 39–40

Nazareth: as hostile to Jesus, 147

Neolithic era, 3, *4,* 13–14, 23, 37. *See also* original matriarchy

neopagan movement: attacks on, 294–95; defense of, 296–97; development of, 292–94; normalization of, 5–6

Neoplatonic thought, 2, 64–65, 226

Nephthys (goddess): death of Osiris and, 64–65, 66; depictions of, *63, 66;* as twin sister of Isis, 61–62

Nergal (god), 48

Nestorius, 153

New Age spirituality, 288

Newman, Barbara, 180, 183–84

New Testament: bridegroom language for Jesus Christ in, 138; cosmologic Christology in, 129–31; father-son language in, 131; "friends" as used in, 333–34n16; Holy Spirit images in, 132–37; infancy narratives of, 148, 150; on Mary, 146–58; on Nazareth as hostile to Jesus, 147; Wisdom in, 127–31

Nicolas I (pope), 160

Ningal (goddess), 45, 51

Ninhursag (goddess), 45, 47–48, 56

Ninlil (goddess), 45

Ninmah. *See* Ninhursag (goddess)

Niqmad II (king), 57

Nisaba (goddess), 42

nonviolence, 284

Norea (disciple): as Eve's daughter, 121; role of, 122, 302; as spiritual power, 116–18; as Wisdom figure, 112

Nothingness, 186

Nut (goddess), 61

planets: qualities endowed by, 107–8. *See also* cosmos and cosmology

Plaskow, Judith, 287

Plato: on afterlife, 100, 106–7; on cosmic hierarchy, 108; as influence, 110, 141, 142, 143, 167

Plutarch, 61, 64–65, 66

Pluto (god), 69–70

Poimandres of Hermes Tresmegistus (text), 108

political alliances: sacred marriage and prostitution in context of, 81–86

political assemblies: as metaphor for relations among deities, 46–47

polygamy, 254, 269

polygyny, 20, 85, 324n32

Poole, Stafford, 212

poor: preferential option for, 217, 218

Porphyry, 335n46

Portage, John, 234

Portugal: colonialism of, 190

positivism, 251–52

Potok, Mark, 295

pottery, 14, 23–24

power: female-identified, in cosmos, 112, 120–22; "greening," 167, 170; kinds of, 283, 308; male, 25, 47–49; *me* (governing power), 46, 50; psychosocial control in, 284. *See also* archonic powers; deities; female power; kingship

prehistoric societies: definition of, 13–14; imagining of, 14–20; interpretations of, 35; as tabula rasa, 14. *See also* ancient societies

preindustrial societies, 313n28

PRI (Party of the Institutionalized Revolution), 216, 217

priestesses: cloistered, 42, 44; in Dianic witchcraft, 280; rejection of dominant, 282–83

prison chaplains, 295

productive work, 19, 38

Proevangelium of James, 151–52, 156, 158, 160

promiscuity: concept of (male), 255, 269; "original," 16, 259–60, 261, 263–64, 265

Pronoia, 112, 113, 120, 329n36

property, private, 39, 43–44, 264–66

prophetic spirituality, 1–2, 109, 309–10n4

prostitutes and prostitution: Inanna as patron of, 81; Israel as wife turned, 82–85; Mary Magdalene as, 122, 330–31n59; origins of, 269; sacred, 56, 82, 319n35

Protennoia, 118–19

Protestantism: Boehme's mysticism and, 226–33; divine and human androgyny in, 10; Harmony Society and, 240–43; Leade's mysticism and, 234–36; Mariology as closed book for, 220, 303; Shakers and, 243–48; Swedenborg and, 236–40; Wisdom symbol in, 9–10

protest rituals, 284

protology, 128–31

proto-Neolithic era, 13

Pseudo-John, 156

Pseudo-Melito, 156

Puritans, 275

Pythagorean culture, 262

Q tradition, 130

Quecholli, maize festival of, 195

queen: use of term, 25, 26

Quetzalcóatl (god): co-optation of, 217–18; Cortés as, 199; earth created by, 197; goddesses paired with, 195; as remembrance of St. Thomas, 214; in second age, or sun, 196; as son of Tezcatlipoca, 193; vulnerability of, 198–99

Qumran community, 128

racial hierarchy, 256, 272–73

racism, 295–96

sexual division of labor, 15, 18, 19

sexuality, 76, 139–40

sexual love/desire: origin of, 115; redeemed in Song of Songs, 86–90; spiritual love joined to, 180

sexual relations: lustful, of Adam and Eve, 243, 245; set aside in contemplative philosophy, 111–12

Shaddai (god), 269

Shaker theology, 243–48

shamanistic traditions: attempts to destroy, 285; neopaganism's affinity with, 294; remnants of goddess religion in, 284; revival of, 282

Shekinah, 96, 96

Shiva, Vandana, 307

shrines: domestic, 28, 30–34, 38; Mithraic, 322n80; Osiris cult, 66. See also temples

Shu (god), 61

Sikhs, 293

Simon Magnus, 330n58

sin: Adam and Eve's, 243, 245; alienation of soul in, 177; death to, 184; gender acquired in, 141–42; healing of, 343n104; original, 158; pains of, 343n104; reinterpretation of, 188; sanctification of Mary and, 160, 162–63

Sixtus IV (pope), 162

Sky (An, god), 45, 46

slaves and slavery, 42–44, 264, 267

snakes, 23

socialism: gender natures ignored in, 272; matriarchal society as liberative hope in, 10, 263–67

Socialist Party of America, Women's National Committee, 267

social justice tradition, 1–2, 5

social movements, 6

social organization, 16–17, 37–40

society: active vs. passive citizens in, 249–50; Greco-Roman, 98–109;

Greek, 1, 72, 327n6; as increasingly hierarchical and centralized, 47; industrialization's impact on, 249; Iroquois, 25; positivism's effects on, 251–52. See also Sumero-Akkadian society; specific types (e.g., matriarchal societies; patrilineal societies)

Solomon (king), 89

Song of Songs (Song of Solomon): as allegory, 137–38; bridal mysticism and, 176–79; Christian commentaries on, 138–42, 223; gender in, 135; sacralization of, 86, 89–90, 325n36, 325n42

Sophia and Sophiology: Bulgakov on, 334n21; female power of, 112, 117; as female "Thought" from the Father, 119–20, 330n54; Harmonist hymns to, 241–43; Leade's visions of, 234–36; liminal role of, 121–22; "mistake" of, 113, 120; redemptive work of, 115; soul's dialogue with, 231–33. See also Wisdom

Sophia of Jesus Christ (text), 122–23, 331n61

soul (anima): ascent of, 184–87; body joined to, 162; as bride, 135, 139–40, 180; as bridegroom, 231; celestial immortality of, 110–11; as co-redeemer, 182; death to, 184; emotions of, 177; gender of, 141–42, 185, 241–43; God's love as creating, 180–82; as God's perfect icon, 165; God's unification with, 112; healing of, 343n104; journey of, 140–41; liberation of, 107–8; as originating beyond cosmos, 108–9; Sophia's dialogue with, 231–33; transformation of, 230–31, 233; tug of war in, 230–31; as warrior-knight, 180; world, 107, 168

Sousa, Lisa, 212

Southern Poverty Law Center, 295

Spain: administrative structure under, 203–4; colonialism of, 190; Meso-american symbols repressed by, 9; rebellion against, 214–15; Virgin of Guadalupe of Extremadura in, 206–7

Sparrow, John, 227

Spirit: depiction of, *136;* elements of goddess worship in, 269; female images of, 132–37

spirituality: complementary, 2; contemplative, 2, 309–10n4; creation-based, 230; ecofeminist, 24, 281, 293–94, 307, 308; Goddess, 3–7, 10, 290, 321n76 (*see also* Goddess worship); New Age, 288; pagan, 1–2, 5, 273, 309–10n4; prophetic, 1–2, 109, 309–10n4; search for earth-based, feminist, 6

Spretnak, Charlene, 6, 21

Stanton, Elizabeth Cady, 267, 270

Starhawk (Miriam Simos): as Goddess feminist, 5; as pacifist, 295; on power, 283, 308; role of, 280–81; teaching of, 286, 355n22; views of, 281–85

Stone, Merlin, 275, 276–77

Sumerian world: slave-owning cities of, 37, 39

Sumero-Akkadian society: class hierarchy in, 42–44; concept of deities in, 44–47, 54–55; goddesses marginalized in, 47–49; Inanna/Ishtar in, 49–56; land ownership in, 43–44; origins of, 42; Song of Songs in context of, 89–90; women's status in, 44

Swedberg, Jesper, 236, 350n38

Swedenborg, Emanuel: background of, 236; followers of, 239–40, 267; on wisdom and love, 237–39

Synagoga (Jewish people), 173

synoptic gospels, 130

Syria. *See* Ugarit (Syria)

Syriac language, 132, 137

Szilagyi, Masika, 277

Tamez, Elza, 217–18

Tanco, Luis Becerra, 213

Tauler, Johannes, 240

taurobolium, 102–3

Tecuciztecatli (god), 197

Tefnut (goddess), 61

"tellurism" concept, 257

temples: administrators of, 44–46; for Baal, 57, 58–59; for Demeter, 70, 71; as focus of urban centers, 42–44. *See also* shrines

Tertullian, 143, 152

Teteo Innan/Toci (goddess), 194, 195

textiles and textile production, 38, 44

Tezcatlanextía-Tezcatlipoca (paired deities), 192

Tezcatlipoca (god), 193, 196, 197, 198–99

Tezozomoc, Hernando Alvarado, 345n36

Thaumaurgus, Gregory, 335n46

theo/alogy: as beginning with experience, 286; Carol Christ's, 286–92; ecofeminist spirituality in, 307–8; integration of process and goddess, 288; proponents of, 6–7; search for sources of, 4–5

theodicy: problem of, 188

Theodore of Mopsuestia, 153

Therapeutae, 95–96, 111–12

Thesmophoria (festival), 71–72

Thomas (disciple): Gospel of, 123, 331n64, 333n5; Quetzalcóatl as remembrance of, 214, 218

Thomas Aquinas, 160, 162

Thoth (god), 66

Tiamat (goddess), 48–49

Tiger, Lionel, 17

Tillich, Paul, 220

Titian, *161*

Titlacauan (sorcerer), 198

Tiwi culture (Australia), 19

Tlaloc (god), 195, 196

Tlaltecuhtli (goddess), 195

Walker, Robert, 294
wall paintings, 28, 30–31
Walls, Neal H., 320n46, 324n24
Wardley, Jane, 243
Wardley Society, 243
warfare, 17, 290
warrior ethic, 295–96, 306
was-scepter, *64*
wealth, surplus, 19–20, 26, 39
Weigel, Valentine, 226
Weisel, Elie, 286
Westermarck, Edward Alexander, 271
White, Anna, 248
white supremacy, 295
Wicca: attacks on, 294–95; Carol
   Christ's views of, 286–89; credo of,
   293; defense of, 296–97; definition
   of, 294, 296; Dianic form of, 279, 282;
   goal of, 279; leadership in, 277–85;
   political activism and, 281, 283–84
will: of humanity, 166; renunciation
   of, 253; resignation to God's, 226,
   230–31
Willard, Frances, 268
Wisdom: background of, 90–91; in
   Boehme's mysticism, 227–33; as
   bride and as bridegroom, 141; as celestial sister, 234–36, 306; as center of
   Trinity, 187–89; Christian church and,
   143, 145; cosmological role of, 94–95;
   as creation of male elites, 91–92; as
   defined by men-God relations, 96–97;
   eternal life linked to, 95–96; female-
   personified, 112, *144*, 165, 303; gender
   of, 137; Harmonist hymns to, 241–43;
   "I am" language of, 131; Jesus Christ
   as, 131, 134; masculinization of, 110–
   11, 131, 223, 302; messianism fused
   with, 128–31; as *ousia* (ground of
   being), 334n21; in Q tradition, 130;
   reclaiming of female, 9–10, 167–68,
   173, 189; in Shaker theology, 243–48;
   Swedenborg on, 237–39; Torah as

manifestation of, 128. *See also* Sophia
   and Sophiology
Wisdom of Solomon: "friends" as used
   in, 333–34n16; relegated to apocrypha,
   223; as source for theological meaning
   of Jesus, 128–31
Witch, Jamyi, 295
witches: depiction of, *224;* Gage's study
   of, 267; instructions for, 279–80;
   labeled as devil worshipers, 285;
   persecution of, 223, 296–97. *See also*
   neopagan movement; Wicca
Witherington, Ben, 333n6
Wollstonecraft, Mary, 250
women: as administrators of temples, 44;
   in Aztec priesthood, 194–95; choices
   of, 5, 306–8; as disciples, 122–26;
   "fall" of, 264; festival for, 71–72; fixed
   "nature" of, 250; idealization of, 252–
   53; legal rights of, 44; marginalization
   of, 2; misogyny toward, 179, 253–54;
   as more loving and less intelligent,
   271–72; oppression/subjugation of,
   266–70; as original human beings,
   275; as passive citizens, 249–50; relegated to domestic sphere, 249–54; as
   workers, 265
women's suffrage movement: ambivalence about, 272; opposition to, 252;
   original matriarchy and, 267–71
Word of God: as creator, revealer,
   redeemer, 130–31; father-son metaphor for, 131, 132; gender absent in,
   141–42; journey of soul and, 140–
   41; milk metaphor for, 132–33, 134;
   Philo's use of concept, 110–11; soul
   as alienated from, 177
work role complementarity, 19–20
World Social Forum, 7
world soul, 107, 168
World Trade Organization, 284
Wright, Lucy, 243
Wright, Rita, 35–36

Indexer: Margie Towery

Compositor: Integrated Composition Systems

Text: 10.25/14 Fournier

Display: Fournier

Printer and binder: Thomson-Shore